Humanitarian diplomacy

Humanitarian diplomacy: Practitioners and their craft

Edited by Larry Minear and Hazel Smith

**United Nations
University Press**

TOKYO · NEW YORK · PARIS

United Nations University Press
United Nations University, 53-70, Jingumae 5-chome,
Shibuya-ku, Tokyo 150-8925, Japan
Tel: +81-3-3499-2811   Fax: +81-3-3406-7345
E-mail: sales@hq.unu.edu
General enquiries: press@hq.unu.edu
http://www.unu.edu

United Nations University Office at the United Nations, New York
2 United Nations Plaza, Room DC2-2062, New York, NY 10017, USA
Tel: +1-212-963-6387   Fax: +1-212-371-9454
E-mail: unuona@ony.unu.edu

United Nations University Press is the publishing division of the United Nations University.

Cover design by Rebecca S. Neimark, Twenty-Six Letters

Printed in India

ISBN-10: 92-808-1134-7
ISBN-13: 978-92-808-1134-6

Library of Congress Cataloging-in-Publication Data

Humanitarian diplomacy : practitioners and their craft / edited by Larry Minear and Hazel Smith.
    p.   cm.
 Includes index.
 ISBN 9280811347 (pbk.)
 1. Humanitarian assistance. 2. War relief. 3. Diplomacy. I. Minear, Larry,
1936– II. Smith, Hazel, 1954–
HV639.H85   2007
363.34'988—dc22   2006028976

Contents

Contributors

Ambassador Lakhdar Brahimi served as Special Adviser to the Secretary-General from 1 January 2004 to 31 December 2005. During his career Ambassador Brahimi has served in a number of diplomatic capacities, including as Special Representative of the Secretary-General for Afghanistan and Head of the United Nations Assistance Mission in Afghanistan; the Secretary-General's Special Envoy for Afghanistan; Under-Secretary-General for Special Assignments in Support of the Secretary-General's Preventive and Peacemaking Efforts; Special Representative for Haiti; and Special Representative for South Africa. Mr Brahimi was Under-Secretary-General of the League of Arab States. Ambassador Brahimi is the former foreign minister of Algeria.

Lizzie Brock worked with Peace Brigades International's Colombia Project between 1999 and 2003, first as a volunteer and then as Coordinator of the Bogotá team. In 2003, she co-conducted a study funded by Terre des Hommes Germany on the effectiveness of Urgent Action Alerts in preventing human rights violations. From 2004 to 2006, Lizzie was director of Nuestra Casa, a Latino immigrant community organization in the San Francisco area.

Antonio Donini is Senior Researcher at the Feinstein International Center (FIC) at Tufts University, USA. He previously worked for 26 years in the United Nations in research, evaluation and humanitarian capacities. His last post was as Director of the UN Office for the Coordination of Humanitarian Affairs (OCHA) to Afghanistan (1999–2002). Before going to Afghanistan, he was Chief of the Lessons Learned Unit at OCHA, where he managed a programme of independent studies on the effectiveness of relief efforts. He has published widely on evaluation, humanitarian and UN reform issues. In 2004 he co-edited a volume on *Nation-Building Unraveled? Aid, Peace and Justice in Afghanistan* (Kumarian Press) and he has written several articles exploring the implications of the crises in Afghanistan and Iraq for the future of humanitarian action (see the FIC website at ⟨http:// www.famine.tufts.edu⟩).

Karin von Hippel is the Co-Director of the Post-Conflict Reconstruction Project at the Center for Strategic and International Studies in Washington, DC, USA. Previously she was a Senior Research Fellow at the Centre for Defence Studies, King's College London, UK, and spent several years working for the United Nations and the European Union in Somalia and Kosovo. Her publications include *Democracy by Force* (Cambridge University Press, 2000) and (as editor) *Europe Confronts Terrorism* (Palgrave Macmillan, 2005).

Masood Hyder worked for the United Nations World Food Programme (WFP) from 1984 to 2006. He was WFP Representative and Deputy Humanitarian Coordinator, Sudan, 2000–2002; UN Resident Coordinator, UN Humanitarian Coordinator and WFP Representative, North Korea, 2002–2004; and WFP Representative to the Bretton Woods Institutions, 2004–2006.

Erika Joergensen worked for 18 years with the Danish Refugee Council (DRC), from which she gained her main experience with the integration of refugees and working with humanitarian crises and emergencies. Between 2000 and 2006 she worked with the United Nations World Food Programme, first as the Representative in Armenia and then as the Representative in Nepal. She is presently the Deputy Regional Director for the WFP Regional bureau in Bangkok.

Larry Minear directs the Humanitarianism and War Project at the Feinstein International Center at Tufts University, USA. Since co-founding the Project in 1991, he has conducted and coordinated research on many humanitarian crises. His most recent books include *The Humanitarian Enterprise: Dilemmas and Discoveries* (Kumarian Press, 2002) and, with Ian Smillie, *The Charity of Nations: Humanitarian Action in a Calculating World* (Kumarian Press, 2004).

Nicholas Morris was a staff member of the Office of the United Nations High Commissioner for Refugees (UNHCR) from 1973 to 2001. He served as the High Commissioner's Special Envoy for the former Yugoslavia from June 1993 to December 1994 and for the former Yugoslavia and Albania from April 1998 to April 1999. Prior to retirement he was the UNHCR Inspector General.

David Morton spent most of his career with the World Food Programme (WFP) in Africa and Asia. He was sent to the Democratic People's Republic of Korea (DPRK) as WFP's Representative and UN Humanitarian Coordinator (Office for the Coordination of

Humanitarian Affairs), and later was appointed, in addition, UN Resident Coordinator and Resident Representative for the United Nations Development Programme in DPRK. He served in the DPRK from 1998 to 2002.

'Funmi Olonisakin is Director of the Conflict, Security and Development Group at King's College London. Prior to this, she worked in the Office of the United Nations Special Representative of the Secretary-General on Children and Armed Conflict, overseeing Africa programmes.

Omawale Omawale now lives in Central Florida, where he retired after 30 years in international development, including service as UNICEF Representative in Sierra Leone, Yemen and DPRK, and as a consultant for international organizations including the Caribbean Community Secretariat, the Food and Agriculture Organization, the International Food Policy Research Institute, the University of the West Indies, the United States Institute of Peace and the World Health Organization.

Toni Pfanner, PhD (econ.), LLM, works at the International Committee of the Red Cross (ICRC) headquarters in Geneva, is Editor-in-Chief of the *International Review of the Red Cross*, and teaches international humanitarian law at the St Thomas University in Miami, USA. He headed several major operations of the ICRC and, from 1998 to 2000, was head of the regional delegation for South-East Asia in Jakarta, which also covered East Timor.

André Roberfroid is currently President of the Association Montessori International, promoting the Montessori pedagogy in more than 60 countries around the world. He worked as a field officer and representative for UNICEF in Africa and the Middle East from 1972 to 2000. He served as UNICEF Deputy Executive Director for Programme and Strategic Planning in New York from 2000 until his retirement in 2003.

Claudia Rodriguez worked in Iraq from February 2003 to June 2004. She was in Baghdad until August 2003 as General Coordinator of the international NGO Médecins du Monde, and returned to Baghdad to work for the NGO Coordination Committee in Iraq (NCCI). She then worked for Médecins Sans Frontières (MSF) in the Darfur and tsunami crises. She is currently working for the United Nations Office for the Coordination of Humanitarian Affairs as head of the sub-office in South Kivu, the Democratic Republic of Congo.

Hazel Smith is Professor of International Relations at the University of Warwick, UK. She received her PhD from the London School of Economics and was a Fulbright Scholar at Stanford University, USA, and Jennings Randolph Senior Fellow at the United States Institute of Peace. Professor Smith has worked for UNICEF, the United Nations Development Programme, the United Nations World Food Programme (WFP) and Caritas Internationalis in the Democratic People's Republic of Korea (North Korea) and the WFP in Nepal.

Brian Walker was Director General
of Oxfam 1974–1983; Executive
Director of the Independent
Commission on International
Humanitarian Issues 1983–1985;
President of the International
Institute for Environment and
Development 1985–1989; Executive
Director of Earthwatch Europe
1989–1995; Member of the Standing
Advisory Commission on Human
Rights for Northern Ireland 1975–
1977; Member of the World
Commission on Food and Peace
1989–1995; Chair of the Band Aid/
Live Aid Projects Committee 1985–
1990; Member of the Editorial
Committee of the World Resources
Report 1985–1995.

D. Sena Wijewardane, MA (Oxon),
BCL (Oxon), Bar-at-Law (Middle
Temple), is a member of the United
Nations Administrative Tribunal
(UNAT) – the highest judicial body
within the United Nations. He was
formerly General Counsel for the
United Nations Relief and Works
Agency for Palestine Refugees in
the Near East and the Legal
Adviser at the United Nations
Mission in Kosovo. He was
educated at Jesus College Oxford
and Trinity College Cambridge, UK.
He has published in the *British Year
Book of International Law*.

Abbreviations

AFL	Armed Forces of Liberia
AUC	Autodefensas Unidas de Colombia
BSA	Bosnian Serb Army
CF	Coalition forces (Iraq)
CMT	Country Management Team (UNICEF Sierra Leone)
CPA	Coalition Provisional Authority (Iraq)
CRC	Convention on the Rights of the Child
DPRK	Democratic People's Republic of Korea
EC	European Community/European Commission
ECHO	Humanitarian Aid department of the European Commission
ECOMOG	ECOWAS Cease-Fire Monitoring Group
ECOWAS	Economic Community of West African States
ELN	Army of National Liberation (Colombia)
EU	European Union
FAO	Food and Agriculture Organization of the United Nations
FARC	Revolutionary Armed Forces of Colombia
FDRC	Flood Damage Rehabilitation Commission (DPRK)
Fretilin	Frente Revolutionaria do Timor Leste Independente
HACC	Humanitarian Assistance Coordination Center (Iraq)
IASC	Inter-Agency Standing Committee (UN)
ICJ	International Court of Justice
ICRC	International Committee of the Red Cross
IDP	internally displaced person
IFRC	International Federation of Red Cross and Red Crescent Societies
IGO	intergovernmental organization

IHL	international humanitarian law
IMF	International Monetary Fund
INPFL	Independent National Patriotic Front of Liberia
INTERFET	International Force East Timor
MFA	ministry of foreign affairs
MOU	Memorandum of Understanding
MSF	Médicins Sans Frontières
NATO	North Atlantic Treaty Organization
NCCI	NGO Coordination Committee in Iraq
NGO	non-governmental organization
NPFL	National Patriotic Front of Liberia
NPRC	National Provisional Revolutionary Council (Sierra Leone)
OCHA	Office for the Coordination of Humanitarian Affairs (UN)
OLS	Operation Lifeline Sudan
OPT	Occupied Palestinian Territory
OSO	Operational Support Officer (UNRWA)
PBI	Peace Brigades International
RAO	Refugee Affairs Officer (UNRWA)
RNA	Royal Nepal Army
RUF	Revolutionary United Force (Sierra Leone)
SACB	Somalia Aid Coordination Body
SF	Strategic Framework (Afghanistan)
SPLA/M	Sudan People's Liberation Army/Movement
SRSG	Special Representative of the UN Secretary-General
TIPH	Temporary International Presence in Hebron
ULIMO	United Liberation Movement for Democracy in Liberia
UN	United Nations
UNAMET	United Nations Mission in East Timor
UNAMI	United Nations Assistance Mission for Iraq
UNCHS	United Nations Centre for Human Settlements
UNCO	United Nations Coordinator's Office
UNDHA	United Nations Department of Humanitarian Affairs
UNDP	United Nations Development Programme
UNDRO	United Nations Disaster Relief Organization
UN-Habitat	United Nations Human Settlements Programme
UNHCHR	United Nations High Commissioner for Human Rights
UNHCR	United Nations High Commissioner for Refugees
UNICEF	United Nations Children's Fund
UNIFIL	United Nations Interim Force in Lebanon
UNITAF	Unified Task Force (Somalia)
UNITAR	United Nations Institute for Training and Research
UNOCHA	United Nations Office for the Coordination of Humanitarian Affairs
UNOMIL	United Nations Observer Mission in Liberia
UNOSOM	United Nations Operation in Somalia
UNPROFOR	United Nations Protection Force (former Yugoslavia)

UNRWA	United Nations Relief and Works Agency for Palestine Refugees in the Near East
UNSCOL	United Nations Special Coordinating Office for Liberia
UNSECOORD	United Nations Office of Security Coordination
UNTSO	United Nations Truce Supervision Organization
UNU	United Nations University
WFP	World Food Programme
WHO	World Health Organization
WSC	World Summit for Children

Foreword

Ambassador Lakhdar Brahimi

Diplomacy has been practised differently in different places and at different times in history. It generally involves the ability to define one's own objectives and at the same time to be fully aware of the views, interests, circumstances and objectives of the other side. The negotiations in which the diplomat engages will have a better chance of success if his or her approach is informed by at least a degree of empathy, understanding and, significantly, knowledge of the overall situation.

Negotiation, it must be said, is not limited to the world of diplomacy or international politics. Negotiation is something one does on a daily basis, be it with one's children, with one's spouse or with the plumber waiting to be paid after a house call.

Perhaps like Monsieur Jourdain in Molière's play *Le Bourgeois Gentilhomme*, who discovers one day that he has been speaking in prose all his life without even being aware of it, we too are all negotiators in our daily lives as well as our professional ones without being entirely aware of it. Thus, quite obviously, not thinking of ourselves as negotiators does not mean that we are not negotiating every day.

It seems clear that the pursuit of humanitarian diplomacy, sometimes overlooked when political events are studied, needs to be examined further. Certainly, we need to study more closely the role played by humanitarian workers when they are negotiating access and related humanitarian issues with combatants and other actors in war zones. There is some truth in the assertion that negotiations in pursuit of humanitarian goals must necessarily differ to some extent from purely political deals that are the product of a traditional negotiation process. Humanitarian principles, again, must necessarily set the agenda for the negotiations conducted by humanitarian actors. Thus, it is important that those working in the international field recognize and give some space to their humanitarian colleagues.

At the same time, it is also clear that the relationship between the humanitarian and the political-military actors, and their roles, is a two-way street. Just as important as humanitarian principles and the respect thereof are the goals pursued by political and military actors. It is inevitable that the space operated in by humanitarian actors and political ones, although separate, will overlap in some areas. What is needed when that inevitable overlap takes place is mutual respect and deeper understanding of each other's motives and goals. Working for durable peace and negotiating humanitarian access are equally honourable goals; they also complement each other.

At the end of the day, the ultimate goal is the betterment of the people that we in the international community have set out to help. Mutual respect between and among various international actors is key, but even more fundamental is the long-term sustainable return to peace and prosperity of conflict-ridden zones. In pursuance of this goal, the short-term (often humanitarian) and the long-term (usually political) goals must be harmonized to positive effect.

Although much of this may be fairly obvious, the daily issues we face in trying to manage these processes in the effort to help people on the ground are much less so. The conflicts and areas covered in this volume are tremendously complex; the studies are wide-ranging and thorough. In the case study on Afghanistan, for example, we are reminded that obtaining humanitarian access not only meant dealing with the Taliban regime; it also meant the employment of a cohesive and coordinated strategy between UN and non-UN humanitarian actors. Such a strategy was reached not immediately but only after some time and experience gained in the country. As the author notes, even such a course of action had its limitations, chief among these being the attitude of the regime, which was affected by its own isolation and world view, including in the later phase after 11 September 2001.

Another notable case is Iraq, perhaps even more pronounced in the complexities and moral dilemmas thrown up in the wake of the US-led invasion and occupation of the country. The Iraq study raises the very serious question of how humanitarian actors can avoid sacrificing humanitarian principles and norms at the altar of "operationality". Gaining access to areas where there may be real need and, at the same time, being perceived as collaborating with those who have entered the country illegally throw such issues into sharp relief. Predictably, and somewhat inevitably, there are no real answers here, and one suspects that non-governmental organizations and others, including humanitarian actors of the United Nations system, may have to (or will, in any case) accommodate to the existing reality as they stumble along. This is even more telling in environments where the main donor(s) and the transgressor(s) of international law are sometimes one and the same party.

The case of the United Nations Relief and Works Agency (UNRWA) is substantially different. UNRWA is one of the longest-standing and the largest of the humanitarian agencies of the United Nations, and it remains to date the main provider of services in the areas of health, education and relief for needy refugees in the Occupied Palestinian Territories. (The role of the governments of Lebanon, Jordan and Syria are more significant as service providers vis-à-vis their respective populations of Palestinian refugees.) As such, UNRWA has some of the closest ties to the people it is mandated to support and assist. This perception also means that it is often accused, especially of late, of providing cover to those engaging in violence, which in turn clearly affects its ability to be a humanitarian advocate with the occupying authorities. The author of the UNRWA case study brings out here the resultant tension between assisting and advocating for a people who have been refugees for over five decades and trying to ensure full humanitarian access to them courtesy of the occupiers.

None of the other cases studied in this book is any easier. Each comes with its own particular, problematic permutations. I thus commend the individual authors for being brave enough to undertake this valuable and useful study. The fact that most of them are also humanitarian practitioners adds a sense of realism and immediacy to their analysis. I also congratulate co-editors Larry Minear and Hazel Smith for the lessons, conclusions and recommendations they draw from the work of their co-authors. The resulting volume will feed and enrich the debate on these important issues in the coming years.

Introduction

Larry Minear and Hazel Smith

This volume offers a series of intimate glimpses into the day-to-day complexities of mounting and maintaining humanitarian activities in some of the world's most conflicted, intractable and remote settings. Readers will visit 14 different theatres in Asia, Africa, the Middle East and Latin America during the Cold War and the post–Cold War periods. The activities reviewed include not only the provision of emergency succour but also the protection of basic human rights.

As an aid to understanding the challenges faced and the experiences recounted, this volume offers the concept of humanitarian diplomacy. This we understand to encompass the activities carried out by humanitarian organizations to obtain the space from political and military authorities within which to function with integrity. These activities comprise such efforts as arranging for the presence of international humanitarian organizations and personnel in a given country, negotiating access to civilian populations in need of assistance and protection, monitoring assistance programmes, promoting respect for international law and norms, supporting indigenous individuals and institutions, and engaging in advocacy at a variety of levels in support of humanitarian objectives. Humanitarian diplomacy involves activities carried out by humanitarian institutions and personnel, as distinct from diplomacy exercised by traditional diplomats, even in support of humanitarian activities.

Having introduced the concept of humanitarian diplomacy, we must quickly qualify it. As pointed out by Ambassador Lakhdar Brahimi in his Foreword, most humanitarian practitioners do not think of them-

1

selves as diplomats. Diplomacy is a specialized function carried out by a special category of personnel. The duties and obligations of official diplomats and the conduct of their functions are clearly framed by international law and custom. Behind the discomfort of humanitarian officials with the diplomacy label is the fact that diplomacy involves regular interactions with host political officials, be they state or non-state actors. Whereas the portfolio of diplomats is eminently political, humanitarian agencies seek to establish and maintain their non-political bona fides.

The experiences recounted in this volume display humanitarian agencies at work in highly political and politicized settings. From the rich data and analyses provided, readers will themselves be able to reach a judgement about the extent to which the term "humanitarian diplomacy" is appropriate to describe the activities conducted. The first chapter of the book therefore provides an analysis of the craft of humanitarian diplomacy, building on recurring themes from the following 14 case studies. The second chapter compares and contrasts humanitarian and traditional diplomacy.

In addition to breaking new intellectual ground in introducing and testing the concept of humanitarian diplomacy, this volume is innovative in its use of practitioners as both the subjects and the objects of the research process. We have quite intentionally asked humanitarian officials themselves to function as policy analysts, reflecting on activities for which they themselves had major operational responsibility. We did this in part because scholars have not had the sustained access to some of the geographical areas in times of conflict or, for that matter, to the internal documentation that chronicles agency experience. We also chose this course of action because practitioners, as major actors in these settings, have an important perspective to contribute. The reflection process in which they are engaged may also play a useful role in the lesson-learning efforts of their organizations and the humanitarian sector as a whole.

Enlisting practitioners into policy analysis, however, edges some of them onto unfamiliar ground. Even senior officials, accustomed to write reports that are primarily descriptive, are less familiar with the task of examining policy options, assessing the impacts of strategies adopted or rejected, or moving from the very specific circumstances encountered and decisions taken to identify lessons of wider import. To guide the reflection process as well as to ensure a certain comparability among case studies, the editors and contributors agreed a template for the preparation of their chapters. Each chapter accordingly has five sections: context, operational issues, obstacles and opportunities, negotiations, and wider implications.

Some of the authors chafed more than others under these strictures, and there remains a certain unevenness from one chapter to the next.

We hope, however, that the results of the template structure will assist readers in making sense of the experiences shared. Some will want to read the volume from the top, following the presentation of the case studies continent by continent. Others will gravitate to a chapter of special geographical appeal. Readers with specific policy interests – for example, in identifying the problems encountered by humanitarian organizations or in assessing what may have been sacrificed, if anything, in the pursuit of humanitarian access – may wish to read a given section of each chapter back-to-back.

This volume is the product of a strenuous research process that began in 2002 when the design of the undertaking was agreed and funding was provided by the United Nations World Food Programme (WFP), the United States Institute of Peace and the United Nations University (UNU). Discussions of the entire group of authors in Bangkok in March 2004 helped establish the analytical framework and sort out certain methodological issues. Discussions among a smaller group of authors in Rome on the occasion of a lessons-identified workshop hosted by the WFP in November 2004 helped refine the approach further and identify crosscutting issues and tentative conclusions.

In the intervening period, during which our manuscript has been reviewed and critiqued by the United Nations University Press, the situations described in a number of the case studies have changed, whether for the better or the worse. Since each of the chapters represents a "snapshot in time" of a particular humanitarian initiative, we have not asked the authors to update their analysis to accommodate late-breaking developments. For the most part, recent events do not change the analysis already offered, although they may highlight the importance of some of the options earlier embraced or discarded.

We see this volume as a contribution to a growing literature on the exercise of humanitarian action. It seeks to inform practitioners in their exercise of the craft of humanitarian diplomacy. It will also interest diplomats, many of whom have no working understanding of humanitarian principles or of the need for protecting the independence of humanitarian action. In addition, it should provide information for the concerned international public, on whose informed support sustained and effective humanitarian action depends.

Acknowledgements

We wish to express special appreciation to the chapter writers. Their experience, enthusiasm and painstaking drafting and redrafting have enriched not only their own chapters but also the volume as a whole.

We also wish to thank the humanitarian agencies for facilitating their involvement and for enabling them to make use of potentially sensitive material. Thanks to individual and institutional engagement, this undertaking has already played a role in the wider lesson-learning effort in which the humanitarian sector is now engaged.

We are grateful to the main institutional underwriters of this project: the United Nations University and the United Nations World Food Programme. The project also benefited from a generous grant from the United States Institute of Peace. The United Nations High Commissioner for Refugees (UNHCR), the United Nations Relief and Works Agency (UNRWA) and the International Committee of the Red Cross (ICRC) underwrote the costs of attendance at the two authors' workshops by the contributors from their ranks. We also offer a special word of thanks to Ambassador Lakhdar Brahimi for agreeing to write a Foreword to the volume and to Asif Khan of his staff for his role in the process. The perspective of a respected international diplomat on the interface between humanitarian and classic diplomacy is particularly illuminating.

Numerous other individuals have made important contributions. At the United Nations University, Ms Yoshie Sawada provided ongoing administrative support. We would also like to thank all in the UNU Peace and Governance Programme and at the UNU Press for their support. At the WFP, particular thanks are owed to Valerie Guarnieri, who assisted in the project at all of its design and implementation stages. We also wish to thank Nicholas Crawford and Sarah Laughton for their interest in identifying and applying lessons from the study to WFP programmes. We would like to thank the United Nations Office for the Coordination of Humanitarian Affairs (UNOCHA) in Tbilisi, Georgia, and Ingrid Kolb-Hindarmanto of Unicef Georgia for their kindness in arranging a research visit for Hazel Smith in June 2004.

Part I

Craft and concept

1

The craft of humanitarian diplomacy

Larry Minear

In this volume, humanitarian practitioners treat readers to a rich set of experiences. The 14 crises reviewed span a quarter-century, from the Vietnamese occupation of Cambodia in the late 1970s and the civil war in Lebanon in the 1980s to the current crises in Colombia, Afghanistan and Iraq. The chapters provide vignettes of humanitarian officials carrying out a variety of diplomatic functions in support of their programmes. Those functions include negotiation of humanitarian access to vulnerable populations, promoting respect for international law and norms, combating a culture in which violations occur with impunity, supporting indigenous counterpart individuals and institutions, and engaging in advocacy with political authorities at the local, national and international levels.

The experiences demonstrate a full range of successes and failures – from the opening up of Cambodia during its occupation by the Vietnamese and the mounting of programmes under the reclusive authorities in North Korea, on the positive side, to frustration by the terms of engagement in Somalia and the blockage of access to civilians in the Maoist-dominated regions of Nepal. In some instances, successes were a function of shrewd decision-making and well-managed programmes; in others, of serendipity. In some cases, failures were a function of factors over which humanitarian actors had little or no control; in other instances, the humanitarian apparatus itself was poorly managed and failed to capitalize on opportunities as they arose.

Gaining immediacy from their presentation by practitioners themselves, the experiences offer, for all of their diversity, a set of variations on several recurring themes. This chapter explores some of those themes, both in their own terms and in their wider implications. As analysts of activities in which they themselves played lead roles, the authors of individual chapters have provided a fascinating behind-the-scenes perspective on events. At the same time, their experiences need to be subjected to more thorough-going scrutiny and placed in a broader context.

The themes examined include the appropriateness of the term "humanitarian diplomacy" for the activities described, the nature of the interlocutors with whom humanitarian diplomats deal, the issue portfolio that humanitarian diplomacy addresses, the tensions between and among humanitarian principles and the pressure for making trade-offs, the comparative advantages of various agencies and actors for different tasks, the levels at which such diplomacy functions, and the ingredients of success and failure. This chapter concludes with some thoughts about the future evolution of humanitarian diplomacy.

The concept

Perhaps the most pervasive theme in the 14 case studies concerns the nature of humanitarian diplomacy, its relation to diplomacy of a more traditional sort and its links to the operational activities of humanitarian organizations and the wider issues of peace and war.

The concept

The concept of humanitarian diplomacy itself is a bit awkward. Asked whether they see themselves as diplomats, most card-carrying humanitarian officials would reply in the negative. In the words of a handbook prepared by the Centre for Humanitarian Dialogue, "[m]ost humanitarian workers negotiate in some way every day but few have thought to recognize this core activity as a conscious skill and so seek to refine and develop it across their organization".[1] For many aid workers with frontline or headquarters responsibilities, diplomacy is viewed as something well beyond – and quite separate from – what they do. It is a more specialized activity, dealing with the broad issues of war and peace. It is a function of states carried out by trained professionals, not the preoccupation of aid agencies and their personnel.

To be sure, commonalities exist between the negotiations and other diplomatic functions carried out by humanitarian personnel, on the one hand, and the practice of diplomacy of a traditional sort, on the other. As discussed in Chapter 2, core diplomatic activities such as communication, information-gathering and negotiations are hallmarks of humanitarian diplomacy and of traditional diplomacy as well. Both crafts are highly consensual in nature and approach; both are central to the well-being of at-risk populations. Like their colleagues with political portfolios, UN humanitarian officials carry *laissez passers*, symbolizing their diplomatic entitlements and immunity (representatives of non-governmental organizations travel on normal passports). Beyond these commonalities, however, lie significant differences. Indeed, as the authors of these case studies agreed in discussions in Bangkok and Rome, the differences in the functioning of diplomats and humanitarian personnel were more numerous and more illuminating than the similarities.

Diplomats function within a "regime", understood as a set of "social institutions composed of agreed-upon principles, norms, rules, and decision-making procedures that govern interaction of actors in specific issue areas".[2] Having had their postings vetted with the authorities in advance, they present their credentials on arrival and act on instructions from their capitals, conveyed with specific rules of engagement and time frames and overlaid with expectations of regular and detailed reporting. Diplomats in a given country-in-crisis represent something of a "community". They undertake joint initiatives on issues – formerly political and military matters but now increasingly economic and sometimes even humanitarian – of interest to their respective governments.

Traditional diplomacy is conducted within a framework of sovereign states, with the Vienna Conventions of 1949 providing the canons of acceptable and unacceptable professional behaviour. Cautious by nature, diplomats who overstep the normal bounds may find themselves declared persona non grata (or "PNGed"). The contents of diplomacy as well as its form are the affairs of states. Diplomatic démarches, as well as day-to-day diplomatic interactions, reflect national interest and realpolitik. Diplomats have multiple issues within their portfolios, only some of which are humanitarian in nature; humanitarians, by contrast, have a more focused agenda in which humanitarian interests are generally first and foremost.

Diplomacy carried out by humanitarian interests, by contrast, is not framed by as well established a regime. To be sure, international humanitarian, human rights and refugee law provides a rubric of obligations to which governments have agreed. There has been significant progress in recent years in making such obligations clearer and more compelling, particularly in the areas of human rights and of internally displaced persons. Most governments have signed a series of conventions and other agreements promoted by UN and regional governmental organizations (e.g. the European Union). Nevertheless, the existing frameworks in the humanitarian domain by and large still lack the enforcement provisions of other international regimes such as intellectual property or trade. Governments experiencing major political or humanitarian crises have developed a litany of rationalizations for their frequent failures to implement agreed obligations in the humanitarian domain. In point of fact, the scoff-laws of international humanitarian norms face few penalties.

In addition to functioning in a still evolving landscape without clear ground rules and sanctions, humanitarian diplomacy is marked by an urgency that does not regard sovereignty with the deference of traditional diplomats. In the canon of most diplomatic corps and most foreign service handbooks, the treatment of a nation's civilians has traditionally been the sole discretion of the relevant state authorities. Only recently has the failure to exercise the positive obligations of sovereignty come to be viewed as a matter with implications for international peace and security, thereby opening up to international review and redress such practices as the massive violation of human rights and the widespread denial of access to people in grave need.[3]

In contrast to its better-established counterpart, humanitarian diplomacy is more improvisational and ad hoc, more opportunistic and *ad hominem*. The vaunted humanitarian imperative does not open all doors. When push comes to shove, humanitarian institutions have limited muscle. They lack the authority and the capacity to impose economic or military sanctions, although they on occasion recommend their imposition.

How many legions has the pope or, in this instance, the International Committee of the Red Cross (ICRC)? It is not that humanitarian interests are without high cards to play, although they may lack recognized trumps. It is rather that reliance on moral suasion puts a premium on compelling presentations of the humanitarian case, unreinforced by clear penalties, or threats, for non-compliance. Nor do aid agencies make or enforce the rules of the game. The suspension of the airlift in Sudan, and its explanation to the authorities as driven by a concern for staff safety rather than as punishment for Khartoum's policies, illustrates the extreme delicacy with which aid agencies approach muscle-flexing. The vulnerability of the international effort in Bosnia to abuse by all parties placed aid organizations in a weak position to insist on humanitarian principles.

In implementing what they understand to be the humanitarian imperative, humanitarian officials are more prepared than are their counterparts in the diplomatic corps to take risks and to acknowledge the reality of failure, given the obstacles they confront. Aid officials often find themselves caught in a vicious cycle of persuading the political authorities to take responsibility for the suffering in which their governments' policies are implicated. Since humanitarians control few of the elements that create suffering, they see their frequent failure to ease the pain as "going with the territory" within which they function. Where traditional diplomats generally operate in the shadows and place discretion high in the panoply of their professional skills, humanitarians are more prepared to "go public" when necessary in the interest of humanitarian goals, reaching out to the media to mobilize the force of public opinion against recalcitrant authorities. Examples abound in the coming chapters.

That is not to say that humanitarian officials, in their effort to carve out space for their agency's activities, may not on occasion be PNGed. Witness the expulsion of several agencies from Sudan in the dark days of 1988, when the authorities were unwilling to allow access for aid programmes or to tolerate the resulting criticism of, and pressure on them for, their failure to do so. More recently, in November 2004, the Khartoum authorities gave Oxfam-UK and Save the Children-UK their walking papers in response to their public criticism of Sudanese government actions in Darfur.[4] One agency seeking visas for its personnel there attributed delays to the authorities' disgruntlement at the publication of a critical opinion piece by an expatriate staff person who had just returned home.

The humanitarian playing field is seldom level. The political authorities have an arsenal of weapons for expressing their displeasure with insistent humanitarianism: the denial of visas or delays in the clearance of relief shipments through customs are but two potent examples. Even at their most persuasive, aid officials proffering mercy are ultimately at the mercy of governments. Usually, however, the dynamics of the interaction are such that what humanitarians do – or seek to do – rarely elicits formal diplomatic censure. Against the backdrop of more cautious traditional diplomacy, the activities of humanitarian personnel in the diplomatic sphere are especially noteworthy.

The parameters

From discussions among the authors of the chapters in this volume has arisen a useful distinction between "capital D" Diplomacy and "small D" diplomacy. The former involves what professional diplomats do: negotiate agreements to avoid, reduce or bring an end to conflict; mobilize international pressure in support of the rule of law; and lubricate the machinery of the relationships among states. Working within the humanitarian sphere, professional diplomats may also create new agencies and institutional frameworks. The formation of the United Nations Relief and Works Agency (UNRWA) and the creation of an international peacebuilding rubric for Somalia are described in this volume. Also in the area of Diplomacy, a study by the United Nations Institute for Training and Research (UNITAR) examines the experience of Special Representatives of the UN Secretary-General (SRSGs) in greater detail, in the humanitarian as well as the political and peacekeeping spheres.[5]

Whereas "capital D" Diplomacy tends to be high-level and formal, "small D" diplomacy is more terrestrial – even pedestrian. It covers a host of humanitarian functions of a more day-to-day sort. It functions in the middle range of activities between, on the one hand, arranging for the safe passage of humanitarian materiel and personnel past a given road-block and, on the other, locating and contracting for aid agency office and warehouse space or setting up bank accounts to allow for agency transactions. These workaday functions, however essential to the success of humanitarian programmes, are not "diplomatic" as such, although they involve negotiations between international personnel and local authorities. In the broad middle range are activities such as the negotiation by the United Nations Children's Fund (UNICEF) of agreements with the multiple factions in Lebanon so that vaccinations of children could take place across the country, and the efforts of the United Nations High Commissioner for Refugees (UNHCR) to create a path for its convoys through the 90 checkpoints between Zagreb in Croatia and Sarajevo in Bosnia-Herzegovina.

Small D diplomacy may overlap with Diplomacy. That happens when, for example, humanitarian practitioners themselves play a role in negotiating terms of engagement in hot-war or post-conflict situations, or, conversely, when diplomats are enlisted in the process of expediting the granting of aid worker visas. The case studies on Cambodia (Chapter 6) and the former Yugoslavia (Chapter 16) illustrate those processes in action.

Few of the reviews in this volume, however, involve capital D diplomacy, such as in the setting up of the basic terms of engagement between international humanitarian actors and the often multiple sets of authorities in countries in crisis. The review of UNRWA in Chapter 3, for example, takes as its point of departure the existence of the Relief Works Agency, itself the result of an exercise in Diplomacy that the chapter notes only in passing. It then examines the agency's stewardship, through a half-century of adversity, of its mandate for Palestinians, a period during which the negotiated arrangements were tested, adapted and strengthened. The Iraq case study (Chapter 5) describes efforts by humanitarian organizations not to broker a peace agreement between the Coalition Provisional Authority (CPA) and the insurgents in Falluja and Najaf but simply to arrange access for the essentials of survival of the embattled civilian population during military action by the CPA.

Most of the chapters describe the cultivation of relationships that goes on as part of the process of nurturing basic agreements already reached by virtue of Diplomacy. In North Korea (Chapter 9), the nurturing process occasioned daily headaches for programme managers. Official displeasure was conveyed by simply severing all communications with a given international agency for a time. In the case of Nepal (Chapter 10), aid agencies confronted a special challenge. On the scene by virtue of development mandates, they were called upon on a daily basis to find ways to deal with an unravelling political crisis, a volatile situation with major implications for the capacities of the Nepalese people to meet their daily needs. Access to people in need throughout the country was a precondition for programmes of emergency succour, which for the time being had to take precedence over longer-term development work.

Humanitarian organizations have widely differing attitudes toward their own missions and obligations as related to Diplomacy and to diplomacy. Some take pains to stick to their humanitarian knitting, exercising (but also minimizing) the small D interactions with host authorities in which they are daily engaged. They downplay the political dimensions of their activities in an effort to protect the perception of their neutrality. Perceptions of partiality or partisanship can place humanitarian actors and those they seek to assist in danger, as experience in Afghanistan (Chapter 7) and East Timor (Chapter 8) demonstrates. Perceptions of favouritism may also wreak havoc in relations with host authorities, in the attitudes of local populations, in dealings with governments and constituencies on the resource-providing end, and in the respect commanded by humanitarian emblems in highly politicized settings. The Iraq chapter provides a close-up description of the ongoing difficulties of protecting the integrity of humanitarian activities from association with the highly unpopular occupation. Those efforts were largely unsuccessful.

A second set of agencies embraces the challenges of small D diplomacy as a necessary ingredient in support of effective activities of protection and assistance. Some do so in one-to-one dealings with the authorities whereas others seek a certain protective cover through support of humanitarian sector-wide representations to the authorities. The experience of aid agencies in North Korea offers a case in point. With each departure of an aid group from the scene (sometimes voluntary, other times less so), the remaining agencies regrouped and reaffirmed the appropriateness of their chosen approach to managing their interactions with the authorities. Or again, the broad set of interlocutors with which Peace Brigades International was in daily touch underscored the agency's view that nurturing access to card-carrying diplomatic actors in Colombia and in capitals around the world is a key to the success of its humanitarian mission.

A third set of aid groups is more forthright in supporting Diplomacy. These agencies reason that the humanitarian enterprise must not just be about the relief of suffering and the protection of civilian populations against abuse. It is also obliged to address, and/or support efforts to address, the root causes that make for deprivation and abuse. An illuminating example is provided by the experience in the former Yugoslavia (Chapter 16), where the UNHCR, in the person of its very visible High Commissioner, Sadako Ogata, became closely involved in international efforts by the United States, the European Community and the United Nations to find a negotiated solution to the breakup of the former Yugoslavia. Yet the range of criticisms levelled at the refugee agency – from failing to help people exercise their right to seek asylum to supporting ethnic cleansing – suggests the perils of association with diplomatic undertakings. Embracing Diplomacy, while eminently logical from a conceptual point of view, is accompanied by clear risks to the integrity of agency activities.

The process and the players

The actual process of humanitarian diplomacy is quite different from traditional Diplomacy, both in its day-to-day activities and in the nature of those who participate. The role of principles merits review, as does the nature of the interlocutors with whom humanitarian officials by necessity interact.

Principles and trade-offs

One of the reasons the concept of humanitarian diplomacy is an uneasy fit in describing what humanitarian personnel do is that Diplomacy involves a process of trade-offs, of tough bargaining between adversarial interests in the search for common ground. Humanitarian action, by contrast, would seem to be informed by humanitarian law, norms and principles, with ostensibly little or nothing to trade. In negotiating space for assistance and protection activities, should a humanitarian official be prepared to make compromises? If so, of what sort and to what extent?

What common ground exists between the imperatives of succour and the practices of rights-abusing governments or insurgencies? What are the carrots and sticks of humanitarian diplomacy? What are the pros and cons of "blaming and shaming" and the effective alternatives to going that route? "In humanitarian situations", observes the handbook on negotiations mentioned earlier, "there are often real obstacles to obtaining principled agreements because the values and interests they [that is, humanitarians] defend ... are often profoundly incompatible with those of their military and political counterparts."[6]

The relatively low ranking of humanitarian priorities, especially when high-level issues of national security and state survival are at stake, places humanitarian interests at a decided disadvantage. Speaking at an off-the-record session in late 2004, one senior UN official posted to an African country in crisis reached for a card-playing analogy to describe his plight. He had been, he said, dealt a weak hand from a stacked deck. When sitting down at the negotiating table with his opposite number, what, after all, can an aid official expect to extract, and at what price? Compromises are the essence of negotiation. The fear of the negotiator – diplomat, labour relations lawyer and aid agency executive alike – is that, in the give-and-take process, compromise will turn out to be a matter of "I give and you take". What do the experiences chronicled in this volume suggest about humanitarian principles and the extent to which they are negotiable?

Many humanitarian organizations view principles as their North Star. The ICRC has its seven. Numerous agencies subscribe to a Code of Conduct that articulates key principles.[7] In some specific emergencies – Sierra Leone, the Sudan and the Democratic People's Republic of Korea are examples – aid agencies hammered out statements of the principles that they sought to affirm in their activities. Some humanitarian agencies, even those that are signatories of the various codes, are essentially pragmatic, treating principles as "for reference only". Still others, although they would not describe themselves as "unprincipled", certainly make no pretensions to "stand on principle" in selecting their crises for involvement or in charting their in-country courses of action. "Opportunistic" or "entrepreneurial" might serve as non-pejorative labels.

Humanitarian principles include such fundamentals as impartiality (assistance according to the severity of need), neutrality (activities without political or other extraneous agendas) and independence (the obligation to resist interference with key principles). Each principle is to one degree or another under stress when humanitarian organizations seek to carry out their mandates in settings of armed conflict.

- *Impartiality* is tested by situations such as the former Yugoslavia, when UNHCR, in exchange for access to Muslim areas, was under continuing pressure to distribute relief supplies from the Sarajevo airlift to Serbian populations in amounts exceeding their proportionate need.[8]
- *Neutrality* comes under pressure when assistance is viewed as taking sides in a conflict, either by aid agencies, which are perceived as supporting one protagonist, or by recipient authorities, which seek to parlay assistance into international endorsement of their cause. Again, the Iraq experience is a case in point.
- *Independence* is jeopardized when agencies are denied the necessary freedom to conduct operations and monitor distribution. The constraints faced by the World Food Programme (WFP) and associated agencies in North Korea constituted a threat to independent humanitarian action.

There are, in the nature of things, fewer tensions in so-called natural disasters.

Faced with the tensions between cardinal precepts and operational constraints, different agencies attach different meaning and value to fidelity to principles. The Afghanistan experience, Chapter 7 points out, indicates three approaches to dealing with the Taliban: principled, accommodationist and "duck and weave". The first, exemplified by UNICEF, advocated a forthright change in policies clearly at variance with the UN Charter. The second, with the World Health Organization and the United Nations Office for Project Services as cases in point, was committed to engaging with the authorities on technical issues with an eye to achieving an easing of restrictions over time. The third, the preferred strategy of many non-governmental organizations (NGOs), sought to finesse such matters by working directly with affected communities. UNHCR and the WFP tended to alternate between the first two positions, depending on the issue and circumstance. To one extent or another, these approaches recur in situation after situation, with the spectrum of agencies arrayed accordingly.

Reflecting upon experiences such as those presented in this volume, humanitarian organizations have revisited the content and importance of principles. Some have concluded that once sacred tenets such as neutrality pose an unnecessary impediment to the conduct of humanitarian activities and to the diplomacy necessary to support them. Some have come to view what were once called principles as the means to an end, the end being the establishment of trust and the winning of consent of at-risk populations. In this interpretation, the validity of principles is tested by their fruits. Rather than using principles as a benchmark for weighing the conditions imposed by belligerents – and, for that matter, by donors – some agencies have shifted the burden of proof to those who would withhold engagement or reject the resources available. Others retain principles as setting a benchmark and they select whatever option comes closest. The case studies provide new data to enrich this debate about the relevance of principles, among both practitioners and outside analysts.

A further complication in an analysis of the role of principle in humanitarian diplomacy is that the institutional politics of the humanitarian enterprise affect the views and approaches of the organizations involved. Agencies that take too principled a stand, whether in Afghanistan or elsewhere, may find that they have dealt themselves out of the action. Not only have they then failed in their humanitarian mission; their own insistence has led them to opt out of the fray. What price fidelity to principle, the pragmatists ask, given the risks of self-marginalization and constituency backlash? Principles, the argument goes, should be devices for energizing activities of assistance and protection, not for frustrating them.[9]

But pragmatism has its own set of problems. Pragmatists risk being forced to make ever greater concessions to the authorities. The comment of a UN official on his dealings with the Yugoslav authorities in the early 1990s illustrates this conundrum. The opening hole is small when the screwdriver is inserted, he noted of the initial concessions made. After a few turns of the screwdriver, however, the screw begins to bite and the damage is more obvious.[10] As humanitarian action has moved into areas of greater physical insecurity, agencies have been confronted with the need to "review the bidding"; that is, to clarify the circumstances in which they will be prepared to suspend or terminate activities. As suggested by the discussions of North Korea, Sudan and Iraq, a shifting admixture of considerations, including staff and beneficiary safety and the need for institutional profile, comes into play.

So dangerous is the potential erosion of humanitarian principle and so misleading the concept of bargaining for access that some agencies avoid the term "negotiations" altogether. Peace Brigades International (PBI) informs its interlocutors in Colombia of its presence rather than negotiating access for its staff. Although UNICEF did "negotiate" in its initiative to secure the release of child soldiers in Sierra Leone, the official involved described what he "gave away" as involving nothing at the level of principle, only a bit of favourable publicity to the government authorities that cooperated. PBI, by contrast, was uneasy with the idea that the Colombian authorities would receive any kudos at all for meeting their acknowledged obligations.

However defined, fidelity to principles is hardly a panacea. That is illustrated by a 1993 exchange between an ICRC delegate and the Serb authorities over access to minority Muslim populations. She pleaded her case on behalf of international humanitarian law and the principles of the Red Cross movement. "We know your principles, and we will make you change them," she was told. She responded, "We believe in our principles. They have been good for 125 years."[11] Taking a similar approach, UNICEF in Lebanon operated on the basis of expecting the factions to meet their humanitarian obligations. More often than not, Chapter 4 confirms, the agency was rewarded for its faith that those groups would choose to be associated with the provision of services for children.

In some settings, principles or the interpretation of principles clash. In Cambodia, the NGO Consortium was acting upon clear humanitarian principles in mounting relief efforts within the country. In deference to those same principles, UNICEF and the ICRC postponed action, seeking what they considered minimum commitments from the authorities to their access and freedom of movement to monitor distribution of supplies. NGOs operational within the country were critical of those agencies running programmes in refugee camps along the border under the oversight of the Khmer Rouge. Conversely, NGOs working in the camps were critical of agencies operational in Cambodia for their lack of independence and their perceived "operational links to partisan actors".

Invocation of hard-and-fast principles can be the enemy of action. Instead of debating principles with the Taliban and embarrassing them for not caring about "our" principles, Chapter 7 on Afghanistan recalls, some agencies sought practical ways to get girls into schools. Instead of insisting that the authorities free all child soldiers, Chapter 13 on Sierra Leone notes, UNICEF concentrated on the younger ones, including their need for rehabilitation. This sort of "humanitarian pragmatism" can be based on principle without being immobilized by it. Not to take such an approach, say its proponents, is to make the perfect the enemy of the good, an unthinkable irony in a world in which the good needs all the help it can get. In other words, from the standpoint of an individual who stands to receive emergency aid, a humanitarian bird in the hand may be worth a flock in the bush.

At the end of the day, the ultimate card in the high-stakes negotiation game involves suspending or withdrawing operations. But here, too, complications abound. The withdrawal of humanitarian operations can represent a victory for principle or a defeat for the agencies and their needy clientele, as in "Let them eat principles". Conversely, accepting as a price for sustaining aid activities the constraints on humanitarian space that the authorities impose can have short-term benefits but be a recipe for future failure. Offering "incentives" to the belligerents in exchange for access may represent a slippery slope and can compromise the integrity of a humanitarian initiative.

Events in Bosnia suggest that the pivotal decision by humanitarian agencies – and their point of maximum leverage with the authorities – was whether or not to engage in the first place. Once that decision is made, the weight of on-the-ground presence of personnel and materiel greatly narrows the options available to practitioners. At that point, the idea of suspending or terminating operations may become "self-indulgent", with the needs of beneficiaries jockeying for position with the scruples of the agencies. Yet the progression seems a recurring one: that, in the face of efforts by local authorities to divert or control, humanitarian activities may over time lose their focus and impact. Indeed, the authorities may with time become more adept at manipulating humanitarian access for their own purposes.[12] The chapters in this volume demonstrate the need for agencies to be clearer in their thinking about principles and the trade-offs associated with them.

Interlocutors

The experience of practitioners also underscores distinctions between traditional and humanitarian diplomacy with regard to those with whom such officials normally engage. Whereas diplomats typically deal with states, humanitarians must find ways of engaging non-state actors such as the insurgents in Colombia or the myriad factions in Lebanon. In a colloquy at the Council on Foreign Relations in New York several years ago, the late Sergio Vieira de Mello, as Under-Secretary-General for Humanitarian Affairs the ranking UN aid official, commented on his unenviable task as the point person for negotiating international access to civilians living within the jurisdiction of the limb-amputating Revolutionary United Front in Sierra Leone. Who are these shadowy people with whom I am forced to negotiate for access to the nation's civilians?, he asked with evident frustration. How do I know whom to deal with and how can I hold them accountable for what they promise me?

Reprobate or otherwise, the people with whom humanitarian officials negotiate – be they insurgents or sitting political authorities, upstarts or internationally recognized actors – are frequently not the real power brokers. "It was never clear", recalls the writer of Chapter 9 on North Korea, who the "higher authorities" were to whom the interlocutors with humanitarian organizations deferred, "or whether it was an excuse to refuse difficult or unwanted requests ... Neither the humanitarian community nor the diplomatic corps were ever able to access these 'higher' officials." The Sudan experience was much the same (Chapter 11): "Behind the hard men negotiating with the United Nations are harder men pulling the strings." Similarly, the writer of Chapter 7 on Afghanistan recounts a double frustration: first, that it was often difficult to find the appropriate Taliban official with whom to negotiate; and, second, that the agreement then negotiated failed to command respect throughout Taliban-controlled territory.

In some settings depicted in this volume, the interlocutors of international organizations have precious little humanitarian literacy regarding international institutions, obligations and procedures. Yet quite the opposite is also the case – counterparts intimately familiar with the nuances of international law and their obligations. Chapter 3 confirms the high level of professionalism in the Israeli foreign ministry among officials to whom UNRWA aid staff related. Although Israeli government policy disputed the applicability to Israel (as the occupying power) of the fourth Geneva Convention on the protection of civilians, diplomats in the ministry quietly acknowledged their government's obligations. Similarly, in the early 1990s, Iraqi foreign ministry officials, many of them educated in prestigious law schools abroad, made a compelling case against the international sanctions imposed on Baghdad through detailed references to international humanitarian law.

The growing importance during the post–Cold War era of belligerent "non-state actors" as erstwhile partners in humanitarian dialogue has led policy makers and practitioners alike to monitor their functioning and, where possible, to acquaint them with their obligations. One such occasion was a conference held in Geneva in late 2004 under the auspices of a consortium, Geneva Call. Viewing the topic of "An Inclusive Approach to Armed Non-State Actors and International Humanitarian Norms" as an opportunity to advance its own mission as stewards and disseminators of international humanitarian law, the ICRC participated in the meeting and gave a keynote speech.[13] With the active support of aid groups, other conferences have brought the protagonists in particular crises together in efforts to negotiate an end to various conflicts.

The task of humanitarian diplomacy is complicated by the reality that what the agencies have on offer by way of relief assistance and protection to civilian populations is not always considered a desideratum by their negotiating counterparts. "Given a choice between humanitarian aid and progress towards ending aggression", observes the author of Chapter 16 on the former Yugoslavia, the Bosnian government "would choose the latter, even at the price of more suffering in the short term". Similarly, many Kosovo Albanians supported NATO bombing even at the expense of the disruption of urgent aid activities.

In each instance, the humanitarian calculus of the belligerents was weighted differently from what the agencies would have preferred. The lack of priority accorded by such actors to their own populations places international humanitarian organizations in the awkward and perhaps ultimately untenable position of ostensibly caring more for such persons than do the authorities themselves.

Institutional dimensions

The conduct of humanitarian diplomacy as depicted in the country case studies that make up this volume raises a series of institutional issues for humanitarian organizations themselves. They include the issues portfolio selected, the levels at which activities are carried out, the comparative advantages of certain kinds of agencies, and the skills needed among practitioners.

Portfolios

The specific issues around which humanitarian diplomacy is exercised include the tasks of assessing the needs of civilians in distress and of monitoring their changing situation over time; ensuring protection of the human rights of a vulnerable population; arranging entry to the country and the countryside for programme staff and headquarters colleagues; facilitating reasonably unobstructed communication with indigenous counterparts; promoting greater observance of international humanitarian law; reining-in abuses directed with impunity against civilian populations and aid workers; and laying the groundwork for ongoing activities. Just as humanitarian diplomacy involves far more than negotiations, so negotiations involve a wider array of objectives than simply ensuring access.

A good example of humanitarian diplomacy's expanding and changing issues portfolio is provided by UNRWA, as chronicled in Chapter 3. Historically, negotiating and maintaining access for the distribution of "relief" to Palestinians have been at the centre of the agency's title and activities. Nowadays, however, its brief also includes responding to the demolition of homes and economic assets such as olive groves, challenging the meting out of collective punishment, and keeping Palestinian needs to the front and centre on the international screen. One creative device to implement this portfolio during the first intifada was the creation of the position of Refugee Affairs Officer (RAO). The position was initially opposed by the government of Israel but has eventually become an accepted and essential monitoring and protection device. The RAO portfolio in turn involves humanitarian diplomacy in its multiple aspects.

A recurrent challenge involves the protection of the integrity of humanitarian activities from abuse. During the second intifada, UNRWA was forced to step up efforts to counteract the campaign waged against its work. In doing so, however, it built on measures instituted much earlier. The allegations levelled against UNRWA – that its camps were used as staging areas for attacks against Israelis and Israel, that its ambulances were being used to transport weapons, and so on – have been made against other humanitarian programmes, including those in Iraq. In the service of successful programmes in highly politicized settings, therefore, one of the tasks of humanitarian diplomacy involves acting to pre-empt charges of partiality and working to increase knowledge among beneficiaries and others of the nature and purpose of the assistance provided.

Another recurring issue faced by humanitarian organizations in such settings is the fragility of the security situation. In some cases, insecurity is used by the belligerents as a rationalization for denying access to humanitarian personnel and operations. That was the case in Sudan, Nepal and Iraq (during the time of the Coalition Provisional Authority). In other cases, concern for the safety of humanitarian personnel leads to measures by the agencies themselves to restrict their presence and operations. Self-imposed restrictions are described in the chapters on Afghanistan (Chapter 7), Iraq (Chapter 5) and, as regards UNICEF and the ICRC, Cambodia (Chapter 6).

The case studies provide evidence of a variety of responses to security constraints. Some organizations turned to international military and peacekeeping personnel to ensure the safety of aid personnel. Examples are provided from East Timor (Chapter 8), Lebanon (Chapter 4) and, during one particular period, Liberia (Chapter 12). Other agencies preferred to keep their distance from the military, at most encouraging military personnel to provide security for at-risk populations rather than for humanitarian personnel themselves. At various times in recent history, Liberia and Afghanistan offer cases in point. Perhaps the most distinctive approach is that of Peace Brigades International, which, rather than lamenting insecurity as a reason for restricting its own access, views insecurity as the very reason for deploying its staff in Colombia (Chapter 15). For most agencies, however, the provision of security is both a major motivation for their engagement and a constraint upon it.

Levels of activity

The case studies provide illustrations of humanitarian diplomacy being carried out at a variety of levels. These range from the local (negotiating convoy passage past a particular checkpoint) to the global (e.g. encouraging the Security Council to address issues at the country or generic level). Whereas the concept of "capital D" diplomacy applies to the arena of interstate relations, the case studies have by design concentrated more heavily on operational challenges. What does the experience reviewed suggest about the relative importance of an operational focus? Given the globalization of issues and relationships, to what extent does a country strategy need to be set within a global framework?

Much of the experience chronicled in this volume confirms the value of negotiating at the most local level possible. This strategy benefits from the immediacy of urgent concerns and from the first-hand knowledge of the actors, avoiding the delays that often accompany efforts to engage higher-level authorities. The Lebanon experience suggests that the absence of high-level outside political involvement over a period of two and a half years contributed to the successful mounting of UNICEF's immunization initiative. In the instance of North Korea, US tendencies to micro-manage the food aid programme in the service of political objectives themselves created problems. The mixed benefits of high-level involvement in operational matters are confirmed by a senior official of the US Agency for International Development with responsibilities for Afghanistan in the post-9/11 period. "The good news is that a lot of high-level U.S. policy makers are interested in Afghanistan," he said.

"The bad news is that a lot of high-level U.S. policy makers are interested in Afghanistan ... If Afghanistan were Liberia, we'd have a lot easier time managing the crisis."[14]

Some obstacles encountered locally, however, cannot be resolved without going up the line. It would also be unfair to conclude that high-level humanitarian diplomacy is necessary and valuable only for high-profile crises. The necessity of such diplomacy not only in Bosnia, Afghanistan and Iraq but also in Liberia, Somalia and Nepal is confirmed by the case studies. Of course, the results can be either positive or negative in any given setting. The experience of Liberia illustrates the difficulties experienced by humanitarian organizations as a result of the off-again, on-again interests of major powers. The Yugoslav review underscores the need for political action to address the causes of the conflict, noting at the same time that politicians used humanitarian activities as a cover for political inaction.

Among humanitarian actors, the ICRC has made perhaps the most thorough-going institutional commitment to humanitarian diplomacy. The thrust of its work is at the field level, where ICRC delegates have considerable autonomy in managing negotiations with belligerents and in making determinations regarding the continuation or withdrawal of programmes and personnel under threat. ICRC headquarters resources are at the disposal of field staff, including those in its Humanitarian Diplomacy (formerly International Organizations) division. The ICRC uses "humanitarian diplomacy to make states aware of problems and issues of humanitarian concern, and shares these concerns with the international community".[15] Its broader representations, however, support and reflect its operational presence and speak to the specifically humanitarian dimension of the given problem. Chapter 8 on East Timor, written by an ICRC official, in describing earlier activities takes pains not to create problems for its continuing endeavours.

Perhaps the most dramatic example of multi-level activities and the need for synchronicity among them is provided by Peace Brigades International in Colombia. In the interests of providing protection to communities and individuals exposed to political violence, PBI uses a spectrum of "objectives, expectations, types of relationships, and forms of interaction" with different actors that form "an interlocking web of preventative political pressure". Thus the disappearance of a leader in a remote area of Colombia – at what some agencies call the "deep field level" – is immediately flagged by the PBI network as an item of concern for regional and national civil and military authorities in Colombia, for donors in their respective capitals, for UN agencies, and for other humanitarian and solidarity groups. In some instances this strategy has gained the release of the disappeared; in others, it has not.

Serious structural problems sometimes impede the information-sharing and other support functions necessary to maintain safety and promote continued access. As one moves from the headquarters level to national capitals, regional sub-offices and ultimately individual communities, the knowledgeability of staff in many agencies regarding international humanitarian law tends to lessen even as staff familiarity with the local context increases. Systematizing and nurturing institution-wide memory regarding agency experience in the various aspects of humanitarian diplomacy present a major challenge. Indeed, as noted below, approaching humanitarian diplomacy as a multi-layered activity has major implications for the resource commitments of the agencies and for the skill sets of staffs.

In tackling its work in Afghanistan, the NGO Care had more than 20 staff persons engaged at least part time in advocacy or, broadly speaking, humanitarian diplomacy functions. These included the executive director, who on occasion contacted the US Secretary of State; Care personnel within Afghanistan, who kept the lines of communication open to the Afghan authorities and with other governments and humanitarian actors in Kabul; officials in Care headquarters in Atlanta and also in Washington and Kabul with responsibility for liaison with the media and governments; and Care staff in New York, who liaised with the UN Security Council and UN member states.

One of the values of humanitarian diplomacy that extends beyond the operational scene is its implicit acknowledgement that the context for humanitarian work is far wider than the specific "humanitarian" niche and the tasks within it. This wider contextualization is illustrated with particular clarity in the study on Liberia (Chapter 12), where the absence of humanitarian sensitivities in the Cease-fire Monitoring Group of the Economic Community of West African States (ECOMOG) directly complicated the work of aid agencies. Keeping a wider framework in mind is important in tamping down grandiose expectations for humanitarian action, whether by political actors or by humanitarian organizations themselves. As detailed in Chapter 5, members of the NGO Coordination Committee in Iraq paired (a) a focused effort at negotiating humanitarian access with the Coalition and Iraqi authorities with (b) broader efforts to protect humanitarian space. The former were more successful than the latter.

In a number of the country studies, organizations expected that successful diplomacy would bring an end to a given conflict and would set up durable structures to nurture peace and reconciliation. Anticipating that their own work would be of short duration as part of an effort to buy time for political solutions, they often focused advocacy efforts in support of global-level diplomacy by other actors. That was the expectation in Bosnia, where the UN High Commissioner for Refugees initially believed that the need to help in Srebrenica and other "safe areas" would last for only a few weeks. This was also the case with UNRWA, where a short-term crisis became a chronic emergency and where the "works" aspect of the agency – the resettlement of Palestinians in neighbouring countries – became impossible, requiring improvisation instead. Humanitarian groups face a recurring problem of becoming bogged down in chronic emergencies, extended in time by virtue of the failure of traditional diplomacy to address underlying problems. And, as noted earlier, humanitarian options have a way of narrowing as emergencies become more protracted.

Comparative advantages

The case studies offer glimpses of a full range of institutions engaged in humanitarian diplomacy. These include first and foremost members of the UN system: UNICEF in Lebanon and Sierra Leone, UNHCR in the Balkans, UNRWA in the Occupied Territories, and WFP in Sudan, North Korea and Nepal. But international NGOs are also deeply engaged: witness the NGO consortia in Cambodia and Iraq and also Peace Brigades International in Colombia. The Red Cross movement too is a major actor, as the ICRC's role in East Timor demonstrates. In fact, as the crisis worsened throughout 1999, the ICRC was the only outside actor present on the ground. An array of case studies wider still would doubtless add to the mix other genres of humanitarian institutions such as bilateral aid agencies and indigenous NGOs.

What are the comparative advantages of these various types of agency in humanitarian diplomacy? Is former WFP Executive Director James Ingram accurate in his rather unorthodox view, reflecting his own role in negotiating access to Ethiopia, Tigray and Eritrea in 1990 and to Sudan in 1991, that the United Nations' humanitarian agencies should not necessarily be the preferred instrument for humanitarian diplomacy? "The head of a major NGO trusted by the parties and known to be apolitical", observed Ingram, "may have done as well [as did WFP], providing the political circumstances are right."[16] He urges that other actors be suited up to fill the void created by a UN aid apparatus that is often hamstrung by member states and their political agendas. At the same time, he prefers humanitarian agencies to concentrate on operational activities, leaving to the political side of the United Nations "the prevention and settlement of conflicts among states".[17]

The experience in Cambodia would seem to illustrate his point. The NGO Consortium succeeded in arranging access at a time when the ICRC and UNICEF had failed to do so. Were the political circumstances, in Ingram's formulation, "right"? Active opposition from the United States and the United Kingdom was offset by strong support from states including the Scandinavian countries, the Netherlands and several others from the Continent and the Caribbean. NGOs were able to succeed at "capital D" diplomacy, opening Cambodia to humanitarian action that UN agencies then joined. The catalytic role played by NGOs soon gave way to a broader effort involving an array of agencies whose capacities, in their totality, were more in keeping with the magnitude of the needs. A more negative result obtained in Liberia, where for years assistance and protection suffered as the United Nations' humanitarian agencies remained largely on the sidelines, the United Nations itself ceding the ground to ECOMOG, which on occasion actually strafed international aid operations. Chapter 12 accordingly urges earlier UN diplomatic involvement and greater accountability for those regional actors pressed into humanitarian service.

Individual sets of actors clearly have distinctive mandates and preferred terrains, which may prove advantageous or disadvantageous as the case may be. "The way an organization works", observed one of the authors in the Rome discussion of humanitarian diplomacy, "is key to the story". UN agencies are generally expected to be present in each and every complex emergency, even though the United Nations' outreach is often limited to areas controlled by representatives of UN-recognized member states. The case studies of UN involvement in Lebanon, North Korea and Sudan are good examples of responses to situations in which UN organizations found ways of overcoming political constraints.

But UN agencies, despite membership in the United Nations system, have different individual specificities. UNHCR, a treaty body authorized by the Refugee Convention of 1951, has stipulated duties in the area of human rights protection that are not subject to review by UNHCR's Executive Committee. The WFP, by contrast, is subjected by its Executive Board to country-by-country, project-by-project review, a process that tends to diminish the humanitarian space it might otherwise enjoy in politically charged settings. UNICEF, thanks to considerable resources generated by its national citizens' committees, has revenue sources that represent something of a counterweight to the funding it receives from governments.

The ICRC's mandate and juridical status thrust it into situations of internal armed conflict, a role exercised over the years with impressive consistency and success. It is demonstrably better suited to function in such settings – the East Timor chapter suggests as much – than are the humanitarian organizations of the UN system. In fact, Nepal provides an instance in which UN field staff, in the absence of the necessary authorization from headquarters, have been reluctant to deal directly with the

Maoist insurgency, even in support of humanitarian access to the wide areas the rebels control. Individual NGOs have more latitude than does the ICRC in picking and choosing where they will become operational, even though for their own institutional reasons they may seek to respond to all of the major crises.

Given the variegated nature of the agencies and actors engaged, the conduct of humanitarian diplomacy is at least as much a function of the international players involved as it is of the particular emergency itself. The task of protecting civilian populations, for example, is a generic challenge common to the 14 crises surveyed. The task is tackled quite differently, however, by virtue of the agency or mix of agencies involved in a given crisis. In the Occupied Palestinian Territories, protection is the responsibility of UNRWA and its RAOs, in Bosnia of UNHCR and its protection officers, in Colombia of Peace Brigades International and other humanitarian and solidarity groups, in East Timor of ICRC delegates, and so on. Different agencies also have differing comparative advantages according to the type of conflict involved. Moreover, agencies have a lot to learn from each other, and policy makers, too, can be more guided by considerations of comparative data than they have been to date.

In recent years, the international playbill has lengthened as newer actors have edged, or been thrust, onto the humanitarian stage. Prominent among them, as revealed in the Iraq and Kosovo experiences, are for-profit contractors and, in the civil-military arena, international and regional military and peacekeeping forces. Chapter 12 highlights some of the relationships at the interface between humanitarian agencies and ECOMOG in Liberia, while Chapter 14 reviews the blurring of lines in Somalia with humanitarian agencies associated with the presence of the United Nations Operation in Somalia (UNOSOM) and Unified Task Force Somalia (UNITAF). A minor theme in the case studies involves the activism of private institutions and individuals – the Carter Center and the Centre for Humanitarian Dialogue are examples – who are increasingly actors on the world humanitarian stage in their own right. Again, examination of a wider selection of country situations would give more profile to private sector initiatives.

The skill set

What are the personnel and resource implications of taking on the challenges in the area of humanitarian diplomacy portrayed in these case studies? What can be learned from experience to date?

Humanitarian diplomacy has been conducted by agencies and individuals for years. An observation by a senior UN official of his agency's experience surely applies to most such organizations. "WFP has been successfully employing humanitarian diplomacy for decades", noted Stanlake Samkange in opening a workshop to discuss the findings of the present volume. "Yet we have yet to capture these skills and knowledge and make them a core competency among all of our staff and partners."[18] The aforementioned handbook on negotiation for humanitarian practitioners has a similar starting point. Negotiation is "a critical transferable skill in all humanitarian work," notes Hugo Slim in his Preface, "but one that was not well understood by humanitarian workers and, in general, one that was very poorly resourced by the agencies that employ them".[19]

Indeed, the implications of tackling the challenges of humanitarian diplomacy seriously and successfully involve building the occasional talents of individual staffers into the core competencies of entire institutions. One of the early devices employed by WFP in upgrading the skills of its staff has been to seek to develop better historical memory regarding its own experience in humanitarian diplomacy.[20] WFP's discussions at the level of its board have been another element in its strategy. As a result, member governments that are stakeholders in the agency's work have given their imprimatur to the exercise of humanitarian diplomacy in support of its operational programmes.[21]

In the final analysis, the skills needed for effective humanitarian diplomacy are as specific as they are extensive. Discussed in greater detail below, they include an understanding of international humanitarian law, a sense of the drivers and dynamics of a given conflict in its own cultural setting; an ability to provide leadership across the diverse and often inchoate humanitarian sector; a familiarity with past efforts, successful or otherwise, to open up and maintain humanitarian space; a battery of interpersonal qualities; and a keen sense of timing. In addition to cultivating these skills among staff, an agency may need to affirm a broader institutional commitment to the other ingredients as well. This volume depicts some of these skills being brought to bear on tough-nut situations, and also the risks of improvisation.

In addition to investing in the selection and cultivation of top-flight professional staff, humanitarian agencies face other challenges that require commitments of an institutional sort. Those that stand out are the Care commitment in Afghanistan to multi-level advocacy and the new visibility accorded by the ICRC to its traditional humanitarian diplomacy brief. Although the panoply of assets that Care deployed in support of its Afghan programme could not be lavished on each and every crisis, the investment was clearly called for in the particular circumstances. Given the stakes involved in doing it right, doing humanitarian diplomacy on the cheap is not the way forward.

The need for increased investments in training personnel was also flagged in the Report of the UN Secretary-General's High-level Panel on Threats, Challenges and Change. Reporting in late 2004, the group made the following recommendation: "United Nations humanitarian field staff, as well as United Nations political and peacekeeping representatives, should be well trained and well supported to negotiate access" to civilians in armed conflict settings.[22] This provision, which acknowledges a role for negotiations on the humanitarian side of the house, was incorporated into a multifaceted 10-point programme of action proposed by the panel.

Concluding reflections

It is tempting to view each country situation as one-of-a-kind, each outcome the product of particularistic factors. However, the experiences presented suggest a number of recurring elements that influence the outcomes of humanitarian diplomacy, for better or worse. Success seems to correlate positively with such factors as the cohesiveness of the humanitarian sector, the presence of seasoned and creative practitioners, the utilization of institutional experience and memory, in-depth knowledge of the political environment and cultural context, the creation of trust, the careful demarcation of what is negotiable, and access to a durable reservoir of political and public support.

Success, it seems, is often a function of a cohesive humanitarian sector, whereas failure frequently reflects a lack of coordination among the agencies active in a given crisis. In Lebanon, UNICEF cultivated and enjoyed the support of many agencies on the scene, and in Cambodia the NGO Consortium was able to speak authoritatively for its 33 member agencies in dealings with Hun Sen. Cohesiveness of the sector makes nuanced strategies possible, as in the good cop/bad cop approach that proved effective in Sierra Leone. Front-line staff in Freetown, with a keen understanding of the problems on the ground, were able to orchestrate the weighing in of "headquarters heavies" in ways that strengthened their own hand. In other instances – Sudan is a telling example – divisiveness among humanitarian agencies undermined efforts to represent concerns to the authorities with a single voice. In Afghanistan, high-flying personnel from headquarters with their own agendas competed with and undercut the work in the field of staff personnel already hard-pressed even before the imposition of a remote control overlay.

The presence of seasoned humanitarian practitioners also bears a positive correlation with success. Such persons are able to bring to the challenges their best professional judgement, combined with the experience of their agency. They generally work to establish the widest possible network of contacts and to adapt earlier experience to the latest challenges.

The assignment of practitioners with previous front-line experience to new crises was one of the lessons learned from the conflicts of the 1990s. It represents a major but still uncompleted change from the previous pattern of assigning junior officials to the most remote and exposed positions. In the Kosovo emergency and thereafter, humanitarian personnel found themselves working with colleagues from earlier crises, facilitating the development in-country of close working relationships among veteran officials.[23]

The accounts of the authors of the case studies are by design coloured by their personal involvement in the events they analyse. That is indeed appropriate, for many successful humanitarian initiatives bear the marks of the individual practitioners who conceived and implemented them. In this context, the conclusion of a review of evaluations conducted in 2003 is noteworthy, if a bit surprising: peer influence is more closely linked with operational success than are aid agency policies and procedures themselves.[24] However, insufficient evidence is presented in this volume to substantiate the view of some that a lack of training in the essentials of humanitarian negotiations is a major factor in the failure of such efforts.

Understanding the political and cultural environment is also of the essence of successful humanitarian diplomacy. Although a bit impressionistic, there is some evidence to suggest that knowledgeable humanitarian officials with long-term service in given areas have a better sense of political forces and dynamics than persons sent from the United Nations' departments of political affairs and peacekeeping operations.[25] The tackling of issues when they are "ripe" for settlement – a key element in successful diplomacy, both humanitarian and traditional – requires discerning judgement on the part of field staff. The case studies may also be read to suggest that, although there may be some no-win situations in which it remains impossible to persuade the political authorities to do the humane thing, even in the most dire surroundings the resourceful practitioner may be able to open at least some humanitarian space.

Humanitarian undertakings, often necessitated by suffering caused by political authorities, may well need political reinforcement in order to succeed. Thus humanitarian organizations have an interest in early and deep involvement by the political side of the UN house, as the Liberia situation demonstrates, if only by default. Yet how such engagement can take place without compromising the independence of humanitarian action is something of a conundrum that is currently the subject of debate among a wide array of officials, humanitarian and diplomatic/political alike.[26]

The creation of trust with the belligerents emerges as a *sine qua non* of successful initiatives. Success in freeing child soldiers in Sierra Leone required good working relationships with the country's military forces as well as contacts with the president and first lady. Not only the UNICEF representative but also his spouse played a role in establishing and capitalizing upon such trust. Years of routine visits by Peace Brigades International helped establish its personnel as known entities and to build relationships that proved useful in situations of duress. Being a known quantity did not avoid serious threats against PBI and staff, however.

Trust is often a function of the transparency with which humanitarian actors proceed. Although transparency is high in the humanitarian pantheon of values and many agencies practise full disclosure, there are circumstances in which some agencies impose clear limits. The ICRC's refusal to supply information on abuses of international law to the International Criminal Court and to other judicial bodies is an instance of the maintenance of confidentiality being viewed as essential to continued prison visits and other protection and assistance activities. The ICRC's decades of work in Indonesia positioned it well to set up shop in East Timor, particularly at a time of high political tension, when other international agencies lacked the necessary credibility with the authorities.

Framing an issue in human terms has also proved an important decision that has played a role in the success of humanitarian initiatives. UNRWA's network of clinics and schools positioned it well to monitor the human toll taken by the intifadas and to publicize the suffering of ordinary civilians involved. The ICRC's work with the victims of landmines gave it unquestioned authority to testify before national policy makers and parliaments on the need for an international convention to ban landmines. Advocacy groups by contrast did less well in mobilizing action around international trade in small arms, an issue that, they realized in retrospect, they had failed to frame in clearly human terms.[27]

Humanitarian diplomacy is most likely to succeed in situations in which the trade-offs made are few. Eroding the core principle of impartiality through distributing relief supplies disproportionately to some communities comes at a price. The conclusion of the case study on Yugoslavia, where agencies strayed from a strict adherence to impartiality in the interests of lubricating access to communities in desperate need, may well be writ much larger: "Humanitarian negotiations have a greater chance of success if it is clear to all parties that there are things that are not negotiable."

Finally, a reservoir of political and public support can be a key factor in successful humanitarian diplomacy. Although the United Nations may have an advantage in the extent to which it can mobilize broad donor support for humanitarian initiatives, the impediments that it encounters in engaging in high-profile, contested settings are also formidable, as its initial sidelining in Cambodia demonstrated. UNICEF's successful functioning in highly politicized Lebanon, however, suggests that not all contested situations are unworkable for all UN organizations. For their part, NGOs may be able to generate an even larger quotient of international concern of a humanitarian character and translate this into political pressure for access.

Humanitarian diplomacy is in a process of evolution. It is coming into its own at a time in post–Cold War history when traditional diplomacy is in eclipse and more muscular approaches to international problem-solving are in fashion. It is a craft that is part and parcel of successful efforts to assist and protect at-risk populations, therefore having a certain "flavour of the month" appeal in some quarters. Yet, as noted, it fits somewhat uneasily with the self-understanding of practitioners and with the traditional concept, now undergoing revision, that humanitarian action and actors must studiously keep their distance from the political arena.

The emerging craft of humanitarian diplomacy takes shape at a time of tensions, both conceptual and operational, between matters political and humanitarian. Within the United Nations, the debate about "integration" seeks to position humanitarian activities as one set among several (trade, development, conflict resolution, democracy promotion and the like) that contribute to international peace and security. Within the wider humanitarian family, however, views differ markedly regarding the dangers of such instrumentalism and the need for preserving the independence of humanitarian action. The case studies in this book suggest that the conduct of humanitarian diplomacy may represent an investment in effective programmes rather than necessarily a politicization of them.

Some practitioners of humanitarian action and of traditional diplomacy alike believe that "humanitarian diplomacy" is best left to card-carrying diplomats. The record does not bear out their contention. Many professional diplomats are unfamiliar with humanitarian principles, organizations and culture. This is true of some who function as Special Representatives of the UN Secretary-General in specific conflicts or post-conflict arenas. It is also true of some who serve as UN Resident Coordinators charged with ensuring the coordination of all UN economic and humanitarian programmes within a given country. Many such persons exhibit a tendency to instrumentalize assistance and protection activities, treating them as arrows in a larger quiver that also includes economic sanctions and military force.

It is a tantalizing hypothesis that successes such as those chronicled in this volume will reawaken traditional diplomacy from its languor and reinvigorate the status of consensual approaches to problem-solving. However, testing the hypothesis is beyond the purview of this volume. It is without doubt the view of the authors, however, that conflicts are not inevitable and that a global humanitarian enterprise, reinforced by the presence of a significant humanitarian diplomacy component, will be needed for the foreseeable future.

The experiences examined by the case studies, and the discussions held along the way among the practitioner-authors, suggest that the generation of support for humanitarian operations, and for trouble-shooting when needed, is an element too important to be left to professional diplomats or to others who often lack a basic understanding of the principles and specificities of the humanitarian enterprise. The framework within which formal diplomacy is conducted is focused on state actors and perceived national interests. The humanitarian imperative has a different logic and framework, dynamic and urgency.

Organizations committed to effective assistance and protection efforts are thus well advised to recognize the value of a judicious exercise of humanitarian diplomacy in support of their bread-and-butter activities. Of course, they are not diplomats and should be wary of overreaching into the realm of traditional diplomacy. Indeed, they are well advised to acknowledge that engagement in areas and on matters beyond their competence and capacity may risk compromising their credibility as well as their effectiveness. Yet they have an undisputed institutional interest in the success of higher-level efforts of formal diplomacy that seek political solutions to the underlying causes of human distress.

With regard to their own operations of humanitarian assistance and protection, however, there can be no doubt. "Humanitarian actors are not always the best diplomats," concludes one of the authors, but "they are the best on offer." "Where agreement is possible," adds another, "it is more likely when negotiations are left to the humanitarians."

Notes

1. Deborah Mancini-Griffoli and André Picot, *Humanitarian Negotiation: A Handbook for Securing Access, Assistance and Protection for Civilians in Armed Conflict*, Geneva: Centre for Humanitarian Dialogue, 2004, p. 6.
2. Oren R. Young and Gail Osherenko, *Polar Politics: Creating Environmental Regimes*, Ithaca, NY: Cornell University Press, 1993, p. 1.
3. See, for example, *The Responsibility to Protect: Report of the International Commission on Intervention and State Sovereignty*, Ottawa: International Development Research Centre, December 2001.
4. See also Larry Minear, "Lessons Learned: The Darfur Experience", in Active Learning Network for Accountability and Performance (ALNAP), *Annual Review of Humanitarian Action 2005*, London: ALNAP, 2005.
5. The UNITAR Project for Briefing and Debriefing Special and Personal Representatives and Envoys of the UN Secretary-General was established to preserve and pass on lessons and experience and to ensure that they are used to refine and enhance UN peace operations. The project has produced a first edition (for UN use only) of a book entitled

On Being a Special Representative of the Secretary-General and a set of DVDs of interviews with SRSGs. Three SRSG seminars have been held to date.

6. Mancini-Griffoli and Picot, *Humanitarian Negotiation*, p. 25.

7. For a review of operational standards as they reflect on principles, see the special issue of *Disasters*, Vol. 28, No. 2 (2004), *The Sphere Project: Humanitarian Charter and Minimum Standards in Disaster Response.*

8. See, for example, Mark Cutts, *The Humanitarian Operation in Bosnia, 1992–95: Dilemmas of Negotiating Humanitarian Access*, New Issues in Refugee Research, Working Paper No. 8, Geneva: UNHCR Policy Research Unit, May 1999.

9. For an examination of the various institutional factors that influence decisions affecting continuation in, or withdrawal from, a given crisis setting, see Ian Smillie and Larry Minear, *The Charity of Nations: Humanitarian Action in a Calculating World*, Bloomfield, CT: Kumarian, 2004.

10. The comment is taken from a discussion of "Dealing with Belligerents Who Defy International Humanitarian Law", in Larry Minear et al., *Humanitarian Action in the Former Yugoslavia: The U.N.'s Role 1991–1993*, Providence, RI: Watson Institute, 1994, p. 80.

11. Ibid., p. 78.

12. One agency working in Darfur noted privately in late 2004 that the Khartoum government had adopted a divide-and-conquer approach, playing some national sections of its federation off against others.

13. For a report of the meeting, see *An Inclusive Approach to Armed Non-State Actors and International Humanitarian Norms: Report of the First Meeting of Signatories to Geneva Call's Deed of Covenant* at ⟨http://www.genevacall.org/resources/testi-publications/gc-nsa-report-05.pdf⟩ (accessed 28 March 2006).

14. Ian Smillie and Larry Minear, *The Quality of Money: Donor Behavior in Humanitarian Financing*, Medford, MA: Humanitarianism and War Project, April 2003, p. 9.

15. See ⟨http://www.icrc.org⟩.

16. James Ingram, "The Future Architecture for International Humanitarian Assistance", in Thomas G. Weiss and Larry Minear, eds, *Humanitarianism across Borders*, Boulder, CO: Lynne Rienner, 1993, p. 188.

17. Ibid., p. 192.

18. Opening remarks, Workshop on Humanitarian Diplomacy, Rome, 2 November 2004.

19. Preface, in Mancini-Griffoli and Picot, *Humanitarian Negotiation*, pp. 9–10.

20. See, for example, WFP, *Food Aid in Conflict Workshop Report*, Rome, 2002, and WFP Office of Evaluation, "Thematic Evaluation of Recurring Challenges in the Provision of Food Assistance in Complex Emergencies: The Problems and Dilemmas Faced by WFP and Its Partners", 1999.

21. WFP's financial and programmatic contribution to the present volume is another example of its effort to promote the craft among its staff and beyond.

22. *A More Secure World: Our Shared Responsibility. Report of the Secretary-General's High-level Panel on Threats, Challenges and Change*, New York: United Nations, December 2004, section XII, para. 236.

23. Larry Minear, Ted van Baarda and Marc Sommers, *NATO and Humanitarian Action in the Kosovo Crisis*, Providence, RI: The Watson Institute, 2000.

24. Active Learning Network for Accountability and Performance (ALNAP), *Annual Review of Humanitarian Action in 2003: Field Level Learning*, London: Overseas Development Institute, 2004, p. 50.

25. An earlier study concluded that it is often preferable to elevate a trained humanitarian professional to the level of SRSG than to orient an SRSG to the essentials of humanitarian principle and practice. See Greg Hansen and Larry Minear, "Waiting for Peace: Perspectives from Action-Oriented Research on the Humanitarian Impasse in the Cau-

casus", *Disasters*, Vol. 23, No. 3 (1999), pp. 257–270. This issue is also the subject of research being carried out by the Humanitarianism and War Project, Humanitarian Agenda 2015: Principles, Power, and Perceptions.

26. See, for example, the special issue on humanitarian aid and intervention of the journal *Ethics and International Affairs*, Vol. 18, No. 2 (2004).

27. Don Hubert, *The Landmine Ban*, Providence, RI: The Watson Institute, 2000.

2

Humanitarian diplomacy: Theory and practice

Hazel Smith

The role of humanitarian actors is to save lives and ameliorate suffering. Whether or to what extent humanitarian actors achieve these goals can be due to a number of factors, from a topography that might make communication and transport more or less easy, to the prevalence of corruption and insecurity in distribution chains, to the availability of funding, the expertise of staff, etc. A significant factor in meeting humanitarian objectives, however, is the capacity of humanitarian officials to negotiate access to beneficiaries and to secure protection both for recipients of assistance and for staff in the context of often very sensitive political and sometimes military environments. These difficult security environments are frequently complicated by and sometimes constituted by multiple authority structures. Humanitarian actors working within the context of fragmented authority structures composed of actors with contested political legitimacy will often therefore have to come to agreements with a diffuse set of sometimes unpredictable partners. These multiple interlocutors may be in conflict with each other and may not share common interests or values with humanitarian actors.

Humanitarian officials are not alone in engaging in tough international negotiations to achieve policy implementation. International business, journalists and other groups also engage in serious policy dialogue in times of conflict in difficult international environments. Hence it is not just humanitarian officials but journalists, employees of commercial businesses and religious people who are sometimes dragged into international conflict as unwitting "players". One grim result is that humanitarian officials and other non-combatants in some, though not all, theatres of conflict are considered legitimate targets for murder and kidnapping by perpetrators who portray these heinous acts as of a political nature directly designed to influence the course of the conflict. The spread of a norm whereby humanitarian officials and others are seen as legitimate targets creates a spiral of danger as criminals take advantage of new legitimation that they use as a cover for kidnapping for ransom by claiming "political" objectives.

What perhaps makes humanitarian diplomacy singular is that, wittingly or not, humanitarian agencies and the officials who represent them have been increasingly caught up in the major international conflicts of the post–World War II period as significant actors in their own right. As the chapters in this book demonstrate in such varied settings as Cambodia, Lebanon and Sierra Leone, humanitarian agencies have entered into negotiations with the most senior political officials, sometimes influencing the course of conflict itself. The objectives of humanitarian diplomacy at this level may very well collide with the interests not just of the host country government but of major international actors. The high-level interest by the United States and the United Kingdom in humanitarian activities in Cambodia and the Democratic People's Republic of Korea (DPRK – more commonly known as North Korea) and their attempts to influence these activities, as also demonstrated in this book, show how humanitarian diplomacy can become an activity that is difficult to separate entirely from the realm of high politics.

Humanitarian officials who strive to maintain the credibility and impartiality of their agencies and their work also can engage in humanitarian diplomacy in a very different sense – eschewing any linkage with high politics but recognizing that the political environment can be managed to facilitate the humanitarian enterprise. Chapter 4 on Lebanon and others in this book also show that the humanitarian enterprise can be facilitated when humanitarian diplomacy demonstrates that the objectives of humanitarians can coincide with the interests of major political actors.

Not all would agree about the core conceptualization of humanitarian diplomacy – including those engaged in the practice. In this chapter, therefore, I first introduce three different but not mutually exclusive conceptualizations of humanitarian diplomacy. After considering conventional understandings of diplomacy in terms of the actors involved, objectives, functions and methods, I assess in what ways humanitarian diplomacy, in terms of the three conceptualizations outlined, can be considered as sharing any features with conventional diplomacy.

I conclude by arguing that humanitarian diplomacy is a distinctive, discrete and limited enterprise. I also conclude, however, that the practice of humanitarian diplomacy could benefit from systematized incorporation of some of the analysis and techniques known to diplomacy in general. Equally important, successful humanitarian diplomacy has something to teach contemporary diplomacy in its ability to negotiate compromise, to use persuasion and to seek and obtain genuine non-zero sum solutions in what are often seen by outsiders as intractable conflicts.

Humanitarian diplomacy – A contested concept

Humanitarian officials and the agencies they represent sometimes have different ideas of what constitutes "humanitarian diplomacy". At least three concepts can be discerned as analytical "ideal types". In practice, of course, individual humanitarian officials may veer between all three understandings of humanitarian diplomacy – using different understandings at different times to help explain different circumstances. The three ideal types here are used simply as an analytical device to indicate broad clusters of differing models or concepts of what is understood as humanitarian diplomacy.

The first notion of humanitarian diplomacy is as an *oxymoron* – a contradiction in terms. Humanitarians do humanitarian work and diplomats do diplomacy and these are two separate and sometimes contradictory activities. By contrast, the second notion of humanitarian diplomacy is as a *common-sense* description of what humanitarian officials do in the field on a day-to-day basis. Humanitarian officials negotiate to get the job done and that is a fact of life. A third idea is of humanitarian diplomacy as a *necessary evil*. There is an acceptance that humanitarian activities sometimes risk over-politicization, along with a relatively phlegmatic understanding about its inevitability. The argument is that diplomatic negotiations with third parties are sometimes necessary in order to achieve humanitarian goals.

An oxymoron

Humanitarian actors carry out their responsibilities with particular regard to international humanitarian law. Humanitarian agencies have limited objectives. They cannot resolve conflict by themselves and their contribution is to provide assistance to those harmed by conflict such that very basic rights – usually those to life, food, shelter and health – are threatened. In contrast, states and state representatives (the diplomats) pursue the multiple interests of states abroad. These may very well include ethically acceptable policies such as development cooperation but, because the state's interests are multifarious and in the first instance include security, the state can also pursue ethically more objectionable policies. These might include discrimination against foreigners through tight immigration policies, deregulation of business such as to permit less oversight over labour practices abroad (for instance to ignore child labour), or a refusal to intervene to prevent genocide abroad, as in Rwanda in the mid-1990s.

If an intrinsic part of humanitarian activity is considered as "diplomacy", then this might imply that humanitarian actors are suborning their missions to broader political interests. States, on the other hand, have competing interests and, should commitments under international humanitarian law collide with, for instance, the necessity to maintain strategic control of oil or energy supplies, then humanitarian law may be the casualty. By definition, humanitarian agencies do not have these competing interests to consider, and therefore cannot be seen as comparable international actors to states. This is an important perspective, although a counter-argument from democratic states might be that as rule-bound entities, as a matter of constitution and practice, they abide by international and domestic law, including fulfilling their obligations to individuals in times of war and conflict.

The question for those troubled by the concept of humanitarian diplomacy, with its intimation perhaps of the politicization of humanitarian activity, is how to maintain "humanitarian space" while at the same time acknowledging that humanitarian agencies engage in politically sensitive environments in which the stakes and the penalties for getting it wrong are high. How can humanitarian actors achieve their objectives and at the same time maintain their humanitarian integrity? Masood Hyder eloquently summarizes the essence of this approach to humanitarian diplomacy in Chapter 11 in this volume, which provides a case study of Operation Lifeline Sudan. He argues that "[n]urturing humanitarian space is the essence of humanitarian diplomacy. Its objective is to save lives, to alleviate suffering and to uphold humanitarian principles."

Common sense

Some humanitarian officials are less worried about the term humanitarian diplomacy, arguing that humanitarian diplomacy in international conflict is simply a fact of life. This is because the enormous increase in humanitarian activity in the post–Cold War period – including both militarized humanitarian intervention and the implementation of extensive international operations to maintain basic supplies to civilian populations – has taken place in zones of "natural disaster", most visibly in countries and regions that require support as a consequence of the deleterious consequences of political conflict. One consequence is that humanitarian officials inevitably encounter political sensitivities in the implementation of humanitarian operations – sensitivities that cannot be avoided if the operations are to be carried out successfully. Some of these sensitivities may have been foreseen, but many of them may have been either unanticipated or unexpected.

Humanitarian officials have had to work round these political sensitivities simply in order to secure the effective implementation of humanitarian operations. They have therefore been forced into practising diplomacy with host governments or powerful non-state or non-governmental actors in order to achieve operational ends. Humanitarian officials thus engage as a matter of course in the practice of diplomacy in a very old-fashioned sense. They are official representatives involved in world politics who attempt to achieve objectives through peaceful means – employing the arts of persuasion, negotiation and compromise to attain those goals. The question for the "common-sense" approach is not, therefore, whether or not humanitarian agencies should engage in humanitarian diplomacy but the more practical question of how to manage negotiations better. The contribution by Omawale Omawale on his experiences negotiating the demobilization and rehabilitation of child soldiers in Sierra Leone (Chapter 13) strongly argues that both humanitarian actors and state diplomats have something to learn from the successful practice of humanitarian diplomacy as international negotiation. Omawale argues (page 299) that humanitarian diplomacy should employ reliable and incontrovertible information; be based on some established international convention to which the negotiating parties subscribe, or on relevant national law; identify some key interest of the other negotiating party that can be satisfied by the negotiation – a win–win proposition; identify a strategic ally either as an entry point or as a supportive resource during negotiation; use a lead negotiator who brings to the table some credit or credibility with the other negotiating party; involve other like-minded entities or individuals as parties to the negotiation wherever possible; propose solutions to any problems the other negotiating party has to acknowledge; and engage in a collaborative negotiation whenever possible.

A necessary evil

The last group of humanitarian actors shares the uneasiness of the first in wishing to circumscribe and protect the humanitarian sphere. They also consider that humanitarian negotiations inevitably take place in conflict zones and that humanitarian officials need to be appropriately prepared and trained so as to make technically better interventions in humanitarian diplomacy. This group also views the intervention of humanitarian actors in international conflict – as actors who will inevitably have either a direct or an indirect role to play in political conflict – as inevitable and, sometimes, morally defensible. Perhaps representative of the peacemaker approach is André Roberfroid, who argues in Chapter 4 on the Lebanon that successful humanitarian diplomacy requires both impartiality and credibility of the humanitarian actors and good diplomatic skills for successful implementation. Yet he also notes that humanitarian diplomacy does not stand alone in its connection to the major political issues of international diplomacy and conflict. Roberfroid argues, for instance, that "[a]lthough UNICEF's humanitarian projects had no formal relationship to the conclusion of the conflict, they did play a role in buying time for the diplomats, preparing public opinion for peace and progressively softening the positions of the warring parties" (page 106).

Conventional understandings of diplomacy

Hedley Bull, a major twentieth-century theorist of international relations, provides a conventional idea of what constitutes the institution of diplomacy, with institution here understood as "a set of governing arrangements". Bull argues that diplomacy is "the conduct of relations between states and other entities with standing in world politics by official agents and by peaceful means".[1] Bull's conceptualization of the institution of diplomacy therefore encapsulates ideas about *actors* (who "does" diplomacy) and *process* (how and why it is done). The major actors are states although, for Bull, "not only ... states ... other political entities with standing in world politics [such as the] agents of the United Nations, of other general international organisations may be said to engage in diplomacy".[2] The key processes involve the use of "peaceful means", which for Bull constitute the institution of diplomacy. Harold Nicolson, whose text on diplomacy remains a standard for practitioners and theorists alike, also reminds us that diplomacy is not about making policy but about negotiating policy implementation.[3] Conventional analysis does not deny that diplomacy has always been a necessary instrument in preparations for, the conduct of and the settlement of war, but makes the point that diplomatic practices, by their nature, are peaceful. This is a different activity from coercive diplomacy, which specifically seeks to force compliance rather than to persuade and to impose solutions rather than to seek compromise.

Non-diplomacy – the case of coercive diplomacy

In the post–Cold War era, with the shift towards the use of military force as a primary instrument of conflict resolution, it is not surprising that we see a new research field of "coercive diplomacy".[4] Diplomacy still takes place, it is argued, but a significant shift in practical usage is noticeable from diplomacy as the classic instrument of achieving peace through negotiation in the direction of attempting to secure agreements through the use of threats.[5] The term "coercive diplomacy" refers to the fact that, for some powerful states (for instance, Russia in Chechnya and the United States in Iraq), the institution and practices of diplomacy are now most significant as a subordinate instrument of war rather than as a primary instrument of peace.

The use of the qualifier "coercive" strips the concept of diplomacy of its intrinsic utility, which is to explain how international political entities achieve objectives through peaceful means. If force or the threat of force is allowed as a fundamental means of persuasion in conflict, it becomes unnecessary to use the concept of diplomacy as an analytical tool. It is enough to argue that states merely negotiate as a complementary aspect of war-making – sometimes with the effect of avoiding war and sometimes with the effect of making war-making more successful. "Diplomatic negotiation" to support war-making is a contradiction in terms.

Allowing war-making or the threat of war to be legitimated by use of the term "coercive diplomacy" is not just or only a question of semantics. The legitimation of a new norm of coercive diplomacy contributes to making the world more dangerous because it helps to legitimize force as a primary instrument of dispute settlement. If the term can be captured to include the use or the threat of force, diplomacy as a peaceful method of dispute settlement risks being shunted off the political agenda. In pragmatic terms, policies guided by coercive diplomacy may be less successful in achieving the peaceful settlement of disputes than policies that make concerted diplomatic efforts. This is because, if the international actor making the threats is not to lose credibility, both with that specific adversary and in the wider international system, it must make good on those threats should talks with adversaries break down.

Diplomatic actors

The key diplomatic actors are representatives (official agents) of states and of other international actors. They may have different objectives but they are bound together by their common attribute of "representivity".

The variety of diplomatic actors

The scholarly and practical literature of diplomacy demonstrates a wide variety of understanding about what or who constitutes the core actors in diplomatic practice. Some commentators are emphatic that it is only states that count as engaging in diplomacy – implying that other international actors may negotiate but they do not engage in professional diplomacy.[6] Others are willing to include intergovernmental organizations (IGOs) as diplomatic actors.[7] Few conceive of non-governmental organizations (NGOs) as diplomatic actors, although, almost paradoxically, there is some openness to recognizing that individuals may contribute to diplomatic efforts. Individuals may engage in private or "non-official" diplomacy or have an official role as a special envoy of public international organizations or governments.[8]

If states are conventionally understood as comprising the core actors in diplomacy, not all states have been willing players in the global diplomatic system. For instance, the post-1917 Soviet Union initially rejected any participation in the diplomatic system. It is fair to say, however, that revolutionary states have rarely remained aloof for long from diplomatic intercourse with other states. In the case of the Soviet Union, revolutionary diplomacy reverted to conventional diplomacy just one year after the victory of the revolution when Georgy Chicherin, an old-fashioned Russian diplomat, took over from Leon Trotsky as the new revolutionary government's People's Commissar for Foreign Affairs.[9]

Conversely, some non-state actors have become fairly uncontroversially accepted as important and conventional diplomatic actors – for instance the United Nations. Other multilateral actors also regularly engage in diplomacy – the European Union being one of the best known. However, the United Nations remains perhaps a special case in its unequivocal commitment to diplomacy as both ends and means – the primary objective is to resolve conflict through the use of peaceful means. Committed to peace through its history, legal framework and institutional development, the United Nations is arguably a diplomatic institution *par excellence*.

Diplomats' objectives

Diplomats negotiate to achieve agreements with partners that by definition do not have identical interests. This is true even when diplomats are negotiating with friendly nations – for instance in the perennial agricultural trade negotiations between the United States and the European Union. The object of diplomacy is to find, within the overall matrix of differing interests, some common ground or at least some perceived common ground. The process entails compromise and trade-offs such that both partners, even while not abandoning important negotiating objectives, sacrifice some interests in order to produce agreements acceptable to all participants.

Diplomacy cannot take place when states and international actors have values and interests so far apart that they prefer the use of military force to achieve their objectives. Nevertheless, there are numerous historical examples of states and international actors with strongly divergent values that have reached agreements that to some extent have satisfied each other's interests. The Strategic Arms Limitation Talks (SALT) between the United States and the former Soviet Union in the middle of the Cold War provide one example of classic diplomacy functioning successfully in these circumstances.

The attribute of "representivity"

Diplomacy is an activity that intrinsically connotes the representation of major international bodies by individuals, irrespective of whether they are directly or indirectly employed by those bodies. The role of the accredited representative is central to diplomatic activity. In many cases the lead diplomat is an ambassador, but other accredited officials (diplomats) can include chargés d'affaires, military, economic and cultural attachés, and other officials recognized by the host government as necessary for the home government to carry out its diplomatic functions. For diplomacy to be successful, the receiving state must be confident that the individual diplomat is representative of the international actor with which it is in dispute. It must also be convinced that the diplomat has the ability to convey high-level messages to appropriate recipients and possesses the capacity, directly or indirectly, to put into practice any agreement entered into by both parties.

In international crises, individuals sometimes seek to play an ad hoc role in political mediation simply by virtue of their presence on the ground. With the cost of air tickets relatively low for Westerners determined to engage in what is sometimes called pejoratively "disaster tourism" and where weak states may not have the capacity, experience or knowledge to assess the representativeness of individual foreigners, these individuals have sometimes attempted a mediatory role way beyond their personal or professional capacities or competence.[10] Lack of representivity can lead to unsuccessful mediatory outcomes even when the participants are distinguished figures, for instance when Edward Heath, the respected former UK prime minister, visited Iraq in 1990 in an attempt to avert the first Gulf war.[11] Activities undertaken by well-meaning individuals do not constitute diplomatic interventions in international crises if their home governments do not support them. This may be because the government does not want to be seen to be offering overtures to countries with which it has difficult relations or because the individual may be cutting across strategic plans already in train.

Diplomatic processes

The processes of reaching diplomatic agreements are various. We can think of processes as consisting of procedures, standard functions and methods.

Procedures

The procedures of diplomacy, or "how" diplomacy takes place, are either bilateral or multilateral. Diplomatic procedures may also follow "old" or "new" diplomatic models. Bilateral diplomacy between just two negotiating partners, although providing a paradigmatic model of diplomatic interaction, has never in practice been the only form of global diplomatic interaction. This is because multilateral diplomacy – involving three or more states or international actors – has continued to be for all practical purposes a necessary and useful response to conflict.[12] The sheer complexity of international relations arising from the institutionalization of the state as the most significant political actor in the international system over the past five hundred or so years, the exponential increase in new states from the twentieth century onwards and the rise in other significant international actors (from global business to international terrorist groups) has meant that multilateral diplomatic interaction has been as much the norm as have bilateral relations.[13]

Multilateral diplomacy today is often institutionalized in international organizations. This again is hardly new. The predecessor of contemporary institutionalized multilateral diplomacy between groups of states was "conference diplomacy". Conference diplomacy as a means of settling disputes and creating post-war peace settlements in a multilateral format both pre-dates and foreshadows the rise of permanent international governmental organizations in the twentieth century. The most notable example was the Concert system of nineteenth-century Europe, which regularly carved up the world between the five great European powers – Austria-Hungary, Great Britain, France, Prussia and Russia – as a way of both avoiding war and settling conflict between these states. The legacy of the Concert system is found in the twentieth-century global institutions, the most important being the League of Nations and its successor the United Nations, both of which were designed to institutionalize conference diplomacy in the service of conflict prevention and the promotion of peace.

The diplomacy that takes place within international organizations has sometimes been referred to as the "new" diplomacy, as opposed to the "old" diplomacy associated with pre-twentieth-century Europe.[14] The term "new" is usually meant to imply diplomacy conducted in an "open" fashion – either in public or with its deliberations written into the public record. In fact the distinction has been less than clear and therefore analytically not very useful from the outset. "Open" diplomacy has very rarely been conducted without a first and parallel resort to some very old-fashioned negotiations indeed in the form of confidential exchanges seeking to achieve "sellable" trade-offs for home governments and domestic constituencies. Perhaps what is more significant about the reference to "new" diplomacy is the implicit reminder about the importance of public opinion as a factor that must be taken into account in the making of foreign policy and in the diplomacy of international actors in contemporary international relations.[15] The general public in both democratic and non-democratic countries expect to have influence over foreign policy in a way that was not normally the case before the early twentieth century.

Standard functions

According to Hedley Bull, the primary functions of representative diplomacy include the gathering of intelligence, communication and negotiation.[16] These are public duties, even if carried out in non-public settings (for instance in the conveyance of confidential information to host governments). They are never private functions in that, for the most part, diplomatic engagement is on behalf of a public organization. The major exception, but perhaps an exception that proves the rule, is when a private person – perhaps an internationally respected business person or ex-official – undertakes a diplomatic initiative as a private person. The aim of such initiatives, however, is always to effect a reconciliation between public international bodies, usually adversarial governments, and, for these "independent" initiatives to be successful, they must have the consent and acceptance of the parties in conflict, even if this is obtained after the intervention has taken place.

Intelligence-gathering is not the same as espionage because diplomatic intelligence may be gathered from open sources such as the media, host government officials and local and resident international organizations and individuals. In the broadest sense, all international organizations engage in the gathering of intelligence as knowledge, simply in order to be able to make informed judgements about the country in which they will be operating or with which they will be negotiating. However, intelligence-gathering is a controversial part of diplomatic activity. States routinely cross the line between legitimate intelligence-gathering activities and what in any ordinary sense of the word can be understood as spying. Officials of international organizations have also sometimes been accused of working for intelligence agencies. What is perhaps more difficult for international organizations to prevent, however, is the knowledge they have collected for legitimate reasons being used by states to inform intelligence estimates.

The function of communication is less controversial. The ancient practice of diplomatic immunity, which was codified in the 1961 Vienna Convention on Diplomatic Relations, was first developed because direct and representative communication between hostile parties could not take place if the representative was routinely killed on entering enemy territory.[17] A core function of a resident diplomat is the transmission of confidential messages. This was particularly important until the mid-nineteenth-century implementation of telegraphic communications, which reduced message transmittal times from weeks to hours and represented a technological development that was arguably much more significant than the invention of email communication.[18] There remains a debate about whether the role of the resident diplomat is less significant in terms of the communication function of diplomacy.[19] What is clear, however, is the value of a resident ambassador in times of crisis when telecommunications with capitals can be technically difficult or intermittent.

The negotiating function is, along with the communication function, understood as providing the very core of the diplomatic institution. A standard textbook states, for instance, that "negotiation is the most important function of diplomacy".[20] A large literature on the technical process of negotiating as well as on the analysis of the experience of diplomatic negotiators is available.[21] For Bull, minimizing friction in international relations means that the use of diplomacy will help to reduce conflict. The function of diplomacy as symbolizing the existence of the society of states is for Bull a reminder that minimal norms of social intercourse between states exist – even between states of very different ideologies. For instance, Bull would not have been at all surprised that representatives of even the most non-conventional governments, such as the Taliban government of Afghanistan, found themselves using the methods of diplomacy and to a certain extent being socialized by the norms of the institution of diplomacy.[22]

Methods

The procedures of diplomacy are underpinned by established diplomatic methods. Some of the most important are the operational professionalism of the diplomat; the employment of ostensibly opaque language; and the use of confidentiality and publicity as appropriate and relevant.

Personal and professional conduct

Diplomatic conventions, although often apparently archaic and contrived to non-diplomats, perform a signalling function that can convey important messages to other international actors. These messages may be given and received through written means, for example letters, faxes and emails. Successful diplomacy, however, often relies upon the "non-verbal" communication that takes place through personal contact. The nuanced messages that can be achieved through symbolic interaction are particularly important in relationships between potentially or actually adversarial negotiating partners where, Berridge argues, "it is so necessary to relieve the inevitable tension of a diplomatic exchange by gracious social ritual and acts of hospitality".[23] Diplomatic methods rely on what in other circumstances would be considered social and personal activities, which assume a political significance in terms of the communication and negotiation functions of the diplomat. A refusal to acknowledge a colleague in the diplomatic corps at a social function in a third country, for instance, is likely to be interpreted not as an individual act but as a message that one country does not recognize or have diplomatic relations with the other country. Conversely, a semi-public social conversation, of even a trivial nature, between diplomats representing international actors in conflict with each other could indicate to observers that relations between the two were improving.

The scholarly literature discusses the personal attributes and demeanour of the diplomat insofar as these can contribute to the successful practice of diplomacy. The individual's trustworthiness and credibility are considered important, not just for their intrinsic ethical value but because of the political significance attached to the personal conduct and language of diplomats as, in most instances, symbolizing and signalling the attitude of the state or international actor by which the diplomat is accredited. For Nicolson, the essential qualities of a successful diplomat are truthfulness, precision, calm, good temper, patience, modesty and loyalty.[24]

Nicolson also notes that the personal failings of a diplomat can contribute to the failure of the diplomatic mission. For Nicolson, the worst of these is vanity.

The dangers of vanity ... can scarcely be exaggerated. It tempts him to disregard the advice or opinions of those who may have had longer experience of a country, or of a problem, than he possesses himself. It renders him vulnerable to the flattery or the attacks of those with whom he is negotiating. It encourages him to take too personal a view of the nature and purposes of his functions and in extreme cases to prefer a brilliant but undesirable triumph to some unostentatious but more prudent compromise. It may prevent him, at some crucial moment, from confessing to his government that his predictions or his information were incorrect. It prompts him to incur or to provoke unnecessary friction over matters which are of purely social importance. It may cause him to offend by ostentation, snobbishness or ordinary vulgarity. It is at the root of all indiscretion and of most tactlessness.... It may induce that terrible and frequent illusion ... that his own post is the centre of the diplomatic universe and that the Foreign Office is both blind and obstinate in ignoring his advice.[25]

Language

Diplomatic methods include the deliberate use of language that appears to outsiders to be bland and understated. Yet it is perfectly decipherable to insiders as regards the message intended to be conveyed – by gradations in emphasis ranging, for example, from "viewing with concern" (i.e. a declaration of war is not yet likely) to viewing an action as "an unfriendly act" (i.e. a declaration of war is likely).[26]

Confidentiality

Early twentieth-century debate about diplomacy concentrated around the slogan of "open covenants openly arrived at". Advocates of the principle included United States President Woodrow Wilson and the Bolshevik revolutionaries. These opposing states both argued that World War I, internationally perceived as a pointless and avoidable conflict because of its historically unprecedented loss of life in the cause of very few apparent gains, was the result of a lack of public oversight of the activities of remote and out-of-touch nineteenth-century statesmen. In practice, both capitalists and communists soon found that the exigencies of negotiation forced some modification to the principles of openness and accountability underlying the "new" diplomacy.

Nicolson's solution to the contradiction between the espousal of openness in diplomacy and the perceived necessity for some privacy in the process of reaching agreements was that foreign policy makers should always be accountable to their publics but that diplomats needed to engage in "negotiation [that] must always be confidential".[27] Such a separation of open covenants accountable to general publics from the process through which the covenants are arrived at is now commonplace. Few today would disagree with Hedley Bull's dictum that "negotiation is greatly facilitated if it can be undertaken in private".[28]

Publicity

Although confidentiality may provide the underpinning for successful negotiations, publicity, its antonym, is sometimes useful in the service of diplomacy. It can assist in communicating important messages. It can also be used as an instrument of judicious pressure at different stages of negotiations. One of the lasting legacies of the "new" post–World War I diplomacy is the legitimization of the right of the public to be informed, if not always consulted, on foreign policy and diplomatic interventions. The mechanics of information exchange are generally through media outlets.

In an age of globalized media access, including through the World Wide Web, diplomats and the organizations they represent can efficiently communicate with different interested sectors of international public opinion both in democratic and in authoritarian countries.[29] Press conferences and television, radio and newspaper interviews can perform a number of functions for diplomats. These include the simple transmission of information, the setting out of broad strategies, and signalling changes in diplomatic direction.

Humanitarian diplomacy

Humanitarian officials have functions in common with state diplomats in that they must rely on negotiation, persuasion and dialogue to try to reach agreements with those with whom they may not share values and interests. Humanitarian officials are not, however, state diplomats. State diplomats pursue a multifarious set of interests responding to a specific national interest. International humanitarian officials pursue an international interest in respect of a narrowly focused mission, which is to respond to humanitarian need.

Humanitarianism and politics

To argue that humanitarian officials routinely and necessarily engage in diplomacy is not to argue that humanitarian officials engage in "politics" or, more specifically, political advocacy. There is a very lively debate within the humanitarian community between those whose fundamental ethos includes a commitment to neutrality in conflict, and those who consider it impossible to disassociate humanitarian intervention from political analysis and, sometimes, political intervention.[30]

The debate about whether or not humanitarians should be political advocates raises different issues from that of how humanitarian officials necessarily engage in diplomacy as a direct consequence of operational requirements. Humanitarians as diplomats are not political advocates but political negotiators. In carrying out their negotiating role, humanitarian actors, consciously or not, use the paraphernalia of diplomatic methods, procedures and instruments. They seek to attain objectives that are at once operational – implementing the specific objectives of their aid programmes – and diplomatic, in that they must seek to reach agreement with sometimes hostile international actors using only the instruments of persuasion and non-military dissuasion.

"Humanitarian interventions"

Humanitarians have not generally relied on the use of force to achieve objectives. The instruments of coercion, whether military or economic, are not normally available for humanitarian actors although, as 'Funmi Olonisakin demonstrates in Chapter 12 in her analysis of the Liberian conflict, military forces are sometimes drawn into the humanitarian role of keeping populations alive. In the post–Cold War world, however, humanitarians have found themselves in the uneasy position of working closely with governments that have been prepared to use military force in support of ostensibly humanitarian objectives.

Force has sometimes been used to punish regimes deemed guilty of human rights abuses when the application of political or economic sanctions has failed to achieve the desired goals. These so-called militarized humanitarian interventions have sometimes succeeded in bringing medium-term political solutions to conflict but in the short term have been accompanied by further humanitarian crises that civilian humanitarian officials have been left to resolve. The exodus of Kosovan refugees into Macedonia in the war against Serbia in 1999 is a case in point. Military interventions whose aims include the eventual eradication of regimes that abuse human rights can be successful. The paradigmatic examples are the Tanzanian intervention in Uganda that removed the dictator Idi Amin from office and the Vietnamese intervention in Cambodia that toppled the Khmer Rouge.

The use or threat of the use of force – that is, coercive diplomacy – is not either efficient or commonly accepted as desirable by many humanitarian actors as an instrument of humanitarians. It is inefficient because it is too blunt an instrument to be used successfully as a way of achieving humanitarian objectives. Humanitarian interventions represent failures of humanitarian diplomacy: humanitarian objectives can hardly be said to have been achieved if military force is used – by definition to kill, maim and damage human lives. Another problem with equating humanitarian interventions with high-profile examples of militarized humanitarian intervention is that it allows the more routine, less spectacular and arguably underestimated activities and achievements of humanitarians to be both ignored and unappreciated.

Humanitarians as diplomatic actors

Intergovernmental organizations, particularly the UN institutions and agencies, have had few problems being understood as diplomatic actors. Their senior personnel are in fact recognized under law by conventions that guarantee their rights as international diplomats with the same privileges and immunities as state diplomats. For instance, in Chapter 13 on negotiating the demobilization and rehabilitation of child soldiers in Sierra Leone, Omawale Omawale shows how his diplomatic status as a UNICEF representative helped him enter into direct negotiations with the chairman of the National Provisional Revolutionary Council. In emergency or humanitarian work, because of the sheer scale and scope of in-country operations, the major intergovernmental organizations are also likely to become significant actors in the host country economy and polity as well as the source of important linkages to external state and non-state actors. Humanitarian officials working in a high-profile political emergency invariably find it difficult to step aside from a diplomatic role they are forced to play by the exigencies of humanitarian work itself.

Non-governmental organizations have a more problematic conceptual status as humanitarian diplomatic actors. This is partly because the disparity in their size, objectives, mandates, methods of operation and funding sources means that it is difficult to generalize about the activities of NGOs. Oxfam's negotiations in Cambodia (discussed by Brian Walker in Chapter 6), in which NGO humanitarian diplomacy collided with the interests of major states, are not necessarily representative of all NGO experience. They do, however, indicate that Western states and Western NGOs will not in every instance share priorities and objectives in humanitarian crises. Walker also argues that the Cambodia case provides an example of NGO humanitarian diplomacy proving effective at ensuring that the needy were assisted when efforts from intergovernmental agencies were less so.

Not all non-governmental organizations engaging in mediatory efforts in international conflict, similar to the efforts of private individuals, can be considered to be undertaking diplomatic interventions in the sense of being representative of public constituencies or of governmental opinion. This can be owing partly to size, partly to the lack of accountability mechanisms and partly to the overt or covert politicization of activities. Small non-governmental organizations with a presence in the field in international conflict sometimes consider that they are privy to better-quality information and perhaps have better analytical abilities than their home governments and may therefore attempt to mediate between home and host governments. NGOs may also exaggerate their representative status or their influence in their home capitals to host governments or important political actors. If unsupported by home governments, NGOs may find themselves in difficult relationships with host governments that expected greater returns from the organizations. Some NGOs may also exacerbate conflict when pursuing interventions in international conflict, for instance if they seek to pursue an ideological or political agenda to overturn particular governments.[31]

Multilateral organizations

The conference system of Europe gave way to the League of Nations, which in turn gave way to the United Nations. International governmental organizations are therefore intrinsically diplomatic actors, although diplomatic actors of a special kind. The United Nations of today is the direct inheritor of a tradition of diplomacy that is, at least in theory, multilateral and publicly accountable. At the same time, the United Nations possesses wide functional and global remits, including the provision of humanitarian assistance. Where unresolved or intractable global conflict intersects with large-scale humanitarian needs, UN agencies are usually the only international actor, apart from the Red Cross movement, with the capacity to respond on the scale necessary. It should be unsurprising that UN agencies, including the humanitarian agencies, become, directly or indirectly, pulled into diplomatic processes and interactions.

Humanitarian organizations as representative diplomatic actors

Intergovernmental organizations are composed of member states to which governments send representatives. Intergovernmental organizations are therefore directly representative of governments and to a greater or lesser degree responsive to member governmental pressure. At one end of the scale the intergovernmental European Union, for instance, possesses a relatively high degree of institutional autonomy because of the structural independence of the Commission. At the other end of the scale, the United Nations agencies are directly accountable to the constituent member states.

The major UN humanitarian agencies – the World Food Programme (WFP), UNICEF and the UN High Commissioner for Refugees (UNHCR) – which must rely on direct fundraising from member governments to sustain their programmes, are directly accountable to member states' governments and must sustain strong links with the major industrial states in order to sustain funding and donations. For instance, the food aid programme of the WFP, which is the largest source of grant-based assistance for developing counties among all the agencies in the UN system (as at 1991), is largely based around donations in kind of grain surpluses from developed countries such as the United States.[32]

Non-governmental organizations have their own constituencies, and this is most clear in faith-based organizations such as CARITAS (the humanitarian arm of the Catholic Church), the Canadian Food Grains Bank (a conglomeration of humanitarian organizations connected to Protestant churches) and the Quakers. Some humanitarian organizations have roots in political parties or movements. Non-governmental organizations range in their accountability from those that regularly provide detailed public reporting on finance and operations to those whose funding and management are more opaque. The diversity in non-governmental organizations and their various different audiences and "weight" in their home states and societies can be confusing for host country partners. Host countries may, as a consequence, overestimate or underestimate the diplomatic influence of non-governmental organizations in home countries.

Objectives

States pursue the national interest. Humanitarian organizations by contrast pursue the universal interest of support for individual human beings – the international interest. The objectives of diplomatic practice as a means to achieve goals are, on the other hand, shared with humanitarian diplomacy. To achieve results in sensitive political environments, often defined by hot conflict, humanitarian officials engage in diplomatic negotiations in the sense that they try to effect compromise with partners who have very different values and interests. In other words, they practise classic diplomacy because they engage in "a process in which divergent values are combined into an agreed decision".[33] They engage in policy implementation, not policy-making.

The processes of humanitarian diplomacy

Similarly to state actors, intergovernmental organizations, non-governmental organizations and bilateral humanitarian agencies operate bilaterally and multilaterally. As the chapters in this book indicate, however, it is common for humanitarian agencies to engage in multilateral diplomacy – that is, with one or more negotiating partners. Humanitarian actors often work in states with fragmented authority structures, as demonstrated in Chapter 14 by Karin von Hippel on Somalia and Chapter 4 by André Roberfroid on UNICEF's activities in the midst of the Lebanese civil war.

Core standard functions of humanitarian organizations include the gathering of information or, in diplomatic language, "intelligence", communication and negotiation.

The uncomfortable mandate – the intelligence function

The gathering of information is a problematic function for humanitarian agencies. Information-gathering is akin to intelligence-gathering only in that diplomatic intelligence-gathering is supposed to be only from open sources. The gathering of information, however, can have uncomfortable and sometimes dangerous connotations for humanitarian agencies. International humanitarian agencies need to collect reliable information from host countries for two purposes: first, in order to be able to implement their programmes and activities efficiently; second, to be accountable to donor countries on how they are spending the funds allocated to them by the donor country taxpayers.

The risk for humanitarian agencies is that, by their nature, the major donor nations are the richest and the most politically powerful states in the global system. These states are protagonists in difficult and dangerous global conflicts – for instance, the Afghanistan, Iraq and North Korea crises – in which the major intergovernmental humanitarian organizations are also significant international actors, because of their global mandates, experience and capacities and also because of the material assistance provided and the scale of their activities relative to any other international actor – with the singular exception of Red Cross and Red Crescent operations. NGOs, too, provide information to donors, but because they are normally operating in discrete localities they do not have the capacity to collect and systematize such comprehensive information on host country societies as do intergovernmental organizations.

Through the routine processes of reporting information back to donors, major international humanitarian organizations thereby supply information about the economy and the society of countries that are normally inaccessible to Western governments. Host countries are equally aware that the international organization may be one of the only sources of reliable information to the outside world, including their political adversaries. The host governments of such states may view all such information as highly sensitive because it allows enemies insights into their vulnerabilities. The host government will be aware of the need for large-scale humanitarian assistance, which can only come from the major international organizations, and yet will at the same time be aware of the institutional linkage to major donors, to which they are not likely to wish to convey information about their economy and society.

International humanitarian agencies therefore have privileged access to information simply by virtue of their presence in host countries. This is one reason for sometimes uncomfortable and ambivalent relationships between host countries and international humanitarian organizations. At worst, intergovernmental organizations and NGOs may be viewed with intense suspicion – suspicion that at the extreme could have consequences ranging from constraints placed on humanitarian access to serious threats to the security of staff. Chapter 9 by David Morton on WFP operations in the DPRK illustrates the first scenario. Chapter 4 by Roberfroid on Lebanon, in which he argues that risk is an intrinsic part of the humanitarian enterprise, provides an example of the second.

Humanitarian officials have responded to these sensitivities in a variety of ways. Some have chosen to ignore them as best they can – attempting to concentrate on "technical" issues such as the logistics of food aid deliveries. Others, a minority, have sometimes enthusiastically accepted the links and actively intervened in the intelligence-gathering processes.[34] Others have been pragmatic about the necessary linkage between information-gathering, operational efficacy and donor relations. These officials try to draw a line between information-gathering that is necessary for operational purposes and information-gathering that might be tangential to the humanitarian effort.

Communication: Mixing politics with humanitarianism?

Similarly to diplomatic envoys, resident humanitarian officials perform the function of communicating between host government and headquarters. Senior UN officials possess legal diplomatic immunity, and NGO humanitarian officials benefit from the generally accepted global norm – adhered to often by the most non-conventional regimes, although certainly not all of them – that humanitarian officials, whatever the nationality on their passport or their legal rights, should be treated as *hors de combat*. The convention of diplomatic immunity has not prevented all killing of serving humanitarian officials or diplomatic envoys, in the same way that it has not stopped all killing of state envoys. It remains, however, a significant norm underpinning the humanitarian regime, such that humanitarian officials may often find themselves able to communicate with belligerents in conflict when others cannot. Humanitarian officials, as distinct from business representatives or even religious leaders, seem to be almost universally accorded, at least implicitly, the status that was formerly reserved for accredited diplomatic envoys. Chapter 10 by Erika Joergensen on the conflict in Nepal demonstrates that development and humanitarian actors have in the main continued to be seen as neutral. Lizzie Brock, in her analysis in Chapter 15 of the work of Peace Brigades International in Colombia, also shows how a non-governmental organization has managed to operate in a dangerous environment, partly by virtue of the normative acceptability of its human rights mandate.

The function of communication between host government and intergovernmental organization headquarters can be as problematic for humanitarian agencies as the function of information-gathering. International conflict is often marked by a lack of political or ambassadorial representation between hostile states. Humanitarian officials, employed as they are in the most physically and politically difficult and often dangerous zones of conflict, may then provide the only channel of communication between host governments and important political actors and the outside world. Although most humanitarian organizations eschew any directly political role in conflict, their very presence on the ground can enable necessary political communications between hostile actors. However, when humanitarian and political mandates become blurred, as von Hippel argues in Chapter 14 on UN involvement in Somalia, both humanitarian and political objectives can be jeopardized.

Negotiation

Negotiation is the least problematic function for humanitarian diplomacy. As all our case-study chapters indicate, humanitarian officials have engaged in substantive diplomacy to achieve humanitarian objectives. Examples include the relatively successful negotiations on access to beneficiaries in areas of political conflict with the Taliban government in Afghanistan (Chapter 7) and with the government in the DPRK (Chapter 9). Agreements were reached by using the classic diplomatic instruments of persuasion, promises and threats. In the case of the DPRK, the promise was of food aid and the implied threat was of aid withdrawal. Little attention has been paid to the experiences of humanitarian negotiators, even within internal reporting systems – something that this book seeks to remedy.[35]

Humanitarians and the methods of diplomacy

Humanitarian officials use the conventional methods of diplomacy to a greater or lesser extent. They send signals through their personal conduct and the language they use. They practise the judicious use of confidentiality and increasingly they use publicity, that is, the media, as an ally in achieving objectives. Few humanitarian officials, however, are trained in the personal aspects of the mechanisms of diplomacy. As a consequence, some humanitarian officials feel uncomfortable with the idea that the success of a mission may have as much to do with their personal behaviour as with their technical and professional ability to deliver aid to needy beneficiaries. Humanitarian officials can rarely avoid this part of the diplomatic role, however, because host governments and partners in the host diplomatic community ascribe this role to them. Host governments, in particular, view the personal conduct of officials as reflecting the attitude of the humanitarian agency itself.

It is sometimes assumed that the officials of multilateral institutions, including humanitarian institutions, and the officials of non-governmental organizations are less likely than state actors to engage in private or confidential negotiations with host governments. This assumption is made on the basis that intergovernmental organizations are publicly accountable institutions that regularly produce reports on every aspect of their activities – much of which is conducted in public. Non-governmental organizations are also presumed to be accountable to their stakeholders, which can include donors and board members. In practice, although both intergovernmental organizations and non-governmental organizations may be more accountable to the international general public than are many states and governments, there remains a large area of discretion open to humanitarian officials. This is particularly so for those working in difficult field postings where political sensitivities abound and where publicity may lead to increased danger to life and personal security for thousands of already suffering people, not to mention the officials themselves. Confidential or private negotiations remain therefore as methods used by humanitarian officials.

Humanitarian actors also use the instrument of publicity as part of the armoury of diplomatic methods. For instance, they may use international press conferences to warn of "donor fatigue". One objective may be to raise awareness of a country's needs among an international audience and to appeal for funding. Another objective may be to signal to recipient governments that a lack of cooperation could result in a diminution or cutting off of resources.

The importance of analysing diplomacy for humanitarian actors

Without analysis of the core role of the humanitarian official as diplomat, the humanitarian enterprise will be jeopardized. This is because humanitarians engage in diplomacy often without understanding that this is what they are doing or, if understanding that they are engaged in something more than technical operational implementation, enter into the diplomatic role with reluctance – considering it to be "political" and outside their operational remit. The diplomatic role is an ineluctable aspect of post–Cold War humanitarian work. If humanitarians feel coerced into this role, either because they are untrained in political negotiating or because they feel it is not part of their role to engage in "political" negotiations, they will be less than optimally effective in meeting humanitarian needs.

At the other end of the spectrum, the humanitarian official who is without guidance and training and yet who enters enthusiastically into the role of humanitarian negotiator may equally jeopardize the success of humanitarian operations. Insensitive interactions with host governments or other in-country political actors, or the transmission of naive political analysis to donors, may exacerbate conflict. Humanitarian officials ignorant of the possible diplomatic ramifications of their humanitarian role may even be viewed as spies by the host government and, as happened in a small number of instances in the DPRK to American NGO officials resident in the country, find themselves as persona non grata (PNG) and ejected from the country. In the terminology of the NGO and diplomatic community, they are "PNGed", usually by not having visas renewed.

Oxymoron, common sense and a necessary evil

The three conceptions of humanitarian diplomacy – as oxymoron, common sense and a necessary evil – are not contradictory. Each contributes to our understanding of the phenomenon. A standard understanding of diplomacy is "the promotion of the national interest by peaceful means".[36] Humanitarian diplomacy could, by contrast, be understood as "the promotion of the international interest by peaceful means". Humanitarian actors "do" diplomacy but they do it in a different way from state actors. Nicholas Morris in Chapter 16 in this volume on UNHCR involvement in the Balkan wars notes that "tactics and arguments may be situation specific, but the requirements and reactions of humanitarian negotiators should be predictable.... Surprise and pragmatism are likely to be counter-productive when seeking to ensure respect for humanitarian principles and basic human rights. Humanitarian negotiations have a greater chance of success if it is clear to all parties that there are things that are not negotiable" (pages 360 and 369).

Humanitarian actors have limited objectives and specified aims. They may engage in the processes of diplomacy but they must be very careful to distinguish for instance between "information-gathering", which is a legitimate tool of humanitarian diplomacy, and "intelligence-gathering", which is not. They must also be careful not to allow their communication role with host governments to slip over into a political communication role between host governments and the national capitals of donors – often those same states that are engaged in conflict with the host governments. On the other hand, humanitarian agencies can learn from the practices of diplomacy in that they can improve the negotiating skills of officials and organize training in when the private mode should be used in communication (confidentiality) and when it is appropriate to use the media (publicity) in the service of humanitarian diplomacy.

This volume demonstrates that humanitarian negotiators have achieved their objectives through peaceful means in the most intractable global crises. Classic diplomatic practice, in terms of the practice of state diplomats or "official" diplomats, may have much to learn from the exigencies of humanitarian diplomacy as practised in the post–Cold War era. The successes (and failures) of humanitarian diplomacy may also have much to teach those who have rejected diplomacy as a significant instrument of foreign policy in favour of the prior use of military force as the preferred way of achieving foreign policy objectives.

Notes

1. Hedley Bull, *The Anarchical Society: A Study of Order in World Politics*, London: Macmillan, 1985, p. 162.
2. Ibid., p. 163.
3. Nicolson argues for a fundamental distinction to be made between policy-making and the negotiation of policy – the latter being the function of diplomats. See Harold Nicolson, *Diplomacy*, Washington DC: Institute for the Study of Diplomacy, 1988, pp. 4–5.
4. For a theoretical critique, see Peter Viggo Jakobsen, *Western Use of Coercive Diplomacy after the Cold War*, London: Macmillan, 1998; for a more empirical account, see Robert J. Art and Patrick M. Cronin, eds, *The United States and Coercive Diplomacy*, Washington DC: United States Institute of Peace, 2003.
5. Alexander George, *Forceful Persuasion: Coercive Diplomacy as an Alternative to War*, Washington DC: United States Institute of Peace, 1991; Kenneth A. Schultz, *Democracy and Coercive Diplomacy*, Cambridge: Cambridge University Press, 2001.
6. For Nicolson, for example, diplomacy is "the art of negotiating agreements between Sovereign States" (Nicolson, *Diplomacy*, p. xiii).
7. For an essentially state-centric approach that nevertheless carefully discusses the development of IGO diplomacy and touches on non-state actor diplomacy, see Keith Hamilton and Richard Langhorne, *The Practice of Diplomacy: Its Evolution, Theory and Administration*, London: Routledge, 1995, especially pp. 183–245.
8. On special envoys, see Geoffrey Berridge, *Talking to the Enemy: How States without Diplomatic Relations Communicate*, London: Macmillan, 1994, pp. 101–116.
9. For an informed and thorough discussion of the transformations in Soviet foreign policy, see the seminal E. H. Carr, *The Bolshevik Revolution 1917–1923*, Harmondsworth: Pelican, 1984.
10. This is an under-researched area. The phenomenon was first widely commented on (to my knowledge) in Nicaragua in the 1980s during the rule of the revolutionary Sandinista government (1979–1990). The Westerners who sought a political vocation in Nicaragua – and sometimes to engage in international diplomacy back in their home capitals – were termed, needless to say derisively, "Sandalistas" by the Nicaraguan opposition press.
11. Berridge, *Talking to the Enemy*, p. 27.
12. There is disagreement among scholars about when it is appropriate to talk about the institutionalization of a recognizably modern states system. Bull argues that European

and non-European states interacted in a single international system from as early as the sixteenth century. Hinsley, in contrast, argues that a "new European states' system emerged in the eighteenth century, and not at an earlier date". See, respectively, Bull, *The Anarchical Society*, p. 15; F. H. Hinsley, *Power and the Pursuit of Peace*, Cambridge: Cambridge University Press, 1988, p. 153.

13. Berridge's definition of multilateral diplomacy and the subsequent discussion limit the constitutive actors to states, although there is some slippage with the mention of "states or other agencies" that participate in multilateral diplomacy. See Geoffrey Berridge, "Multilateral Diplomacy", in *Diplomacy: Theory and Practice*, 2nd edn, Basingstoke: Palgrave, 2002, pp. 146–167. For the quote see p. 158.

14. For discussion see Nicolson, *Diplomacy*, pp. 28–40.

15. Bull makes this point contra Nicolson. See Bull, *The Anarchical Society*, p. 176. For an authoritative discussion on these "new" twentieth-century conditions in respect of public opinion and international relations, see Carr on the relationship between power, public opinion and propaganda. E. H. Carr, *The Twenty Years Crisis 1919–1939*, London: Macmillan, 1984, pp. 132–145.

16. These three functions are commonly understood by most theorists as core attributes of diplomacy and are summarized in Bull, *The Anarchical Society*, pp. 170–172. Bull adds two more: "the minimisation of friction in international relations" and "symbolising the existence of the society of states" (ibid., pp. 171–172). These last two attributes do not comprise part of a widely shared understanding of the core features of diplomacy and so are omitted from the definition I use in this chapter.

17. Bull, *The Anarchical Society*, p. 170.

18. For discussion on the advantages and disadvantages of the use of telecommunications in diplomacy, see Berridge, *Diplomacy*, pp. 90–104.

19. Nicolson, *Diplomacy*, pp. 143–144.

20. Berridge, *Diplomacy*, p. 207.

21. See, for instance, I. William Zartmann and Maureen R. Berman, *The Practical Negotiator*, New Haven, CT: Yale University Press, 1982; Victor A. Kremenyuk, ed., *International Negotiation: Analysis, Approaches, Issues*, Chichester: Jossey-Bass: 2002; I. William Zartmann, *Preventive Negotiation: Avoiding Conflict Escalation*, New York: Carnegie Commission on Preventing Deadly Conflict and Rowman & Littlefield, 2001.

22. On Taliban diplomacy, see Paul Sharp, "Mullah Zaeef and Taliban Diplomacy: An English School Approach", *Review of International Studies*, Vol. 29, No. 4, October 2003, pp. 481–498.

23. Berridge, *Diplomacy*, p. 101.

24. See Harold Nicolson, "The Ideal Diplomatist", in Nicolson, *Diplomacy*, pp. 55–67.

25. Nicolson, *Diplomacy*, pp. 63–64.

26. Examples from Nicolson, *Diplomacy*, p. 123.

27. Ibid., p. 138.

28. Bull, *The Anarchical Society*, p. 181.

29. Christer Jönsson and Karin Aggestam, "Trends in Diplomatic Signalling", in Jan Melissen, ed., *Innovation in Diplomatic Practice*, London: Macmillan, 1999, pp. 160–162.

30. For discussion of the debate within the IGOs and the US NGO community, see Larry Minear, *The Humanitarian Enterprise*, Bloomfield, CT: Kumarian, 2002, pp. 75–97. For the Red Cross movement, it is not just possible but essential that humanitarian operations are non-political. For NGOs such as Médecins sans Frontières (MSF) and Action against Hunger (ACF), another prominent French NGO sharing the MSF perspective, there can be no humanitarian interventions without, at the same time, political analysis and advocacy in support of suffering populations and against oppressive governments. For detailed analysis of the ACF perspective on the relationship between humanitarian

work and political advocacy in various emergencies, including the Great Lakes, Sierra Leone, the DPRK, Afghanistan and Iraq, see Sylvie Brunel, ed., *Geopolitics of Hunger*, London: Action against Hunger, 1999.

31. A paradigmatic example of this latter case was the activity of a number of small US NGOs (some supported with US government funding) operating illegally in China in the early 2000s whose avowed aim was to overturn the North Korean government. They advocated the use of military force to do so, yet positioned themselves such as to supposedly "represent" the North Korean people in congressional committees that were influential in deciding foreign policy towards the DPRK. The murky world of US anti-communist fronts remains difficult to penetrate, but some of the websites are useful. For instance, the "China e-Lobby", which campaigns for the end of the communist government in China, also runs a website dedicated to overturning the government of the DPRK; see ⟨http://www.geocities.com/china_e_lobby/WhyNK.html⟩. Groups sharing these views were constant "representatives" at congressional hearings on the DPRK through 2002 and 2003.

32. John Shaw and Edward Clay, *World Food Aid*, Rome/London: World Food Programme/ James Currey/Heinemann, 1993, pp. 1 and 4.

33. Zartmann and Berman, *The Practical Negotiator*, p. 1.

34. I have discussed the links that some humanitarian officials had to the US State Department in Hazel Smith, *Hungry for Peace: International Security, Humanitarian Assistance and Social Change in North Korea*, Washington DC: United States Institute of Peace Press, 2005.

35. The Geneva-based Centre for Humanitarian Dialogue has started work in this area, based around their developing network of humanitarian negotiators. See ⟨http:// www.hdcentre.org/Programmes/nnetwork.htm⟩.

36. Hans J. Morgenthau, revised by Kenneth W. Thompson, *Politics among Nations: The Struggle for Power and Peace*, 6th edn, New York: Alfred A. Knopf, 1985, p. 563.

Part II

The Middle East

3

Protecting Palestinian Refugees: The UNRWA experience

D. Sena Wijewardane

The problem of the Palestine refugees was created by the displacement of some 700,000 Palestinians from their homes during the hostilities in Palestine in 1948 resulting from the creation of the state of Israel and the flight of the refugees to neighbouring Arab countries, where the majority were accommodated in makeshift refugee camps. In response, the United Nations Relief and Works Agency for Palestine Refugees in the Near East (UNRWA) was established to carry out direct relief and works programmes in collaboration with "local governments" and to plan for the future. This chapter reviews the pivotal role played by humanitarian diplomacy in enabling UNRWA to carry out its mission in a highly politicized environment.

Context

For 55 years, against the backdrop of the Arab–Israeli conflict, UNRWA has been engaged in a unique and continuing exercise in humanitarian diplomacy. UNRWA began its activities by focusing on refugee reintegration, but had to develop into a multifaceted organization that provides essential quasi-governmental services such as education, health, relief and social services, and micro-credit to a present-day population of over 4 million Palestine refugees within its five areas of operations – Jordan, Lebanon, Syria, the West Bank and the Gaza Strip. During these years, the Agency has cultivated and protected the humanitarian space within which it operates by resorting to various measures of humanitarian diplomacy with the relevant governmental authorities, ranging from ground-level operational negotiations to intervention at higher political and policy levels, including through the Secretary-General of the United Nations and the UN General Assembly. These measures have included negotiation, moral persuasion, public discourse, and legal and broader institutional responses from both inside and outside the UN system. UNRWA's status as a subsidiary organ of the UN General Assembly has been a significant factor in these responses. An integral part of UNRWA's diplomatic role has been also to persuade its various stakeholders that its actions are constitutionally well founded in pursuit of its humanitarian mission.

The volatile and prolonged nature of the conflict has compelled UNRWA to activate a diplomatic role in a variety of "conflict" situations, including periods of war, of temporary and more prolonged occupation, and of armed insurrection. Particularly in the Occupied Palestinian Territories (OPT) since 1967, UNRWA has faced numerous challenges to its operations and humanitarian access, including challenges to its functioning in the midst of military operations often involving widespread violence and civilian casualties; the urgent need for emergency medical, food and relief supplies for large sectors of the population; threats to the physical safety and security of its personnel; the detention without charge or trial of its staff; curtailment of freedom of movement of staff, vehicles and goods; the misuse, damage and demolition of its installations and premises; and the targeted and, at times, large-scale damage and destruction of refugee shelters. These limitations have impinged on principles of international law and multilateral and bilateral undertakings, including the Charter of the United Nations, the 1946 Convention on the Privileges and Immunities of the United Nations and the Geneva Convention Relative to the Protection of Civilian Persons in Time of War (the Fourth Geneva Convention), which form the legal framework within which UNRWA operates.

For several years after its creation the Agency focused its activities on attempts to integrate the refugees into the areas to which they had been displaced. This policy was found to be unrealistic, largely as a result of political opposition from the host governments and indeed because of the political aspirations of the refugees themselves, whose clear expectation was to be allowed to return to their homes. It led to a gradual shift in UNRWA's programmes from integration to relief and human development activities. By the late 1950s UNRWA had established the blueprint for its long-term operations and institutional services focusing on vocational training, self-support, primary education, primary health care and continued relief for needy refugees. These activities eventually developed into three major programmes of health, education and relief and social services and helped to shape the attitude of the refugees to UNRWA's quasi-governmental role and the expectation on their part that they would be supported and protected until such time as there is a comprehensive political settlement on the question of Palestine. UNRWA today provides education, health, relief and social services to 4.2 million refugees in the five fields already referred to through a network of 652 schools, 125 health centres and numerous other installations. To provide these services UNRWA employs a staff of approximately 25,000, the vast majority of whom are Palestine refugees themselves, making UNRWA by far the largest organization in the UN system in terms of the number of employees and the largest single employer in the region.

From among all the challenges across its 55-year history, this chapter selects for analysis one from each of the two popular uprisings against Israeli military rule in the OPT. During the first uprising – 1987 to 1993 – UNRWA created a programme to facilitate its role in protecting the refugee community in an environment of military occupation. In the second uprising, beginning in 2000, UNRWA undertook a series of measures to protect the integrity of its operations by ensuring humanitarian access in the face of an increasingly systematic and draconian network of military checkpoints and barriers to movement set up by the Israeli military forces as well as to safeguard itself against allegations that its installations and operations were being abused by Palestinian political and military factions.

Since the occupation of the West Bank and the Gaza Strip by the state of Israel in June 1967, UNRWA has, with the consent of Israel, continued to provide its services to the refugees in these areas. UNRWA's swift and prescient action at this point laid the foundation stone for its later efforts in humanitarian diplomacy. On 14 June 1967, in the immediate aftermath of the war, the state of Israel and UNRWA entered into a "provisional" arrangement, known as the 1967 Comay–Michelmore Agreement, which reiterated the continued commitment of the government of Israel fully to cooperate with and facilitate the task of UNRWA.[1] The Agreement also refers explicitly to the application of the 1946 General Convention on the Privileges and Immunities of the United Nations to UNRWA's operations.

Operational issues

The first Palestinian uprising or intifada (to use the Arabic term by which it has come to be universally known) is taken to have begun in the Gaza Strip on 9 December 1987 and continued until the Oslo accords in 1993.

During the whole of this period and especially at the beginning, the question of the protection of the refugees came to command the attention of the international community. After almost 40 years of responding to their needs, UNRWA had by 1987 developed a special relationship with the Palestinian refugees and was seen as the familiar symbol of the international community's commitment to the refugees pending a political settlement in the area. It was a relatively intimate, open and trusting relationship, which had emerged over the years, albeit one that had limitations. UNRWA was not taken by surprise by the forceful expressions of frustration created by 20 years of military occupation and of economic and political stagnation. However, the main operational concern at the time was the "means" of protecting the refugees when armed Israeli military and unarmed Palestinian civilian elements faced each other in daily skirmishes. By contrast, with the outbreak of the second intifada in September 2000 following the collapse of the Israeli–Palestinian peace process, although the safety and security of the refugees were an ever-present issue, this intifada was marked by the use of lethal weaponry by both sides. In particular, the Israeli armed forces' resort to air-borne attacks and assaults with heavy armour made it practically impossible for UNRWA to intercede – as it had done during the first intifada – between the opposing parties, except to ensure access for humanitarian supplies and to insulate its installations from the dangers of abuse from both sides to the conflict.

The first intifada was characterized by large-scale and widespread public demonstrations by the Palestinian population and confrontations with the Israeli army that elicited the use of force and the imposition of a variety of control mechanisms, such as curfews, blockades and the closure of schools and other Palestinian institutions. It was in the refugee camps, which were the main focus of UNRWA's activities and where the inhabitants were generally the poorest and the most politically motivated, that the confrontations were fiercest. Particularly in the camps in the Gaza Strip, with their massive populations (Jabalia camp currently has a population of 104,000, Rafah camp has 96,000 and Beach camp has 76,000), casualties from army gunfire were shockingly high on a daily basis. The appalling living conditions, coupled with legitimate political frustrations, made Gaza an especially fertile field for extremist action. Many refugees were themselves UNRWA employees and UNRWA was acutely sensitive to the operational need to bring home to all its employees the imperative that the provision of UN humanitarian assistance required a stringent commitment to the principles of the United Nations even if the mandate of the organization was focused on providing assistance to one side only of the conflict.

The intifada affected UNRWA directly in two ways. The frequent confrontations, curfews and strikes made the carrying out of normal

UNRWA operations and the rendering of institutional services in the West Bank and the Gaza Strip much more difficult. It was also soon evident to UNRWA, especially through its network of health clinics and schools, that an appreciable and growing number of the refugees were being subjected to indiscriminate and disproportionate violence in these confrontations with the Israeli security forces. Frustration was compounded by personal injuries and human suffering. By way of example, during 1989 at least 300 Palestinian civilians were killed in the OPT, the great majority by the use of live ammunition and plastic bullets. The number of injuries was naturally much higher: during May 1989, UNRWA recorded 2,473 cases of injury in the Gaza Strip alone.

Although the nature of this intifada was very much one of civil disorder, it was faced with a highly trained military force that was supposed to control security and public order. The Israeli military was exceptionally well equipped for its function as a military machine, but it was ill equipped to deal with civil disorder and the emerging humanitarian crisis. It had been trained to fight armies in battle, not children and turbulent youth. Stones – and there were many – hurled at army vehicles could be more than disconcerting to the occupants. They might even be regarded as weapons, but deadly fire was not a suitable or proportionate response. The alternative of water cannons and batons, familiar equipment for crowd control in other regions of the world, was not evident and indeed has never been used.

UNRWA had always been obliged to shift the focus of its relatively scarce resources in order to meet the pressing needs of the refugees at any particular time. In the context of the intifada it had no choice but to respond in a focused manner to the humanitarian crisis that was rapidly unfolding: UNRWA clinics, for example, which had been more used to providing antenatal health care, soon became emergency treatment centres for immense numbers of gunshot injuries.

UNRWA had no executive authority in the Occupied Territories, even if its operations had by now acquired a quasi-governmental character. It was the occupying power that was responsible for ensuring a secure environment to enable UNRWA to carry out its humanitarian assistance to the refugees. The occupying forces were, however, heavily embroiled as a party in the conflict. The total absence of any riot control mechanisms and the non-observance of the Geneva Conventions left the question of protection of the population wide open and led to a dramatic increase in the number of casualties. It soon became clear to UNRWA that the first imperative was to acquire accurate statistics about the injuries to vulnerable categories of refugees. Only with such information could advocacy and action be prioritized. UNRWA immediately established a casualty database so that it could make well-informed decisions and its policies, advocacy and interventions on behalf of the refugees could be based on concrete and demonstrable facts that the international community had a right to know and that UNRWA envisaged it had a responsibility to provide. UNRWA clinics were widespread throughout the OPT and the Agency had well-established institutional links to all the major hospitals. The casualty database, refined as time went on, served the aims of UNRWA's humanitarian diplomacy well. It came to be seen by the Agency's major donors, by commentators and by other humanitarian and human rights organizations as an authoritative source of information on the rapidly mounting casualties and as a firm basis for debate and diplomacy.

Five years previously, in the immediate aftermath of the 1982 invasion of Lebanon, UNRWA had not been able to make a difference to the tragedies that took place in the Beirut refugee camps of Sabra and Shatila. By 1987, however, a very different situation presented itself in the West Bank and the Gaza Strip. This time the "very presence" of the United Nations could make a difference to emerging humanitarian needs. The events in the camps in Lebanon were still vivid in the minds of the international community, and the clashes, this time between a relatively defenceless civilian population and a heavily armed occupation force, were being played out on television screens worldwide on a daily basis. UNRWA made use of this opportunity in exercising its responsibility for humanitarian diplomacy. Security Council Resolution 605 of 22 December 1987 requested the Secretary-General to assess the situation and to make "recommendations on ways and means for ensuring the safety and protection of the Palestinian civilians under Israeli occupation". The resulting report – often referred to as the "Goulding Report" – was of significance in the development of UNRWA's protection programme in the Occupied Territories.[2]

To a large extent this report reflected ongoing UNRWA operations and the speedy responses it was making on the ground. It also served to distinguish what was feasible in the circumstances from what was not. The report clearly delineated four principal means by which the protection of the Palestinian people, including the refugees, could be secured, although it pointed out that, "[i]n the long run, the only certain way of ensuring the safety and protection of the Palestinian people in the occupied territories ... is the negotiation of a comprehensive, just and lasting settlement of the Arab–Israeli conflict acceptable to all concerned". Pending such a political settlement, the most effective way of ensuring the protection of the civilian population was for Israel to apply in full measure the provisions of the 1949 Fourth Geneva Convention Relative to the Protection of Civilian Persons in Time of War.

Four different concepts of "protection" were distinguished in the report, thereby lending much-needed clarity to operational issues:

(a) protection can mean physical protection, in the sense of providing armed forces to deter, and if necessary fight, any threats to the safety of the protected persons;

(b) protection can mean legal protection, in the sense of intervention with the security, judicial and political authorities of the occupying power by an outside agency in order to ensure just treatment of an individual or a group of individuals;

(c) protection can take a less well-defined form, called in the report "general assistance", in which an outside agency intervenes with the authorities of the occupying power to help individuals or groups of individuals to resist violation of their rights and to cope with the day-to-day difficulties of life under occupation, such as security restrictions, curfews, harassment and bureaucratic difficulties;

(d) protection could also take the more intangible form of "protection by publicity" afforded by outside agencies, including the international media, whose mere presence and readiness to publish what they observe may be beneficial for all concerned.

Of these four protection mechanisms, UNRWA was specifically requested to enhance its "general assistance" capacity through the addition of extra international staff in the OPT to, *inter alia*, intervene with the occupying power in an effort to provide a modicum of "passive protection" to the Palestinians. Thus, what UNRWA had already initiated with limited resources, using available existing international staff from its headquarters in Vienna and the Field Offices in West Bank and the Gaza Strip, who were drawn away from their normal duties to perform these additional tasks, received a much-needed boost with the establishment of a separately funded programme specifically dedicated to this activity. The timing could not have been better. In a key passage in the report, the Secretary-General stated: "I believe international staff can at present play an especially valuable role. It is usually easier for them to gain access to Israeli authorities in emergency situations; and their mere presence at points of confrontation has a significant impact on how the civilian population (including UNRWA Palestinian staff) is treated by the security forces and helps it psychologically by making it less exposed."[3] Member states were urged to respond generously to funding appeals. The Agency's embryonic Refugee Affairs Officer (RAO) programme – so called deliberately to present an innocuous title and a low profile – had become an integral component of its "programme of general assistance and protection".

The RAO programme began in January 1988. The goals were two-fold: (1) to facilitate UNRWA operations in the difficult prevailing circumstances of the intifada; and (2) to provide a degree of passive protection for the refugee population. The two goals are of course closely related, since UNRWA's operations are of an essentially humanitarian nature. For example, an RAO who assisted an UNRWA ambulance evacuating wounded Palestinians for medical attention was both facilitating UNRWA operations and providing protection. At any given period, there were 21 RAO teams operating in the OPT. The formal duties of the RAOs included the following:

- to circulate throughout the OPT on a frequent, though unannounced, schedule for the purpose of observing and reporting to the respective Field Office any unusual or abnormal circumstances;
- to visit Agency installations in the OPT and to report any disruptions in Agency operations;
- to visit camps and other areas under curfew, and to report to the respective Field Office on any problems affecting the welfare of the population;
- to ascertain and report as accurately as possible the names, ages, refugee status, circumstances and other appropriate information relating to Palestinians killed or wounded as a result of hostilities in the OPT;
- to liaise with local military governors and civilian administrators of the occupying power on matters affecting the Agency's operations or the welfare of the refugees; and
- to visit UNRWA staff members detained by the occupying power to find out the grounds for their detention and the quality of treatment accorded to them.

The prosaic language of a UN job description conceals the manner in which the RAOs were expected to, and did, achieve their goals. In principle, they provided protection by their presence as internationally recruited UN officials who were expected to be independent and impartial at scenes of tension and unrest. UNRWA had equipped them with vehicles that were linked by radio 24 hours a day to the Field Offices in Jerusalem and Gaza, thus enabling rapid communication and deployment to trouble-spots. Accordingly, teams of RAOs were constantly touring and operating in the West Bank and the Gaza Strip. The relatively small distances helped although, in the West Bank, the somewhat greater distances than in the Gaza Strip created logistical difficulties in making their presence felt as immediately as might have been desired. The programme was effective also because of the extraordinary infrastructure that UNRWA had built up over the years in terms of offices, vehicles and supporting staff in a limited geographical area. As a result, for the first time in UN history, the white Volkswagen estate flying the UN flag and carrying the RAOs and their local assistants on their tours of the troubled camps, villages and towns became a familiar image on television screens and registered in the international consciousness. The RAOs' calming influence in negotiating the withdrawal of military forces or of an over-enthusiastic or potentially riotous gathering was acknowledged. RAOs were seen at UNRWA schools, especially at the beginning and end of the school day when the large numbers of young people entering and leaving schools represented a potentially explosive situation. There was no doubt that the RAOs helped to prevent many violent incidents taking place.

What an RAO could do when violence actually broke out depended on the circumstances. The RAO would seek out the military commander on the spot and try to negotiate a decrease in tension, for example by suggesting that the military unit change its location or achieve its objective in some less confrontational way. Leading figures among the protestors and the population could also be approached because UNRWA was well trusted. Often both sides were happy to see a third party intervene in a situation that, without mediation, would inevitably result in injuries and possibly deaths. Having, it was hoped, achieved some satisfactory result, the RAO might immediately be called away to negotiate access for an UNRWA ambulance carrying wounded persons that was being detained at a military checkpoint or to a military camp to try to obtain the release of children detained and taken there by the army. RAOs might receive these requests and information through the UNRWA field network, but often they came simply from local residents, worried parents or even the army itself as they toured the area on a daily basis.

The RAOs were strictly prohibited from forceful physical intervention in an incident of violence or abuse. It was not their function either to interfere in the intifada or to stand in the way of the maintenance of legitimate security and order. However, they had a humanitarian interest in reducing violence and the indiscriminate and excessive use of force in a highly charged environment. It was therefore sometimes possible imperceptibly to cross the delicate dividing line in the sole interest of averting tragedy. In at least one instance an isolated soldier separated from his colleagues was discreetly moved out of harm's way by an RAO. This very heavy onus on young representatives of the international community was what made the job exciting, demanding and exceptionally responsible.

The general assistance and protection programme became a central feature of UNRWA's programmes in the OPT by the early 1990s. The Agency's legal officers in the OPT, who were an essential part of the administrative support to the programme, were able to gain access to many of the hundreds of local staff members held in prisons and detention centres during this time, to check on their conditions and on the circumstances of their detention.

By 1991, the programme had come to include a "legal aid scheme" run by the Agency with the purpose of helping the "refugees deal with a range of problems of life under occupation", including "sustained follow-up in cases of deaths, injuries and harassment; bureaucratic difficulties in obtaining various permits; discrimination in access to courts of law, welfare benefits, etc.; travel restrictions; and, various forms of collective punishment".

The conclusion of the Declaration of Principles on Interim Self-Government Arrangements in 1993 and the establishment of the Palestinian Authority ushered in a period during which it was thought the RAO programme would no longer be required. Accordingly, the programme was officially suspended in the Gaza field in May 1994 and in the West Bank field in April 1996.[4]

The RAO programme, established by UNRWA in January 1988, had been the major response by the United Nations to the outbreak of the intifada. Over the intervening years the programme had employed some 140 Refugee Affairs Officers. These in general comprised highly educated and well-motivated young people of many nationalities. Many of them went on to hold responsible jobs in the United Nations and with other international organizations, where their experience as RAOs undoubtedly contributed to the development of a variety of humanitarian strategies in emergency situations both within and outside of the United Nations. The programme was widely viewed as having successfully fulfilled the objectives it had set itself.

When the second intifada broke out on 28 September 2000 the situation on the ground was very different and resembled less a situation of public disorder and more an all-out war. There were many similarities with the earlier intifada as well, and UNRWA had a wealth of experience to build on. The need to observe and report impartially was again critically important, especially to obtain the necessary funding to ensure continued humanitarian assistance to the refugee community. The Final Communiqué of the Extraordinary Arab Summit of 21–22 October 2000 demanded that the United Nations "assume responsibility for providing the necessary protection to the Palestinian people" through forming "a force or an international presence for this purpose" and that the international community should take responsibility for the Palestinian people and territory "until such time as the Palestinian people secures the exercise of its inalienable rights in Palestine in accordance with international legitimacy".[5]

Because the peace process was frozen and the Palestinian Authority increasingly resembled a legal fiction rather than an embryonic government, it was a matter of priority to support and safeguard UNRWA's ability to access its beneficiaries and the rights of the refugees to receive UNRWA services, which were being heavily impeded. UNRWA again needed to act with purposive speed and, within weeks of the commencement of the intifada, it allocated its always scarce resources to the establishment of a new emergency programme, called the Operational Support Officers (OSO) programme. This was designed primarily to facilitate the delivery of humanitarian assistance, to secure the safe passage of Agency staff through the military checkpoints and more generally to enhance the proper implementation of Agency programmes in accordance with UN norms. UNRWA was quick to understand the constraints on its Palestinian staff – well motivated, loyal and experienced as they were – in interceding with the Israeli authorities and ensuring that Agency operations suffered as little as possible. The debates on the mandate that had been conducted with the Israeli ministry of foreign affairs (MFA) were now a part of history, and little resistance was expected to the initiation of such a programme. UNRWA could rely on the reputation that the RAO programme had acquired for its strictly humanitarian role and objectivity of action. With these factors behind it, UNRWA proceeded with remarkable speed (generally unusual in UN organizations) to establish a new programme. Although the OSO programme was not mandated or equipped to provide the Palestine refugees with "protection", to the extent that it has assisted in the delivery of essential humanitarian aid to the refugees it contributed again, though in a relatively limited way, to providing the refugees with a form of "passive" protection.

The changed political realities on the ground after September 2000 affected the abilities of OSOs to provide the same type of protection as had their RAO predecessors. Israeli military operations in the Palestinian-controlled areas took the form of strikes, either by heavily armoured units or from the air. It was clearly much more difficult for OSOs to engage in any form of meaningful negotiation with Israeli military forces. The Palestinian police and security forces now had a considerable amount of small arms at their disposal. Clashes now were between two military forces, albeit vastly unequal ones, with little if any room for intervention by civilian third parties.

A new feature was the increasing practice by the Israeli authorities of blockading areas under the control of the Palestinian Authority, resulting in ever greater difficulties of movement for residents of the OPT and for UNRWA itself. To facilitate the freedom of movement of UN staff and of emergency supplies, the OSOs interceded at the multitude of checkpoints that had been set up. UNRWA took on a coordinating role, in respect of access issues, for all the UN organizations working in the Occupied Territories. Regular meetings were held to develop strategies and to maintain pressure on the government of Israel to respect the privileges and immunities of the United Nations. The problems of movement and access have become substantially more difficult with the recent construction by Israel of the apparently permanent "security fence" or wall around the Palestinian-populated areas of the West Bank, the stated purpose of which is to prevent terrorist attacks in Israel.

In a curious twist, the US government later undertook to fund and support the OSO programme, reflecting an appreciation in the international community of the contribution that both the RAO and the OSO programmes had made to stability in the region by ensuring that UN privileges and immunities were properly protected against abuse from all sides to the conflict. By substantially ensuring that Palestinian factions did not abuse UNRWA installations, UNRWA was also able to reduce violations of its premises by Israeli military forces, which used security as a justification for their incursions. This served as an inducement for other factions to keep out. By seeking to avoid a double jeopardy, not only were UNRWA's humanitarian services to the Palestine population better secured, but the prevention of abuse of UN facilities by all parties meant that UN premises and property were properly identified and were used solely for the purposes of UN activities and programmes. One of the central duties of the RAOs and of the OSOs was regularly to visit UN installations in refugee camps to prevent use of these installations in any manner inconsistent with their status as UN premises and to report on any interference. These regular inspections by officials dedicated to these purposes served to lower the opportunity for violence. In the course of 2000, political interest groups criticized UNRWA's close association with the Palestinian community and mischievously alleged that UNRWA had "collaborated with terrorism". These allegations were more easily laid to rest through the initiatives that UNRWA had adopted through these programmes and it received a measure of recognition and trust from the major donor community for having made a contribution to the limited stability in the area.

Obstacles and opportunities

UNRWA's mandate involves a commitment to render assistance to one side in a highly charged ongoing conflict. Israel is an occupying power, perceived as such by the vast majority of the international community, and has not accepted the *de jure* application of the Geneva Convention to the OPT despite having expressed its willingness to abide by the spirit of the Convention. There is an inbuilt resistance on the part of the state of Israel to any generous approach to assistance for a community that is deeply hostile to the occupation and to any liberal interpretation of the various multilateral and bilateral legal texts that are applicable to relations between UNRWA and Israel. The close relationship between

UNRWA and the Palestinian refugee community, although understandable and in fact useful to all interlocutors, has also proved to be an impediment in the discharge of UNRWA's humanitarian mission. Israel frequently makes efforts to portray UNRWA as a Palestinian organization and to underplay the core characteristics of a UN operation. This makes it all the more critical that UNRWA officials act with objectivity and impartiality when discharging this one-sided mandate.

The picture would be incomplete without reference to the continuous working relationship that UNRWA officials at all levels have had with the occupying power, which is probably unique in what has been essentially an adversarial situation. UNRWA officials have on the whole succeeded in maintaining a working relationship with the Israeli military authorities at various levels. But UNRWA's formal point of contact with the Israeli government has been for the most part the Israeli ministry of foreign affairs. Over the years, professional relations have been established with senior officials on the Israeli side and UNRWA's work in the Occupied Territory has generally received sympathy and understanding from these officials. Indeed, the serious debate and dialogue that MFA officials have conducted with UNRWA over a considerable period are testimony to the high standards of professionalism and courtesy in a very trying environment. As in normal diplomatic discourse, the fact that UNRWA had the benefit of interacting with an established ministry of foreign affairs has been to the advantage of UNRWA, in comparison with the experience of UN officials in other parts of the world who in times of conflict invariably have to deal with ad hoc militias and other groups. To UNRWA, this meant that humanitarian diplomacy could be conducted through the usual diplomatic channels and in a more regulated manner.

The legal framework, to which reference has been made above, is central to understanding UNRWA's ability to function effectively in the OPT. UNRWA's status as a subsidiary organ of the UN General Assembly has, it is believed, helped to maintain a relative degree of operational autonomy and independence of action for the Agency. Treaties governing international bodies are generally drafted in specific language and closely define their operative organs, powers and functions. Under the pressure of political events of the day, the General Assembly resolution establishing UNRWA in 1949 was sparing in the guidance it provided to start an organization of such a size and, as it turned out, for a duration not envisaged at the time. The original resolution had been hurriedly cobbled together and thereafter a particular onus fell on those carrying the responsibilities of running UNRWA to persuade their interlocutors at any given time that its actions were justified. UNRWA staff are not members of the UN Secretariat and, because UNRWA reports directly to the General Assembly, it found itself free from the political direction and control of the UN in New York. This too gave it a considerable measure of flexibility and manoeuvrability of action. Unlike the Specialized Agencies of the UN system, for example, and as a subsidiary organ of the General Assembly, UNRWA does not have a controlling Executive Board. This enhanced its relative independence and provided the space for its own executive head to act quickly when the need arose. Successive UNRWA Commissioners-General have wisely used this leverage, together with the Agency's relatively non-specific mandate, in the interests of the Palestine refugees.

The 1967 Comay–Michelmore Agreement between UNRWA and the state of Israel includes a military security caveat, which states that "the Israel Government will facilitate the task of UNRWA to the best of its ability, subject only to regulations or arrangements which may be necessitated by considerations of military security".[6] Since 1967, interpretation of this qualification has been a central issue in all discussions between the Agency and the Israeli authorities aimed at facilitating the operations of UNRWA relating to humanitarian access. Much time and effort have been spent in debating these provisions without any real consensus. The Israeli authorities have consistently argued that the obligations undertaken by Israel toward the United Nations and other member states in the UN Charter and the 1946 Convention were modified by the military security caveat contained in the Comay–Michelmore Agreement. In numerous negotiations, meetings and communications over the years, particularly during the second intifada, the Agency has taken the position that such a caveat cannot have the effect of overriding the UN Charter or the 1946 Convention. Furthermore, the Agency has in its negotiations and discussions with the Israeli authorities argued that the caveat applied only to the immediate aftermath of the 1967 war and that, therefore, the caveat can no longer be relied upon to excuse or justify Israeli erosion of UNRWA's privileges and immunities essential to the performance of its humanitarian mission by a blanket resort to considerations of military security.

Negotiations

UNRWA was obliged to undertake serious negotiations with the Israeli authorities at the time of establishment of the RAO programme. The claim was made by the Israeli MFA that the programme was outside UNRWA's mandate. Nothing in UNRWA's founding resolution, it was claimed, had authorized such a "monitoring" activity – a characterization of the programme that UNRWA strongly refuted. The concept of general assistance and protection came under challenge and UNRWA was told that it should stick to the distribution of rations and other emergency supplies. Protection for the refugees may originally have meant protection from the winter winds and from hunger. But UNRWA had come a long way from tents and soup kitchens. Although protection from illiteracy and disease was still the major priority in the longer term, statistics drawn from the database that UNRWA had established at the start of the intifada amply demonstrated that the pressing need of the day was to reduce the mounting deaths and injuries among especially vulnerable refugee groups, namely the young, women and the elderly. Using concrete statistics and impartial eye-witness accounts, UNRWA was able to demonstrate that weapons had been used indiscriminately and disproportionately. The negotiations were underscored by an emphasis on the interest that the Israeli government itself had in the work of UNRWA and the fact that UNRWA activities in the territory were dependent on the consent of the government. It was, after all, the government's prerogative to withdraw that consent. Although the arguments were conducted mainly by reference to the legal regime governing UNRWA's relations with the government of Israel, what won the day were not the legalities involved but a recognition that the curtailment of military excesses was in the Israeli government's interests too and an acceptance of the integrity of the RAO programme, which was anchored solely in humanitarian motives and total objectivity – albeit in discharging a committed mandate. It came to be tacitly accepted that UNRWA was performing an essential service in the absence of which the situation in the area would deteriorate sharply.

The negotiations were, however, conducted within the legal framework to which reference has already been made and included the obligations arising from the relevant articles of the UN Charter, which form the primary "constitutional" basis of humanitarian space for the United Nations, the 1946 Convention on the Privileges and Immunities of the United Nations, and the primacy of the Fourth Geneva Convention Relative to the Protection of Civilian Persons in Time of War. The importance of the Fourth Geneva Convention as a reference point for humanitarian diplomacy in the Occupied Territory cannot be overemphasized. Ongoing and highly professional negotiations were thus a prerequisite to sustaining the humanitarian space implicit in the creation of UNRWA.

Wider implications

UNRWA's core responsibilities have involved the provision of humanitarian assistance, which had to be discharged in the context of a major international conflict and, since 1967, in the context of military occupation.

The unusually prolonged nature of the occupation has led to a unique and complex set of political issues that are not easily disentangled. Some issues have a colonial flavour, others pertain to human rights, to self-determination, and to the emergence and stalling of a national entity based on an international peace process that is at times frozen. The situation is complicated by religious and ethnic tensions and, more recently, by the "war against terrorism". The obligation and the capability to carry out humanitarian responsibilities through this maze of issues called for a sustained and diverse effort in "humanitarian diplomacy". However, UNRWA's responses to the special challenges of the two intifadas, which have affected later initiatives both within the UN system and elsewhere, constitute only one important aspect of such diplomacy.

In the Occupied Territory itself, the European Union's initiative of establishing a multinational Temporary International Presence in Hebron (TIPH) within the framework of the Oslo peace process drew immediate inspiration and support from the RAO programme. However, the TIPH was restricted in its mandate to "observing and reporting" on events in Hebron and was powerless to intervene on humanitarian grounds to prevent actual injury being inflicted on the population. This rendered this new initiative relatively impotent.

The focus in this chapter on two initiatives that were commenced during the intifadas should not leave the impression that there have not been almost daily demands on "humanitarian diplomacy" in the course of UNRWA's routine work to keep its operations running. There was, for example, a long period between 1967 and the Oslo peace process when UNRWA was in effect the only legitimate authority in the territory "representing", as it were, the interests of the Palestine refugees to the world at large. The weight of this responsibility was felt both within the Agency and outside it and, as earlier observed, UNRWA even came to be perceived by some elements within the occupying power as a "Palestinian" rather than a UN body. This tension required very delicate and diplomatic handling. Such tensions are par for the course in the discharge of responsibilities that are caught between seriously antagonistic components and will always demand not only diplomatic discretion and delicacy, but, more importantly, the highest standards of objectivity and commitment to that ideal. UNRWA had always to keep in mind that its primary obligation was to safeguard its role as the provider of humanitarian assistance to the Palestine refugees. Nonetheless, it could not ignore a variety of ways in which the occupation contravened the framework of humanitarian law applicable in the territory. UNRWA therefore had to develop innovative ways of discharging its responsibilities to protest against and to flag up such contraventions without at the same time putting in danger its core humanitarian functions. In the 1970s and 1980s, the treatment of the refugees in detention centres became highly controversial. Whenever UNRWA staff, many of whom were themselves Palestine refugees, were arrested without charge or trial and were ill treated in detention, UNRWA always took the opportunity to insist that the Israeli authorities uphold the requirements of the Geneva Convention that a civilian population under occupation should be treated with dignity.

Again, UNRWA has regularly protested against the demolition of refugee shelters, both because this is a form of collective punishment and because it imposes an unacceptable burden on UNRWA's own limited resources, given its obligation as a part of its assistance to the refugees to find new accommodation for those who are rendered homeless as a result. These protests have been all the stronger when sometimes even UNRWA installations are damaged or destroyed, often on the ground that they were being abused by Palestinian factions. Since the start of the second intifada, the Israeli Defense Forces have bulldozed more than 1,400 refugee shelters in the Gaza Strip alone, which accommodated some 28,000 persons who have thereby been rendered homeless. Often these demolitions have taken place at night, without any warning that would allow occupants at least to remove their personal belongings. The Israeli authorities have justified these demolitions mainly on security grounds. UNRWA has maintained that, although the Geneva Conventions, for example, take full account of the imperative of military "necessity", the facts have generally not justified such demolitions, which have in reality been a form of collective punishment. When appropriate, UNRWA has claimed compensation from the authorities and the Agency continues to draw the attention of the General Assembly to these contraventions.

In UNRWA, the exercise of humanitarian diplomacy has not been confined to ensuring the movement of emergency supplies when this is impeded or to technically asserting the privileges and immunities of UN staff, but has gone to the core of providing for the welfare of a population that it has been mandated to serve. The UNRWA experience has shown that, in certain circumstances, there is a need for a proactive and programmatic approach. The duty to notify interlocutors when they fail to abide by expected standards and norms must be taken with the utmost seriousness, because failure to do so would lead to a failure to provide the necessary protection and assistance to beneficiaries of humanitarian assistance. If the humanitarian mission is to be effectively discharged, however, a balance has to be struck between, on the one hand, that duty of notification and, on the other, both the responsibility and the need to obtain maximum cooperation from the very interlocutor who is criticized. The delicate balance required in tone and substance makes exacting demands on humanitarian diplomacy. Quality of service and a total commitment to demonstrable objectivity are essential to ensure credibility.

In both intifadas, but particularly during the first, UNRWA's achievements rested on aggressive but objective reporting of the facts and the presence on the ground of high-quality non-partisan UN officials recruited internationally. The whole world thus knew that the facts as reported were based on first-hand observation by UN officials who were committed solely to the ideals of the UN Charter and who had no partisan loyalty to either side. In the politically volatile atmosphere of conflict heightened by phenomena such as were seen during the intifadas, the need to monitor and appropriately control the political inclinations and even agendas of UN staff coming from a wide variety of backgrounds poses significant management challenges. The selection and training of staff are critically important components. In addition, the specific programmes in both intifadas were tailored to ensuring, through regular but unscheduled visits to UNRWA's operational installations, that humanitarian assistance was safeguarded by fully maintaining the integrity of the operation. This time-consuming and tedious process is an essential investment for success. Moreover, it is not an easy task to persuade an internal bureaucracy that the allocation of scarce budgetary resources for these purposes is a priority.

If all goes well, the efforts of such programmes are hidden below the surface and nothing is seen or heard of the protection and integrity they have provided. But when a complaint is made, as in an incident in the Gaza Strip pertaining to the alleged misuse of an ambulance, by which the Israeli government sought to discredit UNRWA, the value of this investment becomes evident. The dividends can also be seen in UNRWA's success in deflecting criticism that it is an accessory to acts of terrorism. These preventive measures have, it is believed, added to UNRWA's credibility and therefore its ability to be effective.

UNRWA's experience, particularly in the OPT, has been marked by a high level of diplomacy. Without this, its humanitarian operations would not have been sustained for so long a period. This illustrates that humanitarian actors can afford to shun the role of "humanitarian diplomat" only at an unacceptably high cost to vulnerable civilian populations. In the spirit of shared experiences, I hope that other humanitarian actors can learn from the lessons UNRWA has drawn over the years in this critical area and become better equipped to face future challenges.

Notes

1. United Nations Relief and Works Agency for Palestine Refugees in the Near East and Israel, "Exchange of letters constituting a provisional agreement concerning assistance to Palestine Refugees. Jerusalem, 14 June 1967", available at ⟨http://www.mfa.gov.il/NR/rdonlyres/E31F7E9F-3214-4EEF-B065-D031F4FF46FB/0/comaymichelmore.pdf⟩.

2. Goulding Report, *Report Submitted to the Security Council by the Secretary-General in Accordance with Resolution 605 (1987)*, UN Doc. S/19443, 21 January 1988.

3. Ibid., para. 38.

4. Address by Peter Hansen, Commissioner-General of UNRWA, to the American University of Cairo, 21 September 2003, para. 11, ⟨http://www.un.org/unrwa/news/statements/auc-sep03.pdf⟩.

5. *Final Communiqué of the Extraordinary Arab Summit Conference held in Cairo on 21 and 22 October 2000*, cited in UN Doc. A/55/513–S/2000/10/10, 23 October 2000.

6. "Exchange of letters constituting a provisional agreement concerning assistance to Palestine Refugees. Jerusalem, 14 June 1967".

4

Negotiating for results in the Lebanon

André Roberfroid

In Lebanon between 1987 and 1990, the United Nations Children's Fund (UNICEF) remained the main UN agency with an implementation capacity and as such was confronted with the challenge of helping children in an extraordinarily complex and dangerous situation. A civil war was devastating the country, killing thousands of people and wounding many more. Basic services such as health, education, water and electricity were regularly disrupted and, at best, operated poorly. There was no government to make agreements with, and no substantive UN support to elaborate an international aid strategy; in short, there was no authority to deal with and the myriad of actors on the ground were not just uncoordinated but fighting each other. The challenge was to protect all children and to give them some chance of healthy development. This was a daunting task to be accomplished with very limited means – a team of less than 100 Lebanese personnel, headed by a single UNICEF international staff member,[1] and an annual budget that never exceeded US$4 million. Clearly, success required many partners on the ground, including the warring factions and many local non-governmental organizations (NGOs). In practical terms, UNICEF had to convince all of them to contribute people, money and, above all, goodwill to facilitate its actions. Plans of action were designed on the basis of humanitarian needs and standards, which was a job that UNICEF had the expertise and experience to do. Actual implementation required diplomatic skills that UNICEF personnel had, for the most part, to acquire on the spot. In practice, this "humanitarian diplomacy" became the precondition for successful negotiations for action.

This chapter demonstrates that the success of negotiations in a conflict environment depends not only on "being neutral" but on convincing all the warring factions that what you are trying to achieve is theirs more than yours. In other words, the warlords must feel not that humanitarians are asking them the favour of being allowed to do their job, but that humanitarians are doing them the favour of helping them to achieve their objectives.

During this period, UNICEF supported the immunization of over 75 per cent of Lebanese children, secured a regular supply of essential drugs to 714 health units and implemented an Education for Peace programme that gave more than 50,000 children an opportunity to relate to each other in a peaceful and positive manner. Many partners had to be mobilized and the numerous warring factions had to agree on a plan of action and contribute people and resources. Negotiations were conducted, almost on a daily basis, over access, control, travel, the distribution of goods and the selection of beneficiaries. Many lessons were learned. Above all, UNICEF learned that credibility is the main element in a successful operation and that the operational objectives must be transparent. UNICEF also learned that communication must be used as a professional tool. And UNICEF learned that humanitarian diplomacy means acting in a dangerous environment and therefore entails risk.

Context

Humanitarian operations are determined by the recent history of the affected area. Their design and implementation are influenced by the decision-making environment. In a war situation, they are constrained by the intensity of the battles. They are conducted with other partners, in this case the United Nations and NGOs. The size and nature of the actions are based on an assessment of concrete needs, in this case an evaluation of the impact of the situation on children. And, lastly, the humanitarian operations must be consistent with the role of the implementing agency, in this case with the role of UNICEF in Lebanon.

Recent history

The Lebanese civil war lasted for 15 years, from 1975 to 1990. It was an extraordinarily complex conflict. It involved many actors, both internally and externally, had a large number of causes and resisted any attempt to explain it in a simple manner.[2] It can be summarized as having three main episodes:

1. A Lebano-Palestinian episode from 1975 to 1977, during which a very bloody and destructive conflict erupted between the Christian militias (supported by Israel) and the Palestinian movement Fatah (supported by a Lebanese progressivist or leftist alliance that was mainly Muslim). Most of the destruction in central Beirut, its division into eastern (Christian) and western (Muslim) areas and the displacement of several hundred thousands of Lebanese occurred during this period.

2. A Lebano-Israeli episode from 1982 to 1984, during which the Israeli army invaded more than half of the country, including Beirut. The violence of the military campaign generated further destruction and displacement; it also put an end to the Palestinian presence as a military force and started the final collapse of the Lebanese government as an independent actor.

3. A Lebano-Syrian phase from 1987 to 1990, which saw the progressive control of the country by the Syrian army and the virtual elimination of the Christian militias. At that time, General Aoun, leader of the Christian enclave, proclaimed himself president of the republic and declared all-out war on Syria. Intensive artillery shelling and tank battles took place in Beirut from March to September 1989. Early in 1990, a fierce and bloody battle between rival Christian forces weakened their fighting capacity and, eventually, secured the total victory of the Syrian army by November 1990. Since then, Lebanon has lived formally in peace.[3] The events discussed in this chapter occurred during this period.

The decision-making environment

For a humanitarian actor, one of the most difficult aspects of the situation in Lebanon was the multiplicity of partners. There was an official, internationally recognized government with virtually no control over the country and hardly any resources to operate a divided and mostly vanished administration. As a UN agency, UNICEF had to maintain a legal relationship with the government recognized by the international community, which at that time was the cabinet headed by Prime Minister Salim Hoss, supported and controlled by the Syrian army. However, a rival government under self-proclaimed president Michel Aoun, which had more effective control over the Christian enclave, was claiming legitimacy and considered any contact with the Hoss team to be illegal. To make matters worse, a puppet authority, established and supported by the Israeli Defense Forces, was claiming legitimate control over the "security zone" along the Israeli border.[4] In addition, two foreign armies were present and active in the country. Since 1976, Syria had maintained a 30,000-strong force which occupied all parts of Lebanon except the southern zone along the Israeli border, which was occupied by the Israeli Defense Forces, and the areas north of Beirut, which were controlled by the Christian militias.

The battles

The struggle between the two rival governments came to a head during March to October 1989. The Beirut area was subject to random shelling and the use of heavy artillery against the civilian population. During this period, more than 1,500 people were killed, over 5,000 were wounded and almost 2 million people were forced to live in permanent and unpreventable danger. Public infrastructures as well as private properties, conservatively estimated at US$2 billion, were destroyed. In search of security, 500,000 people fled the western and southern parts of Beirut to seek refuge in south Lebanon, and another 100,000 moved from east Beirut to the mountainous areas of north Lebanon.

In the mostly Shiite south Lebanon, two rival militias supposedly fighting Israel, Hezbollah and Amal, were essentially killing each other, creating permanent insecurity among a population already affected by the refugees escaping the battle of Beirut. This local war killed hundreds of people, generated thousands of internally displaced refugees and largely contributed to the growing sense of despair and hopelessness prevailing in this part of Lebanon.

In 1990, following a shaky cease-fire, the situation improved in the Syrian-controlled area, but extreme violence erupted within the Christian area. During March and April 1990, elements of the Lebanese army under General Aoun and the Lebanese Forces militia headed by Samir Geagea were embroiled in a bloody, ferocious, destructive and incomprehensible urban war. Tank battles in city centres, mines in the streets, and blanket and untargeted shelling killed and wounded a large but unknown number of people. A greater number of public and private infrastructures and houses were destroyed during that month in east Beirut than during the first 13 years of the war.

The situation was further complicated by the 600,000 Palestinian refugees settled in Lebanon, most of them since 1948. The majority lived in camps established in Tripoli, Beirut, Sidon and Tyre. Although the presence of such a large number of refugees was not the only cause of the civil war, it did significantly contribute to the beginning and the continuation of the war. From June 1985 to March 1988, a major battle known as "the war of the camps" pitted the Syrian army, supported by the Amal militia, against the Palestinian factions. The main camps in Beirut[5] were subjected to continuous heavy shelling for 30 months. Although the situation had since improved, the camps remained a major source of instability and sporadic violence. A very young population, with no prospects for the future, subjected to intense political pressure and totally dependent on aid agencies, is hardly a source of social integration and stability. The extraordinarily complex political environment among the Palestinian communities and the interference of almost every power in the world (state or non-state) further exacerbated the volatility of this situation. At times, up to 14 different factions were active, sometimes violently, among the Palestinian groups in Lebanon.

The UN response

The humanitarian response of the United Nations was coordinated by the United Nations Disaster Relief Organization (UNDRO), with a specific responsibility for the United Nations Relief and Works Agency for Palestine Refugees in the Near East (UNRWA) in support of the Palestinian refugees.[6] De facto, UNICEF remained the only UN agency with a nationwide operational capacity during this period.[7] UNRWA's operational presence was limited to the Palestinian camps, and the role of the other agencies was limited to an occasional non-operational presence and participation in needs assessment missions. For security purposes, regular contacts were maintained with the UN military, essentially the United Nations Interim Force in Lebanon (UNIFIL) and the United Nations Truce Supervision Organization (UNTSO).[8]

Bilateral agencies were absent, but embassies were present and politically active. World and regional powers were busy trying to interfere in the Lebanese chess game. Some were seriously attempting to assist the development of a peace process; others were essentially pursuing their own objectives or protecting their own interests. The game was complicated and largely unrelated to children's concerns, but embassies often had privileged access to local players. When UNICEF needed to negotiate with these local forces, embassies became effective partners.

The NGO response

Non-governmental organizations constitute another group of traditional allies and partners of UNICEF. The security situation had driven most of the international NGOs out of Lebanon, with the notable exception of the International Committee of the Red Cross (ICRC). National NGOs were therefore UNICEF's most important partners. Literally hundreds of them existed in every corner of the country. The vacuum created by the collapse of governmental social services had been filled by local organizations of varying nature, capacity and motivation. Many were faith-based charities, small in size and serving their immediate community. Some were instruments of political parties or factions, assisting their affiliates or utilized to recruit new supporters. A few were created and operated by active militias offering social protection and services to their members. A significant number were established by real criminals attempting to cash in on the international assistance pouring into Lebanon because of the high visibility of the conflict and its impact on world opinion. This was clearly a minefield, but one that UNICEF had to cross in order to reach the people it wanted to assist. In many parts of the country, NGOs were the only organizations with implementation capacity and they had to be considered as privileged partners. Their close links with the de facto authorities on the ground also made them indispensable allies when negotiating.

The impact on children

The extraordinary resilience of the Lebanese population was almost destroyed by 12 years of civil war. The failure to appoint a unified government and the permanent division of the country brought the population to a state of despair. The Lebanese economy survived the first years of the war, but by 1987 it was on the verge of collapse. The national currency was in free fall, generating a deep depression in a population most of whose livelihoods came from trade.

The impact on children was truly dramatic. Access to food, health and education became similar to that of a developing country. Public services ceased to operate and private services were out of reach because of a lack of resources. For the first time since the beginning of the war, children were in immediate danger. Signs of malnutrition were visible in the worst-affected areas. NGOs reported a significant increase in the frequency and severity of childhood diseases. The worst and potentially most damaging impact on children resulted from the extended closure of schools. Educational facilities accommodating over 60 per cent of the school population were closed from March to October 1989, and some were closed during the first quarter of 1990. The school was the only safe and reassuring environment in which children could rebuild their confidence in the adult world. Locked in apartments or shelters away from their friends, forbidden to play, the children's perception of the world was dominated by fear, stress and despair.

The absence of contacts with children of other communities and the effect of adult propaganda generated hate, intolerance and the belief that violence is the natural and only way to resolve differences. With a large number of school buildings damaged by shelling or lack of maintenance and with many teachers displaced or out of the country, an entire sector, which in the past represented the best asset of Lebanon, was in jeopardy. The future of the new generation was at stake.

The children of Lebanon were living in a world where violence was the only solution to any difficulty and where the "other" was always an enemy.

The role of UNICEF

UNICEF had been active in Lebanon since 1953 and throughout the civil war. All the warring factions and the public at large acknowledged that UNICEF remained during the worst episodes of the war and continued to help children everywhere regardless of the political confusion and the lack of security. They also recognized that UNICEF's assistance was distributed wherever possible in a way that was strictly based on accessibility and the demonstrated operational capacity of the partners. Reliability and pragmatism were the two main factors of UNICEF's reputation. From 1980 to 1990, UNICEF became well known in Lebanon for its support to repair and rehabilitate the water supply network, particularly in the areas affected by the conflict. Water reservoirs were rebuilt, pumps and pipelines were repaired or replaced, wells were cleaned or dug, and, where the networks could not be repaired, trucks distributed water. During active military hostilities, such a service was highly appreciated by the people.

As a humanitarian actor, it was important for UNICEF to avoid involvement with political intricacies. It was essential to remain not only neutral but openly outside the game. In all public statements, it was made clear that UNICEF had no opinion on the issues that had led to the civil war. For the humanitarian actors there were no good guys or bad guys. On the contrary, UNICEF's public position was that all parties and actors in this war were wrong for not being able to solve differences in a peaceful manner. UNICEF publicly recognized that every human being living in Lebanon had the right to feel unfairly treated in this environment of violence. In other words, from the humanitarian and, particularly, from the children's point of view, the situation was unacceptable, and nobody holding authority or power on the ground could claim to be innocent.

UNICEF was speaking on behalf of the only truly innocent victims of this disaster, the children of Lebanon. For all practical purposes, from the children's point of view, all parties and factions involved in the civil war were guilty as charged. This was UNICEF's position all along. UNICEF never tried to gain anybody's support, but rather challenged potential partners to deserve its help and assistance. At times this was a tough attitude to maintain, but it was essential to keep freedom of negotiation.

Operational issues

The impact of the conflict on the children of Lebanon was truly devastating. It dictated UNICEF's tasks and challenges. Given the planning difficulties and operational constraints, UNICEF set itself the following objectives:

- to close the vaccination gap and restore a regular immunization service;
- to secure a regular supply of essential drugs in all parts of the country;
- to offer educational and recreational opportunities to all children regardless of circumstances;
- to create encounters between children of various communities, allowing them to get to know each other and to discover tolerance and non-violence;
- to continue emergency repair and maintenance of water supply networks damaged by war activities.

The successful implementation of this agenda required securing the collaboration of a number of partners. This could be achieved only through formal and informal agreements, which had to be negotiated. UNICEF's experience in Lebanon shows that the main issues requiring negotiation and agreement with the warring parties fell into three categories: (i) the safety of personnel and the protection of material assets, (ii) the logistics for distribution and supervision, and (iii) the issue of objective and perceived fairness in the selection of beneficiaries.

Safety and security

Operating in a context of war or civil disorder means accepting a certain degree of risk, including to the life and integrity of humanitarian personnel. The only way to eliminate the risk completely would be to cancel operations. It is always extremely difficult to decide between the need to fulfil the mandate of the organization and the duty to protect its staff.

The challenge was to minimize the risk, while obtaining results that could justify the risks taken. A number of active and passive measures were taken to cope with the danger. They will be reviewed below. However, the most efficient "risk reduction" approach was the perceived image of UNICEF and of its actions. It was essential that UNICEF's activities appeared to all factions as "non-threatening". In other words, it had to be clearly understood that harming UNICEF or its personnel would bring no benefit to the perpetrators. On the contrary, the message conveyed to all partners made clear that the security of UNICEF's staff was not a subject for discussion and even less for negotiation. UNICEF was not prepared to buy its safety, but it was offering assistance to whoever agreed to respect the integrity of its personnel and assets.

As mentioned earlier, a large number of sometimes uncontrolled militias were patrolling most parts of the country. All were affiliated to ethnic, religious or political groups. Each was claiming to be the legitimate representative of its group. It was therefore extremely difficult for UNICEF's Lebanese staff to remain neutral while each of them was ethnically or religiously identified. Many were subject to various pressures to support their group or threatened if they did not. They had to make clear that they were negotiating and acting in the name of UNICEF and under the strict control of the head of mission. On two occasions during the period, two Palestinian staff members took the risk of getting personally involved with some militias. Both were assassinated. This was a terrible reminder that the danger was real. Working only for children and for all children was not just UNICEF's mandate but also the best protection for its staff.

Equipment and supplies were another source of danger. In 1989, UNICEF was operating over 60 cars; warehousing and distributing essential drugs worth over US$2 million; procuring, storing and operating generators, spare parts and pipes for water supply networks worth more than US$6 million; and importing and distributing school equipment and supplies worth nearly US$1 million. These were scarce and valuable assets, and very attractive in a lawless country. Again, the beneficiaries themselves provided the best protection. For example, UNICEF, at the time, was the only regular supplier of essential drugs, and it was made clear that any attempt to steal drugs would put an end to the programme and deprive everybody in the future. The quality of the service rendered was, in fact, the best possible protection for the staff as well as for the properties. The challenge in a conflict situation is to offer services that are so valuable that their interruption would be unacceptable to all parties.

Logistics for distribution and supervision

Moving people and goods around the country was a permanent nightmare. The Beirut international airport and seaport were closed to traffic. Shipping supplies required the use of illegal seaports, one in the south controlled by the Shiite Amal militia and one in the north operated by the Christian Lebanese Forces militia. Most shipments contained valuable drugs, school supplies and technical equipment for water supplies. Very tough negotiations were conducted to enable every shipment to be delivered free of the so-called "tax" that went directly to the militias. Transportation of goods from the ports to stores and to end-users required the crossing of numerous checkpoints, and every passage had to be negotiated. Air shipments, particularly necessary for vaccines, were received through the Damascus airport, generating nightmarish arguments with the Syrian customs bureaucracy. Storage space was often obtained in religious buildings, churches or mosques. Experience proved that the warring parties usually respected such facilities. However, negotiations with the religious authorities were not always simple and often required "give and take".

Total transparency was another prerequisite for effective delivery. UNICEF always let everybody know where it was, where it was going, with what and what for. The slightest suspicion that UNICEF could have anything to hide would have destroyed the confidence that was its best guarantee of safety.

Fairness and beneficiaries

In a volatile environment where factions are fighting for support, recognition and territories, the worst scenario for a humanitarian agency is to find itself entangled in endless discussions about the fairness of the distribution of assistance. It is clearly impossible to find a formula that can be accepted by all. Any attempt to balance assistance among the various communities, religious groups or political factions will end with many accusations of favouritism.

In Lebanon, where the last demographic survey took place in 1947, it was unreasonable to base any assistance on the estimated number of people in need. It was also to be expected that the leaders of religious or ethnic groups or political parties would grossly inflate the numbers. Similarly, in the hope of receiving more funds from the various aid agencies, NGOs would often claim that they were serving many more people than they actually did. UNICEF participated in a number of needs assessment missions with UN and bilateral agencies. The exercise was at best futile, at worst misleading. UNICEF's findings were mostly constructed from subjective guesses based on inflated statements made by biased people.

Yet UNICEF's mission remained to reach all children, all over the country. For this it needed access across front-lines and borders, and it needed the cooperation of all factions. The implementation of the vaccination campaign showed UNICEF a way forward. All children needed vaccines and everybody's participation was required. No child needed more vaccine than another. There was no benefit to a faction to receive more vaccine than was required for the number of children they could actually vaccinate. However, the more they mobilized themselves to make the campaign a success, the more their health facilities would be supported. The more effective they were in delivering services to their own people, the more they would be assisted. The issue of fairness was no longer based on endless and futile discussions about the needs of each group or faction but related to their willingness and capability to deliver services. The negotiation was not about what and how much they would receive any more, but about what and how much they were prepared to do with UNICEF's support.

Obstacles and opportunities

The main obstacle was of a structural nature. Because of UNICEF's very limited capacity actually to deliver assistance, it had to rely on local partners. UNICEF's staff never exceeded 85 in total and its annual budget culminated at less than US$4 million. Without the leverage of other partners' resources, the impact would have been limited to small numbers of children, and the results at national level in terms of child health and education would never have been achieved. The main challenge was therefore to find effective partners in the chaotic environment of a failed state.

Legally, the most important partner for UNICEF is the government. It is with the government that UNICEF must establish the legal relationship that is necessary to obtain formal approval from UNICEF's Executive Board for fund-raising and programme expenditures. This relationship remained largely virtual in Lebanon and was never operational. The administrative infrastructure had practically collapsed and was no longer a potentially effective partner.

The UN development and humanitarian agencies are the natural partners for UNICEF. In retrospect, it can be said that, during the active period of the Lebanese crisis, the UN system adopted a "wait and see" attitude until 1990. A small but well-informed presence allowed the United Nations Development Programme (UNDP), in particular, to be ready to assist the reconstruction phase immediately after the cease-fire.

As we have already seen, security was another major obstacle. The risks were of various natures. Random shelling over urban areas was the most frequent source of danger and the most unpredictable. Appropriate shelters with basic living equipment, food and water were made available in office basements. Staff were assisted to equip their houses wherever possible. Windows were protected with sandbags, and helmets and bullet-proof jackets were distributed and used. This mostly passive protection was complemented by a more active approach based on careful observation of the pattern of shelling and permanent monitoring of local radio. Such information allowed the risks to be minimized when it was necessary to go onto the streets. Nothing, however, could protect the staff against a direct hit. The fact that, with the exception of one minor wound, UNICEF suffered no casualties was more owing to luck than the result of planned protective measures.

Hostage-taking was another feature of the Beirut scene. This particular risk mostly, although not exclusively, concerned expatriate personnel. The fact that UNICEF's head of mission was the only international staff member reduced that danger. Passive protection required moving around with a minimum of two cars, accompanied by bodyguards.

Most of the warehousing capacity of the administration was destroyed by shelling or looted by militias. Safe storage space had to be secured with ad hoc partners. Militias as well as the Syrian or Israeli armies would have been happy to help, but did not offer the required neutrality. The UN military was able to assist, but on a limited scale and only in the southern area patrolled by UNIFIL. One answer to this problem was to use a large number of small stores scattered throughout the regions, therefore avoiding the dangerous attraction created by large stocks of goods.

Transportation inside the country became a major challenge. Lebanon is a small country with a good road network, but front-lines or internal borders cut across many of them. Often what would have been a 50 km trip became a 200 km journey taking 7 hours. The frequency and length of staff movements were reduced by permanently locating a staff member in each region and by operating a "private" radio communication network. Every UNICEF car was equipped with a radio and every staff member with a walkie-talkie. The head office in Beirut was in permanent contact with its entire staff all over the country. This communication network provided not only a higher level of security but also, more importantly, a permanent flow of information on the real situation on the ground.

The difficulty of finding an acceptable formula in respect of a "fair" distribution of assistance remained a challenge. The problems of finding objective ways to assess each partner's capacity, to document actual delivery and to control the use of funds and equipment were daunting. How could UNICEF collaborate and assist without this being perceived as endorsement? How could UNICEF supply the Hezbollah with drugs and medicines and not be seen by the Israeli-backed Christian militia forces in south Lebanon as supporting their enemy? How could UNICEF help the children in the Christian enclave to go to school and not be accused by the Syrian army of taking sides in the conflict?

UNICEF found that the capacity and credibility of the field staff to verify and assess the performance of health and social services was the key to its effectiveness. The traditional needs assessment approach placed the burden of the proof on the humanitarian agencies. UNICEF's new approach reversed the burden of proof. Because nobody could deny the need to vaccinate children, UNICEF challenged its partners to do it, with its support being subject to their proving their capacity to deliver.

Negotiations

UNICEF's observations of rapid deterioration in children's living conditions and lives meant that it could no longer just improve the life of children by repairing a few pipes and pumps. UNICEF's view was that it should aim to make a lasting difference in terms of survival and development.

UNICEF designed a three-phase strategy that entailed (i) immunizing all children, (ii) revitalizing the health services, and (iii) offering educational opportunities in all circumstances. Each of these phases was technically feasible given appropriate training and the supply of necessary inputs. However, successful implementation required the participation of all the available technical manpower in the country, the cooperation of all de facto authorities and the collaboration of all NGOs in the field. This became the object of the negotiation.

Conceptually, the negotiations followed three steps. First, UNICEF had to establish publicly that it was nobody's friend, but exclusively the supporter of the children. Secondly, UNICEF had to demonstrate that it understood the needs and problems of the children and had the expertise and capacity to improve the situation. Thirdly, UNICEF had to offer all partners with field capacity an opportunity to participate, provided they accepted UNICEF's conditions.

UNICEF found that there is no shortcut to gain people's confidence and that credibility can be gained only by practice and over time. UNICEF progressively gained the confidence of the population through its permanent and visible presence, throughout difficult years, in every part of the country. UNICEF was thus also seen as a reliable partner for the de facto authorities on the ground. In addition, the main sources of funding (the US Agency for International Development and the European Community), which were desperately searching for implementation capacity, supported UNICEF because it had demonstrated neutrality and effectiveness over the years.

The immunization campaign that took place between September and November 1987 was the first phase of the UNICEF agenda for children. It involved large numbers of people out in the open, moving to and from the vaccination stations. It required the repair and maintenance of a cold chain covering the whole country, together with a reliable electricity supply. The event was reported as "three days of tranquillity" negotiated in Lebanon under the auspices of UNICEF.[9]

"The days of tranquillity"

The first step was strictly an information phase. In April 1987, about six months before the campaign, UNICEF contacted the official government authorities, the president, the prime minister and the minister of health to inform them of UNICEF's intentions. Although the authority of the government officials was largely virtual, they did represent the legitimacy of the state. They had no objection to the plan and were particularly pleased to know that UNICEF would officially present the campaign as being under their umbrella. Significantly, UNICEF did not ask anything from them, nor did it even mention the words tranquillity, truce or cease-fire.

The next step was to inform the de facto authorities and forces on the ground. The difficulty was to find and meet them all – the militias, the political parties and the religious leaders. If any of them had been missed or forgotten, this could have created a dangerous obstacle. As expected, none expressed any objection. Again, these meetings were strictly for information: nothing was asked, nothing was negotiated, but the meetings were all reported to the press and in various media. This public record was to prove crucial in the last part of the negotiation. The two foreign armies – Syrian and Israeli – that controlled some parts of Lebanon were kept informed by UNICEF HQ through their nation's UN mission in New York. They were simply asked to avoid any major operation on the planned dates. They agreed not to initiate action on these days, but stated that they would remain free to react if attacked.

In the meantime, technical and logistic preparation carried on in the field. A field officer was assigned in each of the 24 districts of the country, with the task of assessing the capacity of the existing public and private health infrastructures and carrying out a quick survey of the immunization coverage. In doing so, the field officers established contact with the various NGOs operating in each district. Crucial negotiations took place to obtain the full collaboration and participation of the NGOs, in exchange for assistance to revitalize their health capacities. These discussions were discreet and practical; they were not reported in the media and were carried out very much on a "give and take" basis. The bottom line was very simple: "We plan to carry out a vaccination campaign in your area. We have assessed your organization as having the capacity to participate. We are prepared to assist you to upgrade your structure if you choose to participate. If you choose not to, fine and good, you stay out." There were no bargains and no arguments. Most NGOs, but not all, decided to participate.

Agreements were signed by which the NGOs would receive cold chain equipment, vaccines and drug supplies, and appropriate training. In exchange, they would contribute to the public information and mobilization drive preceding the campaign, deliver the vaccination free of charge and report the numbers to UNICEF. This "field side" of the negotiation remained unseen from the media and the public, but was essential for the success of the operation. Most NGOs were attached to one faction or another and became UNICEF's best allies in convincing the warring groups to remain quiet during the three-day period. Such an approach could be called a "bottom-up negotiation" in which the discussion took place with the people at the grassroots level, and they in turn convinced their respective leaders to follow through.

It was vital to keep the pressure on the militia chiefs to avoid any risk of a major clash during the operation. During the week before the three-day campaign (early September 1987), UNICEF visited the leaders of the main militias with the following message: "We confirm the operation for next week. We expect your cooperation in refraining from violence during these three days. The national and international media will be informed of our plans and of the fact that you are aware of it and have expressed your willingness to cooperate."

The key factor was that UNICEF did not ask for any formal commitment, which would have been a costly bargain. In a way, UNICEF was calling their bluff in challenging them. By not asking for any agreement, UNICEF was making them face their responsibilities. Any violent incident that took place during these three days would be seen locally and internationally as a deliberate attempt by militias in Lebanon to sabotage an action that could only benefit children. It was reasonable to believe that local leaders would see more advantage in refraining from active violence than taking the risk of being accused of harming children. This is a noticeable difference from a diplomatic negotiation. A humanitarian action may achieve an anticipated result by acting directly on the ground without the need to negotiate a formal agreement.

At the same time, UNICEF contacted local radio stations and newspapers, as well as the BBC and Radio France International, to announce the event. The BBC picked it up immediately and made it a breaking-news event. A massive nationwide communication campaign literally flooded the country with radio and TV ads and thousands of posters. Most religious leaders agreed to contribute by calling on their followers to vaccinate their children. The public "noise" added to the pressure on the factions, making it almost impossible for them not to participate. And it did work: the three "days of tranquillity" were actually respected (21–23 September 1987). Between 75 and 80 per cent of the Lebanese children were immunized against the main childhood diseases. Those working in and around the health services realized that positive action was possible even in the misery of war. For the first time since the beginning of the civil war, Lebanon was in the news positively.

The successful outcome resulted from a collective effort, in which it was impossible to single out one faction more than another. For many, particularly young people, involvement in the operation seemed to generate a dramatic change of perspective. The worst was no longer the only future for Lebanon and the best was no longer impossible. UNICEF had demonstrated that a humanitarian agency could dare armed groups to contribute to a common humanitarian goal. The negotiation that took place did not involve trying to reach consensus among parties by bargaining, but was a challenge to all to do the right thing. The success of this campaign was a first illustration for UNICEF of the fact that involving antagonistic parties in the pursuit of a superordinate goal (in this case a humanitarian one) can unite them to the extent that they can stop fighting, if only for a few days.

UNICEF's view was that the visible momentum created by the immunization campaign should be maintained. Health workers attached to public and private sectors, to political parties or militias, or to NGOs were upbeat and asking for more. The field officers in the districts were telling UNICEF that the partners on the ground were ready to participate in new activities. In early 1988, UNICEF confronted its partners with a new challenge: to revitalize the health services for the whole population by securing regular and free access to 44 essential drugs.

Bringing essential drugs to the population

Prior to the war, a district-based network of health clinics had served the needs of the population, but many of these had fallen under the control of the factions or had been destroyed. Capitalizing on the success of the immunization campaign and its renewed ability to deliver countrywide assistance, UNICEF was able to supply these essential drugs to 725 clinics in every district of the country and control their usage. The number of beneficiaries came close to 100,000 families, a significant number in a country of fewer than 2 million people. The technicalities of this project were somewhat complex and the World Health Organization supported UNICEF in this endeavour.

In this project, UNICEF had to negotiate locally for safe storage and transportation as well as controlled distribution. In Lebanon in 1989, drugs were as rare as gold and therefore a very attractive commodity. Safe storage was a serious matter. Protection by force would have been costly and inefficient. Again, UNICEF opted for a participatory approach. It established a central store in the basement of a mosque in West Beirut. Again, publicity was the only protection. All factions were informed and knew that, if anything happened, the programme would immediately stop and everybody would lose. Transportation to the districts was organized in the same manner, with total transparency: everybody was informed about when and where the trucks would pass. Throughout the period until the end of the war no serious incident occurred. Some trucks were searched but not a single box of drugs disappeared. This does not mean that the militias suddenly became concerned with humanitarian issues. They needed the drugs for themselves and for the people under their control, and there was no other way to secure a regular supply. People knew that this service was available; therefore no one dared to be accused of stopping it.[10]

As with the immunization campaign, the success of the drugs project contributed to securing the perception of UNICEF as a reliable partner.[11] However, although the service to the population was effective and appreciated, it did not profoundly change the situation or bring hope for a better future. It did not contribute to a process that could lead to an end to the hostilities. Two vital questions were permanently in the minds of UNICEF personnel in Lebanon: what could be done to halt the complete isolation in which children were forced to live; and what could be done to help prevent children from repeating what their parents had done, which had already resulted in 15 years of war.

Education for peace

Isolation in shelters, road blocks and checkpoints were the physical manifestations of more profound barriers between people. Children's perceptions of others were also limited by ignorance and biased by propaganda, by fear and by their own parents' paranoia. How could these barriers be dismantled? Education was the obvious medium through which to achieve a change of attitude, but schools were closed most of the time. UNICEF's view was that a new, creative educational opportunity was necessary. UNICEF wanted to give children a chance to meet one another, to learn together and to practise new attitudes and behaviours, with the aim of convincing them that their apparent differences were not a handicap but a privilege. That was the genesis of the Education for Peace project. The goal was to mobilize the children and youth of Lebanon as agents of change for building peace, while simultaneously giving young people a chance to realize their potential. The idea that children should meet with one another led to the idea of organizing summer camps.

In February 1989, UNICEF contacted about 50 established NGOs – most with a religious affiliation but pre-dating the war – with a proposal to organize summer camps where children from different religions and regions would mix. UNICEF would provide the funding, the logistics and the training for camp leaders if the NGOs were willing to mobilize participants. UNICEF would also guarantee the safe passage of children across the checkpoints. A formal agreement was signed by which each NGO accepted and committed itself to three objectives and criteria. The first was that the summer camps should bring together children and youth from different regions, religions and social strata. The second was that the camps would give youth and children a better opportunity to get to know one another and their country. The third was that youth and children would "live together" in the summer camps in a way that allowed the sharing of human, social and relational values through creative and recreational activities. From the outset, UNICEF was explicit about the peacebuilding agenda. Whereas the immediate purpose of the scheme was to give children an opportunity to learn and play together, away from the shelling, the long-term goal was to change perceptions.

The NGO response was overwhelmingly positive, but the political factions in Lebanese society were less enthusiastic. The project was of less immediate benefit for them and was a potential political risk. After all, most factions were building popular support by exacerbating their differences, and this project was emphasizing the commonalities.

Moreover, the logistics and security concerns involved in getting children together were formidable. UNICEF's target group was primarily the children living in the conflict areas, essentially Greater Beirut, south Lebanon and the Palestinian camps. For obvious reasons, the summer camps had to be organized in safe areas, away from random shelling and military operations. The central part of the Bekaa valley was the best choice at the time. It was occupied by the Syrian army and at the same time under its protection. Transporting children from Christian east Beirut to the Bekaa valley involved crossing several checkpoints in what their parents considered "enemy territory". Bringing children from south Lebanon would entail their leaving the Israeli security zone and then returning; in other words, the tightest border in the region would have to be crossed twice. UNICEF could not possibly "negotiate" safe passage, because there was simply nothing to bargain with.

As with the immunization campaign and the project to supply safe drugs, UNICEF met with all the leaders "for information only". It did, however, have a few trump cards. First, it had the support of 240 local NGOs, most of them attached or linked to the factions in one way or another. Second, it enjoyed extraordinary confidence among the parents, who gave UNICEF their children because they were convinced that it could get them through the front-lines safely. And third, as usual, it had publicity. All the media, within Lebanon and outside, knew that, on a given day, thousands of children would cross the country through front-lines. They also knew that the militias had been informed. Who would stop children from travelling safely to spend a safe time together away from the combat zones? Who would challenge the UNICEF flag, whose protection was trusted by so many parents? It was a dangerous undertaking, and clearly a judgement call. However, UNICEF believed that no faction would dare to be the bad guy. It was certainly risky, but it worked.

In 1989, as the war continued throughout most of the country, 29,000 Lebanese and Palestinian children attended 112 peace camps. In September, a day-long "Peace Festival" in the western Bekaa brought together 700 leaders and 9,000 children. In 1990, 40,000 children attended a total of 215 camps. By September 1991, the programme had reached 100,000 children and had mobilized 240 NGOs representing the entire spectrum of religious, ethnic and regional groups.[12] For many children, this was the first time they had ever met a Christian or a Muslim or a Druze. Suddenly, they were being brought together to live, work, play and eat side by side. It usually took a few days for them to feel comfortable with "the other", but then there was an extraordinary explosion of the will to live together, as if the children had been thirsty for it.

To keep in touch with the children after the camps and to give them a means to continue thinking and reflecting together, a children's magazine called SAWA, the Arabic word for "together", was published and distributed free – 70,000 copies every other month until the end of 1990. The magazine became the main vehicle, in the wake of the camps and while the schools were still closed, for promoting an explicit message of peace. It included stories illustrating children's rights, solidarity, unity and non-violence. An average of 2,500 letters were received from children after each issue of the magazine.[13]

It is impossible to demonstrate whether this exposure to communal life had a lasting impact on the children and contributed to an effective peace process. It certainly had a strong and lasting impact on the 5,000 young men and women who served as camp leaders in 1989, 1990 and 1991. Many had borne the brunt of the war, many had served as militiamen, and some had been directly involved in bloody episodes. They had experienced the excitement as well as the depression created by violence.[14] They were clearly enthusiastic and obviously happy to be involved in such a positive activity. The rule seemed to be that the more extremist they had been during the war, the more involved they became in the programme.

The leaders proved to be the true backbone of the project and UNICEF saw them as agents of change for peace. Through the training programmes, they were provided with the tools and ideas needed for positive interaction with the children. As the programme matured, the scope of activities was broadened to help the leaders reach out into their own communities. In UNICEF's view, their efforts helped public opinion throughout the country to accept the inevitable compromises that came with the peace agreement reached at the end of 1990.

Wider implications

The correlation between diplomatic negotiation and humanitarian action is indirect, but it exists and it plays a role. Why is it that solutions proposed by diplomats are rejected for years and then suddenly become palatable? The UNICEF experience in Lebanon during the last few years of the civil war indicates that conflict resolution depends on changing not only the "balance of power" but also people's support for and tolerance of the war and violence. Diplomats are able to influence the balance of power – that is their main negotiating goal. However, diplomats have very little influence on public opinion. The leaders of factions tend to believe that the balance of power favours them as long as the people under their control continue to think that fighting is the only way to protect their vital interests.

Humanitarian actions demonstrate that there is another way. Practical action, linked to people's daily life, may demonstrate that the vital interests of all the warring groups have a lot in common, and that acting together can be more effective than fighting each other. The lessons learned in Lebanon indicate that a successful humanitarian attempt to influence public opinion should meet several criteria.

Credibility

Legal and de facto authorities, and the people at large, must feel confident that the humanitarian agency has a sound understanding of intricate local politics, societies and cultures. In a war, people are naturally suspicious and wary of propaganda. Statements need to be supported by a record of previous achievements. In other words, an agency that starts operating right at the beginning of a conflict will find it difficult to achieve credibility. A previous and long-established presence in the country is an essential factor. Specialized agencies that are experienced in emergency situations can be effective in strictly relief activities. However, they cannot act as agents of change with an impact on the causes of the situation. Another element of an agency's credibility is the employment of local personnel. The public perceive local staff as understanding their situation. They speak the language and live the problems within their own families. At the same time, local personnel must have a good knowledge of the agency's values, policies and practices.

In short, credibility requires a long-term presence in the country, preceding the crisis, a significant proportion of local staff, in positions of responsibility, and a documented record of successful achievement. In an analogous manner to a diplomat who is taken seriously as the representative of a powerful country that has the capacity to intervene, a humanitarian negotiator is effective only as the representative of an organization that has already demonstrated that it can have a durable and positive impact.

Setting objectives

For an agency to have an effective impact there must be some support for the agency's projects among the people and their leaders. At the minimum, support means sharing the main objectives, which must in turn be public, simple, realistic and technically feasible. Funding sources must be transparent. If belligerent factions are to work towards a common objective, it is essential that the process of formulating this objective is open and transparent. The possibility of a hidden agenda, however remote, kills confidence. Unrealistic targets or wishful thinking also feed suspicion.

Building alliances

The best allies are to be found on the ground. Local organizations that deal with people's daily lives are most likely to share humanitarian objectives. They must be considered and treated not as "beneficiaries" but as partners because, in the field, they are the primary actors. International humanitarian agencies can contribute to the formulation of a common objective and to the mobilization of financial and material resources, but action remains the privilege of the local groups. Public credit for success must also go to those who work for common goals. Results are achieved by convincing people on the ground to share objectives, assisting them with implementation and building the self-confidence that they themselves can achieve success in meeting objectives.

Communication

Exposing the parties to the conflict to the judgement of the public is the best way to exert positive pressure. Conversely, the threat of exposure in the national and international media can help to prevent potentially negative influences on meeting humanitarian objectives. Agencies need to publicize what activities are planned, when, where and how. Because political parties are very sensitive about their image and reputation, media attention can be used to reinforce the positive if warring parties are seen to cooperate in humanitarian action. Conversely, a real threat is provided by the potential of adverse publicity should factions obstruct or prevent such activities. Communication is the true negotiating instrument of humanitarian agencies.

Daring

Risk is inherent in war and conflict. If security concerns outweigh the will to intervene, the humanitarian actor will necessarily cease to be a partner in conflict resolution. The only alternative left to the diplomats will become military intervention.

Looking back at UNICEF's experience in Lebanon, it appears that:
- UNICEF had the credibility of many years of activity and a large national personnel;
- simple and measurable objectives were publicly announced and appropriately funded;
- local grassroots organizations were mobilized around these objectives;
- national and international media were fully cooperative.

None of this would have been sufficient, however, if UNICEF had had to wait for guaranteed security for its staff before initiating action. Humanitarian agents are peace builders, and by their nature operate in dangerous environments. Facing danger in order to build peace is not the sole prerogative of the military.

Conclusion

Negotiations may mean something very different to the diplomat compared with the humanitarian. The purpose of diplomatic negotiations is to reach an agreement among parties who differ on a given issue. In the context of active hostilities, the agreement might be a cease-fire, buying time for more negotiation, or a settlement ending the conflict. Diplomacy is about trying to change the positions of the parties in order to bring them closer to each other. Negotiations are successful when each side is convinced that it is giving up less than the other. The diplomatic negotiator will guide each party to look at its future with due consideration to the existing balance of power. Identity, power, force and wealth will be elements of the negotiation.

Humanitarian negotiations, in contrast, are about the immediate survival and well-being of people. The purpose is not an agreement between parties but an acceptance by all sides that humanitarian action may take place in the areas or among the people under their control or jurisdiction. Any agreement reached is not between the parties but between the humanitarian agency and each party. The arguments used in the negotiations deal with human rights, humanitarian needs and the survival of individuals. Diplomatic negotiations are often secret, whereas humanitarian negotiations gain by being public. The public image and indeed the reputation of each party is at stake and must be used by the humanitarian agency to apply pressure when needed. Diplomats avoid the media and journalists, whereas humanitarian negotiators make use of them.

Beyond the direct impact of assisting people in need, UNICEF in Lebanon had an ambition to play a modest role in the process leading to a resolution of the conflict. At the same time, it was confronted with the recurrent and serious question: was it helping the belligerents to continue the war by making the consequences tolerable to the population? In other words, was UNICEF a partner in crime by alleviating the suffering of the non-combatant population? Most humanitarian operations have to confront this very difficult question, usually without a satisfactory answer. Critics were sometimes harsh, claiming that, by assisting clinics and schools run by Hezbollah or the Lebanese Forces, UNICEF was in fact helping terrorists. UNICEF was also often criticized for giving more assistance to NGOs than to government agencies, and therefore undermining the long-term recovery of the Lebanese administration. UNICEF was accused of being too ready to accept the necessity of dealing with the bad guys. In addition, maintaining a presence in every part of the country was a very costly undertaking. Many observers considered this cost exorbitant.

Some of these criticisms were probably justified. However, it was UNICEF's judgement that achieving results required unconventional ways and means. UNICEF was also painfully aware that its role, although probably useful, was primarily palliative at a time when there was a crying need for ideas that could contribute to a longer-term solution.

The results were not insignificant and, I believe, were worth the risk and the criticism. The immunization campaign proved to the public and the leaders that positive action for the people was still possible, across the lines and the parties. The essential drugs project proved that such positive action was durable. The Education for Peace programme proved that the hate, fear and intolerance generated by war and violence could be overcome.

Intensive diplomatic negotiations led by Arab League representative Lakhdar Brahimi eventually succeeded in bringing an end to the civil war. Although UNICEF's humanitarian projects had no formal relationship to the conclusion of the conflict, they did play a role in buying time for the diplomats, preparing public opinion for peace and progressively softening the positions of the warring parties.

Notes

1. I was the UNICEF Representative in Beirut from 1988 to 1990.
2. For a comprehensive analysis of the Lebanese conflict, see Georges Corm, *Liban: Les guerres de l'Europe et de l'Orient. 1840–1992*, Paris: Ed. Gallimard, 1992.
3. For historical reference, see David Gilmour, *Lebanon: The Fractured Country*, London: Sphere Books, 1987; Robert Fisk, *Pity the Nation: Lebanon at War*, London: Andre Deutsch, 1990; Kamal Salibi, *The Modern History of Lebanon*, London: Delmar New York Caravan Books, 1977.
4. After the first invasion of Lebanon in 1978, the Israeli army maintained a military occupation of a so-called security zone between the Israeli border and the Litani river. This occupation lasted until 2001.
5. Sabra, Shatila and Burj el-Barajneh.
6. UNDRO was replaced in 1992 by the Office for the Coordination of Humanitarian Affairs (OCHA).
7. During the period reported here, the UNICEF team in Lebanon consisted of 1 international staff member and 85–90 national staff. About 25–30 officers were permanently stationed in the various provinces and the rest were in Beirut.
8. UNIFIL was created in 1978 following the first Israeli invasion of Lebanon. UNTSO was set up in 1948 as the first peacekeeping operation established by the United Nations to monitor the cease-fire following the first Arab–Israeli war.
9. *UNICEF Beirut Annual Report*, New York: UNICEF, 1987.
10. *UNICEF Beirut Annual Report*, New York: UNICEF, 1988 and 1990.
11. UNICEF Executive Board, E/ICEF/1988/P/L.29.
12. *UNICEF Beirut Annual Report*, New York: UNICEF, 1989 and 1990.
13. Greg Hansen, *SAWA/Education for Peace: Uniting Lebanon's Children and Youth during War*, Cambridge, MA: The Collaborative for Development Action, June 1995.
14. For a provocative analysis of the impact of violence on youth, see Patrick Meney, *Même les tueurs ont une mère*, Paris: Ed. de la Table Ronde, 1986.

5

Negotiating the legitimacy of humanitarian action in Iraq

Claudia Rodriguez

This chapter analyses the extent to which humanitarian diplomacy was useful in resolving the operational constraints faced by non-governmental organizations (NGOs) in Iraq as a result of limited humanitarian space. Two cases are analysed as examples of a macro and a micro level of humanitarian diplomacy: negotiating the legitimacy of humanitarian action vis-à-vis the occupying forces and the Iraqi authorities; negotiating access to cities under siege by Coalition forces and non-state actors. The chapter reflects on the experience of the NGO Coordination Committee in Iraq (NCCI) from its inception in April 2003 to June 2004.

Following an introduction to the context of the Iraq crisis (March 2003–December 2004), I outline the main operational obstacles faced by NGOs on the ground. On the basis of the two case studies, I reflect on the different approaches taken in negotiating day-to-day, symptomatic problems compared with wider policy concerns. I highlight the limitations of ad hoc approaches in resolving problems arising from policy objectives. Finally, I emphasize the importance of operational and principled unity amongst actors in an environment where crucial issues such as the legitimacy and acceptance of the humanitarian community could not be taken for granted.

Context

Four contextual factors determined international NGOs' efforts at humanitarian diplomacy in Iraq after the second Gulf War: the Coalition occupation and rule in Iraq; the resulting insecurity in the country; the humanitarian impact of the war; and the role of the different humanitarian actors present before and after the war. These factors were pertinent because they reflected the ambiguous political environment in which NGOs were operating; the increased insecurity that threatened their presence; the relevance of their presence to the needs of a distressed population; and the conflicting roles assigned to a variety of players attempting to respond to these needs. The section concludes with an introduction to the NCCI and its efforts at humanitarian diplomacy.

Occupation and rule in Iraq

After months of threats and a long military build-up, the Coalition forces (CF), led by the United States and the United Kingdom, launched "Operation Iraqi Freedom", which resulted in the invasion of Iraq on 20 March 2003. Although the United States claimed it was acting in accordance with international law, an overwhelming majority of governments and world public opinion thought otherwise. Nevertheless, having defeated and overthrown Saddam Hussein's government in March 2003, the Coalition forces began their rule over Iraq in April 2003, as the Coalition Provisional Authority (CPA). They retained political authority in the country, while giving symbolic powers to a hand-picked Iraqi Governing Council. In June 2004, the CPA announced that it had "transferred sovereignty" to a newly formed Interim Government and that elections in January 2005 would create a fully democratic Iraq.

The occupation, however, led to brutal confrontations between the occupying forces and those opposing them. The violence had a negative impact on every effort made by the various parties towards building a viable future for the country and its inhabitants.

The initial post-war phase – from April to roughly August 2003 – was characterized by chaos, an institutional vacuum, disruption of the system and the creation of pockets of vulnerability. The situation quickly developed into widespread insecurity owing to the rapid emergence of a broad and vigorous opposition to the occupation. Criminality and insurgency dominated Iraqi streets. Hundreds of Iraqis were kidnapped for ransom and attacks against the Coalition forces or anyone (including Iraqis) viewed as collaborators increased day by day. The Coalition forces were under constant attack and were unable to guarantee protection to essential civilian structures let alone minimal security to the wider Iraqi population.

When the CPA, hostage to its own security mechanisms in the "Green Zone", handed symbolic powers to the Iraqi ministries, the Iraqi authorities were not provided with the means or the resources to carry out their tasks effectively.[1] By April 2004, two clear fronts had opened against the Coalition forces: a Shiite revolt in the south, led by the al-Mahdi army, and a Sunni insurgency in the so-called "Sunni triangle". As Iraq's political sphere moved towards key dates (the transfer of authority and elections), the determination of certain factions to destabilize this process sharpened considerably. Insecurity became widespread and, as the numbers of affected Iraqis increased, so did the challenges facing the international aid community in maintaining a presence and responding to the country's rising needs.

The humanitarian impact of the war

The post-war humanitarian situation in Iraq needs to be understood in relation to the years of punishing economic sanctions and domestic repression by the government of Saddam Hussein. The impact of the war and the subsequent destabilization of the country once the occupation was established compounded the problem.

Even before the war, Iraq was, in humanitarian terms, a country in distress. The Gulf War of 1990–1991 was followed by 13 years of economic sanctions, which resulted in extreme poverty among the general population, high unemployment levels, worrying malnutrition rates, and decaying essential services, particularly water, sanitation and electricity. The introduction of the UN Oil-for-Food Programme in 1996, the largest humanitarian programme ever implemented, cushioned the fall. However, 70 per cent of the Iraqi population, mostly urban, remained particularly vulnerable and completely dependent on state-run services: monthly food distribution, access to health care and other basic services.

Although the second Gulf War was short-lived and did not result in the widespread humanitarian emergency that many had feared, the vulnerability and dependence of the population on government services that existed before the conflict only increased further. The institutional vacuum that followed the fall of the previous government, together with crippling levels of looting and banditry, led to a widespread breakdown of essential services affecting the mass of the population. This situation inevitably worsened once open confrontation between the Iraqi resistance and the occupation forces started in April 2004. Hundreds of families were displaced as a result and, in the case of Fallujah in November 2004, the city was almost totally destroyed, thereby aggravating the needs of its inhabitants.

Humanitarian roles before and after the war

Prior to the war, Iraqis had little experience of humanitarian work in the sense of principled, neutral, impartial and independent assistance. After the war, the Coalition assumed control of the humanitarian response and the reconstruction process. Both these factors meant that traditional humanitarian agencies had great difficulties asserting themselves as legitimate humanitarian actors, and their failure to do so had dramatic consequences in terms of the security of humanitarian personnel.

The humanitarian landscape before the war was characterized by the role of the Iraqi government, which was responsible for the largest humanitarian operation through its implementation of the Oil-for-Food Programme (OFFP).[2] The United Nations' role was to oversee the imposition of sanctions as well as to supervise the OFFP. Apart from that, there were fewer than 20 Iraqi NGOs operating in Iraq (mostly in the Kurdish areas) and fewer than 10 international NGOs (in governmental Iraq).[3] In other words, the Iraqi population knew little, if anything, about independent humanitarian work.

The number of actors involved in humanitarian assistance and reconstruction rose dramatically after the war. UN agencies and over 100 international NGOs had prepared to respond to what was anticipated would be a major humanitarian disaster. The traditional pattern of response, however, had changed from previous contexts. The fact that the UN Security Council had not supported the war meant that it was given no role in leading the humanitarian and reconstruction process. Instead, the Bush administration decided to put the Pentagon in charge of relief efforts and let the US military take the lead in coordinating them. Military units and for-profit contractors were given major humanitarian and reconstruction roles. UN agencies and international NGOs were marginalized from their traditional function.

It was within this context that the NGO Coordination Committee in Iraq sought to represent the international NGO community and the interests of its constituency (the Iraqi population), negotiate acceptance as actors, and create space and legitimacy for their actions.

The NGO Coordination Committee in Iraq

The NGO Coordination Committee in Iraq (NCCI)[4] was established in April 2003 by a small group of NGOs in response to growing concerns about preserving humanitarian space and safeguarding the neutrality, impartiality and operational independence of humanitarian activity within the framework of the occupation. The UN withdrawal after the attack on its Baghdad headquarters meant that the NCCI assumed many of the coordination responsibilities that had been performed by UN agencies. Its constituency fluctuated around 50 per cent of the 115 international NGOs present or operational in Iraq. It included all the major US and European NGOs, although many declined membership either because their geographical area was not covered by the committee or because they could not abide by the code of conduct and charter designed by NCCI members. Through its main office in Baghdad and sub-offices in Amman, Basra and Erbil, the NCCI attempted to establish an independent forum for humanitarian agencies in which issues of concern would be identified and discussed. A facilitator and not a representational body, the NCCI was, nevertheless, often mandated by the NGO community to represent its views and concerns vis-à-vis the CPA, the Iraqi authorities and other players.

The main roles of the NCCI – as defined by its Charter and the evolution of needs – were those of gathering information (on beneficiary requirements, developments, legislation, etc.), representation (of the international NGO community), negotiation (with third parties) and communication (addressed to the international NGO community and to third parties). The humanitarian diplomacy of the NCCI fluctuated between two levels: seeking concrete, case-by-case solutions to NGOs' main operational constraints; pursuing a more process-oriented engagement with different players for wider, sustainable and more principled objectives.

Operational issues

The three most critical operational constraints faced by NGOs involved security, access and coordination. Security and access were crucial because, first and foremost, they affected the Iraqi population in terms of protection and access to basic services. They also constituted a serious impediment to humanitarian agencies' ability to respond to the needs of the population. Coordination, or its lack, also had an impact on the efficiency and effectiveness of humanitarian actors' activities and performance.

Security

Security affected operational activities in two ways. On the one hand, especially in the early stages of post-war Iraq, criminality negatively affected the capacity of hospitals, primary health care centres and governmental warehouses to deliver services to the population because their equipment, furniture and drugs were constantly stolen by looters. NGOs nevertheless continued to operate in this environment and to provide support to these structures, since only their goods and not necessarily their personnel were targeted. On the other hand, by early 2004, random criminal acts became a secondary threat following the increase in attacks by organized groups against the Coalition forces and any organizations or individuals seen as collaborators.

Aid agencies gradually felt more targeted, which meant that movement and, therefore, access to certain groups of the population and/or areas became increasingly difficult as time went by. Agencies faced difficulties not only in delivering goods but in performing needs assessments and monitoring their results, an essential element in determining the relevance and accountability of their interventions.

The threat to NGO operations was aggravated in April 2004 when two city fronts opened in Fallujah and Najaf and armed confrontations between the Coalition forces and Sunni and Shiite insurgents affected large numbers of civilians. The international community's capacity to respond to the needs of the displaced was severely challenged when 40 foreigners from 12 different countries were kidnapped by insurgents. Many NGOs had temporarily to relocate their international staff to neighbouring areas and thus had to redefine their response mechanisms. Hostage-taking and executions of foreigners continued to be a problem and were the main reason for the gradual decrease in NGO presence, reduced operational response, and the eventual closure of relief programmes in the country.

Access

The access of civilians to basic services and of humanitarian agencies to support civilian structures was mainly restricted by security problems as the physical movement of goods and people became increasingly risky. Confrontations between insurgents and the Coalition forces in cities (especially in the case of Fallujah and Najaf in April) exacerbated the difficulties of access as parts of the cities came under the control of one party or another and ongoing hostilities required the agreement of both parties for humanitarian agencies to access the population.

Coordination

Given the many actors engaged in humanitarian activities in post-war Iraq, NGOs soon realized the necessity of coordinating not only between themselves and their traditional partners (the United Nations, the International Committee of the Red Cross and national NGOs) but also with the other actors involved (military units and contractors were engaged in activities very similar to those traditionally undertaken by humanitarian agencies). Within weeks of starting operations in the country, NGOs were reporting overlapping and duplication of efforts between them and the "humanitarian arms" of the occupying power, i.e. military units and contractors. The situation was somewhat ironic given the large financial resources being made available for the reconstruction of Iraq, the vastness of the country and the huge range of needs, from large infrastructural rehabilitation to addressing particular vulnerable groups in the communities.

The occupying power had maintained the leading role in humanitarian and reconstruction efforts and thus coordination activities were mainly organized by the Coalition forces and on their premises, rather than by civilian structures (such as ministries) in non-militarized locations. This created a problem for the perceived neutrality of aid agencies and for their security. Other problems derived from the lack of any organizational capacity to collect all the information regarding players' actual and future activities as well as a reluctance to make this information too public for security reasons.

Obstacles and opportunities

Adding to the above operational constraints, and undermining NGOs' ability to negotiate increased security, better access and improved coordination, was the limited humanitarian space available to NGOs. The lack of humanitarian space resulted from a series of policies adopted by the Coalition vis-à-vis humanitarian aid as well as from the international NGOs' differing approaches in responding to these policies. Moreover, owing to the absence of the United Nations and the weakened status of the Iraqi authorities, there was no credible neutral third party to take the lead in coordinating humanitarian efforts. The resulting blurring of lines and confusion amongst the Iraqi public adversely affected the NGOs' ability to operate in the country.

Limited humanitarian space

By "humanitarian space", the NCCI and the international NGOs understand a conceptual space distinct from the political arena and a framework within which independence, neutrality and impartiality guided and defined humanitarian action. Also referred to as "the humanitarian operating environment",[5] the notion suggests that adherence to these key operating principles represents the critical means by which the primary objective of relieving suffering wherever it is found can be achieved. The concept implies that maintaining a clear distinction between the role and function of humanitarian actors and those of the military is the determining factor in creating an operating environment in which humanitarian organizations can discharge their responsibilities effectively and safely.

Occupation policies towards humanitarian aid

The policies adopted by the Coalition concerning humanitarian aid were the most significant cause of the shrinking of humanitarian space in Iraq. To list a few raised by the NCCI:

NGOs have seen their operating space diminish as a result of a number of factors including, the increased use of humanitarian aid as a political tool including labelling entire military campaigns as humanitarian missions, the provision of assistance through for profit groups (private contractors), adulteration of the concept of civil society to become equal to sub-contractor, cooption of the community approach by certain elements within the armed forces, and so forth. The earlier highlighted behaviours have created a sense of confusion among the Iraqi public who are no longer able to differentiate between independent humanitarian agencies, private contractors and Coalition Forces. Needless to say that has dramatically increased our insecurity in the context of Iraq.[6]

Military contingents of the Coalition forces would often declare their mandate to be a humanitarian one and denounce losses of soldiers as attacks against humanitarian workers. These examples of the misuse of language and abuse of the term "humanitarianism", although probably intended to make the military presence and occupation more user-friendly to the population, did not serve that purpose and negatively affected the profile of genuine humanitarian actors present in the country. Humanitarian actors, moreover, often felt that their cause had been appropriated by the Coalition to further political aims. In declaring NGOs to be a "force multiplier" and "an important part of our combat team", Secretary of State Colin Powell stripped NGOs of their independent and neutral character and implied that NGO motivations were indistinguishable from those of the Coalition.[7]

The engagement of military forces in direct assistance (i.e. the face-to-face distribution of goods and services) further contributed to the blurring of lines. Internationally accepted UN guidelines proclaim the desirability of humanitarian work being performed by humanitarian organizations and exclude the military from delivering assistance directly to the population. This is the only way to retain a clear distinction between the normal functions and roles of humanitarian and of military stakeholders.[8]

The previous Iraqi public distribution system had suffered disruption as a result of the war, but the structures for the distribution of food rations and the provision of health care were still in place and functioning. This meant that direct assistance by military forces was not necessary because civilian options were available. Yet military forces would regularly engage in quick-impact relief activities with the aim of "winning hearts and minds". Their objectives were to gain community goodwill, to guarantee positive media coverage and thus to contribute to the overall success of the military campaign.

These objectives were problematic for several reasons. First, "hearts and minds" operations are designed to maximize security and normally target potentially "friendly" groups rather than those most in need. Second, the engagement of the military in the provision of assistance makes it difficult for opposing parties and the population to distinguish between independent humanitarian organizations and occupying military forces. Finally, to be workable, the provision of assistance by the military requires close two-way coordination with combat units.

The engagement by the Coalition forces of for-profit groups (contractors) to carry out humanitarian activities also caused problems. Although these were civilian bodies, they were not accountable to internationally recognized humanitarian principles and operational standards. They were not neutral, or independent (they reported to the Coalition forces and pursued their objectives) or impartial (they acted on pre-established contractual agreements and not on the basis of need). They were, furthermore, heavily armed or protected by military escorts and thus perceived by the population as a civilian branch of the Coalition forces. NGOs feared that, by extension, they too would be considered as an instrument of the Coalition.

NGOs were also concerned about the types of activities undertaken by military units and for-profit groups. These bodies took on tasks usually considered to be humanitarian assistance activities (in particular, health care, the provision of clean water and involvement in rural areas) as well as activities normally carried out by international rights-based groups (such as education and empowering national civil society), rather than maintaining a focus on large infrastructural rehabilitation projects. It seemed to NGOs that their terminology, activities and community-based approaches for engaging the population were being high-jacked in the pursuit of political objectives. Again, to the population of Iraq, NGOs could be increasingly perceived as indistinguishable from the other players – even though the differences remained substantial.

The issue of Iraqi civil society was, perhaps, the most telling. The Iraqi Assistance Center (a Coalition force unit in charge of liaising with the aid community) established an NGO support office in the Green Zone where Iraqi NGOs could seek guidance and financial assistance. This resulted in military officers coaching and training emerging Iraqi NGOs on issues ranging from civil society, to how to carry out a needs assessment, how to prepare proposals and how to carry out food distribution. As far as international NGOs were concerned, these issues were better left to experienced, non-belligerent, civilian bodies, which would also be able to contribute to a principled approach to the emerging Iraqi civil society.

Differing NGO approaches to the Coalition forces and their policies

International NGO approaches to this situation varied considerably, mostly because of an overarching confusion about how to work with the occupying power. This confusion led to varying degrees of adherence by NGOs to traditional humanitarian principles. The subsequent partial erosion of humanitarian standards had a further negative influence on the ability of the NGO community, as a whole, to obtain wider acceptance by the population.

NGOs were not sure how to operate and work under the auspices of an occupying power that many of them regarded as illegitimate. NGOs sought to hold the occupying power accountable for its responsibility under international law to the Iraqi population and the security of aid workers. Ideally, the role of the occupying power should have been limited to establishing law and order – leaving humanitarians to get on with humanitarian work. Such a distinction might have allowed the occupying power to focus on re-establishing national security, which would have had the double effect of improving the security of aid workers through disassociation of NGO activity from Coalition forces' activity. This did not happen, however, and questions about how NGOs should cooperate with the occupying power did not find a coherent response. Some NGOs recalled their experience in Kosovo, where military and humanitarian agencies worked side-by-side successfully. Other NGOs saw great dangers in this form of collaboration in terms of their perceived neutrality and independence. This latter group of NGOs attempted to define and defend a separate humanitarian agenda from that adopted by the occupying power.

The collaboration of some NGOs with the Coalition forces, manifested by their agreement to participate in common projects, to accept funds and to accept military escorts and protection, led to serious divisions within the aid community. The NGOs embracing collaboration did so for a variety of reasons. They might have been acting under donor pressure, driven by competition with contractors, protecting their institutional survival, or considering the purely pragmatic operational purpose of getting the job done. For other NGOs, though, getting the job done that way (at the cost of compromising their basic humanitarian principles) was too high a price to pay.

The absence of neutral leadership of humanitarian efforts

The problem of the blurring of lines, the lack of adequate coordination and the confusion of roles, which led to increased insecurity and problems of access, could have been partly resolved if humanitarian assistance had been seen to be led by a credible and neutral third party distinct from the occupying power. This could have been either the United Nations or the Iraqi authorities. Neither was able to take on this role.

Because the UN Security Council refused to endorse the Coalition invasion and occupation, Washington decided to ignore international calls for the United Nations to take over the civil administration after the war, and retained complete control over relief and reconstruction efforts. Fearing that this militarization of aid would affect their perceived neutrality and independence, NGOs still hoped that the United Nations would serve as a buffer between them and the occupying power.

Critics had warned against the United Nations being identified with the "illegal" war and occupation. Nevertheless, after Security Council Resolution 1483, a Special Representative for Iraq was appointed and the United Nations assumed some responsibilities. In August 2003, UN fears were confirmed by the bombing of UN headquarters in Baghdad, which killed 15 UN staff, including the Special Representative. The United Nations then pulled out of Iraq. It maintained a minimum role for the planning of national elections as well as a restricted operational presence through the activities of national staff. Under these conditions, the United Nations could not take a lead role in coordinating humanitarian action. In the absence of a UN presence, international NGOs had no alternative but to deal directly with the occupying power.

The Iraqi authorities did not have the capacity to assume the role of leading humanitarian efforts. Offices had been damaged during the war and looting did the rest. Their upper management was denuded by the de-Ba'athification process imposed by the occupying power, which adversely affected the availability of skilled resources and institutional memory. Most importantly, the Iraqi authorities were not given the means by the occupying power to develop such a coordinating capacity. Their decision-making powers were unclear and they were not provided with the financial and material resources that would have enabled them to carry out such activities successfully. NGOs nevertheless considered the Iraqi authorities to be the legitimate leadership and, from the initial post-war stages, sought to work with them for coordination purposes and operational collaboration.

Confusion amongst the Iraqi public

The mixed and blurred roles between and among the CPA, the Coalition forces, CF contractors and NGOs, together with the lack of adequate leadership, meant that outsiders were perceived by Iraqis as upholders of particular interests rather than of the universal rights of Iraqis. "Why are you here?" an NGO worker was asked by a representative of an Islamic group while attempting to explain the role, principles and modus operandi of NGOs. "Iraq has money, it was a rich country until the sanctions [i.e. Western intervention]. It has the resources and the capacities: people are well trained and educated ... What the people need is for foreigners to leave and let Iraqis run our country. We know how to do it."

A further irritant was that many Iraqis believed that NGOs were using Oil-for-Food (that is, Iraqi) money to fund their operations (as was the case with the United Nations prior to the war).

NGOs' normal security strategy depends on the acceptance of their presence and activities by the population. The confusion of the Iraqi public therefore had serious implications for the security of NGOs and their ability to maintain safe and unrestricted access to local communities.

Negotiations

The rationale behind the humanitarian diplomacy of the NCCI was that international NGOs ought to be able to operate in Iraq in a secure fashion, with unrestricted access to the population, and do so effectively, through adequate coordination. To achieve this, the NCCI had to address the underlying causes of the obstacles to the integrity of humanitarian action and, at the same time, support the day-to-day work of the agencies with practical solutions. NGO diplomacy thus had both a macro-level and a micro-level objective: the first was to reverse the narrowing of the humanitarian space available for NGO action and to protect the legitimacy of humanitarian activities; the second was to secure access to those in need of assistance. These objectives employed different negotiating modalities. This section discusses both levels of negotiation and concludes with an analysis of the outcomes of negotiations, the most important of which was the "crisis of legitimacy" of NGOs in Iraq.

Protecting the legitimacy of humanitarian activities

At a macro level, the NCCI concentrated much of its efforts on protecting the integrity of humanitarian action in the highly politicized and militarized circumstances of the occupation. To do so, the NCCI engaged with different relevant actors, mainly the Coalition forces, the Iraqi authorities and the United Nations. The approaches used with the different players were, respectively, bilateral negotiations, operational cooperation and advocacy. All these options were oriented towards engaging each party in affecting the various policies that had brought about the narrowing of humanitarian space in the first place.

Negotiations with the Coalition

From its inception, the NCCI met numerous times with representatives of the Coalition Provisional Authority (CPA) and the Coalition forces to discuss the contribution of occupation policies to the lack of a distinctive humanitarian space. The NCCI raised NGO concerns and made concrete demands, namely:

1. the need to improve coordination between military units, contractors and the NGO community in order to avoid duplication and to avoid their being perceived as similar entities;
2. the need for these coordination activities to take place within ministries (or directorates in the Governorates), not only to empower them to perform their responsibilities but also to avoid the security implications of NGOs' attending meetings in CF premises and running the risk of being externally perceived as "collaborators";
3. the need for military units to use clear distinctive military marks on their vehicles;
4. the need to transfer CF activities for the support of the emerging Iraqi civil society into the hands of civilian bodies.

Negotiations were usually bilateral, continuous and open. Some had positive outcomes in terms of intentions: the Iraqi Assistance Center (IAC) and the Humanitarian Assistance Coordination Center (HACC), both of which were part of the Coalition forces, were responsive and welcomed the NCCI's positions. More often than not, however, solutions to these issues were beyond their reach. For example, they did not have the organizational capacity to obtain feedback from all military units themselves. Nor did they have the capacity to influence contractors' behaviour. In Basra, for example, the Coalition forces were sensitive to the fact that it was dangerous for NGOs to enter their compound and they offered to travel to NGO premises. This solution, however, was accepted with great reluctance by NGOs because none wanted military escorts outside their offices. In respect to national NGOs, the IAC finally offered to transfer its civil society project to civil organizations (both the United Nations and the NCCI were asked whether they were willing to inherit it). However, taking over the project was perceived as too compromising and likely to blur the lines between military and humanitarian objectives even further.

These were "lose–lose" types of negotiation, not only because the NCCI usually had nothing to bargain with, but also because the solution proposed for one problem would often create further, different problems. The NCCI regularly sat at the negotiating table and, though able to highlight problems, was often unable to propose "win–win" scenarios or better alternative solutions to the current dilemmas. Both parties had the objective of assisting the Iraqi population, yet, whereas the Coalition forces thought it could be possible to do this collaboratively, NGOs thought each party should restrict its actions to what it knew best: NGOs providing assistance and the Coalition forces providing security. That decision, however, needed to be made at levels far higher than the

NCCI and its CF interlocutors. The role and engagement of the military in humanitarian activities were matters of higher policy that could hardly be affected by negotiations in the field.

Operational cooperation with the Iraqi authorities

Negotiating cooperation with the Iraqi authorities took a different tack. NGOs had two interests in these negotiations. The first was to liaise with the authorities so as to avoid having to do so with the CPA. NGOs understood that this was a symbolic action, because every minister was backed by a CPA adviser who would actually define policies. The second interest was that, because the Iraqi authorities would be the inheritors of power after the occupation, NGOs wanted to take the opportunity to distinguish themselves, their roles, their guiding principles and their modus operandi as a first step in their quest for humanitarian space.

The general approach of the NCCI was to engage the Iraqi authorities – through relevant ministries – as the NGOs' legitimate counterparts to which NGOs should report and with which they should coordinate (as opposed to the CPA). By so doing they hoped to increase the transparency and accountability of international NGO actions in the country.

In all technical and operational matters, the NCCI maintained regular communication through the constant reporting and sharing of information on NGO activities, needs identified, technical recommendations, etc. The results were successful. Ministries often reported that NGOs and UN agencies were the only parties informing them of activities. Although later meetings suggested that the Iraqi authorities did not fully understand NGO mandates, at least vis-à-vis the Iraqi authorities, the distinction between NGOs and other actors was made clear through this constant contact.

Advocating with the United Nations

NGOs sought an active and substantive role for the United Nations in pushing the issue of "humanitarian space" to the top of the agenda in Iraq. Although aware that many problems were not within the direct control of the United Nations, NGOs strongly felt that the United Nations was most suited to raise them with all concerned parties and hence press for behavioural and policy change. In particular, the NCCI expected the United Nations to remind all participants in the UN Drafting Committee (a significant number of which were members of the Coalition in Iraq) of the very clear and explicit contents of the March 2003 "Guidelines on the Use of Military and Civil Defence Assets to Support United Nations Humanitarian Activities in Complex Emergencies".[9]

Following Security Council Resolution 1546 (2004), which requested "member states to contribute assistance to the Multi National Force

(MNF), including military forces to help meet the needs of the Iraqi people including humanitarian assistance", the Office of the Deputy Special Representative of the Secretary-General (SRSG) of the United Nations Assistance Mission for Iraq (UNAMI) issued a modified version of earlier "Guidelines for Humanitarian Organisations on Interacting with Military and Other Security Actors in Iraq" in October 2004.[10] This document addressed relevant issues of civil–military relations for humanitarian action in Iraq, as well as considerations regarding areas in which humanitarians and military and other security actors might need to coordinate. Again, although these were positive steps, the guidelines did not tackle the decisive issue of military engagement in humanitarian activities.

Securing access to those in need

At the micro level, the humanitarian diplomacy of the NCCI concentrated on the day-to-day constraints in the field, in particular the lack of access to Iraqi communities, largely owing to security considerations. Once again, the Coalition forces were approached. On this issue, however, non-state actors such as insurgents or Islamic groups from civil society sector were also included in the negotiating effort. Two approaches were taken. The first was to liaise bilaterally with each group. The second was to use public information mechanisms to exert pressure on the major stakeholders. The sieges of Fallujah and Najaf in April 2004 are used here to illustrate the process of these negotiations.

Negotiations with the Coalition forces

When the Coalition forces blockaded Fallujah and Najaf, access had to be negotiated with them in advance. Another issue was the occasional attempt to prevent aid convoys from moving without a military escort. The NCCI made a formal request to the Coalition forces to open a "humanitarian corridor" to allow NGOs to enter the cities independently. The Coalition forces responded by establishing a mechanism for "convoy clearance" – although this required 48 hours' notice. This arrangement did not work very well because NGOs relied on informal contacts in the cities to let them know when the internal situation was secure, and this could vary from day to day. Despite expressing this concern, there was no further room for negotiation. Sending the request, processing convoy clearance and obtaining a stamped approval with relevant contact information for commanders in the field took quite some time. These conditions forced some organizations to seek alternative routes that were controlled not by the Coalition forces but by insurgents. Negotiations for access thus had to be carried out with them as well.

Negotiations with non-state actors

Negotiating access with insurgents in control of areas and roads required an extensive network of national contacts. Prior contact was not possible because the NCCI did not know their structure of command and did not have a central person with whom it could establish contact. Thus, intermediaries in the form of sheikhs had to be used. Obtaining their assistance, however, required establishing some degree of credibility and legitimacy, which was obtained through the provision of assistance by NGOs. Mosques within the cities and in villages outside the cities hosted displaced families that had fled the military confrontations. NGOs provided support to these mosques in the form of goods and supplies to address the needs of internally displaced persons.

Coordinating with sheikhs raised questions about the neutrality of international NGOs. However, not only was collaboration the most efficient way of providing assistance to families but it also resulted in a network that proved vital for international NGOs to obtain access to the cities with some guarantee of security. NGOs would pass on information about their movements to the sheikhs, who would then tell the different resistance groups that these movements were to take place.

As international NGOs established their credibility as humanitarian actors, they were issued with letters in Arabic for each international staff member, stating their humanitarian profile and requesting protection. These included letters stamped and signed by groups such as al-Sadr's Mahdi army, the Office of Grand Ayatollah Sistani, the Iraqi Islamic Committee and the Olama' Islamic Council. Nevertheless, even these contacts and negotiations were not always sufficiently reassuring. On one occasion, three international NGO national staff transporting medical supplies and an ambulance were kidnapped by insurgents. Their release was negotiated by the sheikh responsible for an improvised clinic set up in one of the mosques with which they were working. According to the sheikh, the reason for the incident was that the Coalition forces had previously organized ambulances to evacuate urgent medical cases from the city and had taken wounded insurgents straight to the US Marines, paying 25,000 Iraqi dinars to Iraqis willing to do the job.[11] The insurgents had thought the NGO was doing the same.

Although negotiating access this way was successful on an ad hoc basis, it was too unpredictable and subject to too many factors that could seriously threaten the security of NGO personnel. A more consistent and reliable approach was needed. Thus, NGOs resorted to the use of public statements and communiqués to exert pressure on the warring parties to deal with this dilemma.

Public communiqués

All relevant information received from the field, in terms of reports on the situation and response actions, was collated by the NCCI and framed in daily Situation Reports, which were then sent to all humanitarian actors, including NGOs, the International Committee of the Red Cross and UN agencies. They were also sent to donors and the Special Representative of the Secretary-General (SRSG) for Iraq. These communications were designed to inform higher-level decision makers about developments in the field and to try to obtain support for the resumption of peaceful negotiations among the parties in conflict.

NGOs initially used discreet, formal means of raising issues of concern with the Coalition forces and the CPA through letters addressed to Ambassador Bremer (the head of the CPA) and informal communications with the different commanders in the field. Given the lack of success in bilateral negotiations for the suspension of hostilities, for solutions to the various reported violations of international law and over issues of humanitarian access, NGOs used public communications to reinforce these efforts. These included NCCI press releases, representing all NGO members, sent to the media and to NGO headquarters. The outcomes of this approach were also mixed. Agreeing on a statement that would both denounce the situation diplomatically and state the facts objectively was no easy task. A consensual document signed by most NGOs was finally agreed,[12] but the attempt to be representational made the document much too long and too late for it to have any impact.

Different negotiating modalities

These two examples of humanitarian diplomacy reflected two problematic concerns. The first was a deep-rooted crisis of legitimacy and the second was a symptomatic constraint – in this case, limited access to the Iraqi population. Humanitarian diplomacy thus had two different objectives. The first was to create a sustainable safe environment in which to operate. The second was to obtain day-to-day access to the population. Each objective involved negotiating with different players and required different approaches. In the first case, the negotiations were with formal bodies such as the CPA/Coalition forces and the Iraqi authorities. In the second case, negotiations were with informal bodies such as the insurgents and Islamic civil society groups.

Basic factors such as the degree of formality in correspondence and the type of information exchanged between NGOs and other actors depended on whether NGOs were negotiating formally or informally with the CPA and Coalition forces or informally with other actors. The emphasis on the role of the negotiator also differed. Sometimes an expatriate was used as the key negotiator (usually with formal bodies); sometimes a national staff member was the preferred negotiator (especially in negotiations with non-state actors); sometimes NGOs preferred to use intermediaries such as the United Nations and religious groups as "buffers" in their dealings with the Coalition forces and insurgents, respectively.

Approaches also varied in terms of the "rhetorical tools" used for negotiations. NGOs sometimes alluded to the "high moral ground" obligations of parties to respect international humanitarian law and international human rights law. At other times, NGOs reverted to a "complicity approach" – suggesting that all parties shared the objective of benefiting the Iraqi population. Negotiations were most often successful when small, concrete objectives were outlined and requests were made face-to-face. Most importantly, negotiations could achieve results only when interlocutors actually had the power to respond to requests. Petitions that needed a response at higher levels often remained unanswered. The challenge therefore became to find the right means to approach the upper levels of decision-making hierarchies directly.

Negotiating approaches were the result of trial and error. The NCCI had no notion that the negotiations it was carrying out amounted to humanitarian diplomacy and certainly had no prior preparation, knowledge of techniques or training for undertaking these activities. It had, thus, no specific awareness of the importance of the process or how this process could have been better informed and better planned.

The Iraq context suggests that many factors, beyond diplomatic techniques, influenced the NGOs' ability to negotiate. One factor concerned the originating country of the NGO and the nationality of its staff. French NGOs, for example, always felt more "protected" than those from Coalition countries, because France had not supported the war. Another factor was whether or not the NGO had a presence in Iraq before the war, and also whether or not it had stayed during the war. Some in the international community believed, for instance, that the evacuation of all UN staff during the war contributed to sections of the Iraqi population viewing the United Nations as biased towards the alliance.

The amount of time spent in the country was also significant in terms of understanding the context, the culture and the people. The processes of negotiation and liaison were helped by a knowledge of Arabic, familiarity with "hospitality" procedures and an ability to work through "informal hierarchies". Conversely, NGOs with security personnel from military backgrounds had better access to information and, in security matters, were able to gain access to more important contacts within the

Coalition forces than were civilians. The NCCI's success was dependent on the extent to which it was able to offer a united, organized and knowledgeable approach to negotiating partners. How far the NCCI was able to engage its interlocutors on the issue of its legal rights and obligations and of the actions expected from its interlocutors also reflected the NCCI's competence as an actor.

Outcomes: The crisis of NGO legitimacy

It is hard to measure the achievements of NCCI's humanitarian diplomacy. This was because, almost a year and a half after the war, the majority of humanitarian actors had left the country and were closing their projects owing to their inability to operate safely. Between April 2003 and June 2004, however, the NCCI may have contributed positively to increasing the information base (and thus to improving the decision-making activities) of NGOs present in the country. It was also successful in creating a spirit of community, dialogue and exchange amongst NGOs. It maintained open communication lines with relevant parties and brought pressing needs to the negotiating table. In the wider context, however, these were small victories. In addressing the "symptom" of blocked access, often humanitarian agencies were able to negotiate ad hoc interventions only on a case-by-case basis. Their broader efforts at protecting the integrity and legitimacy of humanitarian work in Iraq were less successful.

The NCCI cannot be blamed for being unable to control events well beyond its purview, including the agenda of insurgent groups. That said, the NCCI did miss opportunities to address elements clearly within its sphere, most particularly the "crisis of legitimacy" of humanitarian action in Iraq. This "crisis of legitimacy" arose because the NGO reliance on the conventional principles of neutrality, impartiality and independence and distance from military and political influence was severely challenged in the post-war context. The Iraqi population did not see a separation between NGOs and the occupying forces.

The NGOs gave insufficient consideration to Iraqis' lack of prior experience of international NGOs or their negative perceptions of the aid community. This is not to say that all Iraqis were prejudiced against the relief community, especially beneficiaries and those who worked closely with NGOs. The central problem was that representative sections of the population did not know enough about the humanitarian community and NGOs did not adequately explain their guiding principles or their modus operandi. Moreover, by adopting a low-profile approach,[13] NGOs did little to help people to distinguish military actors and subcontractors from independent humanitarian actors.

The low-profile approach arose from NGOs' inability to reconcile their internal divisions. International NGOs' divergence over very basic humanitarian principles and their attitudes towards the Coalition forces meant that NGOs could say nothing about their principles, mandates and modus operandi that could apply to the whole NGO community. The NCCI could not draw up communiqués, articles or press releases addressing the population on behalf of the wider NGO community because there was nothing that could be said about one NGO that would apply to all. Perhaps NGOs themselves contributed to what the SRSG described as the "loss of innocence of the humanitarian community".

Wider implications

The NGO experience in Iraq raises fundamental questions about the practice of humanitarian diplomacy in highly politicized contexts and in conflict situations, including (i) the use of military assets in humanitarian action, whether in support of humanitarian efforts or in providing assistance directly; (ii) the implications of military engagement for the future of principled humanitarian action; (iii) the importance of no longer taking for granted a population's acceptance of humanitarian actors per se; (iv) and the role of coordination mechanisms in encouraging a unified principled approach to humanitarian action and in developing improved means of communication with local populations.

Some may argue that the Iraqi experience is too particularist in the policy-driven obstacles to humanitarian assistance, because political interests do not affect most other contexts to the same degree. At a time, however, when the "war against terror" has extended political interests to other areas – an example being the expansion of the security agenda to failed states – the use of humanitarian action for political ends may increase. Faced with similar patterns of humanitarian leadership by non-UN or civilian structures and the increased role of military and for-profit actors in leadership and direct assistance, similar negative consequences for the creation of humanitarian space can be expected. Humanitarian agencies therefore need to consider the choice between principles and pragmatism carefully.

Some contend that a "back to basics" approach is called for in which principled humanitarianism becomes, once again, the guiding framework. Others argue that it is "not the time to invest in yet more interminable debates to 're-define humanitarian action' from first principles. Nor is it time to form a square and defend humanitarian values. They are simply not that threatened. Instead, it is time to get decisive about where we can and cannot operate and get innovative about how we do things."[14] In either case, the humanitarian agenda needs to identify and respond to humanitarian objectives in a way that is distinctive and different from the response to broader security or political objectives.

Nor can one any longer assume that humanitarians will be welcomed and protected by local populations as unconditional "good-doers". The humanitarian enterprise has come to be too associated with negative connotations of Western, neo-colonialist values. The aims, guiding principles and modus operandi of humanitarianism will thus need to be better outlined and more widely shared with beneficiary populations in order to gain greater adherence. Through such a regenerated engagement, humanitarian diplomacy could prove useful in altering policies and realities on the ground that impede safe and unrestricted access to populations in need. The creation of the NCCI suggested that the NGO community was willing to engage in such a process in Iraq. Coordination brought about a certain degree of operational unity, which influenced NGOs' capacity to reach the negotiating table and address issues relevant to their work. More could have been achieved to negotiate a wider acceptance and legitimacy of the NGO community if the principled divide had been overcome. Although the likelihood of this happening is somewhat utopian given the heterogeneous nature of NGOs, some improvements could be made if at least the most important NGOs agreed to take part in this process.

As humanitarian scenarios become increasingly politicized and insecure, as actors proliferate and as the traditional principles of humanitarian action erode, improved coordination mechanisms may serve as a means for humanitarian agencies to put their own house in order. NGOs could perhaps find unity in the common principles that should define their actions. They should also make a unified stand to pursue an array of humanitarian issues through diplomatic means. Initiatives such as the guidelines on civil–military relations produced by the UN Office for the Coordination of Humanitarian Affairs need to be promoted and made better known.

Humanitarian coordination should, however, be seen as distinct from the integrated approach that seeks to harmonize the different agendas, including the political, peacekeeping, humanitarian and development agendas, of agencies in any one country. Coordination is needed to facilitate the definition of individual agendas, and in particular to maintain the humanitarian agenda as separate and distinct.

Conclusion

Whether consciously or not, humanitarian agencies use certain methods of traditional diplomacy, such as information-gathering, representation and carrying out negotiations, to overcome the wide range of obstacles they face in the field. This chapter has reflected on the limits of humanitarian diplomacy as carried out by the NGO sector in Iraq in the absence of the United Nations. I have shown that humanitarian diplomatic engagement was useful in achieving small, specific gains, such as ad hoc access and improved collaboration. I have also shown, however, that NGO diplomacy was unable to influence policy and obtain enduring solutions to recurring problems, in particular the narrowing of humanitarian space. I have suggested that one of the main reasons for the failure of humanitarian diplomacy in Iraq was the lack of a unified and coherent humanitarian agenda and the lack of adherence by the humanitarian community to common humanitarian principles. I would also suggest that better coordination, built on common and articulated humanitarian agendas, is the prerequisite for successful humanitarian diplomacy and action in the future.

Notes

1. The CPA established its offices in a vast area in the centre of Baghdad including one of Saddam's palaces as well as a hotel and a conference centre. This area was known as the Green Zone, suggesting it was the only safe area in the city. Despite being heavily fortified and guarded, the Green Zone was constantly under attack. Most CPA officials lived and worked in the Green Zone and rarely left it.
2. After the first Gulf War, the United Nations imposed sanctions on Iraq that prohibited imports of military value and banned oil exports in order to deny Saddam Hussein money to rebuild his army. When it became apparent that Iraq's civilian population was suffering great hardship, the sanctions were eased. The Oil-for-Food Programme (OFFP) allowed Iraq to export oil under UN supervision, with the revenues to be used for food, medicines and other necessities. By virtually all expert accounts, the sanctions (backed by UN weapons inspectors) and the Oil-for-Food Programme achieved their major goals: Iraq's programmes to make chemical, biological and nuclear weapons disintegrated, and the health of the civilian population improved. Right from the start, however, Iraq found ways to circumvent the sanctions. Analysts estimate that Iraq generated some US$11 billion in illicit revenues. Responding to allegations of corruption, the UN Secretary-General appointed an independent investigation on 21 April 2004 into the alleged misuse of OFFP funds. The investigation resulted in the Volker Report, the first Interim Report being released on 3 February 2005 (Independent Inquiry Committee into the United Nations Oil-for-Food Programme, *Interim Report*, at ⟨http://www.iic-offp.org/documents/InterimReportFeb2005.pdf⟩). The results of the report are mixed. On the one hand, it suggests that the majority of violations were carried out outside of the programme framework. On the other hand, it suggests that the management and procurement of the fund were not sufficiently transparent and accused certain people of responsibility for utilizing their position to pursue personal interests. See ⟨http://www.unausa.org/site/pp.asp?c=fvKRI8MPJpF&b=387757⟩ (accessed 2 May 2006).
3. "Governmental Iraq" is an informal term for the 15 provinces that were controlled by the government, as opposed to the 3 northern Kurdish provinces (Dahuk, Arbil and Sulaymanihyah), which were given semi-autonomous status through the Oil-for-Food Programme and had their own governmental structures separate from central government (see Security Council Resolution 986 (1995)).

4. For more information on the NCCI, see ⟨http://www.ncciraq.org/sommaire.php3⟩.
5. United Nations Office for the Coordination of Humanitarian Affairs (UNOCHA), "Guidelines on the Use of Military and Civil Defence Assets to Support United Nations Humanitarian Activities in Complex Emergencies", March 2003, p. 3, ⟨http://ochaonline.un.org/DocView.asp?DocID=426⟩.
6. "NCCI Statement HACC Luncheon (08-05-04)", ⟨http://www.ncciraq.org/article.php3?id_article=135⟩.
7. See John S. Burnett, "In the Line of Fire", *New York Times*, 4 August 2004, ⟨http://www.globalpolicy.org/ngos/credib/2004/0804fire.htm⟩ (accessed 2 May 2006).
8. UNOCHA, "Guidelines on the Use of Military and Civil Defence Assets to Support United Nations Humanitarian Activities in Complex Emergencies", p. 9.
9. NCCI, "Bullet Points for Mr Ross Mountain, SRSG a.i. for Iraq – UNAMI: Humanitarian Space in Iraq & Security of Humanitarian Personnel on the Ground", May 2004, available at ⟨http://www.ncciraq.org/IMG/doc/NCCI-Bullet_Points_for_Mr._Ross_Mountain_-_Humanitarian_Space_in_Iraq_05-04_.doc⟩.
10. "Guidelines for Humanitarian Organisations on Interacting with Military and Other Security Actors in Iraq", 20 October 2004, reproduced at ⟨http://www.reliefweb.int/rw/rwb.nsf/db900SID/HMYT-66BQU7?OpenDocument⟩.
11. NCCI, "Crisis Situation Report", 13 April 2004 (SitRep 14.04.04), available at ⟨http://www.ncciraq.org/article.php3?id_article=104⟩ (US$1 = 1,462 dinars).
12. NCCI Statements on the Falujah Crisis – Spring 2004, ⟨http://www.ncciraq.org/article.php3?id_article=135⟩ (accessed 2 May 2006).
13. The NGOs' low-profile approach was characterized by an intentional effort to minimize the visibility of their presence and activities. Unlike in most other humanitarian contexts, NGOs in Iraq removed all signs of identification in their offices, houses and vehicles, and avoided making public announcements or statements as well as any action that might draw attention to themselves.
14. Hugo Slim, "A Call to Alms: Humanitarian Action and the Art of War", Geneva: Centre for Humanitarian Dialogue, 2004, p. 2.

Part III
Asia

6

NGOs break the Cold War impasse in Cambodia

Brian Walker

In 1979, Cambodia faced a major humanitarian crisis. While international attention was focused on the needs of Cambodians who had fled to refugee camps in Viet Nam and along the Thai border, the situation within the country was critical. The authorities installed by the government of Viet Nam allowed virtually no international access to civilians requiring assistance and protection, except by permission and through the capital city of Phnom Penh. Stepping into the breach, a non-governmental organization (NGO), Consortium for Cambodia, negotiated access and mounted humanitarian programmes in an undertaking originally opposed by United Nations agencies and the International Committee of the Red Cross on the grounds that the regime refused to allow aid to flow across the Thai/Cambodia frontier and expected to provide too little independent access to agencies to monitor needs and programmes. The former was standard practice; the latter proved not to be a real problem because the Consortium's leaders had considerable skills in national and international negotiation and were able rapidly to prove their expertise on the ground. They thus became acceptable to both the Consortium's constituent members and the Phnom Penh government. The Consortium initiative was accepted by most humanitarian agencies and subsequently was credited with having broken an impasse that reflected the international aftermath of the recent Viet Nam War.

Time line of key events	
1963–1968	US war in Viet Nam includes the bombing of Cambodia's Ho Chi Minh Trail
1970	Right-wing coup topples King Sihanouk; the United States invades Cambodia; puppet ruler Lon Nol installed
April 1975	Pol Pot and his Khmer Rouge army empty capital city Phnom Penh at gunpoint, directing its people to work in the fields
November 1978	Viet Nam invades Cambodia to topple Pol Pot and stem the flow of Cambodian refugees into Viet Nam
June 1979	A consortium of NGOs decides to deliver basic aid supplies to Cambodians not under Khmer Rouge control
October 1979	Consortium agreement authorizes delivery of aid up the Mekong River to Phnom Penh or into its airport, but forbids entry of assistance across the Thai/ Cambodian border. The agreement becomes the model for arrangements with the United Nations, the ICRC and other agencies
1989	The Vietnamese army withdraws from Cambodia, leaving Pol Pot and his depleted army north of Siem Reap
May 1993	The United Nations High Commissioner for Refugees oversees elections
June 1993	Results of elections endorsed by the UN Security Council; Hun Sen confirmed as prime minister
15 April 1998	Pol Pot dies of heart failure
October 2004	King Norodom Sihanouk retires from the throne; his son Samdech Norodom Sihamoni accedes to the throne peacefully

Context

The circumstances in Southeast Asia in the latter part of the 1970s were complex and largely impenetrable. Nonetheless, a response was demanded to the genocidal war pursued in secrecy in Cambodia from April 1975 until November 1978, when Vietnamese forces invaded Cambodia to destroy the Maoist Khmer Rouge. They remained until 1989. The Khmer Rouge, a centralized, Stalinist-type dictatorship led by Pol Pot, was supported by an inner core of intellectuals, some of whom had been educated in the West. They included Ieng Sary, Khieu Samphan and Son Sen.[1]

Khmer Rouge soldiers had previously attacked Viet Nam across their common border, and Viet Nam had responded once before. The November 1978 Vietnamese invasion of Cambodia, however, was in response to written and verbal requests for armed help from Cambodians led by Heng Samrin and Hun Sen, who had decided to break ranks and to oppose the tyranny of Pol Pot.

Viet Nam's military response had been influenced by the political and economic pressure exerted by the 300,000 refugees who had fled from Cambodia into Viet Nam during this period, coinciding with the outflow of Vietnamese "boat people". Most of the Cambodian refugees had been held in re-education camps, where they were guarded, fed, clothed, provided with medical services and, in some camps and to some degree, indoctrinated by Marxist Vietnamese. In the wake of the US war against Viet Nam (1963–1968), Viet Nam had become an international pariah. The legacy from the war in Viet Nam was a difficult one, including over 58,000 American deaths[2] and as many as 4 million Indo-Chinese deaths.[3] Moreover, although victorious in its war with the United States, Viet Nam was regarded as the arch-enemy of the US-led Western alliance. That alliance made political and diplomatic capital out of the exodus of the Vietnamese "boat people", moving quickly to provide succour and refuge to those fleeing by boat, canoe and raft across the South China Sea. By the same token, the alliance withheld assistance from those under Vietnamese occupation within Cambodia and from those within Viet Nam.

Alarmed by the extent of suffering that remained unaddressed, the Consortium for Cambodia was formed in 1979 by 33 NGOs drawn from a variety of countries and traditions, including Western Europe, North America and Australasia. Leading the initiative was Oxfam.[4] The Consortium secured an initial budget of US$40 million, which was more than Oxfam's worldwide budget. The Consortium was motivated by a commitment to assist people in Cambodia – the humanitarian imperative – notwithstanding the policies of the Western alliance.[5] The Consortium faced a daunting series of operational issues, whether logistical, institutional or political in nature, including the consequences of the secret bombing of Cambodia's "Ho Chi Minh trail" in the US war with Viet Nam.[6]

Operational issues

The *Oxford Dictionary of Historic Principles* defines "diplomacy" as "the management of international relations by negotiation carried out by Ambassadors or Envoys". Somewhat more cynically, but not unreasonably, it then offers Stubbs' definition of an ambassador as "[t]he man who was sent to lie abroad for the good of his country".

The problem for Cambodia in 1979 was that diplomacy had ceased to function as Cambodians tried to shake themselves free from the genocidal excesses of the Pol Pot regime. The Cold War dictated that UN agencies should not recognize the newly emerging regime of Heng Samrin because it was backed, seemingly, by Viet Nam, which was judged to be in the Soviet camp. However, being economically poor itself, Viet Nam was unable to underwrite the economy of Cambodia or the policies of Heng Samrin's government.

In 1979, European NGOs did not regard themselves as part of this equation. Their loyalty was to human need (humanitarianism) and not to Cold War ideology. Thus, after a period of 10 months when they tried to persuade their governments and the specialized agencies of the United Nations to respond to human need in Cambodia, the NGOs decided to act unilaterally. They needed to convince their publics, who were their donors, that a relief programme on the ground was feasible, open to reliable negotiation and would respond to the needs of suffering Khmers. Such a programme could proceed quite apart from international politics. People and their communities could be helped, while the diplomatic log-jam remained obdurate and immovable – a process that pushed humanitarian morality into the background. The dilemma for the UN agencies, of course, was that their funds were provided largely by the donor governments of the Western alliance.

The relief programme demanded constant, negotiated diplomacy from day one when the first relief aircraft flew into Cambodia's air space to land at its principal airport. This had been stripped by Pol Pot's forces of all landing technology, including even the passenger steps, as well as essential equipment such as the generator needed to re-fire any aircraft engine for take-off. Alternatives had to be painstakingly negotiated. From that juncture, everything sought by the Consortium on one side, and by the government on the other side (e.g. handwritten entry visas, press passes for journalists, hotel accommodation and security therein, freedom of travel in safe areas, vetting processes for journalist applicants, the size and nature of the proposed relief programme, how to cope with foreign evangelical NGOs, the Consortium's own control mechanisms consistent with the highest professional codes of conduct, as well as the government's own controls and oversight), had to be patiently negotiated with understanding and cultural sensitivity.

The first question for the Consortium leaders was which areas, starting with the capital city of Phnom Penh, were relatively safe for mounting a humanitarian relief programme. Secondly, what were the priorities within that programme? Thirdly, how could that programme grow to embrace major infrastructural priorities such as Phnom Penh's water supply and medical facilities – as well as seeds, hoes, water pumps and food aid? Fourthly, how could the Consortium monitor its own programme safely and to normal standards of managerial efficiency? Fifthly, what rules of the game would apply from the outset to the media, where and by whom? Sixthly, where would supplies be purchased from in a world divided by the Cold War? Finally, what relationships ought/could the Consortium have with Viet Nam and with neighbouring Thailand?

Against this background, each point of which had to be negotiated, humanitarian organizations in Cambodia faced a number of constraints. One was the requirement for a critical mass of aid capacity equal to the need on the ground. Another concerned the resistance of the United States and its allies to assistance provided to Cambodians under the authority of a government installed by Viet Nam and recognized by the Soviet bloc.

Given the unwillingness of the United States and its allies to respond to human need in Cambodia, one of the major preliminary issues to be addressed was to find an NGO or consortium of NGOs with sufficient operational capacity and political influence to mount an initiative. The core group proved to be a coalition that had been formed during the mid-1960s with representatives from the League of Red Cross and Red Crescent Societies (Licross) and other major voluntary agencies (volags), including Oxfam, Catholic Relief Services and the Lutheran World Federation, which also represented the World Council of Churches. The initiative for this coalition had lain with the League and Oxfam.

Early in 1978, UN Secretary-General Kurt Waldheim asked the Licross-Volag Committee on Disasters to receive his Under-Secretary-General Brian Urquhart to discuss aid to post-war Viet Nam. At its meeting in Geneva, the group received a shopping list running into hundreds of millions of dollars for capital projects, including roads, bridges, railways, airports, hydroelectric plants, harbours, reforestation schemes and huge population resettlement projects, all of which were outside the scope of NGOs. Nevertheless, the Committee agreed to look at the extent of human suffering in Viet Nam to see what it might do.

Accordingly, the head of the Consortium visited Saigon and Hanoi in 1978, with extensive field missions around both cities, including the Mekong delta, and then to the Chinese border north of Hanoi. Viet Nam's Marxist government provided a "minder" from Aidrecept, which was part of the Vietnamese Foreign Office and supplied a vehicle, interpreters, food and accommodation during the mission. Aidrecept would serve as focal point for any NGO activity that might ensue. During the three-week mission, the head of the Consortium drafted a paper at the request of the authorities defining the key characteristics of NGOs and how they might operate in Viet Nam. This paper would become the framework within which NGOs would function in future years.

The head of the Consortium was also invited by Foreign Minister Nguyen Co Thach to attend a special meeting of the diplomatic corps in the foreign ministry. In the presence of about 50 international diplomats, the foreign minister said:

We have noted, Mr. Walker, how at every meeting over the last fortnight, you have stressed the difficulty you face in responding to our needs in the light of adverse Western publicity surrounding the "boat people". We understand your dilemma but are surprised that at no point have you asked a single question about our own refugees from Cambodia. They number about 300,000 people. Nor have you asked any questions about the requests for intervention we have had from those Cambodians who oppose Pol Pot and his clique who have caused immense suffering in Cambodia, and who are responsible for this mass exodus. It far exceeds the boat people.

Turning to the diplomatic corps, the foreign minister made three points: first, that this refugee burden was intolerable; second, that, unless the international community decided by October 1978 to intervene in Cambodia to support the anti-Pol Pot forces, then – his third point – "Viet Nam will have no option but to invade Cambodia in response to human suffering and its consequences". These grim words were a warning to Western governments. No mention was made of the cross-border incursions by the Vietnamese into Cambodia from 1975. In a follow-up visit with Dr Thach, the head of the Consortium arranged for an NGO visit to the Cambodian refugee camps in Viet Nam to be undertaken by an Oxfam staffer who spoke Vietnamese.[7]

The response of the Licross-Volag Committee was two-fold. First, it encouraged Oxfam to accept the invitation to become operational in Viet Nam, re-establishing a field presence in North Viet Nam as had existed in South Viet Nam throughout the war with the United States.[8] Oxfam was the first post-war NGO to do so, and was soon followed by other NGOs. Second, the Committee explored the allegations about the outflow of Cambodian refugees flagged up by the Vietnamese foreign minister. It was known that something uniquely tragic was being enacted in Cambodia: that 600,000 Khmers had been killed in the 1970–1975 civil war, and that millions of displaced people were on the move inside Cambodia and across its national boundaries. Rumours were beginning to circulate about "Year Zero" under the bizarre policy pursued by the Khmer Rouge – in April 1975 its guerrilla troops had emptied Phnom Penh at gunpoint. In February 1976 *Le Monde* had published a series of articles by a French priest living in Cambodia, Father François Ponchaud, followed in 1977 by a book.[9]

If the first operational issue was the need for agency capacity to provide assistance, the second involved the political tangle that would make it difficult to do so. The tangle had elements of regional policies as well as international realpolitik.

The secretive and remote Cambodian leader, Pol Pot, held that only when all foreign influences were purged from society would the natural Cambodian Phoenix rise from the ashes, liberated to return to the mystical power and creativity (the "Angkar") that he claimed had inspired the magnificent fourteenth-century Angkor Wat civilization. The foreign influences he had in mind ranged across ideas, belief systems and ideology to their physical manifestation in religion, education, libraries, schools, universities, forms of marriage and procreation, the economy and the (non-Khmer) physical artefacts such as the motor car, the television, the sewing machine, the factory, the bank note and the refrigerator. The "Angkar" became the mystical authority legitimizing the policy of repression and destruction. The essence of this thesis had earned one of the Khmer Rouge leaders, Khieu Samphan, his doctorate from the Sorbonne, conferring the stamp of approval from Western academia. Once it had been refined in the jungles, this thesis was implemented by the Khmer Rouge on the ground from 1975 onwards with a relentless ferocity of nightmare proportions. This form of human enslavement is so grotesque that it seems to remain unrecognized as a category even today.[10]

Before 1975 there were 8 million Khmer people. Of these, 1.5 million were killed in the insane regime of terror after the population of Phnom Penh had been forced at gunpoint to walk to the countryside to become the "new people". Henceforth, they would be rural labourers. The city infrastructure was dismantled, stone by stone, book by book, car by car, riel by riel. People living in the north and those living in the south were swapped over by decree and family units were broken up. The concept and practice of marriage were banned. Love was replaced by party and country. The "Organization" became responsible for children. Men and women were selected at random by the state to procreate. All mentally and most physically disabled civilians were murdered. Of the 450 medically qualified staff that functioned prior to Pol Pot, only 50 or so managed to survive in the country, mainly disguised as peasants.

When I first entered Phnom Penh in 1979, a city that had grown to house an estimated 5 million people now contained at most 15,000 people, made up of soldiers, civil servants and a handful of Vietnamese advisers. To walk its deserted streets, catching discarded and useless bank notes blowing through the air like lost leaves in the wind, was a Kafkaesque experience. Many pavements were lined with banana trees planted by the regime to provide a source of fruit to city dwellers – but this imaginative idea paled somewhat when we learned that more often than not a human corpse was buried beneath each tree as fertilizer. In Cambodia fact proved to be stranger than fiction.

In November 1978, responding to the destabilizing impact of Cambodian refugees at home and to a plea from middle-ranking Khmer Rouge cadre leaders such as Heng Samrin, Hun Sen and Kom So Mol, Viet Nam invaded Cambodia. Another factor was the unambiguous refusal of the international community to answer Viet Nam's plea for help. A terrible war of attrition ensued. The retreating Khmer Rouge army implemented a "scorched earth" policy that was total in effect – from the systematic and widespread destruction of villagers' fishing nets to the dismantling of Phnom Penh's Roman Catholic cathedral and many Muslim and Buddhist temples.

In 1979, President Heng Samrin's government was installed in Phnom Penh by Viet Nam. Its writ kept pace with the front-line of the Vietnamese forces as they pursued the retreating Khmer Rouge, who gradually fell back to Pailin in the Cardamon mountains and then north to Siem Reap province. Their final redoubt did not fall until April 1998 when Pol Pot died. They had remained a thorn in the flesh for the Heng Samrin and Hun Sen governments for 19 years. As a result, the questions of sovereignty and what constitutes a government became points of dispute between UN agencies, supported by their donor governments, on one side and the NGO Consortium, supported by its publics, on the other. The former saw the lack of political legitimacy of the authorities as a reason to withhold assistance; the latter sought to mount a humanitarian response to human need regardless of international politics.

Obstacles and opportunities

International political opposition to the Vietnamese-installed communist regime in Cambodia created formidable obstacles for international humanitarian organizations seeking to act on their mandates. Within a month of the takeover by the putative Heng Samrin government, a covert political agenda designed to frustrate work on the ground had emerged. It led to a host of difficulties for the Consortium. Among the obstacles were the lack of political acceptability of established aid agencies to the Cambodian authorities and, conversely, the lack of acceptability of the putative government itself to the United States and its allies.

International law requires that relief agencies respect international boundaries and present themselves in any country requiring humanitarian assistance with the approval of the host government. The stamping of a passport symbolizes this approval: without it, one is illegal, regardless of rank. Reciprocating the US-led refusal to recognize the legality of the Phnom Penh government, the authorities would not extend that welcome to the two key agencies of Western donor countries – UNICEF, designated the "lead" agency by the United Nations, and the International Committee of the Red Cross (ICRC). Conversely, the Cambodian authorities were designated a "puppet" regime of the invading Vietnamese army. As a consequence, the UNICEF and ICRC delegations in Phnom Penh were in effect held prisoners in their hotel, forbidden to travel or to implement any aid programme until the political log-jam was broken.

Bearing in mind the refugees flooding into Viet Nam and Thailand and the horror stories beginning to trickle out of Cambodia, the Licross-Volag Committee in Geneva faced a dilemma. Its allegiance was to suffering humanity, not to the governments of the Cold War. For 10 months (1978–1979) its members had read reports from the Red Cross as well as by the British academic Malcolm Caldwell (who had gained access to Cambodia only to be murdered in 1978 in his Phnom Penh hotel) and by scholars Elizabeth Becker and Richard Dudman. They had lobbied governments, the European Economic Community (EEC) and the United Nations in favour of humanitarian action on the ground. The United States remained obdurate and was supported by the United Kingdom: recognition would not be extended to another Marxist puppet government whose writ extended just beyond its capital city and could be extended further only by virtue of the invading army of Viet Nam. This argument had a compelling political logic, but it did nothing to help the suffering people of Cambodia.

In May 1979, with the full backing of the members of the Licross-Volag Committee in Geneva and of the EEC's powerful and widely representative NGO Liaison Committee formed in 1975, Oxfam formally took a decision to engage in Cambodia. By August it was ready to hire a jumbo-jet transport plane in Luxembourg, fill it with aid supplies and fly it into Phnom Penh under the Oxfam flag. As noted above, Pochentong airport had been ravaged by the Khmer Rouge army. All its equipment had been destroyed and so the pilot and Consortium crew had to over-fly the airport to let the heavily armed soldiers on the ground see them plainly as being unarmed. On landing, without knowing the Khmer language, they had to explain who they were, what they were carrying, offer some reassurance as to their interest in humanitarianism, negotiate how their supplies could be off-loaded, how their passports might be stamped giving permission to be there, how they might themselves get from the aircraft to the ground (15–20 feet without a ladder), how prior to take-off they might re-fire the aircraft's engines in the absence of a generator, give some idea of their potential support for the new government and its people, and finally emphasize that their independence of government was axiomatic. The act itself was humanitarian diplomacy with a sledge hammer. In view of the claim by the international community that any aid sent to Cambodia could not be distributed and would almost certainly find its way to Viet Nam, Oxfam's senior field officer was directed to negotiate with the Heng Samrin government so that Oxfam would be able to distribute and monitor relief supplies according to its normal standards of oversight and security. Indeed, further inputs would depend on the success or failure of that requirement. Those negotiations took place immediately with the authorities – to the satisfaction of both.

Oxfam spent three weeks assessing the human misery and supervising the distribution of the initial shipment to camps and villages dotted in and around Phnom Penh. Oxfam staff met and exchanged intelligence with the UNICEF and ICRC delegates. Oxfam also liaised with journalist John Pilger, whose article "The Killing Fields of Cambodia" in September 1979 alerted the world to what had been going on.[11] On behalf of their New York and Geneva headquarters, the UNICEF and ICRC delegates expressed anger at Oxfam's action, which, they claimed, cut the ground from under their efforts to negotiate access. Speaking privately as individuals, however, they approved, lamenting that Cold War politics were inhibiting them from making the humanitarian response that they knew ought to be made.

Based on this initial experience, a small Oxfam team was sent to supervise aid distribution and assess the scale of the longer-term operation. Negotiations took place with Hun Sen, elected Cambodia's foreign minister in January 1979, and the minister for agriculture, Kom So Mol. A verbal agreement was struck and implemented immediately. More aid was called for and the plans offered by Kom So Mol in respect of seeds and food supplies were forwarded to Bangkok and from there to Oxford, and then distributed to the Consortium members for approval. Another flight followed within 72 hours.

On arrival, three things were apparent. Massive external media coverage triggered by Pilger's "Killing Fields" article had alerted European and North American populations to the disaster and its scale, stimulating an enormous public response. Second, the refusal of the Phnom Penh government to allow the UN relief operation to begin its work would inevitably cause a reaction, with pressure placed on NGOs by their governments and the United Nations to fall into line. Third, there was a dispute among Oxfam staff about the extent to which a large-scale famine might be under way, for which neither food nor seed grain was available. The fact that an Oxfam staff member had initially spoken of famine conditions was later modified to hunger and malnutrition following a mission to Siem Reap and Battambang escorted by the Vietnamese military, which failed to find widespread famine. This episode led to some questioning by the international media of Oxfam's professionalism. The dispute was a gift to opponents of humanitarian action in the United States and the United Kingdom.

Although there was evidence that the US government was working to frustrate the NGO-led aid response, on occasion the connections were more subtle. In an effort to cut costs and shipment time, the Consortium held talks with the government of Singapore seeking permission to purchase relief supplies in Singapore and to hire open barges that a powerful sea-going tug would tow across the South China Sea and up the Mekong through Viet Nam, and so to Phnom Penh. Both the Singapore government and the Viet Nam government agreed to this plan. A few days into the operation, however, the stevedores went on strike. In subsequent negotiations with their leaders, it transpired that "strange men" had asked to meet them. They had argued that the supplies were not going to Cambodia at all, but to Viet Nam – Singapore's enemy. "Strange men" meant non-Singaporean, white men who had not been seen before, or since. The supply line was eventually re-established, but the three-week delay proved costly in human terms.

Politics also swirled around the Consortium's decision to purchase rice for Cambodia from China as well as from Thailand, Italy, India and Singapore. The initial year's relief programme was based on the assumption that, if the peasant farmers of Cambodia could become self-sufficient in seed rice from the first harvest, the malnutrition problem would be capable of resolution. China was the only rice exporter with available stocks of the variety that was most acceptable to the Cambodian palate. But not only was China Maoist and part of the perceived "enemy" of the international community; it was in armed dispute with Viet Nam on its northern borders. Following negotiations with Oxfam, China agreed to supply rice provided it was off-loaded in Bangkok and then re-loaded at the purchaser's cost before onward shipment to Phnom Penh. This way China felt that most people need not know it was the supplier.

Almost immediately, two stories appeared in the Asian press. The first reported that the food grain had been poisoned by the Chinese so as to embarrass Vietnamese overlords: those who ate it would die. The second reported that the seed grain had been heated to make it impossible to germinate. Would history show that the Consortium had been guilty of distributing poisoned food aid? Would an entire year's crop be lost because the seeds were dead? Neither eventuality materialized. However, aid agencies must beware of being caught in such crossfire when the humanitarian imperative encounters high-stake political interests.

Another example of the risks to aid agencies involved the alleged abuse of the Consortium's fleet of 300 white trucks, purchased from funds donated by UK children in response to an appeal on BBC children's television programme "Blue Peter". Cambodia had only 48 trucks following the Khmer Rouge retreat and, anticipating charges of mis-use or corruption if Cambodian trucks were involved in the aid effort, the Consortium had each of its own vehicles painted white and boldly numbered. In 1980, a reporter in Saigon broadcast on BBC radio that he had just seen proof positive of the redirection of Consortium aid (textile machinery) from Cambodia to Viet Nam carried by a Blue Peter truck and seen loading at a factory in Saigon. Upon checking, however, it was proved that the textile machinery had been mistakenly addressed by the Japanese donor to Saigon. Its intended destination was a factory in Cambodia that the Khmer Rouge had destroyed but which was the sole producer of cotton cloth in traditional Khmer colours and design, which was needed to replace the black pyjamas imposed on the population by Pol Pot. Far from abducting the aid, the Vietnamese authorities had advised Phnom Penh to come and collect it.

The effectiveness and credibility of the relief programme were proved in several ways. For example, in September 1979, the government appealed urgently to the Consortium to find a supply of Khmer script typewriters for official use because all typewriters had been destroyed by Pol Pot. It seemed an impossible task: who other than Khmers would manufacture Khmer script? Yet, without Khmer script, how could the government function? Oxfam discovered a small supplier in India who had once traded in Phnom Penh and who could supply redundant machines to get the infrastructure going again.

Another example involved the Australian navy. Armed pirates in the South China Sea had discovered that picking off small groups of Vietnamese boat people could bring rich returns as refugees exchanged their life savings for small-volume, portable riches – gold, precious stones and ivory. Piracy became a refined and established trade. How vulnerable were aid convoys, with massive barges full of food and medical supplies, machinery and agricultural inputs? In fact, the Consortium's barges were never attacked or boarded. The Consortium discovered after the fact that someone had ordered the Australian navy to monitor its sailings from Singapore and, using tracking radar, to remain over the horizon out of sight, but then to heave into view if pirates threatened to close in on the barges.

In short, humanitarian organizations in major emergencies face a variety of risks, particularly in settings where the political stakes are high. These demand considerable anticipation, shrewdness and resourcefulness on the part of aid personnel. But, above all, functional integrity is essential. Moreover, as the Cambodia experience confirms, what appear to be obstacles may prove to be opportunities.

Negotiations

The NGO Consortium that sought to mount a major relief effort in Viet Nam-controlled Cambodia faced a series of difficulties in negotiating access for NGO personnel. The fact that it was proceeding in the face of the active opposition by key governments and without the support of humanitarian institutions heightened the difficulties encountered.

Foreign Minister Hun Sen took an active role in the 1979 negotiations and sought to advance a number of objectives. Minister for Agriculture Kom So Mol likewise drafted and then negotiated the costed plan for seeds, agricultural implements, water pumps and food aid with Consortium officials. The most difficult issue proved to be the location of village clinics. These were basic to the country's healthcare system but the government would have preferred them to be focused on hospitals in Phnom Penh and other major towns.[12]

Hun Sen also insisted that the government in Phnom Penh must be recognized by the Consortium as legitimate and as the government of Cambodia. After all, it performed sovereign functions: its troops held the airport, river and seaports; its officials examined all passports and stamped them, or, more accurately (because Pol Pot had destroyed the official stamps), wrote in long-hand in Khmer script permission to stay. Second, and most importantly, no relief supplies were to be delivered across the so-called "land bridge" – the Thai/Cambodian border. That would make aid a political act of destabilization because hungry Khmer peasants would flock to the border for food. Aid should either be flown direct to Phnom Penh's Pochentong airport or be sailed up the Mekong River through Viet Nam to Phnom Penh's port. To do otherwise risked destabilizing his government by limiting its writ to Phnom Penh. Later, the Consortium negotiated permission to use the southern seaport of Sihanoukville. Transport and distribution questions were complicated by differences between French colonial maps and traditional Cambodian maps.[13]

The Consortium took the position that international law required that aid should not cross borders willy-nilly but should be agreed with the authority in power. If air flights to Phnom Penh and the Mekong River route were the negotiated and authorized routes, the Consortium should stick to them. Later, many organizations – UN and non-governmental, but not the Consortium – disregarded this convention. Some engaged in a cynical attempt further to destabilize the population north of Tonle Sap Lake, thereby hoping to demonstrate that the Phnom Penh government's writ did not cover all of Cambodia and hence that it was not the government of Cambodia. Illegal food distribution centres were set up on and across the Thai border, encroaching on Cambodian sovereignty as far inland as Battambang. A host of border "refugee" camps were established/tolerated by the Thai authorities. Many were controlled by armed Khmer Rouge soldiers. Their purpose was essentially political, acting as a magnet to hungry people living in the Cambodian hinterland who were then indoctrinated inside the camps as part of the food distribution process. The Thai military controlled all activity on the border for 12 years.[14] The arrangements allowed anti-Cambodia politicians to argue that the government in Phnom Penh had little control outside the city limits and was not therefore really a government at all. From such a position, covert operations could also be mounted in favour of the Khmer Rouge and against the "puppet" regime in Phnom Penh. Although the Consortium's officials held talks with the Thai government to stop aid from being passed illegally across the border, they were wholly unsuccessful in this respect. In other areas, the Thai government helped the Consortium on numerous occasions.

After initial discussions with Foreign Minister Hun Sen, the head of the Consortium drafted an understanding along the lines agreed, which was signed the following day by them both. The Foreign Office typed the agreement, unaltered, in Khmer, French and English.[15] The international relief log-jam had been broken, not by the agreement itself, but by the subsequent experiential proof that humanitarian aid could be securely sent and distributed inside Cambodia. The terms provided for independent supervision by NGOs of the distribution of aid, contradicting the view of UNICEF, the ICRC, Western governments and sections of the media that aid would be siphoned off to Viet Nam. Each NGO member of the Consortium accepted the monitoring and other obligations, which were carried out in detail first in and around Phnom Penh and then, as the Vietnamese pushed the Khmer Rouge towards the north and west, in an ever-widening arc. None of this was easy and there were daily frustrations. Language was a major problem, so were the war and its aftermath – how close ought staff to get to the fighting lines? For years Khmers had been forbidden to take decisions or to act on their own initiative. The transition to a more normal society made the Consortium's task of monitoring and even agreeing aid flows at once difficult, frustrating and daunting. But progress was made. On-site monitoring embraced the crucial rebuilding of the water treatment facility for Phnom Penh and the city's textile plant for the manufacture of traditional Khmer cloth. The rehabilitated railway from Phnom Penh to Kompong Speu was used immediately to distribute food, tools, water pumps and seeds to peasant farmers and for setting up village health clinics. Modern, high-capacity water pumps were installed to repair the complex and historic system of dykes and dams destroyed by Pol Pot during his retreat.

The integrity of the humanitarian operation depended upon close and continued scrutiny by the Consortium NGOs. Following the original agreement with Hun Sen, NGO officials were able to negotiate the right to assess needs as far as the war would allow and to travel with aid supplies as they were distributed directly to the people – again insofar as the war and its aftermath allowed. The Cambodian authorities accepted that the strength of the NGOs lay in their independence and integrity. Their credibility in the eyes of the British and the broader international public hinged on their unfettered access to people in need and the regular updating of their constituencies. The process was difficult and time consuming, but little by little it worked. Certainly by early 1980 a measure of genuine trust had been established between the government and the Consortium. The Consortium was able to disprove on the ground the arguments advanced publicly and in discussions by the US State Department and recycled by the UK Foreign Office justifying their prevailing policy of non-intervention. Human suffering could be relieved efficiently, despite the political context within which it took place.

The Consortium also took steps to ensure that its members respected the apolitical approach that it had negotiated. The Consortium refused membership to certain evangelical Christian relief operations, mainly from the United States and Australia, which soon arrived with transport aircraft and telecommunications equipment that they erected without permission. However, so huge were their budgets that the Phnom Penh government chose to ignore their covert operations or judged itself to be immune to the results.

As the Consortium mounted its operations in the autumn of 1979, an international black propaganda campaign sought to discredit the Consortium in general and Oxfam in particular. Recurrent articles in the international press lampooned the NGOs as innocents abroad, manipulated by the wicked communists, disloyal to the best interests of the Western democracies, and unable to understand the complexities of international aid and the huge political issues said to be at stake. Despite the criticism, however, public support not only remained rock solid, it increased. The churches, universities, trades unions and general public rallied behind the NGOs' work in packed meetings, in correspondence with newspapers, and in sacrificial giving. According to one survey, over 80 per cent of the UK population supported Oxfam's work.[16] People trusted the members of the Consortium rather than the media or the politicians.

Complicating matters further, in September 1979, Hun Sen made the agreement with the Consortium the model for the United Nations, the ICRC and other aid agencies wishing to work in Cambodia. When the United Nations and the ICRC demurred, Hun Sen castigated the international agencies for playing politics when human needs were clear and announced his intention to expel both UNICEF and the ICRC forthwith. The head of the Consortium interceded with Hun Sen on grounds that the minister was making the Consortium's job impossible. NGOs could never repair Cambodia's entire infrastructure alone, or secure the millions of tons of food aid that would be needed should the first harvest fail. Should he persist with the expulsions, the Consortium would have to consider suspending its own work. Hun Sen repeated his threat but there were no expulsions and that is where the matter ended.

Indeed, in the coming months UN agencies and the ICRC signed their own agreements with the authorities, modelled on that of the Consortium. Regular UN pledging conferences were held and programmes were launched that soon dwarfed those of the Consortium.

Wider implications

Members of the Consortium took satisfaction that they were able to break the political impasse that had stymied humanitarian assistance to people in Cambodia, while retaining their own integrity and professionalism throughout. The Consortium remains, arguably, the most successful Consortium in the history of NGOs. Indeed, the pivotal role played by NGOs in 1979 was something of a harbinger of the more prominent role they would assume in the post–Cold War era. As NGOs "came of age", they would be consulted increasingly by governments and multilateral agencies and would play a growing part in the implementation of humanitarian activities. They would be sought out for membership of humanitarian activities and invited to join official delegations and needs assessment missions.

However, their increased prominence was not an unmitigated blessing. In the decades since the NGO Consortium responded to the genocide in

Cambodia, the world has witnessed similar atrocities in the Balkans, Rwanda, the Congo, Afghanistan, the West Bank/Israel, Darfur, Burma and northern Uganda. During these years the clear distinction between the role of the NGOs and that of governments and UN agencies has become blurred. Although the higher profile carries advantages to governments and the United Nations in terms of their public constituencies and opens extra funding to NGOs, NGOs' independence has been severely compromised. NGOs today are, if anything, less likely to be able to respond to new crises as they did in Cambodia. But, surely, the loss of revenues that would accompany a distancing of NGOs from governments is worthwhile in terms of their capacity to respond positively and ethically to genuine humanitarian need.

Even the wealthiest of NGOs can deal only in "penny packets" of aid compared with the United Nations, the World Bank or the bilateral agencies. But the scale of cash revenues is not of prime importance. Instead, acting catalytically is: articulating humanitarianism as a kind of conscience to governments, multinationals and the general public remains the best role for NGOs. NGOs can also experiment with new ideas in the field. Historically these have included, for example, oral rehydration therapy, the Oxfam biscuit, mass-produced generic medicines for the poor, and "barefoot" doctors and nurses. Each is a humanitarian act whose implementation depended on diplomacy. NGOs can help to educate their public constituencies in matters of humanitarianism in the twenty-first century – as the success of the *New Internationalist* magazine, used worldwide by teachers today, testifies. Evidence of their ability to cooperate with competing NGOs is required, therefore, if humanitarian diplomacy is to be as effective as it could be.

In retrospect, the Consortium's experience confirms that humanitarian initiatives that challenge perceived political interests can expect to be drawn into the political cross-fire. The week before Christmas 1979, in an effort to counteract the propaganda onslaught, Oxfam convened a major press conference in London to update the media on developments and to answer concerns. The turnout was large. Senior journalists, including John Pilger and William Shawcross, were in attendance.[17] The questioning was intense. Afterwards, the senior *Financial Times* correspondent confided privately that the high turnout and the repetitive nature of the questions raised were not accidental: "We were all summoned to the Foreign Office yesterday to be briefed on Cambodia. What you have told us is the opposite of what they told us. They told us you cannot freely distribute aid, that the Vietnamese are in control, that most aid ends up in Saigon, that you cannot travel outside Phnom Penh, and are not free to supervise your operation. You have said the opposite. All of us now must decide which of you is telling the truth." Most endorsed the Consortium's version. The *Sunday Times* published both stories, leaving its readers to choose between the two.

In a not dissimilar episode, the late Alistair Cooke's Christmas Sunday broadcast on BBC radio in 1979 included an attack on Oxfam, citing its alleged naivety and foolishness, despite its good intentions. A long-time supporter of Oxfam, who on more than one occasion had lent the NGO his name for fund-raising purposes, Cooke said he had formed his negative judgement on the advice of a former senior US State Department official. The UK's ambassador to the UN Security Council, Sir Anthony Parsons, would later express his personal satisfaction at the path-finding work of the Consortium, in effect disassociating himself from the propaganda campaign.[18] Clearly, the Consortium's humanitarian undertaking was the object of high-level political consternation and active opposition in some quarters but of appreciation in others.

Also in retrospect, the agreement between the Consortium and the Cambodian authorities merits review. Was it adequate to ensure effective access to people in need for international agencies, or did it concede too much to the authorities? Here the key point involved the Consortium's agreement not to use a "land bridge" for bringing aid into Cambodia from Thailand. Oxfam itself insisted, however, that it was free to help in refugee camps inside Thailand, provided it did so from Bangkok and with that government's permission. It allocated over £250,000 to that programme – a massive grant then for an NGO.[19] Other NGOs did likewise. Although some (UN) face was lost, the humanitarian-driven policy worked.

Nonetheless, a book published in 1986 by Maggie Black, UNICEF's press officer, held that the Consortium "agreed as a condition of a relief effort not to feed Kampucheans up on the Thai border under the protection of the [Khmer Rouge]".[20] As explained above, members of the Consortium, including Oxfam, provided substantial amounts of aid to refugees in carefully selected camps on the Thai side of the border, although the Consortium itself respected, impeccably, the agreement not to mount a cross-border aid operation from Thailand into Cambodia. The issue, in fact, was never one of "aid up on the border"; rather it was one of "aid across the border". The distinction is crucial. Black's assertion that the Consortium's decision to work in Cambodia undermined the opportunities for UNICEF and the ICRC to do so was contested by the Consortium, which pointed out that the other aid agencies made their own judgements about the conditions of their engagement. In 1992, in another publication, Black would call the Cambodia initiative Oxfam's "finest hour".[21]

In the early 1970s Cambodia was a failed state. Today, states in crisis include many hot-spots around the world. Complicit states not only condemn their own human populations to immense suffering, they represent, for one reason or another, a threat to world peace and global security. Somehow professional humanitarianism has to cope with these challenges in a special way. Perhaps an élite corps of highly experienced diplomats should be designated to focus on such states and to recommend to the UN Secretary-General, and through that office to the member states, how the world community can manage such situations without compromising international humanitarian law or damaging global security. Adequate support budgets would be essential and the best of sustainable development techniques would need to be implemented.

Meanwhile, UN agencies have tried to learn some of the lessons of Cambodia. The Executive Director of UNICEF, James P. Grant, appalled at the sidelining of the United Nations' lead agency in Cambodia in 1979, set in train policies designed to ensure that UNICEF would never again fail the children it was created to protect. Those changes have, by and large, held up. The notable exceptions are the 5,000 child soldiers – some under 10 years of age – taken by the Tamil Tigers in Sri Lanka, and the thousands of boy and girl soldiers abducted over a period of 18 years in northern Uganda to become part of the notorious Lord's Resistance Army.[22]

For Cambodia itself, 25 years on, there are grounds for hope. UN-supervised elections in May 1993 introduced a genuine element of democracy to Cambodia. The economy is beginning to grow – although Cambodia has not recovered its status as the rice bowl of its region. Modern Cambodia is an active member of the Association of Southeast Asian Nations – strengthening the whole of Southeast Asia.

In 1998, Pol Pot died, and a process of peace accompanied by a draining away of violence, albeit besmirched by widespread corruption, offers grounds for hope. There remains the potential for a trial whereby remaining Khmer Rouge leaders such as Khieu Samphan and Duch Kang Tek will be brought to task. In October 2004, King Norodom Sihanouk abdicated as Cambodia's God King (a non-hereditary kingship) but, with the approval of the Hun Sen government and on the recommendation of the Throne Council, his son Samdech Norodom Sihamoni acceded peacefully to the throne. This augers well for the future, building on those first faltering footsteps taken in 1979.

Notes

1. David P. Chandler, *Brother Number One: A Political Biography of Pol Pot*, Boulder, CO: Westview Press, 1992; also Henry Kamm, *Cambodia*, New York: Arcade Publishing, 1998; Serge Thion, *Watching Cambodia*, Bangkok: White Lotus, 1993.

2. Robert S. McNamara, *In Retrospect*, New York: Times Books/Random House, 1995.
3. Noam Chomsky, *Rogue States*, London: Pluto Press, 2000, p. 169.
4. The original Oxfam appointments to the Consortium were myself as Chair and the lead field representative; Secretary – Roger Newton; Treasurer – Hugh Belshaw; Field Director – Malcolm Harper; Disasters Officer and Water Engineer – Jim Howard; Medical Advisor – Tim Lusty. The Cambodian government contact was Men Near Sopeak, who today is Communications Director of the Cambodian Red Cross. The Cambodian minister who liaised with the Consortium was the Canadian-educated Kom So Mol. Today he is Hun Sen's link to the Royal Palace. The Viet Nam liaison officer in Phnom Penh was Mr Nhan of the Vietnamese foreign ministry.
5. William Shawcross, *Quality of Mercy*, London: Simon & Schuster, 1984, offers a different interpretation of the Consortium, but also see Thion's critique of the Shawcross analysis in appendix 2 of *Watching Cambodia*, and Chomsky's *Rogue States*.
6. Christopher Hitchens, *The Trial of Henry Kissinger*, London: Verso, 2001, pp. 34–40.
7. The Oxfam staffer was Helen Stevens.
8. Andrew Clark was the resident Oxfam field director for the whole of Viet Nam. During the war he operated in the border region, travelling around by bicycle.
9. François Ponchaud, *Cambodge Annee Zero*, London: Penguin Books, 1978.
10. Kevin Bales, *Disposable People*, Berkeley: University of California Press, 1999.
11. John Pilger, "The Killing Fields of Cambodia", *Daily Mirror*, 12 September 1979.
12. Harish C. Mehta and Julie B. Mehta, *Hun Sen: Strongman of Cambodia*, Singapore: Graham Brash, 1999.
13. Thion, *Watching Cambodia*, p. 73.
14. For a discussion of humanitarian dilemmas posed by the border camps, see Mark Frohardt, Diane Paul and Larry Minear, *Protecting Human Rights: The Challenge to Humanitarian Organisations*, Providence, RI: Watson Institute, 1999.
15. "Proposal for an NGO Consortium to provide food, medical, agricultural relief, and other aid to the people of Kampuchea (Cambodia)", 17 October 1979, signed by Hun Sen for the People's Revolutionary Council of Kampuchea and Brian Walker for the Consortium.
16. Dr W. Davies of the Manchester School of Business Studies and an Oxfam trustee surveyed and advised the extent of public interest.
17. Pilger and Shawcross represent the two extremes of media attitudes to Cambodia in the 1979–1985 period.
18. Occasional meetings with Brian Walker in New York in 1982 and in London in 1985.
19. Josephine Raynal, *Political Pawns*, Oxford: Refugee Studies Programme, Queen Elizabeth House, 1989.
20. Maggie Black, *The Children and the Nations*, New York: UNICEF, 1986, p. 392.
21. Maggie Black, *A Cause for Our Times*, Oxford: Oxfam, 1992, p. 235.
22. See, for example, Susan Makay and Dyan Mazurana, "Where Are the Girls?", Rights and Democracy, Montreal, Canada, 2004.

7

Negotiating with the Taliban

Antonio Donini

This chapter deals with the United Nations' efforts to negotiate humanitarian access and space with the Taliban, the de facto rulers of most of Afghanistan from 1996 to September 2001. I examine the constraints and opportunities encountered by the United Nations and the wider assistance community. The Taliban period coincided with innovative attempts by humanitarian actors, under the leadership of the United Nations, to operate in a more coherent and principled manner than in other crisis countries. I show how this more unitary approach initially strengthened the hand of the United Nations in its negotiations with the Taliban but led to a stalemate later on. Conversely, ad hoc or uncoordinated negotiations allowed the Taliban to manipulate the relationship with the aid community to their advantage. Some lessons of wider relevance are identified: the advantages of having a clear negotiating posture and strategy but also the structural limitations of negotiating with an abusive regime whose ideological and practical frames of reference were at loggerheads with those of the United Nations and the international community. The chapter shows the advantages of quiet diplomacy over public posturing and of "duck-and-weave" approaches over direct confrontation. Finally, I highlight the tension between local and HQ-driven negotiations and argue that the latter often fail because too much static – political issues with no direct relevance to the negotiation at hand – interferes in the communication between the parties.

Context

The Afghan crisis spans a quarter-century – from the Soviet invasion in December 1979 to the emergence, since the attacks of 11 September 2001, of an embattled externally supported regime seeking peace amongst the spoils of war. During this period, humanitarian action remained a constant, although its ability to provide assistance and protection to those in need – whose numbers have ranged from 3 million to over 10 million – has ebbed and flowed according to the vagaries of conflict, external intervention and the international community's fickle attention span. Humanitarian action in Afghanistan thus has a long history, which has been affected by, and has intersected with, the political, military, human rights and socio-economic dimensions of the crisis. As in other contexts, humanitarian action itself has been more or less principled, politicized or instrumentalized depending on the interests of superpowers, donors and local actors as well as the humanitarian agencies' ability to orchestrate a coherent and coordinated response.[1]

The negotiation of humanitarian access was high on the United Nations' agenda from the moment it appeared on the Afghan scene after the UN-brokered Geneva Accords of April 1988, which set a timetable for the Soviet withdrawal and were supposed to usher in period of peace and reconstruction. The first steps were diplomatic in form but distinctly non-traditional in substance: in July 1988, the first UN Coordinator for Afghanistan, Sadruddin Aga Khan, negotiated a "humanitarian consensus" with the Kabul government and the various mujahedin factions.[2] Through this formal undertaking to allow the United Nations – and,

Time line of the Afghan crisis	
December 1979	Soviet intervention
April 1988	Geneva peace accords
February 1989	Last Soviet troops leave Afghanistan
April 1992	Fall of the Najibullah Soviet-backed regime
1992–1996	Civil war; triumph of warlordism
Autumn 1994	First operations of Taliban in southern Afghanistan
September 1996	Taliban enter Kabul; control two-thirds of the country
1996–1998	Taliban extend grip on west and north of the country
October 2001	Collapse of Taliban regime
December 2001	Bonn Agreement; transitional government established

by extension, the non-governmental organizations (NGOs) – to operate throughout the country on the basis of need, the government gave implicit recognition that the United Nations could work on both sides. This was a ground-breaking agreement; in previous crises humanitarian assistance had in all but a handful of cases formally been limited to affected population groups who had crossed into neighbouring countries.

The "consensus" covered arrangements for working cross-border from neighbouring countries and cross-line from government- to mujahedin-held territory and vice versa. There were provisions for giving both sides advance notice when missions entered the country or crossed lines. With a few basic precautions – never go anywhere unannounced; respect the "no leap-frogging principle"[3] – the United Nations obtained reasonably good access by road or air to most parts of the country. Moving staff and humanitarian goods cross-line – e.g. from warehouses in government-held cities to mujahedin-controlled rural areas – became routine. It was not always easy, and of course both sides wanted to manipulate or take advantage of the assistance, but by and large the rules of the game were respected. One of the rules, respected by all save a handful of fundamentalist commanders (and their non-Afghan minders), was "do no harm to foreign aid workers".

The "consensus" also established the humanitarian credentials of the United Nations. These had been tarnished, in the view of the Pakistan-based international NGOs operating cross-border inside Afghanistan, by the fact that the United Nations had retained a presence in Kabul, where it implemented a handful of assistance projects in cooperation with the government, throughout the Soviet occupation. The United Nations was seen initially as "pro-Kabul", whereas the NGOs had developed close links with mujahedin groups (and the Pakistani secret services who controlled access to the border), and were thus seen as affiliated with the "muj" cause. Over time, the NGOs also benefited from the "consensus" as they started to see the advantages of the facilities and the opportunities for expanded humanitarian action provided by the United Nations: access by air to remote places, access for humanitarian commodities through the then USSR to northern Afghanistan, warehousing, office and residential facilities in the cities – a vast improvement over travel by horse and donkey from Pakistan, pressures from abusive and manipulative commanders and insalubrious accommodation in flea-infested mujahedin bases.

One of the paradoxes of humanitarian action in Afghanistan is the diminishing ability, over time, of humanitarian agencies to access populations in need. Things started to deteriorate after the fall of the Najibullah regime in April 1992. The ideological stakes of the *jihad* against the Soviets disappeared and the war became a brutal internecine struggle for power. Humanitarian work became more difficult because of the confusion, shifting alliances, growing volatility and insecurity. After their sudden appearance on the Afghan scene in late 1994, the Taliban, using terror tactics, brought a modicum of stability in the areas they controlled but also a change in one of the unwritten rules of Afghan war. Unlike their various predecessors who did not interfere too much with the movements of humanitarians, the Taliban were much more prone to deny access to populations controlled by their enemies. As a result, humanitarian work became much more difficult and the need for a negotiating framework more urgent.

Operational issues

This section analyses the environment in which negotiations took place during the period in which the Taliban controlled most of the country, the different positions within the aid community on how to deal with the Taliban and the negotiating framework that was eventually put in place.

During the Taliban years,[4] negotiating access to areas or groups in need was always high on the agenda of the UN Coordinator for Assistance to Afghanistan and a frequent source of frustration for UN agencies, NGOs and donors alike. Unlike the "cross-border" years, and the subsequent period of internecine mujahedin fighting, humanitarian space became tenuous in many areas and deliberately under attack in others. The Taliban's predecessors had accepted humanitarian actors as relatively neutral and impartial players. Assistance was not a factor in the war or something they should fight over. For the Taliban, however, the targeting of civilians and the denial of access and humanitarian assistance became integral parts of their war strategy, as we shall see below.

During the gestational period, from the Taliban's first skirmishes around Kandahar in late 1994 to the capture of Kabul in September 1996, the nature and significance of the Taliban phenomenon were poorly understood by the aid community. The Taliban were "just another faction", albeit one that had bizarre and profoundly discriminatory practices. Their behaviour was not anything too unusual by Afghan standards. Dealing with their leaders in Kandahar was difficult – they had limited knowledge of the workings of the aid community, they were unaccustomed to dealing with foreigners, they had an oral culture with little appreciation of written undertakings, their chain of command was confusing, and internal sharing of information between departments or localities was poor or non-existent. But then dealing with faction leaders such as Dostom, Rabbani and Hekmatyar had never been easy. After the Taliban entered Kabul, things started to change, if for no other reason than their policies became clearer as they established themselves in hostile territory outside their Pashtun homeland. Their practice in dealing with women, their Islamic rigour and the various restrictions they imposed were not so different from those of other mujahedin groups (including the internationally recognized Rabbani government). The difference was that such practices had now been elevated to policy – the policy of the Islamic Emirate of Afghanistan – which was proclaimed to the world through sometimes obscure edicts (*firmans*) bearing the signature of Mullah Mohammed Omar.

Moreover, the nature of the conflict changed. Although abuses against civilians were nothing new in the Afghan context, as the various battles for control of Kabul in 1992–1994 had shown, there was now a quantum leap in the level of targeting of civilians by the Taliban. At the same time, the outside world became more conscious of human rights abuses or at least more rhetorical that human rights violations were unacceptable. Many observers were led to conclude that such abuses were a deliberate ingredient of the Taliban war strategy. This was confirmed by the string of massacres perpetrated by the Taliban between 1998 and 2001 in their attempts to force the remaining opposition enclaves into submission. The forces of the Northern Alliance (NA) were not particularly benevolent towards civilians – they had shown during the mid-1990s how predatory and abusive they could be – nor were they less brutish on the battlefield, where they made indiscriminate use of landmines (whereas the Taliban had pledged to ban their use and refrained from using them). But it is fair to say that, partly because it had less territory under its control and was mostly in a defensive mode, the NA did not resort to the widespread killings, scorched earth tactics and forced displacement that came to characterize Taliban military offensives.

When the Taliban controlled only the south and east of the country, the conventional wisdom in the aid community was that the Taliban would not last. They were not taken too seriously as interlocutors, partly because they did not show much interest in the workings of the humanitarian agencies, partly because of the huge cultural gap, which made most conversations with them a dialogue of the deaf. There was also an in-built imbalance because the Taliban saw themselves as a moral force fighting against the corrupt rule of the mujahedin factions whereas aid workers, in the main, saw the Taliban as one faction – a particularly retrograde one – among others. Such was the strained atmosphere in which negotiations took place between the Taliban and the aid community to secure access and humanitarian space. Initially, UN agencies and NGOs approached the Taliban separately and without a clear or coordinated agenda. Individual agencies obtained protection for their premises and staff, access to vulnerable groups and relative freedom of movement.

Most aid workers saw the closure of girls' schools, the ban on female employment, and the imposition of beards, burkas and compulsory prayers as temporary measures dictated by the political economy of the Taliban's brand of *jihad*, that is, as measures to control the population rather than as a structured political agenda.

This proved not to be the case. When the Taliban took Kabul and showed that their intention was to reinforce rather than loosen the discriminatory measures that they had imposed in their heartland of southern and eastern Afghanistan, which by and large corresponded to the local mores of the mostly rural population who lived there, the aid community found itself wrong-footed. Although the Taliban were sometimes clumsy in articulating their views, it became clear that they had an agenda – to win the war, to obtain international recognition and to set the rules for aid agencies – whereas the aid agencies did not. Individual actors – UN agencies, NGOs, visiting donor delegations – discussed a variety of operational and policy issues with Taliban officials whose real power and influence were unknown and with little or no coordination among themselves. As is often the case, institutional survival trumped principles: many agencies were all too happy to secure approval for their own particular projects without any consideration for the wider issues.

There were three main positions in the assistance community (and among donors) on how to deal with the Taliban: principled, accommodationist and "duck-and-weave".[5] The first openly advocated change in the Taliban policies inimical to the values of the UN Charter and internationally recognized norms and sometimes threatened withdrawals or conditionalities. The proponents of the second position were ready to engage, preferably on technical issues and with Taliban technocrats (such as there were), hoping that pragmatic arrangements would lead to a "softening" of the Taliban over time. The third sought to avoid dealing with the Taliban as far as possible by working directly with communities and counting on their support (and on the ability of community leaders to extract concessions from the Taliban). Lines were by no means drawn in the sand and the same agency could experiment with different approaches in different locations at different times. Generally speaking, during 1996–1998, the United Nations was split between an accommodationist camp led by the World Health Organization (WHO) and the United Nations Office for Project Services (UNOPS) and a principled camp led by the United Nations Children's Fund (UNICEF) and the UN Coordinator, with the technical agencies – the Food and Agriculture Organization of the United Nations (FAO), the United Nations Human Settlements Programme (UN-Habitat), the United Nations International Drug Control Programme (UNDCP) – trying to weave around the Taliban. Some agencies, such as the United Nations High Commissioner for Refugees (UNHCR) and the

World Food Programme (WFP), were hard to pin down, confrontational one day and accommodating the next, depending on local arrangements struck between their staff and the Taliban leaders or on dictates from their HQs. Most NGOs tried to work directly with communities and eschew formal contact with Taliban officials at the central level.

For example, WHO initially had no qualms about working with the Taliban in the health sector despite the discriminatory environment that prevailed. The Taliban had heavily compromised women's access to health by insisting on separate hospital buildings for male and female patients and prohibiting male doctors from examining female patients. Nevertheless, WHO's argument was that, by engaging with them, the Taliban diktats would soften (they eventually did, but it is hard to tell if this was the result of engagement or of the more principled approach and open condemnation of other agencies, including UNICEF, working in the health sector). Memorable spats occurred at UN inter-agency or donor meetings, with public indictments of WHO that forced it, somewhat reluctantly, to change its tune.[6] The WFP, on the other hand, took a very hard line dictated from HQ – which was seen as impractical and culturally insensitive, if not counterproductive, by most aid workers on the ground: if projects could not demonstrate that they benefited men and women in an equal manner, they would be terminated. Some were. When it was realized that, regardless of the Taliban restrictions, Afghan women could not possibly participate in food-for-work projects such as road repair, more flexible attitudes prevailed. The Taliban were quick to take advantage of the confusion in the aid community's ranks and ably blew hot and cold or played one agency against the other.

The United Nations' ability to present a more united front vis-à-vis the Taliban improved significantly with the introduction of the Strategic Framework (SF) as the key tool for defining the United Nations' overall political, humanitarian and human rights objectives in Afghanistan. The aim of the SF was a more coherent and unitary approach to the UN system's work in Afghanistan. It was both a framework for principled action as well as a process that involved all UN agencies directly and the NGO community somewhat more indirectly, through the agreed structures for coordination and common programming.[7] The SF was predicated on the assumption that better communication between the assistance and political wings of the United Nations, on the one hand, and a strategy based on clear humanitarian and human rights principles to which all parts of the UN system would formally subscribe, on the other, would yield better results in dealing with the Taliban than the scattered approaches of the past.

As such, the SF and its corollary – "speaking with one voice" – became the template for negotiating with the Taliban. The UN Coordinator's

Office (UNCO), to which the responsibility of implementing the SF was assigned by the UN Secretary-General in September 1998, became the central hub for principled engagement with the Taliban. The fact that some of the modalities of the SF were binding for UN agencies, in particular the requirement that individual agencies not discuss issues of principle with the Taliban, greatly strengthened the UN negotiating position. These coordination arrangements were more robust than in any other crisis situation. By and large, until September 2001, significant levels of principled engagement in Afghanistan were achieved, at least on the assistance side, despite the fact that initially many UN agencies were deeply resentful of the approach, which they saw as an effort to clip their wings. Donor governments, on the other hand, were very supportive – an important factor in agency compliance.

Some of the ups and downs of negotiations with the Taliban are discussed in the following pages. Negotiations were held at a variety of levels: by the UN Coordinator with the Taliban leadership in Kabul or Kandahar; by UNCO regional coordinators in their respective areas; by more junior or local staff at Taliban checkpoints or with village-level officials. Although negotiations were sometimes cordial, they often rambled on and success was elusive. Talks with technocrats or on logistical issues were easier to handle. Discussions with military commanders or ideologues tended to be more difficult. Often, despite efforts to "keep politics out of the discussion", negotiations would stumble on hot political issues. In some cases, the UN political wing scuttled delicate negotiations. Depending on the opportunities it saw to advance a stalemated peace process, the political United Nations would court the Taliban to bring them to the negotiating table, only to lambaste them publicly when this did not work, thus complicating the task of those who were dealing with them every day on assistance, protection and access issues.

For example, when, in January 2001, the UN political mission learned through UN humanitarian colleagues that there had been a massacre in a particular district in Hazarajat, the head of the mission, without informing his humanitarian colleague, took the initiative of raising the matter directly with the Taliban foreign minister, thereby putting the humanitarian sources at risk and jeopardizing the ongoing negotiations that the UN regional coordinator was patiently conducting over access for food convoys to the area. Access was denied and negotiations had to start again from scratch. Thus, the clash between different UN cultures can have serious humanitarian consequences.

For UN agencies on the ground, and to some extent for the NGO community, the importance of a unitary and principled approach in dealing with the Taliban became increasingly self-evident: given the circumstances, it was the best possible strategy for effective humanitarian action. Progress was slow, negotiations were difficult, but not engaging would have resulted in even more suffering and less access. Confrontation, when it had been tried, had backfired, and threatening the withdrawal of aid was not an option that aid workers were prepared to consider, both because leaving would have worsened the plight of ordinary Afghans and because the Taliban leadership did not seem to care about the well-being of civilians. As one moved away from Afghanistan, however, perspectives changed. UN headquarters and certain member states, the United States and Russia in particular, as well as the media, often had little sympathy for the nuances of the field, whose approach was seen as unduly "accommodationist". As we shall see below, this HQ–field dichotomy tended to make negotiations more difficult.

Obstacles and opportunities

The main obstacles to successful negotiation between the United Nations and the Taliban were of a cultural nature. Cultural fault-lines within each camp were an additional complicating factor. I discuss these in this section.

The SF provided a template for principled engagement and therefore negotiation. The rationale on the UN side was that engagement would provide a better environment in which humanitarian needs could be met, that the Taliban would come to understand and respect the principles and modus operandi of assistance agencies, and that interaction with the aid community would bear fruit in terms of an "opening up" of the regime. By and large in 1999–2000, the consensus within the donor community supported this approach. Donors and the UN Coordinator regularly worked together, including through joint démarches with the Taliban leadership and public statements to ensure that the Taliban received the same message. As we shall see, the results were mixed.

Before looking at specific examples of negotiations, it is necessary to understand where the two sides were coming from and where they wanted to go. On the UN side, this was relatively straightforward: there was a body of law – international humanitarian law (IHL) – governing humanitarian assistance and protection activities, to which agencies could refer, and a sort of jurisprudence – a tradition built upon years of experience working in complex emergencies – as well as a specific rulebook for Taliban Afghanistan – the do's and don'ts derived from the principles of the SF.[8] Whereas the humanitarian players – the UNCO, the UNHCR, UNICEF and the WFP – were at least in theory familiar with the law, the understanding of issues of principle among UN staff varied greatly. Even greater variations existed among NGO staff. Many staff were totally unfamiliar, and sometimes uninterested, in the basics of IHL and, until 1999, there was no specific training.[9] The situation in development-oriented agencies – WHO, FAO, the United Nations Centre for Human Settlements – was generally worse. In some agencies, principles were seen as an obstacle to operationalism – the desire to get things done. And, of course, there was no training in the complex art of negotiation. The result was confusion, at least initially. It was difficult enough to reach common positions among UN heads of agencies meeting in Islamabad on the objectives and strategy for a particular negotiation, but ensuring that all agency staff in the seven duty stations inside Afghanistan would toe the same line or speak in harmonious voices was sometimes near impossible. The SF was a useful tool, but there was no mechanism to enforce it. Local staff often made local arrangements with the Taliban, which were not in line with the central policies of the United Nations (or, for that matter, with those of the Taliban).

In terms of what needed to be negotiated, again the United Nations was relatively clear. The core purpose of humanitarian action is to ensure that the rights held by individuals under IHL are promoted and respected by the authorities controlling populations affected by conflict and crisis. Typically, humanitarian actors seek to reach this objective by advocacy with the authorities concerned (and also with the international community to provide the resources required) and by substitution, in other words by acting in lieu of the authorities when they are either unwilling or unable to provide assistance and protection themselves. Both advocacy and substitution require engagement with the authorities, but substitution often requires sustained negotiation.[10] For the United Nations, therefore, the terms of engagement were self-evident (even if there were internal differences or specific negotiating positions on different issues). It assumed that the Taliban had a similar understanding of the purpose and nature of negotiations. This was a serious mistake: the perspective of the Taliban was radically different.

To begin with, the political context as seen by the Taliban was at loggerheads with the UN view. UN humanitarian agencies do not recognize belligerents. For them, the Taliban constituted an armed group, among others, that happened to control most of Afghanistan. The Taliban saw things very differently: they were the legitimate rulers of the country, not only because they controlled most of it but more importantly because they had a "god given" mandate to do so. Mullah Omar was the "Commander of the Faithful", Afghanistan was an Islamic Emirate – what could have been more legitimate than that? Similarly, whereas to the United Nations the Taliban seemed "unprincipled" in their apparent neglect of the welfare of the population they controlled and in the treatment of their enemies, the Taliban's own view was that whatever they did was based on a strict interpretation of religious principle and coloured by their duty to wage *jihad*, an obligation that trumped all others. As a result, they were often incapable of engaging with or even understanding what the humanitarian folk had to offer. Their "Allah will provide" attitude obviously clashed with the "welfarist assumptions of humanitarians".[11]

Culturally, as well, the world views were incompatible. The issue of gender equality was, and is, central to the identity and rhetoric of the United Nations (although all too often it does not practise what it preaches[12]). For the Taliban, but also for the average rural Afghan whom they sought to represent, the role of women in society is defined by tradition and religion in a very conservative way. When in July 2000 Mullah Omar issued Edict No. 8 banning the employment of Afghan women by aid agencies, except in the health sector, the United Nations and the NGOs were shocked by the substance of the edict but also by its offensive language, which accused the aid community of practising immorality or even encouraging prostitution. But for the Taliban, according to their own frame of reference, accusing the United Nations of "polluting" Afghans made a lot of sense. This was fully in line with their identity, their world view and what they thought their society should look like.

Moreover, there were other factors that made negotiation not only difficult but also unpredictable. Decision-making by the Taliban was obscure to the outsider but had its own internal rationality. The Taliban saw themselves not as a party or a government but as a movement. Decisions, particularly on matters of policy and on how to deal with the foreigners, were discussed at many levels, often in a collegial manner as in the traditional *shuras* (councils). The United Nations tended to meet and negotiate with Taliban "moderates", or such they were thought to be. These in turn had to negotiate with other levels of the leadership, including of course religious zealots, military commanders and assorted "hard-liners" in Kabul and Kandahar. Seniority in the government – having the title of "minister" – was no guarantee that the "higher levels" in Kandahar would support a discussion held in Kabul on a technical issue. "Difficult" matters would not be sorted out because officials in Kabul were reluctant to raise them with Kandahar for fear of appearing to be ideologically unsound. There was a regular pattern of Taliban officials giving "deniable permission"[13] to agencies for a particular activity, including for example the non-objection of a local district chief to the establishment of a girls' school, but refusing to agree in writing or in public for fear of being pilloried by more senior ideologues or the religious police.

There were internal cultural tensions in the UN camp as well. The SF helped to harmonize the humanitarian and human rights perspectives. As for the development agencies, they were by nature reluctant to fall into line, at least initially. Their automatic reflex was to "think long term" and treat the Taliban as a legitimate government. Their tendency to promote capacity-building activities – explicitly proscribed by the SF because they would strengthen the Taliban regime – had to be kept in check by the UN Coordinator. But it was the different world views of the UN political wing, at HQ and in the field, that interfered most often with humanitarian negotiations on the ground. Though the political United Nations had formally subscribed to the SF and its principles, it was institutionally and culturally averse to working and sharing information with its humanitarian and human rights counterparts. In particular, the UN political mission was not mindful of the one-voice policy. This led to tensions and misunderstandings as well as to bad timing of political statements, which impacted negatively on, for example, delicate humanitarian negotiations for access to non-Taliban enclaves.

On occasion, distance from HQ became an obstacle in itself. High-level missions from UN HQ would appear with little advance consultation and engage with the Taliban on sensitive issues – such as gender or human rights violations. They would then issue "feel good" statements pillorying Taliban policies, which would achieve little other than irritating the very officials with whom the UN country team was holding low-key discussions. One example of this was the issuing in 2000 of a statement, grossly exaggerated, on the presence of child soldiers in the Taliban ranks. Another example was the ill-fated high-level mission sent by New York in 1998 to negotiate a comprehensive Memorandum of Understanding (MOU) with the Taliban.[14] This raised huge expectations for the Taliban, including the prospects of international legitimation, but the starting points were on such different levels that the discussions were at cross-purposes. The United Nations learned the hard way that sending a high-level delegation had made the search for compromise more difficult. Moreover, the United Nations was unprepared for failure. It had no "best alternative to a negotiated agreement" (BATNA)[15] – an important element, as we shall see below.

In sum, because the Taliban and the United Nations were operating from such different but, in a sense, equally principled ideological premises, it is no wonder that they often talked *at* each other rather than *to* each other. Both sides tended to demonize the other and to engage in negotiational brinkmanship, with the United Nations often threatening to suspend activities or to leave and the Taliban calling for the expulsion of the United Nations or the NGOs. In their first engagements with the Taliban, UN officials assumed, wrongly, that the Taliban "needed them" and that therefore they could exert some "humanitarian leverage", either negatively ("if you don't accept our rules, we'll leave") or positively ("if you do accept our rules, we'll increase our assistance"). The Taliban reply was predictable and difficult to counter: "If you don't accept our terms, we will do without you. It will take longer, but we don't need your polluting influence." Principles on both sides were often equated with hard-line negotiating positions. Those arguing for flexibility, on both sides, were accused of collaborating.

Negotiations

Accessing internally stuck persons

The Taliban were more forceful than their disorganized opponents and predecessors in keeping tabs on the activities of aid agencies and therefore in denying or restricting access to particular areas or groups. For example, the Hazara minority – Shiite, and therefore seen by the Taliban as pro-Iranian and even by some hard-liners as apostate – and their central highlands stronghold were constantly abused and subjected to Taliban wrath. In 1997–1998, the Taliban imposed an economic blockade around Hazarajat that was lifted only when they occupied Bamiyan in 1998. International protests did little to sway the Taliban, but continuous pressure from the UN Coordinator, the WFP and some NGOs finally resulted in an agreement to allow some food aid into the region, including an airlift operation to Bamiyan. The airlift was not without problems and finally had to be cut short when the Taliban bombed the Bamiyan airfield while the UN plane was on the ground.

Even as they gained a stronger foothold in Hazarajat, the Taliban were not keen for the United Nations to establish a presence there, and least of all in the opposition-controlled (and desperately poor) enclaves such as Dar-e-Souf. In these enclaves and in other remote areas of the central highlands – the so-called hunger belt – hundreds of thousands of internally stuck persons too poor or weak to move, or prevented from doing so by conflict or by Taliban restrictions, were at exceptionally high risk of famine. Needs assessment missions, often able to reach these areas only on foot, reported near-total food shortages, with families surviving on grasses, roots and other famine foods. Scurvy and other malnutrition-related diseases were rampant. Nevertheless, access by UN missions would frequently be denied. Sometimes, after days of uncertainty and shuttling between the ministry of foreign affairs, the ministry of the interior and assorted Taliban back-channels, missions would be allowed to proceed, only to be turned back at Taliban checkpoints before entering Hazarajat. As the drought hit harder in 2000 and early 2001, the conditions in many remote highland areas became more and more precarious.

The Taliban strategy was presumably to deny assistance so as to weaken the Hazara resistance, encourage outward population movement and make the area safer for the Pashtun nomads, who were keen to return to their summer pastures in the highlands from which they had been excluded in previous years by Hazara resistance. The Taliban also repeatedly claimed that "too much" assistance was going to Hazarajat compared with Pashtun areas and they proved impervious to any discussion based on surveys or facts that demonstrated the dramatic levels of need.

The UN Coordinator and his colleagues engaged in almost continuous efforts to unblock the situation so that food and staff would be allowed free access. While the UN Regional Coordinator for Hazarajat engaged the local authorities in Bamiyan in discussions about access both for UN/NGO assessment missions and for food convoys, visits were made by the UN Coordinator and his senior agency colleagues to the highest levels of the Taliban leadership that were accessible to the United Nations, in Kabul and Kandahar, to secure new agreements or the implementation of old ones. When quiet diplomacy did not bear fruit, all other possible avenues were tried: démarches by donors, interviews in the media and, when information about massacres trickled out, statements by the UN Secretary-General. The results were mixed. Taliban military commanders did not want the UN aid agencies in Hazarajat, particularly when military operations were ongoing. They were aware that information on violations was reaching the outside world through civilians fleeing the area and the contacts that aid workers had developed on the ground. It is also possible that the Taliban leadership were concerned by the negative publicity they were getting in the international media and they had to balance the risks of keeping outsiders out against possible exposure by letting them in.[16] In the end, they failed to suppress the information on massacres and, with stops and starts, had reluctantly to agree that assistance could reach the opposition enclaves. Persistence in negotiation therefore yielded some positive results. The occasional unsavoury deal was also struck, as when the United Nations promised to send needs assessments and assistance to areas under Taliban control, which were of a lesser priority compared with Hazarajat, in order to enlist the support of key Taliban officials.

In other cases, persistence was brought to naught by external factors. For example, in November–December 2000 the United Nations and the International Committee of the Red Cross (ICRC) held protracted negotiations in Kabul to gain access to internally displaced persons (IDPs) in the Shomali plain and Panjshir valley who had been displaced by the Taliban advances in the previous months and were stuck in enclaves behind the front-line. With winter setting in, the only access route from the north, over treacherous passes in the Hindu Kush, was becoming impassable. The

IDPs were in a precarious situation and food stocks were low. Finally, on 20 November, after extended negotiations that involved UNCO staff securing agreements from field commanders on both sides to hold their fire, 15 UN and ICRC trucks were allowed to cross into Northern Alliance territory. This was to be the first of several convoys. It was to be followed by some 90 trucks crossing the front-line through a "humanitarian corridor". The next day, however, a comment by the UN Secretary-General's spokesperson in New York about an aerial bombardment by the Taliban in the Panjshir valley, close to an UNCO office, angered the Taliban, who allowed only three trucks to cross. The Northern Alliance was not pleased. As the trucks were returning through no man's land they were shelled by the NA. Although no one was hurt, this in effect scuttled the prospects of any further cross-line deliveries.[17] Again, an intervention from HQ had thrown a spanner in a process that was being successfully managed locally.

Was the mix of denunciation and formal and informal negotiation to secure access the right one? Some have argued that keeping a lower profile (read: not raising the issue of human rights violations against Hazaras and other minority groups) would have been more effective in terms of saving lives, and that mixing the humanitarian and human rights agendas actually reduced humanitarian space.[18] An important point deserves to be made here. In the Afghan context, as elsewhere, it is difficult, if not impossible, to de-link the relief needs of a particular group from the political circumstances affecting their vulnerability and the protection needs that such circumstances engender. The facts that access was denied or that abuses against civilians were committed were integral to the humanitarian condition that the UN Coordinator and his staff were obliged to address.

The allegation that the UN approach was deleterious to humanitarian access did not have much currency in the field. It was raised by the HQ of some NGOs (Médecins Sans Frontières in particular) with the United Nations Office for the Coordination of Humanitarian Affairs (UNOCHA) in New York. Some agencies with reputable track records in Hazarajat initially expressed concern that the United Nations' activism would jeopardize their own activities – but this was from an institutional survival more than from a policy perspective. In the end, the approach for negotiating access was defined in the Regional Coordinating Body for Hazarajat by all the concerned UN and NGO agencies as well as in the UN-led Emergency Task Force, which met in Islamabad where all the key operational players were present, including donors, and where policy decisions on assistance were made. There was thus a division of labour between the humanitarian actors, who focused on fighting for access, and the Human Rights Advisor and the human rights consultative group, composed of UN agencies, NGOs and donors, who dealt with the issue of what to do with the sensitive information that was coming out of Hazarajat from a variety of sources, including Afghan aid workers and witnesses. The UN Coordinator and his office were careful not to condemn the Taliban publicly for alleged abuses because they knew that this might compromise access, but they ensured that the information would be made public by others.

The Humanitarian Operational Requirements

There were many other examples of concerted interventions by the UN Coordinator and aid agencies on access and protection issues. Not all were successful. Not all involved the Taliban. For example, after the Taliban offensive in the Shomali plain north of Kabul in the summer of 1999, access to the IDP concentrations on the Northern Alliance side of the front-lines was possible only by a perilous journey over high mountain passes into the Panjshir valley. Private truckers were asking extortionate rates to deliver urgently needed relief commodities in conjunction with NA commanders who were bent on "maximizing", i.e. taking advantage of the transit of humanitarian assistance. Interventions with the NA leaders, including meetings with President Rabbani, did not bring the rates down. These leaders also fuelled a "numbers game" where the numbers of IDPs were deliberately inflated in order to obtain more assistance.

By the summer of 2000, what had been a process of slow and incremental progress in engagement with the Taliban came to an abrupt halt when Mullah Omar issued Edict No. 8 banning employment of Afghan women by aid agencies except in the health sector. From then on, the relationship went downhill. Given the deteriorating political climate, the bad publicity the Taliban were getting for their abuses and the destruction of the Bamiyan buddhas, and the parallel increase in humanitarian need resulting from the deepening humanitarian crisis that was engulfing most of the country, the focus of the UN country team shifted nearly entirely to issues of access and protection. Issues of constructive engagement were no longer on the agenda.

It was in this context that a last attempt to negotiate an agreement on minimum operational requirements for humanitarian action was undertaken in the spring of 2001. It was dictated by the need for the United Nations and NGOs to find a way of circumventing Edict No. 8 – to which the Taliban themselves showed varying degrees of rigour in its implementation. The thinking was: "let's try to get a clear agreement on basic issues of principle; if this doesn't work, we will have to define our collective conditions for engagement and disengagement." Unlike the MOU, this time the United Nations was better prepared and had a BATNA – an inter-agency agreement on what to do if the negotiations failed.

A draft one-page text – the Humanitarian Operational Requirements (HOR) – containing basic humanitarian principles and conditions under which UN agencies would operate in the country was shared with the Taliban minister of foreign affairs and some of his Kandahar-based senior colleagues. Informal meetings were held between Afghan staff of the UN Coordinator's Office and mid-level Taliban officials where the HOR were explained and a Pashto version provided. Initial positive comments were received in the form of a copy of the HOR with handwritten annotations from the minister. These seemed relatively minor and certainly warranted further discussion, to which both sides agreed.

An inter-agency UN team led by the UN Coordinator travelled to Kabul in April 2001 for a high-level meeting with a delegation of Taliban ministers (foreign affairs, interior and even the ministry for vice and virtue). As usual, the Taliban blew hot and cold. The discussions were acrimonious and further complicated by a simultaneous crisis between the Taliban and the WFP concerning the employment of women in a planned house-to-house vulnerability survey.[19] Confusion arose over the translation of the HOR, with the Taliban claiming that they had never seen the "agreed" translation and even less their own annotations. The talks collapsed when the Taliban insisted that all IHL principles in the HOR should be qualified as acceptable as long as "they did not contravene Islamic precepts and Taliban Emirate policies".

As in the case of the MOU, high-level discussions proved to be unproductive. The United Nations was better prepared this time and refrained from bringing in heavyweights from HQ. It was able to speak with one voice on all the key issues. Not so the Taliban: they were disorganized and spent inordinate amounts of time raising political issues that were not on the agenda or haranguing the United Nations. They became more intransigent as the days went by. It became clear that, although some of the Taliban officials might have individually agreed to the text under discussion, they could not do so as a group, particularly when the hard-liners from the ministries of interior and vice and virtue were present. Any compromise would have been seen as a loss of face on their part.

In the end, the collapse of the negotiations on the HOR had little practical impact for two reasons. The first was that the relationship between the assistance community and the Taliban was steadily deteriorating and expectations that an agreement on the HOR would allow the continuation of some form of pragmatic engagement were low. Indeed, some in the United Nations privately welcomed the failure since it gave them more leverage for arguing for a more confrontational approach. In accordance with the agreed BATNA, UN agencies minimized formal contacts with the Taliban by adopting "duck-and-weave" tactics and focusing on strictly life-saving activities.

The second reason relates to the deepening crisis caused by the deadly combination of drought, displacement and conflict. By the summer of 2001, some 12 million Afghans were at risk of food insecurity, if not famine.[20] The energies of the assistance agencies were focused on the challenges of accessing and moving food into the affected areas, caring for over 1 million IDPs, often living in desperate conditions in makeshift camps, and trying to address the myriad protection problems that arose (not to mention the often thankless task of mobilizing donor support). Nobody had time for the niceties of negotiation with the Taliban at the central level. The focus shifted to the regions and provinces, where hard work and sheer persistence by the UNCO's staff and their agency colleagues were often successful in unblocking issues of access. Local Taliban leaders were also genuinely concerned about the gravity of the situation and welcomed whatever help the United Nations and the NGOs could provide. It helped that the international media started to pay attention and that TV crews visited Herat, Mazar and other affected areas. Interestingly, the Taliban no longer seemed to mind if living beings including women were being filmed. Occasionally, they even allowed themselves to appear on camera. Of course, graft, manipulation and incompetence did not disappear – the Taliban had a keen eye for possibilities to cream off assistance in places such as Herat where the numbers of IDPs were deliberately inflated – but it is fair to say that, in their final months, instances of denial of access became the exception rather than the rule.

Wider implications

What can be learned from negotiating with the Taliban? Strong leadership and coordination seem to be necessary ingredients in successful negotiation. The robust UN coordination mechanisms on the ground during Taliban times were effective tools for facilitating assistance and protection activities. For the Taliban, the fact that there was unity of purpose in the aid community, and donors, UN agencies and NGOs were giving out the same message on issues of access and protection, was a reality that they could not afford to ignore. The Afghanistan experience also points to the importance of pursuing all avenues – quiet and public, local and international – to negotiate access to vulnerable populations. Equally important is ensuring that discussions take place at the appropriate level.

Bringing in "high flyers" from HQ was often counterproductive because it resulted in both sides indulging in rhetoric and political posturing that made the search for practical solutions more difficult. Good communication between HQ and the field on such issues is essential to ensure that consistent messages are given to the concerned authorities.

Culture is a crucial factor in negotiation. UN staff are often not equipped to understand the historical and cultural context that explains the behaviour of their interlocutors. Unnecessary offence may be given by arrogant personal behaviour or institutional posturing. Solid anthropological training or, better still, the routine deployment of anthropologists in UN coordination offices could go a long way to facilitating communication, if not agreement, with abusive authorities. Similarly, more systematic efforts are required to explain "what the United Nations stands for". The Taliban were notoriously confused by what the foreigners wanted because even senior leaders had had no previous exposure to the niceties of humanitarian principles or diplomatic practice. Many were semi-literate or unaccustomed to co-signing agreements in written form. Specialized training, including, crucially, training in the art of negotiation, could help to reduce such relatively predictable obstacles to getting to yes.

Another finding is that the political or cultural battles within the United Nations and between headquarters and the field can have a deleterious effect on the negotiation of access for assistance and protection. UN political staff are generally averse to working with their humanitarian and human rights colleagues. There is an unwritten pecking order that sanctifies the primacy of the political. This results, for example, in the deployment of senior political officers or, worse, special UN representatives with no knowledge of or sympathy for humanitarian practice. Coherence and unity of response, in Afghanistan and elsewhere, do not necessarily mean subordination of humanitarian and human rights concerns to political dictates. Yet, in recent crises, this seems to have become the default approach.[21]

Ultimately, however, the UN strategy had its limits. The Taliban chose to put themselves beyond the pale of negotiations, among other reasons because they increasingly felt isolated and vilified. In the end they tolerated the United Nations because of its humanitarian work but became deeply suspicious about the overall agenda of the aid community. Events since the attacks of 11 September 2001 – and especially the fact that the Bonn Agreement was an agreement among victors – have increased the perception that the United Nations and the assistance community have "taken sides", thereby reducing the acceptability of the presence of aid agencies in resurgent Taliban areas and by the same token increasing the threats for aid workers.

Notes

1. For extensive background on the issues covered in this chapter, see A. Donini, *Learning the Lessons? A Retrospective Analysis of Humanitarian Principles and Practice in Afghanistan*, a report prepared for OCHA, June 2003 (full text available on ReliefWeb at ⟨http://www.reliefweb.int/library/documents/2003/ocha-afg-30jun.pdf⟩, accessed 4 May 2006). See also A. Donini, N. Niland and K. Wermester, eds, *Nation-building Unraveled? Aid, Peace and Justice in Afghanistan*, Bloomfield, CT: Kumarian Press, December 2003. On the politicization of humanitarian assistance in Afghanistan, see also Helga Baitenmann, "NGOs and the Afghan War: The Politicization of Humanitarian Aid", *Third World Quarterly*, January 1990; Fiona Terry, *Condemned to Repeat: The Paradox of Humanitarian Action*, Ithaca, NY: Cornell University Press, 2002.
2. This was in the form of an exchange of letters between the UN Coordinator for Afghanistan and the Afghan prime minister, as well as with the leaders of the alliance of mujahedin parties.
3. When moving from area A to area C, be mindful of the needs and perceptions of area B.
4. On the genesis of the Taliban, see Ahmed Rashid, *Taliban. Islam, Oil and the New Great Game in Central Asia*, London and New York: I. B. Tauris, 2000.
5. Defined as "principle-centered", "tip-toe" and "community empowerment" approaches in Claude Bruderlein with Adeel Ahmed, "Report of the DHA Mission to Afghanistan", United Nations Department of Humanitarian Affairs (UNDHA), May 1997.
6. This was further complicated by the polarized positions of the WHO HQ (more principled) and the regional office in Alexandria, to which the WHO representative reported (accommodationist).
7. On the origins of the Strategic Framework, see M. Duffield, P. Gossman and N. Leader, *Review of the Strategic Framework for Afghanistan*, Islamabad: Afghanistan Research and Evaluation Unit, 2001, and Antonio Donini, *The Strategic Framework for Afghanistan: A Preliminary Assessment*, Islamabad: UNOCHA, 1999, available from the author.
8. The SF was followed by additional agreements – the so-called "Next Steps Papers", which elaborated on the conditions of engagement and disengagement at specific moments in time.
9. The Human Rights Advisor in UNCO established a successful one-week training course for UN and NGO staff on human rights issues, including IHL in 1999.
10. Nicholas Leader, "Negotiation and Engagement in Afghanistan", report prepared for the UN Coordinator's Office, Islamabad, 28 May 2001.
11. Ibid., p. 8.
12. On the UN "gender wars", see Norah Niland, *Humanitarian Action: Protecting Civilians. Feedback from Afghanistan*, prepared for OCHA, United Nations, 30 June 2003 (available on ReliefWeb at ⟨http://www.reliefweb.int/library/documents/2003/ocha-afg-30jun2.pdf⟩, accessed 4 May 2006), particularly pp. 17–18 and 39–43; see also the chapters by Sippi Azerbaijani-Moghadam (on gender) and Norah Niland (on human rights) in Donini et al., eds, *Nation-building Unraveled?*.
13. Leader, "Negotiation and Engagement in Afghanistan", p. 9.
14. The MOU is discussed in some detail in Donini et al., eds, *Nation-building Unraveled?*, pp. 132–133.
15. R. Fisher, W. Ury and B. Patton, *Getting to Yes: Negotiating Agreements without Giving in*, Boston, MA: Houghton Mifflin, 1981.
16. The Taliban were far from monolithic. Some hard-liners actually thrived on the negative publicity; others were genuinely concerned about the attacks against civilians and even

quietly passed on information to aid workers about what was happening in inaccessible areas.

17. For a discussion of instances of negotiation of access to and protection of civilians, see Niland, *Humanitarian Action*.
18. Nick Stockton, "Afghanistan, War, Aid and the International Order", in Donini et al., eds, *Nation-building Unraveled?*.
19. The survey was aimed at identifying beneficiaries for the subsidized bread provided by the Kabul bakeries programme. This was a hot issue because it was assumed that the survey would uncover large-scale diversion of assistance.
20. UNOCHA, "The Deepening Crisis in Afghanistan", August 2001, document issued by UNOCHA and circulated to donors and the media.
21. For a discussion of the benefits and risks of integrated approaches, see the special issue of *Ethics and International Affairs*, Vol. 18, No. 2, 2004.

8

Principled humanitarian action in the East Timor crisis

Toni Pfanner

The East Timor experience has been described as a "tremendous humanitarian success".[1] Within weeks of the beginning of the crisis in 1999, the deployment of a UN-authorized force enabled a major humanitarian emergency operation to respond to the massive displacement of population and widespread destruction and plundering. After 25 years of Indonesian rule and within 2 years of an overwhelming vote in favour of independence in September 1999, a new state was born.

This chapter focuses on four distinct periods during the East Timor crisis: (i) the period immediately preceding the referendum (July 1998–April 1999); (ii) the pre-ballot period (May–August 1999); (iii) the outbreak of violence following the referendum (September 1999); and (iv) the post-ballot period (October–December 1999). Each of these phases followed its own pattern and had its specific problems. Events in Indonesia, which were under way in parallel during one of its most turbulent times, heavily influenced the rapid developments in East Timor.

Humanitarian diplomacy in a given context involves an entire strategy to at best prevent or at least resolve humanitarian problems. This strategy includes humanitarian negotiation, but this is only one of the many means of communication used to influence the actors in a humanitarian crisis. This chapter demonstrates that a particular feature of the humanitarian diplomacy of the International Committee of the Red Cross (ICRC) is the link to the legal framework governing situations of armed conflict. The ICRC mostly operates in armed conflict, which prevailed in East Timor. As one of the main implementing actors of the Geneva

Conventions for the protection of war victims, the ICRC uses a variety of means of humanitarian diplomacy on a daily basis to persuade parties to an armed conflict to abide by the law. The preferred mode of action is confidential dialogue and persuasion, in particular in the area of visiting prisoners. Within this framework of a balance between security interests and humanitarian considerations in the midst of armed conflict, the ICRC tries to defend the interests of the victims of these situations.

It does this by following the Red Cross's fundamental principles of impartiality and non-discrimination, which are essential elements of every humanitarian action. In addition, and in contrast to many other governmental and non-governmental organizations (NGOs), the ICRC's humanitarian action aims to be independent from political actors and to abstain from taking part in the political and military endeavour that forms the context of its operations. This principled action influences all its humanitarian diplomacy and operational modes. The crisis situation in East Timor towards the end of the twentieth century exemplified the ICRC's attempt to maintain its distinctive character.

Context

In the eighteenth century, the island of Timor was divided between the Netherlands and Portugal. The Netherlands took the western half, which became part of the Dutch East Indies and then, after World War II, part of Indonesia. The eastern half became a Portuguese colony. East Timor remained under Portuguese rule until the mid-1970s. After Portugal's "carnation revolution" in 1974, the empire disintegrated and the colonial ruler hastily ditched East Timor.

The strongest political party, Frente Revolutionaria do Timor Leste Independente (Fretilin), took control of East Timor and declared East Timor an independent state in November 1975. However, Indonesian troops invaded East Timor on 7 December 1975, and in July 1976 President Suharto signed a bill integrating East Timor into Indonesia and making it the twenty-seventh province. During a full-scale war, Indonesian forces gradually gained control over the entire territory. Aerial bombardments generated widespread suffering, especially in the countryside, but urban resistance by "clandestinos" also caused heavy losses among the Indonesian forces. A massive war-related famine in 1979 affected at least 300,000 people.

Even though the war was officially over by the beginning of the 1980s, sporadic large-scale military operations did occasionally occur, often in response to attacks by the military wing of Fretilin against Indonesian soldiers, and these operations affected the civilian population. The focus of resistance groups, however, shifted from open military attacks to largely unarmed resistance.

In a stunning reversal of policy, on 27 January 1999 the newly appointed Indonesian President, B. J. Habibie, raised the possibility of independence for East Timor. Eventually, on 5 May 1999, the United Nations and the government of Portugal and Indonesia signed an agreement that provided for the United Nations to conduct a ballot that would determine the future of East Timor. The announcement took everybody by surprise — the East Timorese, Indonesian politicians and the military, the international community, as well as the ICRC.

At the outbreak of hostilities in 1975, the ICRC had appealed to the Indonesian and Portuguese authorities to respect the Geneva Conventions.[2] The ICRC was legally entitled to act in East Timor under the mandate conferred by the Conventions, but it could obviously deploy in East Timor only with the agreement of the Indonesian authorities. It was not until March 1979 that the ICRC was allowed into East Timor for the first time since the Indonesian occupation to undertake a year-long relief programme launched jointly with the Indonesian Red Cross. No other international organization was allowed to be present in East Timor and non-Indonesian NGOs were not allowed to operate either.

Within the framework of visits to political prisoners in Indonesia, the ICRC also had access to prisoners arrested and sentenced because of their involvement in the East Timorese conflict. The main category of prisoners visited comprised the so-called GPK prisoners (disturbance-related prisoners).[3] Sentenced prisoners and those awaiting trial had been included in an agreement between the ICRC and the Republic of Indonesia of 1977 (revised in 1987). Many East Timorese were transferred to prisons outside the island, mainly to Surabaya and Jakarta. However, some prisoners remained in East Timor and the first visits to them took place in 1982.

As from 1993, the Indonesian authorities allowed a limited but continuous de facto presence of the ICRC in Dili, the capital of East Timor. The office that was finally established was dependent on the delegation in Jakarta. The ICRC had an established presence in the Indonesian capital based on a "seat agreement", which regulates the immunities and privileges of the institution and its personnel. However, this bilateral international agreement does not regulate the activities of the institution, apart from emphasizing their humanitarian character.

Operational issues

Until 1999, the ICRC focused primarily on protection-related activities. These included visits to East Timorese detained within and outside East

Timor and working on behalf of the local population to improve their living conditions and protect their basic rights. In addition, health programmes and water sanitation projects were carried out jointly with the Indonesian Red Cross.

The period prior to the referendum (July 1998–April 1999)

The "reformasi" period in Jakarta resulted in a complete change in the military and police personnel directly involved in the East Timor conflict. The police increasingly assumed a more prominent role in ensuring security. An informal cease-fire was agreed upon by the military and the resistance, East Timor remained calm, and expectations of the reform process were extremely high.

When four people linked to the security apparatus were apprehended and killed by members of the resistance in the small village of Alas at the beginning of November 1998, the military started a large-scale military operation. In the middle of the tripartite negotiations in New York between the United Nations, Indonesia and Portugal, the usually confidential ICRC reports on this issue to the Indonesian authorities became a source of public dispute between the parties to the tripartite negotiations, East Timorese leaders and the ICRC. This indicates the difficulty of carrying out sensitive and disputed humanitarian activities in the public limelight.[4]

These events were followed by the emergence and the arming of pro-integration groups closely linked to families of influential officials. Each area had its own militia, and sometimes also paramilitary groups.[5] The first casualties were reported at the beginning of January 1999. The death toll rose sharply with the announcement of a forthcoming "consultation" of the East Timorese population on belonging to Indonesia. The earlier distribution of arms facilitated the eruption of violence as military-backed pro-integration militias terrorized the population with the aim of influencing the outcome of the vote.

The visit of the ICRC president to Indonesia in February 1999, with the objective of discussing the activities of the institution in several areas of unrest in Indonesia, was overshadowed by the situation in East Timor. ICRC staff in the region remained restricted to five expatriates in East Timor. From mid-March to mid-May, the ICRC delegates were the only expatriates left in East Timor (apart from some long-standing religious personnel). They were also threatened, and making direct contact with hard-core members of the militias in the field was extremely difficult – and dangerous – because of the militias' limited understanding of the role of the ICRC and thus their very biased and negative perception of the ICRC. Interventions by the ICRC with militia leaders did not prevent the occurrence of several serious incidents. Although ICRC delegates remained in Dili, they could no longer leave the capital or even their residences for safety reasons, and it was only with great difficulty that they were able to get some limited help to the victims of the fighting.

Pre-ballot period (May–August 1999)

Starting in the second half of May, the progressive arrival of the United Nations Mission in East Timor (UNAMET),[6] accompanied by numerous journalists, slowly restored calm. Thousands of new Indonesian soldiers were sent to East Timor to ensure that the referendum could take place. A high-ranking Indonesian taskforce guaranteed the relationship between the Indonesian authorities and UNAMET. Because this taskforce was composed of regular interlocutors of the ICRC delegation in Jakarta, the office in Dili had easy access to them. Displaced persons who had fled their homes in fear of attacks were slowly but progressively reached and assisted in areas far from the capital, and, as a result of the improved security situation, they were able to return home.

Simultaneously with the arrival of about 800 UNAMET personnel, several humanitarian agencies also established themselves in East Timor at this time – namely the Office of the United Nations High Commissioner for Refugees (UNHCR), the World Food Programme (WFP) and the United Nations Children's Fund (UNICEF) – together with several non-governmental organizations such as Médecins Sans Frontières. The ICRC operations benefited from its knowledge of the field, its long-standing East Timorese employees and its long-established relations with the Indonesian authorities. On the other hand, the ICRC became one of many humanitarian agencies operating during this period. Its still limited staff of accredited expatriates were able to contribute to resolving humanitarian problems, in particular those concerning detention issues. Assistance programmes were, however, increasingly carried out by other humanitarian organizations.

The last phase before the election was political rather than humanitarian. The focus of the ICRC's humanitarian diplomacy remained improved compliance with international humanitarian law and the preservation of its unique status as an impartial, neutral and independent humanitarian organization. At the same time, it endeavoured to meet the need for coordination with other humanitarian and political players and to secure overall support for humanitarian action. The uncertain outcome pushed the ICRC to prepare for the post-ballot period: one week before the ballot and with a lack of breaking news, the arrival of a large ICRC-rented ship full of assistance supplies made headlines and was a small signal of events to come.

The outbreak of violence following the referendum (September 1999)

In the wake of the 30 August 1999 popular consultation, when nearly the entire population eligible to vote in East Timor turned up at the UN-administered poll to back the independence option, violence of unprecedented intensity broke out, leading to deaths, disappearances, massive displacement of the population and wide-scale destruction of property. Every town and village was affected and virtually no family was spared suffering of some sort.

The attack on the adjacent premises of the ICRC and the Bishop of Dili, Msgr. Bello, and their destruction and burning on the very first day of widespread ransacking and plundering were apparently symbolic, intended to demonstrate that there was no safe haven in East Timor, not even in institutions that had continued to be active throughout more or less the whole period of Indonesian rule. In the 10 days after the attack, all expatriates and all UNAMET personnel had to leave East Timor, sometimes in a dramatic public showdown. An unknown number of people were killed in the aftermath of the referendum and hundreds of thousands of people fled or were forced to flee into the mountains in East Timor or to Indonesian West Timor.

The post-ballot period (end of September–December 1999)

Following a week of intensive negotiations with the Indonesian authorities in Jakarta, the ICRC obtained permission to return to the devastated territory and start assessing humanitarian needs. ICRC delegates returned to East Timor on 14 September, which eventually allowed a meaningful dialogue with the military authorities in East Timor and the redeployment of the ICRC eight days after having been forcibly evicted. With the agreement and help of the newly installed Indonesian military administrator, the ICRC was able to set up its new headquarters in one of the few untouched buildings in Dili, the civilian hospital, which became the first new safe haven of the largely destroyed capital. This gave the ICRC a sound basis to develop its activities not only in the medical field but also in all other fields – especially getting emergency food relief first to the towns and then to remoter areas.[7]

Considering the situation in East Timor to be a threat to international peace and security and acting under Chapter VII of the UN Charter, but with the consent of the Indonesian government, the Security Council authorized the creation of a multinational force (International Force East Timor – INTERFET) in Resolution 1264 of 15 September 1999. INTERFET's task was to restore peace and security in East Timor, to protect and support UNAMET in carrying out its tasks, and to facilitate human-itarian assistance. The Indonesian authorities on their side established martial law on the island and appointed a senior military person, well known to the ICRC, to enforce it.

INTERFET, under the leadership of the Australian Defence Forces, arrived on 20 September 1999 to ensure security on the island. Because security was the primary task of these forces, their deployment was given absolute priority and no humanitarian organizations were allowed to reach Dili from Australia, which led to considerable tensions between humanitarian organizations and the Australian authorities. For two weeks, the ICRC, operating mainly from Indonesia, was the only human-itarian organization in place and it was progressively able to extend its activities to other places than the capital.

The arrival of all major humanitarian UN organizations, in particular the WFP, as well as all major international NGOs, quickly allowed the emergency needs of the population living in East Timor to be met. The emphasis was on the need for coordination as literally hundreds of small humanitarian organizations swamped the island. The United Nations Office for the Coordination of Humanitarian Affairs (OCHA) endeav-oured to coordinate the activities of the numerous international, govern-mental and non-governmental organizations.[8] Rapid progress was made and, especially in the absence of notable military confrontations, assis-tance progressively took on the character of development aid rather than emergency help.

The ICRC quickly phased out emergency relief, although it maintained its medical activities, and concentrated on its traditional fields of deten-tion and tracing people who had disappeared during the turmoil. The In-donesian authorities had withdrawn from East Timor, and INTERFET, and subsequently UNAMET, took over the administration. Under its conventional mandate, the ICRC sought now to protect those who were in the hands of the new rulers of East Timor, especially those arrested by them.

Obstacles and opportunities

The mandate of the ICRC

The ICRC bases its activities on the 1949 Geneva Conventions on the protection of the victims of war.[9] The Conventions give the ICRC a legal mandate in all humanitarian affairs and specifically entitle the ICRC to visit captured combatants (Article 126 of the Third Geneva Convention relative to the treatment of prisoners of war) and civilian internees (Article 143 of the Fourth Geneva Convention relative to the treatment of civilian persons in times of war, which applies also in the case of occupation). Article 5 of the Statutes of the International Red Cross, which were also approved by all states parties to the Geneva Conventions, rules that the role of the ICRC is "to undertake the tasks incumbent upon it under the Geneva Conventions, to work for the faithful application of international humanitarian law applicable in armed conflicts and to take cognizance of any complaints based on alleged breaches of that law".[10]

General approach and activities of the ICRC operations

The Geneva Conventions and international humanitarian law in general set out the rights and duties of parties to, and victims of, armed conflicts. The duty of combatants is to spare the civilian population and medical personnel and to protect prisoners. All victims have a right to humane treatment – the wounded are entitled to be cared for, prisoners to be detained in good conditions, and the population to enjoy the means essential to its survival. The purpose of all activities of the ICRC in situations of armed conflict is to ensure that these rules are applied in practice.

The ICRC does this in two ways. The first is to draw the parties' attention to their obligations as regards the treatment of victims and means and methods of waging war, and to point out any failure to observe these obligations. This approach consists mainly of making contact with all parties to armed conflict and persuading them to comply with the law. Direct contact with the parties to an armed conflict is essential to influence their behaviour. Humanitarian diplomacy, however, includes networking with all possible actors – governmental and non-governmental, national and international, the civil society and other actors likely to be able to influence the parties to a conflict and to have an impact on the humanitarian situation of the victims on the ground. It may require an overall strategy and numerous and various means and initiatives to obtain an improvement in respect of humanitarian law and principles.

The second way is to give victims direct assistance to remedy the inevitable shortcomings observed by ICRC delegates in such circumstances. This aspect of direct action, that is, practical assistance to victims, may involve highly complicated operations and raise problems in terms of choices and priorities. Humanitarian diplomacy in this regard aims at being allowed and able to assist victims without discrimination, even if they are considered "enemies" by a party to an armed conflict. This again involves a network of contacts in order to gain access to the victims and assist them if necessary.

Both the monitoring and the assistance functions are conferred on the ICRC by international humanitarian law, and hence by all the states that drew up and adopted that law. International humanitarian law also gives the ICRC a right to initiate any action it considers appropriate to help victims of conflict. Differing from many other humanitarian actors, the ICRC seeks thereby to orient the goals of its activities by the standards laid down in the Geneva Conventions and refers explicitly or implicitly to them in its interventions.

Although the ICRC had a sound legal basis for its activities in East Timor under the Geneva Conventions, it nevertheless had to negotiate with the Indonesian authorities in Jakarta concerning its presence, its access to the victims and its activities. The "seat agreement" allowed for the establishment of a delegation only in the Indonesian capital. Any ICRC activities, and even more a permanent presence, outside Jakarta and especially in East Timor were subject to authorization by the ministry of foreign affairs. Prior consultations with the main governmental departments, especially the ministry of defence, and their various services were necessary to overcome political and security objections. The fact that ICRC operations usually take place in war situations or internal disturbances explains the sensitive and delicate character of its activities.

Principled action

Every humanitarian action should be inspired only by the desire to help the victims and such action should treat those victims strictly according to their needs and vulnerability, with no discrimination.[11] The ICRC additionally insists that its humanitarian actions are carried out independently from political authorities (the principle of independence) and does not take sides regarding the issue at the origin of the conflict (the principle of neutrality). The institution believes that only then will humanitarian action remain acceptable to all parties to an armed conflict and thus retain its effectiveness. Other humanitarian organizations, in contrast, act on behalf of governments or link their action with a particular political goal.

Moreover, multilateral and, in recent years, regional peacekeeping operations and military operations in general have become more numerous, complex and diverse. They encompass not only military but also political and humanitarian aspects. Since they are inherently political, these operations may often undermine the ICRC's humanitarian action and its underlying principles of impartiality, neutrality and independence and may call for the ICRC to take a position. Its principled action then becomes even more important.

In East Timor, while coordinating its activities with the Indonesian authorities in the first period and with the United Nations and the many governmental and non-governmental humanitarian organizations in the second period, the ICRC tried to maintain its independence from the political players in order to reach the victims. The task of upholding its fundamental principles, and more precisely the perception of the impartiality of humanitarian action, was particularly difficult in a situation such as East Timor. Humanitarian problems arose in the long years of occupation mostly among the East Timorese civilians: interventions were carried out on their behalf and assistance was directed to them. The ICRC often played the role of neutral intermediary between East Timorese civilians and the Indonesian authorities and very exceptionally between the Indonesian authorities and the resistance movement Fretilin and its armed wing Falintil[12] – direct contact with Falintil in East Timor was prohibited. Many of the Indonesian interlocutors and pro-Indonesian East Timorese (pro-*integrasi*) therefore questioned the impartiality of the ICRC (see below).

Coordination

Humanitarian work in some contexts has been characterized by overlapping, insufficient coordination and the ill-defined mandates of the numerous humanitarian agencies involved. Sound consultation mechanisms are therefore essential and the greater efficiency of humanitarian action also contributes to the application of international humanitarian law. The ICRC tries to establish a dialogue with the principal organizations engaged in emergency humanitarian aid programmes, with a view to harmonizing and improving the humanitarian responses and defining a common code of ethics that will make their activities more effective and enhance their credibility.

Negotiations

As mentioned above, the overall objective of international humanitarian law and of the ICRC is for the law to be respected and implemented so that the victims of armed conflicts can benefit from its protection and the effects of the conflicts on the victims are minimized as much as possible.

The parameters of humanitarian negotiations

In general, humanitarian negotiations seek to obtain protection and assistance for the victims of conflicts, for the civilian population and for particularly vulnerable categories of civilians or persons hors de combat, especially prisoners. More concretely, the goal is to obtain treatment and conditions for these individuals that would not prevail without such "humanitarian negotiations". The negotiations are usually linked to the operational activities of the ICRC, which should contribute to achieving these goals.

These operational activities of the ICRC are not restricted to assistance. According to international law, assistance activities by humanitarian organizations are only subsidiary for two reasons: first, the parties to an armed conflict must do their outmost to ensure that non-combatants are not affected by armed hostilities, and, secondly, the parties to a conflict are themselves responsible for assisting the victims under their control. Accordingly, the ICRC tries first to draw the attention of the authorities to their obligations before itself rendering assistance.

The legal framework within which a crisis takes place influences the rights and duties of states. In international armed conflicts, the parties are obliged to accept certain monitoring functions of the ICRC, whereas in non-international armed conflicts and in situations that are not covered by the Geneva Conventions the ICRC can offer its (humanitarian) services but there is no obligation to accept them.

If there is an obligation to let the ICRC act and the authorities accept this view, the negotiation is obviously easy because the maxim "pacta sunt servanda" (pacts must be respected) prevails. Mostly, however, the situation is different. Political and military considerations, reciprocity, confidence, cultural and religious elements as well as national and international public opinion constitute decisive parameters of the negotiations. Most importantly, the timing of an intervention often influences the success of the negotiations. Each humanitarian organization may have different approaches, depending on its character, history and goal.

Humanitarian negotiations in East Timor basically involved two sets of challenges. The first related to cooperation with the political and military authorities, and the second concerned coordination among humanitarian actors, which included UN agencies as well as other organizations.

Negotiations with the political and military authorities

The ICRC's principal operational means everywhere are interventions directed at the parties to the conflict. These démarches are the key to all its activities: on the basis of direct access to victims, the ICRC engages in a bilateral confidential dialogue with the authorities aimed at ending violations of humanitarian law, at preventing further abuses and at limiting their effects, possibly through assistance to the victims.

Interventions or démarches are part of a global strategy of action and were the ICRC's principal tool of negotiation to achieve its overall humanitarian objectives in East Timor. They addressed a wide range of issues in order to remind the authorities of their responsibilities and to call for their action. They related to the establishment of the ICRC (for example, the seat agreement on immunities and privileges), visas for the staff of the delegation (which implied lengthy negotiations), the planning of training for the military in humanitarian law or the protection of the civilian population (comprehensive confidential situation reports to the Indonesian authorities) or individuals deprived of their liberty (interviews with prison commanders, reports on detention conditions and the treatment of prisoners), the conduct of hostilities or behaviour by military or security personnel, the protection of humanitarian workers, and authorization of and information about assistance programmes.

Interventions involved both major and minor acts of communication, both written (*notes verbales*, reports, letters) and oral (telephone calls, interviews, meetings). Minor acts may seem trivial when taken alone but possibly reinforced major initiatives. Such initiatives were ineffective, or even counterproductive, unless other types of communication (indirect contacts, seminars, etc.) were organized beforehand to ensure that the message would be properly understood and followed up afterwards. Serious and urgent problems demanded rapid and strong responses (e.g. expressions of regret for the attack on the ICRC by the Indonesian authorities, authorization to open a hospital) whereas other problems could be solved only in the medium or long term, especially when they were of a structural nature (e.g. structural prison problems).

Interventions took place at local (district of East Timor, Dili), regional (e.g. the military area in Denpasar, also responsible for East Timor) or national levels (Djakarta) or possibly at headquarters level of the ICRC in Geneva. They were carried out variously by a delegate in a village in East Timor, the head of the ICRC office in Dili, the coordinator for protection issues or the head of the delegation in Djakarta or the person responsible for Asia, the ICRC's director of operations or its president. They targeted different publics, but obviously particularly the parties to a conflict directly in charge of the implementation of humanitarian law. These included the ministries of defence, interior and foreign affairs, which were often the liaising authorities for all ICRC activities. The ICRC delegation contacted the authorities at different levels and in different ministries – the executive but possibly also the legislative – and other actors in civil society that had a bearing on the situation. In civil wars, the non-state party to the armed conflict and in particular its military wing are usually the main interlocutors for inducing respect for international humanitarian law, but because of Indonesian legislation they could be contacted only outside East Timor. Similarly, the ICRC established contact with the political and military authorities of the multinational forces INTERFET and UNAMET.

The rhythm and intensity of interventions had to take into account the changes in the political conflictual environment. The ICRC's long-term strategy to improve the situation of the population in East Timor during the last 20 years of Indonesian rule took different and sometimes difficult forms during the run-up to the referendum. The situation was especially hectic during and after the referendum until the emergency phase was over. Obviously, it was more difficult or temporarily even impossible to establish contact with the parties to the conflict during active hostilities. Because of the highly political environment in East Timor and the security issues involved, even minor details often required lengthy negotiations, and decisions on ICRC activities and interventions were taken at very high levels of the Indonesian government.

Bilateral confidential dialogue is clearly the ICRC's preferred mode of obtaining improvements for the benefit of victims of armed conflict or ensuring respect for humanitarian law. The ICRC is thus the only humanitarian organization that systematically bases its actions on persuasion and matters of principle. Confidentiality should help to keep the ICRC's relationship with the authorities outside political pressure and manipulation.[13] The ICRC's longstanding relations with the Indonesian authorities enabled many humanitarian problems to be resolved and were instrumental in allowing the quick return to East Timor of forcibly evicted individuals. Other humanitarian problems, however, could not be resolved despite continuous dialogue at all levels.

The ICRC announces publicly whether it has access to the victims of a given armed conflict and whether or not it can operate in certain contexts. However, public denunciation is used by the ICRC only as a means of last resort, exceptionally and under restrictive conditions.[14] Despite many difficulties, this applied also in East Timor. Only when the ICRC president, following interviews with then President Habibie and the ministers of foreign affairs and defence, failed to influence the Indonesian position of creating and supporting the militias reigning with impunity in East Timor did he publicly warn of an imminent humanitarian tragedy.

In addition to bilateral confidential démarches, the ICRC maintained close relations with governments not directly concerned in the armed conflict and with international and regional organizations, especially with the United Nations and in particular with UNAMET. By sharing non-confidential information on its operations, raising awareness of humanitarian problems and publicizing its concern, the ICRC aimed at mobilizing support for its activities and the plight of victims.

It is important for humanitarian diplomacy to include more general aspects as well and for the ICRC also to promote the dissemination of knowledge of humanitarian law and the importance of respecting it and to promote its position on issues of humanitarian concern. Operational difficulties in one context may have a bearing on other situations and can be tackled only in a global manner. A narrowly understood "operational diplomacy" is only a part of a strategic framework. Humanitarian diplomacy for efficient humanitarian action in armed conflicts also involves general issues such as discussions on principles and may require a widespread mobilization through all means of communications.

In this environment of diplomacy, multilateral cooperation and worldwide communication, the ICRC has to continue its efforts to raise awareness of humanitarian issues in international forums. While taking due account of the respective spheres of competence of political and humanitarian players, it has to promote mutual understanding of objectives and working methods, and thus to develop complementarity.

The example of the hospital

The example of the hospital in Dili is particularly important and illustrative. Although the ICRC had been active in the region for many years, and in spite of a formal agreement with the relevant authorities at the highest level in Jakarta, previous attempts to place an ICRC surgical team in Dili General Hospital had failed. Thus, although there had been no direct ICRC involvement in the hospital before 1999, the ICRC was not entirely new to the context and was familiar with the hospital and its activities prior to the recent events. During 1999, it became clear that, if violence broke out, there would be a vacuum in terms of medical human resources. The ICRC would have to intervene and total substitution of all medical services and hospital management would be the only option in a situation where the health system completely failed.

Initial assessment after the return of ICRC delegates to Dili on 14 September 1999 revealed that, despite the general destruction in Dili, including the ICRC delegation, the hospital was one of the few buildings that had suffered only from vandalism and looting of equipment and supplies. A few East Timorese nursing staff and patients remained, and the hospital compound was sheltering up to 500 civilians who had sought refuge there. As a first step, the ICRC managed to secure protection of the hospital site, patients and staff by the Indonesian Armed Forces (Tentara Nasional Indonesia). This was possible because of its longstanding presence in Indonesia and the relations – including at the highest levels in Jakarta – it had developed over the years.

The ICRC then sought and obtained approval from the Indonesian military authorities to use the hospital as a base for all ICRC activities and as accommodation for the expatriate team. This arrangement gave the ICRC a viable base to start from in the midst of what was otherwise still a highly volatile situation in a destroyed town, at a time when the future evolution of events was anything but certain.

The ICRC's choice of the hospital as a base for its activities was a crucial step in creating a space for humanitarian activities. For the population, it was important to have a visible presence and clear focus for the whole range of ICRC activities. Practical considerations of finding an operational base in Dili, where much of the infrastructure had been destroyed, posed many problems for the numerous NGOs that arrived later. Having an established base at the hospital gave the ICRC a head start. Previous contacts with the Indonesian authorities made negotiation and decision-making much easier in these early phases.

The ICRC focused on protecting the patients, staff and others already sheltering in the hospital by providing emergency hospital services and by preserving the hospital buildings and facilities for the future. The strategy for achieving these protective measures was to create a space for humanitarian activities. First, the ICRC maintained its dialogue with the Indonesian commander to ensure understanding and approval of its work in the hospital and in the country. Secondly, the ICRC placed expatriates in the hospital. Thirdly, the population was informed during field trips that the hospital was functional and that it was safe to seek treatment there. All of these factors contributed to restoring the population's confidence in the hospital. On 29 June 2001, the ICRC handed over the responsibility for and management of Dili National Hospital (formerly known as Dili General Hospital) to the United Nations Transitional Administration in East Timor.

Difficulty in upholding the perception of independence and impartiality

Although the ICRC was able to act independently from the Indonesian authorities, it was much more difficult to uphold the *perception* of its independence and impartiality in the run-up to the referendum. During the whole period, the ICRC tried rather unsuccessfully to distance itself from the political endeavour to organize the ballot. The overwhelming presence of hundreds of UN personnel, both military and civilian, and the sudden arrival of several UN humanitarian agencies and some major NGOs not only overwhelmed the ICRC but led to a situation in which the institution could not distinguish itself sufficiently from organizations with a mandate that was basically political in nature.

The first goal of UNAMET was to calm down the situation in East Timor, gain access to the thousands of East Timorese who had fled from their villages in order to avoid the terror of the militias and get assistance to those in need. Access to victims and humanitarian relief were not just a humanitarian gesture, but a precondition for creating an environment conducive to the peaceful holding of the referendum. They were willy-nilly instrumentalized and perceived as partial by pro-integration East Timorese and in particular the militias.

During this period the ICRC withdrew progressively from the assistance programmes, emphasized its independence in its communications, concentrated its efforts on disseminating international humanitarian law and principles to the military and police forces present in East Timor, and prepared for the events ahead. As usual, independent from the organizational, structural and logistical set-up of the United Nations, the ICRC maintained and developed its own network and logistical infrastructure and consulted with the United Nations without being coordinated by it. The ICRC feared that the uncertain outcome of the plebiscite could lead to major fighting and even to the forcible and disputed division of East Timor into pro-independence and pro-integration areas, and possibly even to the involvement of the United Nations and its military personnel. Numerous contacts were established with political and military actors on all sides, including militia leaders, to prepare for all possibilities. Despite these moves and probably owing to the massive gathering of people seeking protection, the ICRC was the first major target of attack following the announcement of the results, nearly a week before the premises of UNAMET were attacked.

Following the return of the ICRC to East Timor in mid-September 1999, cooperation with INTERFET and UNAMET followed the same principles. There was indeed a possibility that military confrontation might take place involving the multinational forces and militias and possibly even Indonesian military forces. The ICRC had to underline its independence from all political and military actors in order to fulfil its function as a neutral intermediary between possible military opponents. This role soon became relevant as the first militias were arrested by the multinational forces and the ICRC asked to visit them according to its customary practice. It reached an agreement with INTERFET to visit all individuals arrested by the forces. Inspired by the rules of international humanitarian law related to a situation of military occupation, but without recognizing their formal application, the rules on detention contained in the Fourth Geneva Convention served as models for the conditions of detention and the ICRC's visits.

Following the departure from East Timor of the Indonesian authorities in September 1999, the ICRC concluded a similar "seat agreement" with the UN administrator in East Timor, which was in turn replaced by the present agreement concluded with the Timor Leste government.

Coordination with other humanitarian actors

Until May 1999, coordination with other humanitarian actors was not a major issue because the ICRC was the only international humanitarian organization active in East Timor. The ICRC cooperated with the Indonesian Red Cross and easily coordinated its activities with the few non-governmental organizations present in East Timor. With the arrival of several international humanitarian organizations in the run-up to the referendum, coordination became an important issue. Many humanitarian actors – governmental and non-governmental, with different mandates, objectives, areas of expertise and varying resources – arrived in Dili. It was therefore only natural that coordination came to form an intrinsic part of the universal humanitarian effort of the ICRC too, if only to gain overall effectiveness.

As regards international organizations, the ICRC of course most readily enters into relations with those whose attitude or actions are closest to its own. For example, the ICRC is in regular contact with the Office of the United Nations High Commissioner for Refugees (UNHCR) for operational reasons: because the UNHCR's role with regard to refugee law is similar to the ICRC's role with regard to international humanitarian law, the two organizations often work side by side in the field. In the case of the East Timor crisis, under its mandate to protect refugees, UNHCR was mainly responsible for protecting the East Timorese who found themselves in West Timor or in other parts of Indonesia. The two institutions harmonized their activities in Indonesia. The ICRC was active especially in respect to the tracing of missing East Timorese residing both in East Timor and in Indonesia and organized the exchange of messages for those East Timorese separated from their next-of-kin.

In the light of the humanitarian emergency and the invasion of hundreds of bigger and smaller humanitarian organizations, coordination among the humanitarian actors on the island became increasingly important. The ICRC's approach on coordination was based upon regular contact involving dialogue and mutual consultation, both at headquarters and in the field, on operational questions. The basic principle underlying the ICRC's participation in coordination mechanisms and efforts was to seek the greatest possible complementarity with other actors in terms of their respective mandates, expertise and operating methods and procedures. With regard to OCHA, the ICRC contributed to the discussions concerning the elaboration of a humanitarian action plan during the emergency phase, and actively participated in the Geneva launch of the Consolidated Appeals.

Wider implications

In peace-time, the ICRC endeavours in its humanitarian diplomacy to promote international humanitarian law and its universality, respect and development. It seeks to preserve independent and impartial humanitarian action and contributes to its coordination and efficiency. It assures political, operational and financial support for its activities both in situations of armed conflict and in performing a whole series of short- and long-term tasks to prevent abuses and to uphold human dignity.[15]

In situations of armed conflict and also in East Timor, ICRC's preventive efforts do not cease entirely but are transformed into a drive to promote respect for international humanitarian law. Different phases in the East Timorese crisis allowed for the achievement of limited goals, although political and/or military events often prevented the protection of or assistance to the victims of the armed conflict. The *reformasi* period following the resignation of the longstanding Indonesian ruler Suharto brought hope to the East Timorese that they might be able to determine their situation themselves, but also led to a critical humanitarian situation. The ICRC was on the whole the only international humanitarian organization operating in East Timor during this period. Despite its best efforts, it was able to address only a few humanitarian problems because of its severely limited means and serious security problems.

The period leading up to the referendum was overshadowed by the political endeavour to organize the consultation, and even humanitarian organizations were largely instrumentalized to achieve this goal. The ICRC adhered to its principles of independence and neutrality, but could distance itself from the political process only with great difficulty. Following the outbreak of severe violence, the post-ballot period saw the deployment of numerous humanitarian agencies coping with the aftermath of the political process, which primarily called for coordination between the humanitarian actors. Fortunately, armed confrontations between the new military force INTERFET, the militias and the Indonesian military occurred only rarely and the ICRC was able to limit its protection activities to visiting prisoners held under the new administration.

The humanitarian diplomacy used by the ICRC to prevent or at least to resolve humanitarian problems in the East Timor crisis and to work for the respect of humanitarian law encompassed the whole spectrum of communication means, ranging from the usual confidential interventions to negotiations over humanitarian assistance and to exceptional public denunciations. In the light of the important political consequences of the East Timor issue, the ICRC also tried to preserve its distinctive humanitarian and independent character. Whatever the result in political terms, a crisis such as East Timor can never be described as a humanitarian success.

Notes

1. Ian Smillie and Larry Minear, eds, *The Charity of Nations: Humanitarian Action in a Calculating World*, Bloomfield, CT: Kumarian Press, 2004 (in particular the chapter "East Timor: The Perfect Harmony").

2. The situation in East Timor was classified by the United Nations as an occupation (UN Security Council Resolution 384 (1975) and General Assembly Resolution 3485 (1975)).

3. "Geraten Pengacan Keamanan" (disturbers of public order). The best-known category among these prisoners were the G30S/PKI prisoners arrested during the repression of communist movements following the attempted coup d'état in 1965. The annual rounds of visits to these detainees started in 1974. Independence movements in East Timor (ex-GPK/TIM) and in other areas of Indonesia (Aceh, Irian Jaya, Moluccas) were also classed as GPK.

4. See East Timor and Indonesia Action Network (ETAN), "Selected Postings from ... East-Timor: Red Cross Visits East Timor's Alas Region amid Massacre Rumours", 23 November 1998, ⟨http://www.etan.org/et/1998/november/22-30/23redcro.htm⟩ (accessed 24 April 2006); see also the public debate about the disclosure of ICRC reports on the treatment and conditions of detainees held in Iraq (Abu Ghraib) and at Guantánamo.

5. The most famous militia groups were the Aitarak in Dili, headed by Eurico Guterres, the BMP (Besih Merah Putih) in Liquiza, headed by Manuel de Souza, and Mahidi (Mati Hidup Integrasi) in Ainaro/Kovalingo, led by Cancio de Carvalho. The most famous paramilitary group was Halilintar.

6. To carry out the consultation, the Security Council, through Resolution 1246 (1999), authorized the establishment of UNAMET on 11 June 1999. The 5 May 1999 tripartite agreements between the United Nations, Indonesia and Portugal stipulated that, after the vote, UNAMET would oversee a transition period pending implementation of the decision of the East Timorese people.

7. By January 2000, the ICRC had opened a full delegation with 53 expatriates and 284 locally hired staff. In 2002, the ICRC maintained a much reduced presence in East Timor, with 3 expatriates and 20 local staff.

8. At the multilateral level, the ICRC closely followed the work of the Inter-Agency Standing Committee, the mechanism for inter-agency coordination of humanitarian assistance, which is chaired by OCHA and is made up of agencies with humanitarian mandates, the International Red Cross and Red Crescent Movement, NGO consortia and the World Bank. It maintained close relations with the Humanitarian Liaison Working Group in both Geneva and New York, and continued to make a substantial contribution to UN efforts towards efficient inter-agency coordination in East Timor.

9. See the full text of the Geneva Conventions of 1949 and their Additional Protocols of 1997 at ⟨http://www.icrc.org/Web/Eng/siteeng0.nsf/html/genevaconventions⟩ (accessed 24 April 2006).

10. "Statutes of the International Committee of the Red Cross", *International Review of the Red Cross*, No. 324, 30 September 1998, pp. 537–543; see also Marion Harroff-Tavel, "La Diplomatie humanitaire du Comité Internationale de la Croix-Rouge", *Relations internationales*, No. 121, 2005, pp. 73–89, and Jean-François Berger, *The Humanitarian Diplomacy of the ICRC and the Conflict in Croatia (1991–1992)*, Geneva: ICRC, 1995.

11. See International Court of Justice (ICJ), Judgment of 27 June 1986, *Case Concerning Military and Paramilitary Activities in and against Nicaragua (Nicaragua v. United States of America)*, ICJ Reports 1986, pp. 14 ff., in particular paras 242 ff. The ICJ had to examine the question of whether (and which) assistance from the US government to the so-called Contra rebels engaged in a civil war with the government of Nicaragua was legal under international law and what criteria applied. The ICJ declared that the fundamental principles of the Red Cross, namely the principles of humanity and independence, were essential for every lawful humanitarian action.

12. Forcas Armadas de Libertaçao National de Timor Leste.
13. See, for example, Jakob Kellenberger, "Speaking out or Remaining Silent in Humanitarian Work", *International Review of the Red Cross*, No. 855, 30 September 2004, pp. 593–610.
14. See "Action by the International Committee of the Red Cross in the Event of Breaches of International Humanitarian Law", *International Review of the Red Cross*, No. 221, 30 April 1981, pp. 76–83.
15. See the "Operational Activities: Humanitarian Diplomacy" section in the ICRC's 1999 annual report, which outlines what the ICRC understands by humanitarian diplomacy in a general sense, ⟨http://www.icrc.org/Web/Eng/siteeng0.nsf/iwpList74/8A94331BF49856DCC1256B660059124D⟩ (accessed 24 April 2006).

9

Steep learning curves in the DPRK

David Morton

The Democratic People's Republic of Korea (DPRK) is one of the most closed and isolated countries in the world. A distrust of foreigners goes a long way back in Korean history; a siege mentality is pervasive and North Koreans fear that they may be attacked at any moment. When the DPRK government suddenly appealed to the humanitarian community for aid in 1995, no one really knew what to make of it. The international community knew very little about the country or its problems, and there was very limited representation of the donor community in the capital, Pyongyang. For its part, the DPRK knew even less about the operational requirements of aid agencies. The concept of a non-governmental organization (NGO), an organization that was not part of a government structure, was alien to the Koreans, where everything was centralized and there was no such thing as civil society.

It proved to be the start of a long, steep learning curve for both the DPRK authorities and the international aid agencies. Humanitarian workers found themselves using diplomacy to bridge the gaps between actors with widely divergent priorities, working practices and politics. This account covers the period from 1998 to 2002, with particular reference to how humanitarian diplomacy contributed to the efforts of the World Food Programme (WFP) to provide food aid.

In the DPRK, conventional negotiating strategies did not work. North Korean officials demonstrated time after time that they were quite willing to forgo food aid their citizens desperately needed for "reasons" that were impossible for outsiders to fathom – if reasons were given at all.

For humanitarian workers involved in the negotiations, officials appeared to be exercising power in the most arbitrary way. Finding common ground, not just between North Korean officialdom and the WFP but between aid agencies and donor countries that often had diverging views on how to deal with the DPRK, proved to be a major test for humanitarian diplomacy, and important lessons were learned. First, despite the difficulties of operating in conditions of extreme hardship, isolation and hazard, with movements curtailed and in an absence of transparency or access to even rudimentary information, achieving objectives through negotiation was possible. However, as will be discussed in this chapter's first case study – negotiating permission to conduct a nutrition survey – success could take literally years to achieve. Secondly, external pressures and criticisms affected the situation of agencies working inside the DPRK and at times undermined them. Building inter-agency consensus was necessary in order to engage in successful negotiations with a difficult political regime and to justify courses of action to external actors. This process is discussed in the second case study about building inter-agency consensus.

Context

The situation in the DPRK was shaped by the closed nature of the state and the interdependent relationship of its agriculture and industry. The government's failure to cope with economic collapse and natural disasters contributed to the crisis the DPRK faced after 1995. Pyongyang's decision to ask for help was unprecedented and, because it lacked precedents, the international community struggled to respond. In this context, the United Nations' Humanitarian Coordinator played a pivotal role in humanitarian diplomacy.

Politically, North Koreans strongly believe that they live in a small country surrounded by hostile powers. Although an armistice ended fighting on the Korean Peninsula in 1953, no peace agreement was ever concluded between the two Koreas or between the DPRK and South Korea's powerful ally, the United States. Thousands of US troops remain stationed within a 90-minute drive of Pyongyang, along the Demilitarized Zone. Another powerful enemy, Japan, lies to the east.

Geographically, the DPRK is a mountainous country with limited agricultural land. Farming is very intensively managed and requires large amounts of fertilizers. In addition, it relies on a functioning industrial economy to provide inputs for the manufacture of fertilizers and energy for irrigation systems.

Economic development and collapse

In the 1960s and 1970s the DPRK existed successfully within the Soviet orbit. It had a heavily industrialized economy that relied greatly on barter with and aid from the Soviet Union and other Eastern bloc countries. When, in the 1990s, the Soviet Union broke up and the Eastern bloc countries adopted the market system, the DPRK was badly affected. It could no longer barter for the required fuel, inputs and spare parts. This, combined with a dramatic drop in energy production, led to a sharp decline in industrial activity. The shortage of fertilizers and energy for irrigation, a depreciating stock of tractors and tyres, and a shortage of fuel led to falls in agricultural output.

When the severe floods of 1995 hit, the significance was dramatic. Successive harvests were at least 1 million tons short of the minimum survival requirements of the population, over 60 per cent of whom lived in towns and cities.

The industrial decline also affected the provision of clean drinking water – there was not enough power for the water pumps, broken pipes could not be replaced and contaminated water seeped into them, and there were no chemicals to purify the water. Water-borne diseases were prevalent. Hospitals were unheated, medical equipment was antiquated, and international drugs and medical supplies were not available. The result was a combined food and health crisis.

The DPRK's response

The first external indication that there was a problem came in 1995 when the North Korean government appealed for assistance to the humanitarian community, including the World Food Programme (WFP), the International Federation of Red Cross and Red Crescent Societies (IFRC) and Caritas. It seems that the government presumed that it would simply ask for aid and aid would be provided. There was no understanding of how international agencies with responsibilities to donor governments operate. The resulting questions and need for information to assess, monitor and evaluate the situation, as well as facts and publicity to convince donors to support the programmes, seemed to take them by complete surprise – and to some extent was an affront to their dignity and integrity.

The government set up the Flood Damage Rehabilitation Commission (FDRC) to coordinate those international agencies providing humanitarian aid. The FDRC formed part of the ministry of foreign affairs but included officials from other parts of the government. It was with the FDRC that all negotiations took place. According to the established diplomatic corps, the ministry of foreign affairs was weak and did not have the ear of North Korean leader Kim Jong Il or his advisers.

> *The Koreans were very sensitive about certain words. They did not like the term "monitoring", and professed shock that we did not trust them. Other not-appreciated words were the "R" words "reform" and "restructuring". These words were not acceptable because they implied that the present system was not perfect. The Juche (self-reliance) philosophy of the Great Leader, Kim Il Sung, was considered perfect; therefore it could not be reformed or restructured. Another "R" word was "random", as in "random monitoring". This was not acceptable because its application would contravene national sovereignty.*

Hunger hidden away

It was not until 1997, some two years after establishing their offices, that the international aid agencies began gradually to understand the extent and seriousness of the food crisis and the large number of children affected by acute hunger and poor health. Bound by a traditional sense of honour, the Koreans were secretive about their needs and the extent of their problems. This was quite unlike the situation that humanitarian workers usually find themselves in – for example, seeing lines of gaunt starving Ethiopians by the roadside or queuing up outside feeding centres looking for assistance.

In the DPRK, hunger was hidden away. When travelling around the country, all that could be seen were seemingly healthy, albeit stunted, Koreans. There were no obvious signs of hunger. The sick and malnourished stayed in their homes, unseen.

Assessing the situation

Despite travel and monitoring restrictions, aid agencies did begin to assemble a picture of the situation. By 1999, there was no doubt that people received very little food through the public distribution system and were forced to find other sources. Their coping mechanisms included gathering wild foods from the hillsides and fields and "alternative foods", which were produced by the authorities with a combination of a small amount of cereal or grain and whatever else was available, such as ground-up maize stalks, vegetable stalks and roots.

Food shortages were particularly acute in the north-east of the country, where there were large urban populations who had worked in the now defunct industrial sector and were reliant upon a very limited amount of suitable agricultural land. Life was a desperate struggle for survival.

Although household visits by the WFP's field officers were clearly manipulated, nonetheless there were telling details that indicated how badly people needed food. There was a predominance of skeletal teenage girls in north-eastern hospitals (this led to the inclusion of secondary school pupils in WFP feeding programmes). Field officers reported that some mothers were keeping pigs in their houses (one pig hidden in a cupboard made so much noise that it had to be let out). Such animals were so valuable during the food crisis that they would be stolen if they were kept outside. County officials were obviously hungry – the lunches laid on for visiting field officers were clearly eagerly anticipated by all the officials because it meant they had an excuse for a meal. The lunches usually consisted of wild foods such as bracken and edible leaves, and sometimes seaweed if it was a coastal county.

The role of the Humanitarian Coordinator

Although it is obvious in retrospect that the food situation was really very bad, at the time its seriousness was the subject of controversy. In 1998, many of the donor countries that were providing humanitarian assistance were frustrated by the different messages coming out of the DPRK. Some NGOs said there was a crisis, others that there was not. By late 1998 two NGOs had already withdrawn from the country and another was just about to depart. Those that withdrew were critical of the agencies that had decided to remain.

There was thus an immediate need to encourage the humanitarian agencies to reach a consensus so that a credible position could be presented to the outside world. In the DPRK, the best-placed person to do this was the UN Humanitarian Coordinator. Humanitarian Coordinators are appointed by the Under-Secretary-General for Humanitarian Affairs, who headed the UN Office for the Coordination of Humanitarian Affairs (OCHA). Humanitarian Coordinators are appointed in countries with complex humanitarian crises in order to provide leadership and coordination on humanitarian issues. In practice, the Humanitarian Coordinator can easily be ignored or bypassed, but in this context the position was pivotal in the conduct of humanitarian diplomacy for two reasons: first, the Humanitarian Coordinator had established better access to higher-level officials within the FDRC and so could have more influence than other agencies; and, secondly, from this position it was possible to spearhead inter-agency consensus-building.

In the DPRK capital Pyongyang, a weekly inter-agency meeting was chaired by the Humanitarian Coordinator and attended by all UN agencies, NGOs, the European Commission and donor representatives, and served as the main forum for coordination and discussion of all humanitarian issues. On occasion the Humanitarian Coordinator was asked on behalf of the inter-agency group to take up issues with the government and, in general, the government accepted the Humanitarian Coordinator as spokesperson for the community.

Operational issues

The main issues of concern for the small humanitarian community of UN agencies and NGOs revolved around the very restricted operating conditions that obtained in the DPRK. Some parts of the country were off-limits; the number of foreign staff permitted by the Koreans was insufficient; agencies were not able to conduct true random monitoring and spot checks; and there was a serious lack of reliable data and information. Furthermore, ensuring the safety and well-being of humanitarian workers was a major concern. These constraints map onto the main operational considerations of humanitarian organizations: access to the population; assessing, monitoring and evaluating the effects of programmes; ensuring compliance with agreed agendas; coordination and implementation of programmes; and the need to justify decisions, actions and activities to donors. Such considerations are closely interrelated: restrictions in one area have a deleterious effect on the others. For example, access to the population was essential to assess what aid was needed, whether it arrived and had been given to the intended beneficiaries, and whether it had the desired result – which was in turn the justification for additional future aid.

The role of humanitarian diplomacy was to find ways to ease these restrictions in order to maintain the humanitarian space. As such, it was these issues that became the chief objects of negotiations with the DPRK authorities.

Access to the population

One of the greatest hurdles was that aid workers were denied access to about 25 per cent of the country, representing about 15 per cent of the population. There was no way of assessing the needs – if any – of the people in these areas, although the general consensus was that conditions were unlikely to be any better than those in the accessible areas. The inaccessible areas were mainly the mountainous counties in the north and those down the central mountain range. Although there was a general trend towards gradually increasing access, at the same time some areas that were accessible became inaccessible, and vice versa, for no clear reason.

Access to official information

Equally serious were difficulties in accessing official information and data. Agencies had to formulate their assistance programmes based on information of uncertain quality and reliability provided by the government and on whatever else they could find out from other sources.

The capabilities of aid agencies to assess, monitor and evaluate their programmes are fundamental to their ability to carry out their work successfully. The paucity and poor quality of the information and data provided by the Koreans made it very difficult to measure whether the aid was having any positive impact, and this in turn created difficulties for agencies that had to deliver viable answers to the donor community about their programmes. Throughout this period, there was concern about whether aid was reaching all the intended beneficiaries, predominantly children and mothers, or whether some people were being excluded for any reason.

However, agencies were not permitted to conduct random monitoring of programmes or spot checks, which are the normal means to determine that aid is properly used. Negotiating permission to carry out nutritional surveys of children in the accessible areas of the country in order to assess vulnerability and the impact of their programmes was a major priority of the WFP and the United Nations Children's Fund (UNICEF).

> National security overrides every other consideration in the DPRK. If there was a choice between external aid and national security, there was no contest: national security would automatically prevail. This was why certain parts of the country were off-limits; this was why information was restricted. Even giving us a list of beneficiary institutions was perceived to have national security implications.

Communications

Establishing communications, both within the country and with the outside world, is a priority for aid agencies, for reasons of security and for basic logistics. In the DPRK, setting up any kind of functional system proved to be a major challenge. Telephones, the obvious means by which to communicate with the outside world in real time, were unreliable and tightly controlled and, although the WFP managed to establish a functioning email system, it was plagued by the poor quality of telephone lines and the resulting very slow data transmission speeds. The installation of satellite facilities that would enable access to the Internet and provide voice and data communications was not permitted.

It is normal procedure for UN agencies and NGOs to equip their vehicles and sub-offices with long-distance radio communications (HF) or, failing that, with satellite phones. However, the DPRK authorities would permit neither, for reasons of "national security". This became a major worry because the possibility of a serious road accident outside Pyongyang was high. Roads in the countryside were very poor, turning almost entirely to gravel not far outside Pyongyang. There were very many steep mountain passes with precipitous drops and no safety barriers. Road traffic mainly comprised ancient lorries with poor brakes and bald tyres. If staff were injured while travelling, there was no way of communicating or of bringing the injured person to Pyongyang.

Health and safety issues

Ensuring the health and safety of staff is a priority for any responsible employer, and agencies and NGOs are no exception. Making provisions for the treatment of staff in the event of serious illness or injury that cannot be treated locally is an essential task for all agencies.

As a matter of course, in almost all operating countries throughout the world UN agencies and NGOs have agreements with international air ambulance services to provide medical evacuation (medevac) services in order to quickly fly sick or injured staff to hospitals in major centres. In the DPRK, health practices were decades out of date and far below international standards, so setting up a medevac contingency plan was of paramount importance. However, the ministry of foreign affairs was not able to guarantee that an air ambulance aircraft would be permitted to land at Pyongyang in an emergency. Only the military authorities could give flight clearances for foreign aircraft, and this could take 48 hours or more. This was clearly unsatisfactory. A further stumbling block was that the Koreans considered that their medical facilities could handle any medical problem, thereby negating the need to take people out of the country for treatment.

Staff living conditions

The WFP staff posted to the sub-offices led a tough existence. The sub-offices consisted of a few rooms in a hotel, and the interpreter stayed in the same hotel. North Korean hotels tended to be dark, gloomy and almost completely empty. The food was monotonous and sometimes scarce. In winter, the hotels were very cold – the WFP had to remove its staff from Hyesan, in the far north, when temperatures reached −38°C and the plumbing froze.

But the most serious problem was that staff were not able to leave the hotel premises without the interpreter, who, at the end of the working day and at weekends, often left the hotel. Being confined to a cold, gloomy hotel for a whole weekend did nothing for morale. This issue was constantly raised, but the Koreans responded that this was "for the safety of the staff".

> *All travel outside of the capital was with an obligatory driver, provided by the army, and an interpreter or "minder". The minder was responsible night and day – he, or occasionally she, stayed in the same hotel and interpreted during meetings with officials or beneficiaries. If anything went wrong, for example if you left the hotel on your own and walked around the town unsupervised, or took photographs, then your minder would be accountable to "the authorities". As a result, the minders usually took no chances and played safe by restricting movement as much as possible.*

Obstacles and opportunities

Aid agencies operating in the DPRK in the mid-1990s were confronted with a novel situation: here was perhaps the most isolated country in the world, which had very little knowledge or understanding of the outside world, struck by a crisis that was hidden for reasons of pride, misunderstanding and/or national security.

There were opportunities for successful negotiation in the DPRK, but they were few and they emerged from increasing knowledge of the country itself. And although humanitarian diplomacy, as practised through continuous negotiation and bargaining, could achieve a great deal, ultimately there were some obstacles that could not be removed because they arose from contexts and beliefs that were fundamentally incompatible and unchangeable.

The humanitarian imperative may have been the chief driver of the aid agencies, but other actors followed competing, if equally deeply held, agendas. For the North Koreans, all aid agency requests and demands were received through a filter of mistrust and suspicion and weighed against their overarching priority – national security. For some observers there were deeper political motives expressed as concerns that assistance would prop up a regime they did not wish to support. Different world views led to contradictory opinions about what the DPRK needed to resolve its crisis.

Secondly, there were issues that were structural in nature that made maintaining the humanitarian capacity for action difficult. Government recalcitrance over permitting access to the countryside, to information, to visas, was a product of the closed and bureaucratic nature of the North Korean state itself. The absence of consensus within the NGO community also hampered activity, but this is a fact of life when different constituencies come together: inevitably there may be an agreement on ends but not on means.

Thirdly, there were problems in implementation that flowed from the problems of competing agendas and structural weaknesses. It was difficult to design a programme of action in the absence of knowledge and agreement, and it was difficult to carry it through given the restrictions involved.

Fourthly, there was the issue of justification. The role played by the humanitarian community in the DPRK was scrutinized, both locally and internationally, and agencies had to be able to provide evidence that their actions and decisions were valid and appropriate.

Contradictory views

Aid agencies were caught between a regime in denial, on the one hand, and an often reluctant donor community on the other.

Officially, the North Koreans said they were experiencing "temporary difficulties" that had resulted from "natural disasters" such as floods and droughts. It was clear, however, that, although flooding and drought had exacerbated the situation, the problems in agriculture were structural. Yet, to admit structural problems would be to challenge the wisdom of the Great Leader, Kim Il Sung, who had died in 1994 but who was so revered that to question his legacy of *Juche* was unimaginable to most North Koreans. They genuinely believed that what had befallen them was indeed the result of natural disasters. This made it extremely difficult to engage in meaningful discussions about the structural changes and development assistance they so badly needed if the country was ever going to emerge from its humanitarian crisis.

On the other hand, international opinion was not positive towards the DPRK, which had test-launched a multi-stage rocket across Japan in 1998. This move was viewed as unduly aggressive. Donors were unwilling to provide development assistance because the prerequisites of policy dialogue, transparency and accountability did not exist. But, without development assistance and support from international finance institutions (the DPRK is not a member of the World Bank or the Asian Development Bank), the country would not be able to extract itself from its dire situation.

Suspicion and mistrust

Suspicion and mistrust of foreigners was intense. Ordinary Koreans were forbidden to interact with foreigners and, despite being invited into the country, the international presence was barely tolerated.

Apart from their diplomats, very few Koreans had travelled abroad and there was little interaction with the world outside its borders. There were no foreign newspapers, and radios and televisions were programmed to receive only local Korean transmissions. Consequently the vast majority of North Koreans did not have the slightest knowledge or understanding of the outside world apart from what they were told, which added to the difficulties of mutual comprehension and negotiation.

The Koreans were very distrustful of the media, which is hardly surprising given that much of it was very critical of the country. In the early years it was almost impossible for journalists and TV networks to get into the country. Because agencies rely on the media to draw attention to crises in order to raise funding, the lack of media coverage of the situation inside the DPRK was a great drawback.

> *We tried to persuade the Koreans to allow in more media, arguing that, if they let the media in, they were more likely to get balanced reporting. If they kept them out, the reports would be produced anyway and were more likely to be very negative. The problem was that the official who took a decision to let in a certain journalist would subsequently be held responsible by the "relevant authorities" if a critical news article appeared. So it was better for them to play safe.*

Lack of information

Lack of access to information of all kinds – from lists of officials to phone lines to gaining clearance for medevac procedures – severely hampered the ability of NGOs to operate.

What would be considered routine information and data in normal circumstances were treated almost as if they were state secrets by the North Koreans. For example, some 80,000 nurseries, kindergartens and schools were believed to receive food aid for children who were WFP's beneficiaries. A list of beneficiary institutions was always promised but never provided, because, the Koreans said, they were having difficulty assembling all the names of the institutions and translating them into English.

Sometimes different agencies were given conflicting information about the same thing, leading to the suspicion that information was being tailored to the specific recipient. This situation undermined the credibility of NGOs and agencies externally.

Travel and visa restrictions

Where aid agencies were allowed access to the population, heavy bureaucratic controls frequently made reaching them difficult. For example, it was impossible to conduct "surprise" monitoring visits or spot checks because travel plans had to be lodged several days in advance. Unless advance notice of travel was communicated to the army, vehicles could not pass the numerous army checkpoints. These restrictions also applied to ordinary Koreans.

Even without the bureaucratic red tape, travel outside Pyongyang was difficult at the best of times. Until 1997, travel to the provinces had to be undertaken by train, not car. The most severe hunger was found in the very large industrial cities along the east coast, where industry had collapsed and there was little other means of support for the population. It was a long and difficult journey to these areas – driving time just to reach the WFP sub-offices at Chongjin and Hyesan was three and four days, respectively, and, as a result, very few foreigners ever saw the extreme hardship in these areas.

The number of international staff was strictly controlled by tightly rationing the number of visas issued, and it seemed that visas were issued in rough proportion to the value of aid that an agency brought in. The maximum number issued to UN agencies and NGOs was 100 visas. Added to this was the problem of the length of time it took actually to issue the visas once they were approved. By simply taking a long time to issue visas, the Koreans kept the number of foreigners down. This also meant that aid agencies had to rely upon locally assigned staff, such as government interpreters, liaison officers and drivers, which sometimes caused problems. Korean-speaking foreign staff were never granted permission to enter the country.

The Koreans used the visa system to intimidate or punish staff, for example by threatening not to renew visas or by keeping them waiting in Beijing, often at their own expense, for a visa renewal. Apart from the head of agency, who was normally granted a one-year visa, visas for staff were issued for two or three months only.

> *Every few weeks, international staff travelled to Beijing and beyond for rest and recuperation, which was eagerly anticipated given the difficult life in the country. Air tickets were collected by the Korean staff. Sometimes they would delay producing the air tickets until the last moment, causing great anguish.*

Opportunities

The DPRK's continued reliance on aid meant that it had to continue to engage with the aid agencies; and, although all the agencies were extremely frustrated by the restrictive conditions they had to work under, the suffering, hardships and pervasive malnutrition of ordinary Koreans were compelling reasons to persevere. Through negotiation, humanitarian agencies were able to learn what worked and what did not. Real progress was made in terms of achieving aims, earning trust, gaining knowledge and, through this, becoming more effective, which in turn increased confidence on both sides.

Over time, staff from the agencies and NGOs gained much better access to the countryside than most diplomats, whose travel was very restricted unless they were providing bilateral aid. Consequently the humanitarian community had a much greater knowledge and understanding of the situation outside Pyongyang than most of the embassies. The World Food Programme was able to travel to the 75 per cent of the country where food aid was being distributed, and had a permanent presence in the provinces through its five sub-offices, although most NGOs were restricted to the western side of the country. With this increased knowledge, so painstakingly acquired, came a greater understanding of the problems facing the country and of people's coping mechanisms, so aid could be more effectively targeted.

Negotiations

For humanitarian diplomacy to be successful, a number of basic conditions have to be satisfied. First, negotiators must know who to talk to and how to talk them; secondly, there should be at least some awareness of what the opposite side is willing to concede, and where it will draw a red line; finally, when negotiating on behalf of a number of agencies or groups, those agencies should have a clear consensus on what the limits and objectives are: internal dissent can weaken the overall position.

Identifying issues

Key issues were identified that were common to all agencies and NGOs in the country. These issues included access to all parts of the country; random monitoring; better access to beneficiaries; access to data and information; access to farmers' markets; a second nutrition survey; arrangements for medical evacuation of staff; radio and satellite communications; prompt granting and processing of visas; more access to the country for the media to facilitate fundraising; and access to the Internet. These comprised a relatively constant agenda for negotiations between the DPRK and the Humanitarian Coordinator. Furthermore, having achieved inter-agency consensus, these issues were put on the agendas of and raised by donor missions, senior agency visitors and senior government officials – including prime ministers and foreign ministers – from donor countries including the European Union.

Negotiating with the DPRK government

In simple terms, the aid agencies had what the DPRK wanted – food and health assistance – and so bargaining power should have been on the side of the agencies, but this was not the case. Instead, the agencies had to negotiate very hard to open their humanitarian space. Humanitarian diplomacy relied on understanding the North Korean negotiating style, identifying when, where and how talks were most productive, and recognizing what the "red line" issues were. Some improvements came about as a result of successful negotiations but also through improved understanding and reduced mistrust.

Negotiating style

In negotiating with the Korean authorities, it did not take long to understand that national security was the top priority and would not be compromised in any circumstances. If it was a choice between aid and national security, then there was no contest. National pride and dignity would not be compromised, and North Korean officials would not give way to pressure as a matter of principle.

Decisions, once made and communicated, were never retracted, which meant that pushing too hard in negotiations carried a high risk. If a confrontational approach was taken, the Koreans became confrontational as well, refusing to budge, and that was the end of the negotiations. On many occasions it seemed that the Koreans disadvantaged themselves with their obstinacy, but this was a price they appeared ready to pay (in fact the price was paid not by government officials but by ordinary Koreans trying to survive in remote parts of the country).

Unsurprisingly, carrots proved more effective than sticks. For example, it might be suggested that, if aid agencies were given more access, the Koreans would receive more aid in the areas that were opened up, thereby offering the Koreans a clear incentive for complying with the request. Using this tactic, gradually some counties became accessible. However, these were usually counties in areas that were not obviously strategic, that is, they were not in the Demilitarized Zone or in the mountainous areas in the centre of the country or bordering China – in other words, the Koreans could give way without their security being compromised.

> *Some critics accused us of being too soft in our negotiations, saying that we should take a harder line. This charge was directed towards WFP in particular because they considered that the large size of its programme ought to give it greater bargaining power. In response to these critics, it was pointed out that we did not negotiate in public and they could have no means of knowing what leverage or pressure we were applying. In fact, a lot of pressure was applied over access and visa issues, but the Koreans were quite willing to hold their ground, and tens of millions of dollars' worth of food aid were forgone as a result.*

Channels of communication

Control over the timing and means of communication was an important part of the manner in which the Koreans negotiated.

All communication between the government and the agencies was conducted through the Korean-appointed liaison officer, who wielded a great deal of power. Most meetings had to be arranged by sending a written request, and agency representatives could never be sure whether such letters were actually delivered – especially if there was any implied criticism of the liaison officer him/herself. On occasion the Humanitarian Coordinator was able to speak on the telephone with his counterpart at the Flood Damage Rehabilitation Commission, who spoke excellent English, but this was very unusual.

There was no question of circumventing the process by, for example, driving to visit the FDRC without an appointment. All government offices had armed guards and no one was permitted inside until someone from the counterpart office came to the door to escort the caller to a special meeting room.

Experience proved that negotiations were better undertaken away from the formal meeting rooms of the ministry of foreign affairs, where there were always many note-takers and interpreters in attendance. It was much better to use the more informal setting of one of the few restaurants in Pyongyang. Many of the more important discussions took place in the informal atmosphere and general hubbub of restaurants where people could talk more freely, and the Korean officials enjoyed being taken to these places, some of which they could not afford to go to themselves. The Korean officials also used this tactic on the aid agencies, inviting staff to dinners at government guest houses.

Deferring decisions

Once the two sides were together, negotiations could begin, but achieving results was another matter. Counterparts sometimes stated that they were not in a position to grant certain requests, which would have to be referred to "the relevant authorities", usually taken to be national security authorities. However, it was never clear who these higher authorities were, or whether it was an excuse to refuse difficult or unwanted requests, or whether some decisions did in fact have to be referred to a higher hidden authority. Neither the humanitarian community nor the diplomatic corps were ever able to access these "higher" officials. In fact, not even a list of officials belonging to the FDRC ever circulated.

> *Over time it became clearer how the Koreans dealt with NGO and UN agency representatives, and even ambassadors, whom they considered "awkward". This might be because they were asking for too much, or talking too freely and critically with the press, or not treating the DPRK and its people with respect. The Koreans simply froze these people out – they stopped all communication with them. There were no meetings and letters went unanswered. The unfortunate representative found him/herself unable to carry out the agency's work. After two or three months of this, the Koreans might feel that enough punishment had been inflicted and gradually resumed communications, or sometimes the representative was withdrawn and a new one sent.*

Case study: The nutrition survey

In 1998, UNICEF, the WFP and the European Commission's Humanitarian Aid department (ECHO), in cooperation with the DPRK government, carried out a nutrition survey of children in the accessible areas of the country. Great care was taken in the design of the survey and in the way it was carried out so that the results would be scientifically valid. This took many months of negotiation. The survey confirmed that malnutrition was extremely serious and provided justification for aid. This was a great breakthrough because it was the first time that agencies were able to get hard, statistically valid data on the condition of children in the country. However, the government would not agree to annual follow-up surveys to assess progress on reducing malnutrition, and this became a constant subject for discussion.

The negotiation process was strengthened by UNICEF and WFP maintaining a united front throughout discussions, and also through pressure applied at higher levels. The need for a second nutrition survey was put high on the agenda of issues to be raised by all important visitors, including the heads of agencies and donor missions and even a visiting foreign minister. In New York, the UN Secretary-General raised it with a very high-level visiting DPRK official.

After fruitless negotiations in 1999 and 2000, in 2001 the FDRC finally agreed to another survey, but one conducted by the government and under its own terms, and requested international support for this. The WFP and UNICEF were wary: they concluded that they would have insufficient control over the process and that any association with the survey could be portrayed as endorsement of the results. They therefore declined to participate and made it clear to the government that any survey the DPRK carried out on its own would not have international credibility. The government survey went ahead and the agencies refused to comment on the results.

Finally, in 2002, it was agreed that a survey with the full participation of UNICEF and WFP would take place and the agencies were satisfied that the arrangements would provide valid results. This is a rare example of eventual success in negotiations, where persistent pressure was applied with high-level reinforcement. But it took four years to achieve! The results of the 2002 survey indicated that the nutritional condition of children aged under 7 years had greatly improved. The results increased confidence that most of the food aid was widely distributed and reaching the young children for whom it was intended.

Other successes

Over time, a number of successes were achieved through negotiations. In 2002, the government finally agreed to allow the installation of a satellite communications system and also sanctioned mobile satellite phones, but only for the office in Pyongyang – when they were really needed in sub-offices and vehicles. The government did agree, however, to the installation of satellite receivers in the sub-offices so that field staff could have some entertainment in the evenings. Another improvement for field staff was the granting of permission to leave their hotels without a minder, although they did not have complete freedom.

There was also progress on the visa issue. It became apparent that the mechanics of issuing visas without undue delay and the short validity of visas were problems that the ministry of foreign affairs ought to be able to resolve without recourse to "higher officials". Visas for staff were extended from two or three months to six months. The length of time needed to issue visas for new staff improved somewhat but was never consistent, and seemed to vary according to the state of the relationship of the agency and the Flood Damage Rehabilitation Commission. The total number of visas never got much beyond 100, with the FDRC citing a shortage of suitable accommodation, but in the end the government built some new apartments in the diplomatic compound that eased the problem.

The WFP managed substantially to improve the quality of information available by establishing a database of each county, combining information provided by the government with information collected by the field officers. The database included information on agriculture and population. The technical subgroups of the inter-agency group facilitated the sharing of information and coordination amongst the agencies. The Koreans had tried to prevent agencies from sharing information amongst themselves, but eventually relented.

The number of WFP monitoring visits increased from 250 per month in 1998 to over 500 per month by 2002. The quality of the visits improved somewhat when the Koreans agreed to focus group discussions with beneficiaries, but pre-notification was still required and random spot checks were not permitted. During monitoring visits to counties, interviews were conducted with county officials, at nurseries, kindergartens, schools and hospitals, and in beneficiaries' homes. Some of the field officers managed to have some limited flexibility in the choice of institutions visited.

The emergency medical evacuation issue was never resolved satisfactorily. However, after 2002, when a medical emergency did occur, the DPRK permitted an evacuation.

Inter-agency diplomacy

Humanitarian diplomacy played an important role in mediating between agencies and between agencies and donors. The aid community in the DPRK faced its own set of crises in 1998. It was under heavy external pressure, being forced to answer charges that aid was being diverted to the military or that it was propping up an unwholesome regime, while inside the country the operating environment remained difficult. Under these pressures, some NGOS were withdrawing.

To counter the deteriorating situation, it was decided that the first task of the UN agencies and NGOs was to identify humanitarian principles specific to the DPRK that would provide common guidance in respective programmes. Agencies and NGOs developed nine humanitarian principles, which were incorporated into the Common Humanitarian Action Plan. This formed part of the UN Consolidated Appeal presented to donors at the end of 1998. The Humanitarian and Development Working Group drew up a matrix that set baselines and tracked progress towards meeting the nine humanitarian principles. Benchmarks were identified, and the matrix was maintained and updated by the Office for the Coordination of Humanitarian Affairs on behalf of all agencies and published in successive UN Consolidated Appeals.

To address the question of access, the first step was to get all agencies to agree to the principle that no agency should provide aid to areas or places that the agency could not access. It was vital for all the agencies and NGOs to have a common position on this when going into negotiations with the government. This fundamental principle was reinforced periodically during the inter-agency meetings and all agencies adhered to it.

Case study: Diverting aid to the military

Several very critical articles started to appear in the media in 1998 after some NGOs left. Those that remained, and particularly the WFP, were accused of perpetuating an intolerable regime and its human rights abuses. It was argued that discontinuation of the aid would speed the collapse of the regime. These critics failed to take into account that NGOs claimed that more than 1 million people had died of starvation in 1996/ 1997 but the regime had not collapsed. Because the aid could not be monitored properly, critics alleged that it was being diverted to the army and to other favoured groups.

These were extremely serious criticisms and the humanitarian community needed to be sure that it was doing the right thing. However, there was no agreement amongst the remaining agencies and NGOs about the overall humanitarian situation in the country or about the effectiveness of aid programmes. More NGOs were talking about withdrawal, partly as a result of their own headquarters reacting to media criticism.

An inter-agency group, chaired by the Humanitarian Coordinator, addressed these issues very intensely over a week in late 1998. The most pressing issue was whether it was better to withdraw from the country, in view of the unsatisfactory operating restrictions, or to stay and try to improve the situation. The conclusions were drafted as a Consensus Statement, together with the names of the agencies and NGOs that supported the statement.

The consensus was that there was a serious humanitarian situation in the country; that the aid was having some positive impact; that the operating restrictions were unsatisfactory but had shown some improvement;

and that much more improvement was necessary. Having agreed this, the decision could be taken to remain engaged and to try to make gradual improvements from within, rather than withdrawing or adopting an approach that would likely lead to confrontation with the DPRK authorities and suspension of programmes. Having a common position was extremely valuable, and the Consensus Statements, which were for public circulation, proved to be useful when talking to donors, the media and the government. The Humanitarian Coordinator remarked at an inter-agency meeting at this time that "it is easier to withdraw than to remain".

Two more NGOs withdrew at the end of 1999 and 2000. As each one left, the inter-agency group renegotiated and reviewed its position, examining where progress had been achieved and where setbacks had occurred and debating whether there was justification for continuing the aid. On each occasion it was agreed that progress had been made and that aid was saving lives. Therefore, although serious operational issues remained, it was better to continue the dialogue with the Korean authorities. An updated Consensus Statement was then issued.

Over time, the balance of in-country belief emerged that there was no major systematic diversion of food aid to the North Korean military. The army was one of the state's designated priority groups and therefore benefited from the domestic harvest. Priority groups took the entire year's supply of food at the time of the harvest, leaving the remainder to be distributed through the public distribution system (PDS) throughout the year. There were other known sources of food, including bilateral aid from China and other sympathetic countries, that could be used to feed the army and other priority groups. Conversely, the bulk of international food aid was maize and wheat, commodities that were not popular with the Koreans, who preferred home-grown rice. Only people who needed to supplement their PDS ration – the really poor and hungry (the ones the agencies wanted to reach) – would eat these foods.

Wider implications

In negotiations between states, diplomats are there to serve the interests of their government or what could be called "the national interest". This defines and limits their course of action. For humanitarian diplomacy, however, the calculation is not "does this serve my agency's interests?" but, rather, "what is the price worth paying to save lives?"

In the DPRK, the answer was that the price demanded, in terms of the severe restrictions placed on the humanitarian community, was worth paying because, on balance, the greater interest of saving lives was being met. A majority of agencies and NGOs took the line that it was better to remain engaged and improve the situation in the DPRK than to withdraw. Furthermore, all negotiations, whether between the agencies themselves, with the DPRK or with external donors and governments, were predicated on this principle of saving lives.

With this principle in mind, humanitarian diplomacy was conducted to enhance the aid community's capacity for action. A number of lessons were learned through the experience that may be applicable to negotiating with other closed states. These include:

- In a highly politicized and uncertain environment, negotiating a joint position or consensus is worth while. A degree of coordination improves bargaining power, mitigates the problems of inadvertently undermining one's own "side" through unilateral action, and provides the possibility of sharing and pooling information and resources.
- Identifying issues that are key, and persisting in applying pressure about them, over time, across different levels of government and through different means, signals to the other side that certain issues are important, not something merely thrown into the bargaining "pot".
- It is important to develop an awareness of the other side's priorities and limitations and their preferred negotiating style. Positions that appear to be illogical or arbitrary may derive from underlying conditions that are not immediately apparent. On the other hand, some will be arbitrary and can be changed.
- Negotiation is just part of the process. Presenting and carrying out a consistent programme (preferably with a consensus behind it) can build confidence and alleviate suspicion and mistrust.

Overall, and very slowly, progress was made in the DPRK, despite the setbacks. Although it was always a case of two steps forward, one step back, the negotiations that took place on humanitarian assistance did nonetheless open the door. This experience can now be built on by governments to improve political interaction with the DPRK.

10

Steering through insurgencies in Nepal

Erika Joergensen

> *I had no idea what I was in for when I agreed to come to Nepal in August 2002. After years of working in emergencies, I thought I was taking on a quiet development post where I would be able to put in a good day's work to make sure that the programmes were running effectively, but then retire to my home at the end of the day to watch the sun set, not too worried about what tomorrow might bring.*

The major reason for engaging in humanitarian diplomacy is to create and maintain the humanitarian space in which aid activities can take place. Although negotiations occur on a political level, sometimes political objectives clash with humanitarian ones. When humanitarian operations take place in a time of great political instability, new tensions and unanticipated challenges inevitably emerge.

This chapter describes the engagement of the World Food Programme (WFP) in humanitarian diplomacy in Nepal from mid-2002 to May 2004. During this period, a Maoist insurgency that had been simmering for years spread to most of the country. Rebel groups began to tighten control in areas in which development activities were taking place, and government forces moved to reassert their influence. Meanwhile, in the capital of Kathmandu, weak central governments lurched from one political crisis to the next and the entire democratic structure of the country was threatened.

In this situation, aid agencies faced a major dilemma: deciding if and when it was acceptable to bypass government systems and to accept parallel structures in order to fulfil humanitarian imperatives. Such actions ran the risk of weakening the legitimacy of the government while bestowing legitimacy on the parallel – usually insurgent – structures. If badly handled, this could in the long run compromise the development space. The alternative, to cease operations in conflict-affected areas, could put local people at risk and trigger a humanitarian crisis.

In the countryside, the security situation was rapidly deteriorating, both for the increasingly isolated and vulnerable population and for aid workers in the field. Humanitarian principles were not respected: the insurgents stole supplies, demanded registration, extorted "taxes" and banned some development activities. The security forces were suspicious of aid workers and their programmes, fearing they might assist the rebels. Both sides in the conflict violated human rights; even worse, "extreme measures" were being tacitly accepted as necessary, and neither the government nor the Maoist leadership seemed strong enough to maintain discipline over their distant troops.

As the security situation worsened during 2002, humanitarian imperatives increasingly overlapped with the development programmes that were already in place. On the programme side, this included using assistance in conflict-affected areas to help the population retain their assets, sustain their livelihoods and cope with hardships.

Although there was no evidence of a humanitarian crisis, there were concerns that, as areas became inaccessible and as violence escalated, food deficits would occur and emergency assistance would be needed; and there were fears that the provision of such assistance could be made difficult by a central government in denial about its insurgency, and at the local level by the presence of Maoist guerrillas who effectively controlled a growing area of territory. Donors began to question whether it was realistic to continue development work in the context of what was starting to look like a civil war.

For the WFP, its mandate as a UN agency meant that it had to seek government approval when trying to alter its existing programmes to deal with the changing situation, which included seeking some engagement with the insurgents. Therefore, its efforts went far beyond finding ways in which to implement field objectives; humanitarian diplomacy was transacted at the highest political levels in order to gain the necessary recognition that humanitarian imperatives transcended political ones and would be respected by all sides – the government, the Maoists and the Royal Nepal Army. The only leverage available was the mandates of the non-governmental organizations (NGOs) themselves and the assistance they could provide.

Context

The central purpose of this section is to provide, first, background to the political crisis and the insurgency, and its impact on the population; and, secondly, a brief account of the activities undertaken by international agencies in Nepal and the challenges they faced as the insurgency escalated.

The political background

The Kingdom of Nepal's feudal structures were replaced relatively recently: in 1990 it became a constitutional monarchy with an elected prime minister presiding over a Council of Ministers whose members were appointed from the elected parliament. Although democratic structures were thus in place, the functioning of the inexperienced elected government had not been very successful, leaving a political vacuum at the heart of the country.

Under the constitution, the king served as head of state and supreme commander of the Royal Nepal Army (RNA), which in turn had strong cultural and traditional links to the monarchy. The reigning king, Gyanendra, ascended to the throne following a palace massacre in June 2001 in which 10 members of the royal family, including King Birendra, lost their lives. The mysterious circumstances surrounding the massacre, and a lack of popular affection for Gyanendra, undermined the popularity of and respect for the monarchy.

The staunchest opponent of the monarchy was the Communist Party of Nepal (Maoist). Disillusioned with democracy, it left the political mainstream in 1996 and began to strengthen its support base in the mid-west of the country in preparation for a "people's war". The Maoists were able to capitalize on years of government neglect, failed development projects and increasing poverty that had served both to isolate many communities from government influence and services and to foment resentment among the local population.

The insurgency spreads

The government negotiated a cease-fire with the Maoists in August 2001, a consequence of the political crisis that gripped the country following the palace massacre. Four months later, however, the cease-fire broke down and the government proclaimed a state of emergency. The Maoists launched several successful attacks, in which they overran army barracks in a number of district headquarters culminating in a major attack in

Time line of key events

1991	First democratic elections in Nepal
1996	Communist Party of Nepal (Maoist) leaves political mainstream and launches insurgencies in mid-western district of Rukum
June 2001	10 members of the royal family, including King Birendra, slain. His brother King Gyanendra succeeds him
August 2001	First cease-fire declared
November 2001	Cease-fire breaks down, followed by serious fighting; the Maoists win influence over a significant part of Nepal; state of emergency declared
May–October 2002	Political crisis as party infighting leads prime minister to dissolve parliament and seek new elections; prime minister and cabinet forced to resign; King Gyanendra dismisses elected governments in all districts and appoints prime minister himself; elections postponed indefinitely
January–August 2003	Second cease-fire signed, with occasional violations as peace talks begin; political crisis continues
August 2003	Maoists withdraw from negotiations and fighting resumes. Neither the army nor the Maoists gain full control of the countryside, parliament remains dissolved, and there is increasing public opposition and protests against the king
December 2003	A group of international agencies and embassies in Nepal publish basic operating guidelines for all development and humanitarian assistance in Nepal
January 2004	UN Country Team in Nepal issues *Basic Operating Guidelines* and *Guiding Principles*
April 2004	King promises to hold parliamentary elections in 2005
May 2004	Prime minister resigns

Mangelsen, Acham, in February 2002 that left 107 security personnel dead.

The elected government was unable to reach consensus on whether to extend the state of emergency, so in mid-2002 King Gyanendra dismissed it on grounds of national security and appointed his own people. This further undermined the legitimacy of the state in the eyes of its population.

Whereas initially the impact of the Maoist insurgency had been largely limited to the rural areas of the far west and mid-west, by late 2002 the fighting between the Maoists and the RNA had intensified, affecting most of the 75 districts of Nepal and even making itself felt in Kathmandu. Its rapid spread forced the government, which had tended to ignore the conflict since the collapse of the first cease-fire, into action. Following a series of bombings, which culminated in the assassination of the Chief of Police, his wife and bodyguard in Kathmandu in January 2003, the king, through his special appointee Minister Pun, negotiated a second cease-fire with the Maoists. This lasted until August, when peace talks collapsed and fighting resumed.

By early 2004 the priority was to return to elected civilian governance and put a process in place to negotiate an end to the conflict between the Maoists and the RNA. This was no easy task, because the fundamental demand of the Maoists – to establish a constitutional assembly to draft a new constitution, which could well result in the end of the monarchy – ran contrary to the aims of the political mainstream, the RNA and, of course, the Palace.[1] Meanwhile, the rift between the government and the king (backed by the RNA), on the one side, and the political parties backed by increasingly enraged student organizations, on the other side, widened significantly.

The impact on the population

Statistical facts are hard to collect in Nepal, but it is generally accepted that the conflict had claimed about 9,000 lives by early 2004. There were also numerous reports of beatings, abductions, amputations and murders, attributed both to the Maoists and to the RNA. In 2003 alone, 996 cases of arrest and torture were reported.[2]

The insurgents had a negative impact on the civilian population in the areas they operated in. Although they left most civilian infrastructure untouched, they disabled village headquarters and government buildings, as well as communications towers and bridges, which they claimed could serve military as well as civilian purposes. They exacted forced donations of grain from a population that was already unable to meet its food requirements even in a good year, and imposed taxes on the salaries of teachers, health workers and NGOs in their areas of influence.

The RNA was responsible for at least two high-profile incidents that involved the loss of civilian life. By early 2004, it became apparent that the RNA was increasingly acting on its own authority, rather than under civilian leadership.

The impact on NGOs

In the field, NGOs were confronting problems with both parties to the conflict. The Maoists expelled many NGOs from their areas of control and blocked the implementation of hundreds of government-financed road and water system projects – infrastructure that was critically needed by the civilian population. Their intimidation of government officials, combined with the king's replacement of previously elected local leaders with government appointees who had little standing within their communities, greatly weakened capacity at the local level to implement development projects. Meanwhile, the RNA made some worrying statements accusing assistance agencies of providing tacit support, or worse, to the Maoists.

Assessing the capacity of the population

As dire as the situation was in the countryside, it did not deteriorate to the point where it triggered a recognized humanitarian crisis. When the second cease-fire in January 2003 allowed a relaxation of access restrictions to the Maoist-dominated parts of Nepal, the donor community expected to find a population suffering from major food deficits and in need of emergency assistance. There was some concern that the government would block such assistance, because it had indicated a general reluctance to accept emergency aid related to the conflict. However, both the International Committee of the Red Cross (ICRC) and the WFP were able to confirm that there had been no substantial increase in acute malnutrition or displacement and emergency assistance was not needed; supply lines remained operational and stores were full thanks to an abundant spring harvest. This was an important lesson, indicating that the population of rural Nepal was capable of coping with a certain level of hardship without external assistance. However, it was also clear that, even in normal conditions, the people of Nepal were living on the edge and could ill afford further shocks to their livelihood systems: in 2003, Nepal ranked 143rd out of 175 countries on the UN Development Programme's Human Development Index. The line between subsistence and disaster was particularly fine in the far western and mid-western regions, where there was a long history of neglect and underdevelopment.

The role of international agencies

The donor and assistance community in Nepal was primarily development oriented. Nepal was a major recipient of development aid; more than half of the government income was derived from foreign donors supporting major sectors such as education, energy, agriculture, infrastructure, environment, governance and human rights. Major donor countries included Denmark, the United Kingdom, India, Japan, the United States, Norway and Switzerland. Also present were organizations such as Gesellschaft Technischer Zusammenarbeit (GTZ), the UK Department for International Development (DFID), CARE International and Save the Children. There was representation from many of the United Nations' major development agencies, including the WFP, the Asia Development Bank, the Food and Agriculture Organization, the International Labour Organization, the World Health Organization, the United Nations Children's Fund (UNICEF), the United Nations Development Programme and the World Bank. The ICRC maintained a mission that primarily focused on visits to detainees in prison or army camps and on education of the armed forces and insurgents in international humanitarian law.

Operational issues

The WFP, working in cooperation with the other resident agencies, had two objectives to support field operations: first, to support the peace process and, secondly, to facilitate the implementation of field projects. In order to achieve these goals, the WFP has specific operational objectives for Nepal. These included:
- securing full access to all areas affected by conflict;
- coordinating information-gathering activities through securing cooperation from all parties involved;
- enforcing implementation capacity;
- insisting that respect for humanitarian principles by all participants to the conflict be maintained;
- maintaining local support for programmes.

Facilitating access

In trying to reach their beneficiaries, aid agencies confronted formidable geographical and infrastructural challenges in Nepal at the best of times.

In this period, WFP field staff and their implementing partners faced added danger and uncertainty as the insurgency began to affect most of the country's 75 administrative districts.

Most donor assistance was channelled through district development committees (DDCs) in the district headquarters and/or through village development councils (VDCs). As the security situation grew worse, the king's decision to dismiss elected bodies in the DDCs and VDCs made maintaining access via these structures more difficult.

The WFP was less affected by access constraints than were some other agencies, probably because, when its field presence was established in 2002, the WFP was delivering tangible resources – food and infrastructure – that benefited the same population from whom the Maoists sought support. Nevertheless, two national staff members connected to a WFP project were killed because of their alleged links with the Royal Nepal Army. The Maoists prohibited other organizations with "softer" programmes, such as literacy campaigns and empowerment activities, from working in their areas of control, and throughout the conflict-affected areas many staff were harassed by army and insurgents alike.

To facilitate and maintain access to these areas, assistance agencies had to engage in dialogue with the warring sides. For their part, the Nepal government, the RNA and the Maoist insurgents all had to acknowledge that such dialogue with their opponents was necessary and did not indicate an "allegiance" to one cause or the other. But, even when both the Maoists and the RNA agreed to permit access in theory, in practice it remained problematic because of the terrain itself, the poor or non-existent infrastructure and obstacles placed in the way by the RNA or the Maoists. In some cases, it took great efforts and resources just to reach the district headquarters, and to move beyond them into the villages was sometimes impossible. Many of the district headquarters could be reached only by helicopter; WFP field monitors routinely walked for more than a week in order to visit a handful of projects in villages. Food supplies destined for the remote mountainous district of Humla had to be either airlifted by helicopter or trucked in from the opposite side, through Tibet. Other methods included using porters, mules, trucks or tractors – all of which proved to be very time-consuming and costly.

Information-gathering

Information collection is the foundation of programme activities: in Nepal, it was difficult to plan appropriate programmes in the absence of credible and organized data. Therefore, finding ways to gather accurate and relevant information was an operational issue that plagued WFP interventions and directly exacerbated access problems.

> *When I arrived in August 2002, information seemed completely unsystematic and disorganized. We would hear from one source that 200,000 people were on the move, and the next day we would read in the newspaper that famine was expected in February. The following day a third source would announce that there was no problem at all.*

Enforcing implementation capacity

Most agencies relied on the government as an implementing partner, a system that was developed to support local governance and decentralization as part of the new democracy's capacity-building and improved service delivery in Nepal. However, the national implementation procedures that had been put in place to support development – namely, the mandate to work through district development committees and village development councils for all activities – were not particularly well suited to the situation that was emerging. Restricting aid work to these channels limited the ability to reach the targeted population and, it was feared, would preclude an expansion of activities if needed to address an evolving humanitarian crisis. The WFP began to explore alternative means of implementation. Since the government did not request emergency assistance, many agencies tried to use their ongoing development frameworks to address any needs arising from the conflict.

Members of the international community also largely failed to recognize what was happening. This was partially owing to the remoteness of the affected areas: most agency and donor representatives lived in Kathmandu, which was relatively unaffected by the insurgency in the early period. Furthermore, there was no indication of large-scale population displacements or increases in acute malnutrition or crude child mortality rates. On this basis, agencies such as the ICRC reported that, although the population was living on the edge, there was no humanitarian crisis.

Respecting human rights

The lack of respect for human rights became an increasing problem over the course of the conflict, with both sides committing abuses. On some occasions, government officials made statements that in effect condoned the abrogation of human rights on the basis that extraordinary means were required in extraordinary circumstances. Such impunity ran the risk of giving the impression that human rights violations would be tolerated.

There were daily reports of civilian casualties and regular reports of executions at the hands of both the RNA and the Maoists. Although atrocities were not widespread, they were significant. For example, in an incident in Ramechhap in August 2003, the RNA was alleged to have executed 21 suspected insurgents in their custody, a matter that was not adequately investigated by the government.

The role of local support

Most development agencies were eager to redirect their activities towards addressing and mitigating the root causes of the conflict – thereby indirectly attempting to help peace-building – but very few managed to reach the poorest of the poor. In the experience of the WFP, once programmes began to take off in the most marginalized areas, the local population protected and supported them against obstruction from the Maoists. It was therefore critical to develop better targeting and implementation mechanisms to deliver tangible results and build confidence and to anchor those programmes in the local communities.

At the same time, the international NGOs were challenged directly or indirectly to support the Maoist movement by forced payment of taxes, registration or confiscation/theft of material. It was essential to discuss and understand what types of activities were helpful and what types ran the risk of jeopardizing the communities they were intended to help. For example, although infrastructure projects produced immediate demonstrable results and helped build confidence, the parties to the conflict could of course also make use of this infrastructure.

Obstacles and opportunities

The dynamics of the evolving insurgency began to affect development and aid programmes in ways that presented new obstacles and challenges to established working practices. Humanitarian diplomacy would play a central role in overcoming these challenges as assistance agencies reformulated and renegotiated their activities. Among the major obstacles were bureaucratic constraints, maintaining communications channels, political interference, the lack of intra-agency cohesion, and the violation of humanitarian principles.

Bureaucratic constraints

Development work in Nepal was subject to a grinding bureaucracy. It often took more than six months to agree changes to projects or to clear vehicles through customs, and it sometimes took years for an NGO to receive government approval to operate in Nepal.

It was at times difficult to distinguish between delays that were a result of the conflict and delays that were owing simply to bad governance. The Nepalese state was new and still battling with a lack of experience and competence in public administration. Success was more often determined by personal networks and there was an informal decision-making hierarchy that was not transparent to outsiders. Civil servants were unwilling to make and execute decisions.

> *We wasted enormous amounts of time knocking on the doors of civil servants to get letters, exemptions and etceteras. Our frustration was shared by those government officials who were genuinely trying to streamline procedures.*

In a development context, the need to be patient when dealing with bureaucratic constraints was frustrating. More important were more fundamental concerns that, in the context of an emerging humanitarian crisis, such constraints would hamper the expansion of humanitarian activities and indeed could begin to cost lives.

Maintaining communications channels

A major obstacle was opening and maintaining channels of communication between the aid agencies themselves, and also between the agencies and the warring parties. It was necessary to find ways to work with and through government officials who had limited legitimacy at both national and field levels, and also to work with the RNA. On the other hand, contact had to be maintained with the Maoists to ensure that programmes could go forward, but without becoming complicit in the Maoists' political agenda.

Although the government supported the need to continue development work in the areas affected by the conflict, it wanted to see this work carried out through government channels. These channels had not been particularly effective in the conflict areas in the past; only in rare cases were the very poorest represented on government committees, which were predominantly filled by higher-caste, more affluent members of the community. However, the committees became virtually useless when their elected representatives were replaced by government appointees. These appointees often failed to report to work, either because they feared they would become targets for the Maoists or simply because they lacked engagement.

Another major obstacle in pulling together a coherent effort to address the evolving crisis was the lack of a structured high-level dialogue with the Maoists. The United Nations held discussions with the Maoists only when the government explicitly agreed to them; the last such dialogue took place within the context of the second peace negotiations before they broke down in 2003.

Political interference

In Maoist-controlled areas, no rural projects could be implemented without Maoist approval. At the local level, the Maoists made it clear that they were interested only in projects that delivered tangible results, such as food aid, road construction, immunization and vitamin A campaigns, or water/sanitation interventions. For the most part, WFP activities fit the Maoist criteria; however, the Maoists forced other agencies to leave their areas of control if they were engaged in projects the Maoists deemed antithetical to their ideology. These included more politically oriented activities such as social mobilization, empowerment projects for women and governance programmes. The insurgents also consistently tried to tap into project income, by diverting resources, charging a project tax and/or taxing local salaries directly.

Assistance agencies were also harassed by the RNA, which sometimes suspected them of supporting the Maoists. In January 2004, a member of the Médecins Sans Frontières staff in Jumla was deported following allegations that he consulted openly with local Maoist leaders. These worrying trends not only hindered field work, but also generated concern that the international community would face major obstacles if it needed to scale up activities to address a humanitarian crisis.

The lack of intra-agency cohesion

The development community in Nepal was not a coherent group. Agencies did not routinely pool information and resources. Instead, they cultivated separate, direct relationships with the government and dealt with the Maoists as individual organizations. This allowed the Maoists a certain degree of manipulation of agencies: for example, they would permit only organizations whose objectives were consistent with their own to operate in their areas of control.

The tendency for local NGOs to work alone was exacerbated by the culture of fear that existed in the field. Individual NGOs were particularly worried that other organizations would pass information to the Maoists or to the RNA that would somehow have negative consequences for their programmes or their safety.

> *During a visit to one of our WFP sub-offices, I called a meeting with all local UN bodies, and another with all NGO representatives in the area. Whereas the UN meeting proved to be a successful forum for discussion and became a permanent feature in the area, the NGO meeting was more problematic. Local NGOs were deeply suspicious of the purpose of the meeting and questioned the need for sharing information on a regular basis. One NGO representative said to me: "Why would I tell him what we are doing and give him information. He will just report to the police tomorrow." Such an atmosphere of mistrust would have to be overcome if fuller and more effective coordination between agencies was going to take place.*

Violation of international norms

The government, the RNA and the Maoists did not always respect humanitarian principles and sometimes interfered with assistance activities in violation of international norms and standards. Agencies and NGOs operating in the Maoist areas had a number of problems with the insurgents: they were faced with demands for payment, including of a proportion of project income, as well as illicit taxation of project staff salaries. Theft of project supplies also occurred. There were problems with the RNA too. Occasionally, project user groups would report that they had not received their allocated food, in spite of the fact that the government had confirmed delivery, and sometimes bags of WFP food aid were found in the possession of the RNA, who would not release it.

Negotiations

The pursuit of humanitarian principles through the practice of diplomacy took place at both central and local levels of government. Negotiations also took place with the Maoist insurgents at the local level to try to secure field objectives and development/humanitarian space. Throughout, effective communication with donors and tight coordination and cooperation with negotiation partners such as other UN agencies were a crucial part of the negotiating strategy.

The following case studies illustrate how and why such negotiations took place, as well as their outcomes. The first example is a discussion of the role that high-level humanitarian diplomacy played in the 2003 peace process; indeed, it appeared that humanitarian issues might become a cornerstone of any agreement between the state and the insurgents. The later examples illustrate how the WFP negotiated on various issues concerning field operations, including redressing the lack of credible field information, changing the focus of existing programmes, establishing a Code of Conduct, and working with donors and other NGOs to keep humanitarian goals on the political agenda. Such negotiations, however risky, helped overcome obstacles such as access issues, intimidation of field staff and the need to refocus programmes in order to respond to a changing environment.

Supporting the peace process

A cease-fire was declared in January 2003 and preparations were made to engage in a peace process that looked to be more substantive and promising than the earlier attempt in 2001. From the perspective of the aid agencies operating in Nepal, it appeared that humanitarian concerns were going to be given a high priority and that humanitarian diplomacy could be leveraged to achieve some areas of agreement between the warring parties, as well as to help maintain the humanitarian space.

The National Human Rights Commission of Nepal, along with government representatives, Maoists and members of civil society, designed a code of conduct known as the "22 Peace Stones" to set the tone for the talks. The king's appointee to the talks, Minister Pun, set the agenda. He proposed starting with humanitarian issues, moving on to political issues and tackling military issues only when some agreement had been achieved in the first two areas. The international community stood ready to play a constructive role.

With humanitarian issues at the top of the agenda, it was hoped that initial agreement might have been reached and confidence built fairly quickly. However, it soon became apparent that neither the political parties, nor the Maoist insurgents nor the government actually wanted to take advantage of a humanitarian agenda for confidence-building measures and, in the end, the two rounds of negotiations that took place did not address humanitarian issues. On the margins of the peace talks, the UN Resident Coordinator, with the government's agreement, engaged in some discussions with the Maoist leadership in July 2003. In these brief exchanges, the Maoists made it clear that they were exclusively focused on their political agenda and were not prepared to discuss development issues. They indicated that they would entertain discussion of humanitarian issues only if or when faced with a humanitarian crisis: development issues were not a priority. And, although a Nepal Human Rights Accord had been negotiated and agreed in April 2003, in the end the parties to it would not sign it.

This stance left no room for humanitarian actors to play a role in the peace process, either at the centre, as honest brokers, or at the local level, alleviating the poverty, deprivation and isolation that underpinned the conflict itself.

> *The Peace Stones condemned forced collections of donations in kind or in cash. Although in principle agreeing to this, all parties, including the Maoist leadership, were concerned that the large number of rebels who lived off extortion and robberies would not refrain from such activities. At one point, the WFP was approached informally to discuss the possibility of temporarily providing food aid to this particular group. Our reaction was hesitancy: the project did not appear to sit well with our basic principle of impartial, purely needs-based aid. We were also concerned about the prospect of maintaining a segment of the rebel force intact and ready to resume hostilities. On the other hand, we did not wish to jeopardize the peace process. In the end, we proposed to initiate a bilateral "Food for Arms" programme through which WFP rice would be exchanged for combatant weapons and munitions. Sadly, things did not progress and the cease-fire broke down. Later, the Maoists did appear to have problems in controlling elements of their cadres; some observers argued that one of the reasons for the Maoist pull-out from talks was resentment among cadres over the loss of extortion incomes.*

Establishing field monitoring

To help overcome the information deficit, in late 2002 the WFP decided to set up a field surveillance team to intensify programme monitoring and gather primary data from the field. DFID agreed to provide bilateral funding to support this initiative. Upon receipt of the funds, staff recruitment was undertaken in the districts where the WFP had a presence, a set of templates for data collection was developed, the new recruits were trained and they formally began their work in November 2002. It was concluded that it was important to maintain high visibility so that the WFP's work would be fully transparent to both the RNA and the Maoists. Therefore, in addition to code of conduct letters, the field monitors were issued with WFP caps, vests and t-shirts so that their identity was clear. They started walking around, familiarizing themselves with the villages and making contact with both sides through the local community in order to pass on the message about what they were doing and why. Both the RNA and the insurgents responded positively, indicating that, as long as the assistance reached its agreed target beneficiaries and the operations were transparent, they would not interfere. This early attempt at negotiating suggested that both sides could be amenable to recognizing and respecting humanitarian activities.

By early 2003 there were 30 full-time field monitors, who covered 32 districts. They produced bi-monthly reports that were shared with partners and donors. One monitor was posted at border crossing points to India to observe people movements and check whether this was part of normal temporary migration for economic reasons or a direct result of the conflict. Although some of the monitors were stopped and interrogated, by and large those involved in assistance programmes were spared accusations that they were "spying" for the enemy and, unlike some NGOs, they were not pressed for "intelligence" by either side. However, it remained a risky occupation and a constant concern and debate having local colleagues working in an exposed environment.

To determine key trends and to ensure some level of consensus on the situation in the field, the WFP also set up and chaired a monthly Food Coordination Meeting open to all relevant players.

The QIP programme

In an evolving and difficult situation, it was important that donor countries allowed agencies to adapt existing programmes to address changing circumstances. Most donor assistance was tied up in long-term development programmes, but there was an understanding that aid agencies needed to be flexible. For the WFP, it was crucial and significant that key donors – including the United Kingdom, Norway and Canada – continued to demonstrate their trust and support and engage deeply in trying to support peace-promoting solutions. To maintain donor confidence, the WFP tried to uphold very careful and transparent planning procedures, effective implementation strategies and a proactive attitude.

When information from the field monitors indicated that people in more than 70 village development councils in nine districts of midwestern and far western Nepal were so marginalized that just one more setback would tip the balance, the WFP decided to adjust the focus of its ongoing Nepal Country Programme in order to address their needs directly. Encouraged by the National Planning Commission, which had urged donors to try to intensify implementation of projects in the Maoist-controlled areas, in March 2003 the WFP began working with the government to reallocate 1,500 tons of rice from the WFP Country Programme to what were termed "Quick Impact Projects" (QIPs) in particularly vulnerable areas. The WFP worked with UNICEF, two national NGOs and one international NGO to support simple projects, which were planned together with community members; DFID agreed to cover the NGO non-food costs, and its flexible attitude to this new approach was invaluable for implementation.

To move forward, the government had to sign an amendment to the WFP Country Programme to indicate that it agreed to the change. This process took six months. At the ministerial level, the government appeared somewhat reluctant to see this programme shift to Maoist-controlled areas and away from direct government implementation. After the amendment was finally signed, it took another two months for the NGOs to get to the target areas to set up activities. Thus implementation of QIPs only really got under way towards the end of 2003.

Once the QIPs began, however, the need was evident and the local population received them very enthusiastically. They were grateful not only to receive some help but also for the fact that their difficult situation was finally being acknowledged. Some of the severely affected communities had not been visited by anyone from the government or from development organizations for nine years. Preliminary information from an internal review of the QIPs found that they were timely, well targeted and helpful to the communities, although it remained an open question whether development programmes could continue to run in such an unstable and insecure context.

Although the process of getting QIPs off the ground was a lengthy one, the WFP recognized that it was important not to bypass government systems and create parallel structures. On the contrary, the WFP worked closely with the government to determine who would receive assistance, while anchoring ownership in the individual communities. Furthermore, the cooperation established with the NGO partners proved to be a good experience on which to build further work in the conflict-affected districts.

The Code of Conduct

As discussed above, a major obstacle was maintaining access in the field, owing both to the isolation of some of the communities the WFP was undertaking to assist and also to the difficulties encountered when moving through conflict-affected areas. In some cases, humanitarian principles were not respected and programmes and individuals were put at risk.

To try to overcome some of these problems, as it began to expand its activities in the conflict-affected areas the WFP developed a Code of Conduct as a confidence-building measure in the field in 2002. The purpose of the Code was two-fold: first, to explain the purpose of the WFP presence, and, secondly, to set out clearly what conditions the WFP attached to its provision of aid. By doing so, it was hoped that suspicion and interference could be somewhat mitigated.

The Code explained the mission and objectives of WFP in Nepal and clarified that all WFP equipment, supplies and resources would be used solely for their stated programme objectives. It noted that diversion of resources would be grounds for cessation of WFP support to the district; that no armed or uniformed personnel were allowed to travel in WFP vehicles; and that hiring processes would not to be influenced by political considerations or by ethnic or religious biases. The Code was published in English and Nepali, signed, stamped and laminated, and placed in all official WFP vehicles.

> *Field staff pointed to the Code of Conduct when stopped by the RNA, and on several occasions reported that they found it helpful in lending them some authority and leverage with combatants. I used it when the driver and I were stopped at an RNA checkpoint in the far west. We handed the Code to the RNA soldiers as they prepared to search the vehicle. They read the Code and then let us through without a search.*

There were a number of incidents where the WFP was required to put its Code of Conduct into effect. For example, in December 2003, Maoists looted 6.5 metric tons of rice from the village development council in Phuldev Mandau, Bajura district. In tandem with aid partner GTZ, the WFP immediately issued a press release announcing the suspension of the project in Bajura. Through the local community, the WFP was informed that the Maoists had not realized that the food belonged to the WFP – it had been re-bagged by a private transporter who failed to mark the bags with WFP logos. An investigation found that the responsibility lay with the transporter, who replaced the food. In another incident, insurgents looted a small quantity of rice and, in response, the WFP suspended its project. To compensate, the Maoists agreed to do community work in the villages that were supposed to receive the contribution.

In a more serious incident, in November 2003 the WFP and its aid partners suspended all programmes in Dailekh district after two local women working with an affiliated NGO were abducted and killed by Maoists. The insurgents had accused them of spying and of working for the "imperialists". The local population took action, forcing the Maoists to provide guarantees that aid activities could be resumed according to the Code of Conduct conditions. When the guarantees came, activities in Dailekh resumed.

There were many other examples to underscore the important role of the Code of Conduct in the field. When the WFP addressed issues directly with the Maoists (either via the media or in dialogue in the field), it was possible to achieve an informal agreement. It seemed that Maoist practice regarding development programmes varied from district to district and that the outcome of informal negotiations to a large extent depended on the local commanders. In the absence of a dialogue at the central level on humanitarian issues, such informal and indirect exchanges at the local level were helpful in resolving issues that arose around specific project activities, while the Code of Conduct ensured that conditions were systematically applied across the country.

Establishing operational guidelines

The development of codes of conduct into guidelines became an essential basis for donor cooperation. One significant effort was undertaken by a group of eight donors and bilateral agencies, whose final guidelines expressed many of the same points as the WFP Code of Conduct and provided principles for assistance, including the importance of basing assistance on need; ensuring the direct participation of beneficiaries; and tackling discrimination and social exclusion.

UN agencies in Nepal did not join this initiative because it did not involve consultations with the Nepalese government. Instead, they joined hands as a country team to develop the *United Nations Agencies Guiding Principles* and the *United Nations Agencies Basic Operating Guidelines*, which were very similar to the guidelines issued by the bilateral agencies.[3] These too drew directly on the WFP Code of Conduct for inspiration. The *Principles* affirmed that the United Nations was guided by the principles enshrined in international law, and that it conducted its work in conformity with the principles of humanity, neutrality, impartiality, accountability and transparency in a manner that respected, preserved and promoted the dignity and humanity of the people it sought to assist. The *Guidelines* outlined the purpose and rationale for UN humanitarian and development assistance, the importance of safe and unhindered access, and the responsibilities of states to care for victims of emergencies as well as to facilitate the United Nations' work in such emergencies. The *Guidelines* stipulated clearly that diversion of assistance would not be tolerated, that the transport of armed groups in UN vehicles was not permitted and that intimidation was unacceptable. The text was based on the Geneva Conventions and the Universal Declaration of Human Rights.

Whenever the signatories of the *Guidelines* experienced obstruction of their activities or other violations, they reacted publicly and in solidarity. A case in point was the insurgents' continued demands for taxes on development activities and workers in early 2004. The group of bilateral agencies and the United Nations placed newspaper advertisements urging the Maoists to stop their extortion and warning that, if they failed to do so, activities could be suspended.

Of course, many problems remained. At the operational level, UNICEF tried to set up schools as "zones of peace" and to implement "days of tranquillity" together with the UN Country Team to protect children from violation and abduction by Maoists and to provide urgent supplies and services.[4] For these initiatives to be really successful, both the government and the Maoists needed to agree explicitly to respect the United Nations' *Guidelines* and *Principles*. However, it remained far from certain that they would do so, and this reluctance itself constituted a major impediment to the delivery of assistance.

Applying international pressure

The donor community and humanitarian groups tried to maintain pressure on the highest levels of government in an effort at least to set benchmarks for measuring the progress of the state's own development plans and to identify where performance was falling short.

The donor community was worried not only about the deteriorating security situation but also about the prospect of seeing decades of development efforts and investments undermined by the insurgency. Such concerns were very strongly expressed by a number of key donors that joined the Nepal Development Forum (NDF) in early May 2004. The NDF questioned the government's ability to live up to the ambitions expressed in the Tenth Plan of Nepal's Poverty Reduction Strategy.

The UN Country Team issued a statement based on the UN Secretary-General's message of 22 March 2004. The objective was to share concerns about meeting development goals by highlighting the impact that the insurgency was having on the delivery of programmes. This was the first time the UN Country Team had publicly acknowledged that, because of the conflict, the government did not have access to many areas where development service delivery needed to take place. The statement expressed profound concern about the human rights violations being committed and outlined the significant changes that had taken place in the operational environment since the previous NDF in 2002.[5] The statement also opposed the government's suggestion of an "Integrated Security and Development Programme", stressing that it was fundamentally unsound to combine security and development issues. The donor community welcomed the statement; the government did not; and the statement failed to spark the necessary debate.

Wider implications

Although there were perhaps as many failures as successes in terms of overcoming the obstacles detailed above, through humanitarian diplomacy aid agencies were able to establish parameters within which to continue their work in an increasingly difficult situation – in effect, to define humanitarian space that was to some extent respected by both insurgents and government forces. The fact that a laminated card declaiming a Code of Conduct was respected by soldiers in the field, or that Maoists made good on food stores they had appropriated from aid agencies, attested to the success of moving forward on a negotiated and mutually understood basis. Another, higher-level demonstration of this was the recognition that the United Nations could be a useful actor in any peace process and that humanitarian principles could inform the peace agenda.

More generally, the example of Nepal provided some important lessons for conducting humanitarian activities in the context of escalating political violence. They included:

- When operating in a politically unstable environment, it is vital to keep dialogue possible with all sides while remaining impartial and transparent. A major achievement in Nepal was to gain some acknowledgement from all parties that, for aid agencies, humanitarian principles transcended political ones and that aid was provided on this basis.
- Aid agencies must sometimes decide whether to bypass official systems and work with parallel structures. Such decisions depend on the individual mandate of the organization and the situation it confronts. Nevertheless, to choose is to confer or deny legitimacy for such structures, and this can have long-term consequences that must be balanced against short-term exigencies.
- Building human capital by strengthening, engaging and making responsible local community organizations can embed humanitarian activities in the local population. The beneficiaries of programmes can support and protect them more effectively than can external actors, and they can play an important role in influencing negotiations.
- Continually monitoring and collating information from the field is important and helps the aid community determine scenarios for contingency planning and intervention. The view from the centre can be quite different from the view on the ground. Communities in Nepal demonstrated great resilience but also showed that, in some cases, the line between subsistence and crisis was very thin.

- Establishing and publicizing objectives, principles and conditions of aid provision can help build confidence in areas where aid agencies are operating.
- There is a need to be flexible on the part of donors and within aid agencies themselves so that they can adapt quickly and effectively to rapidly changing situations.

In the period discussed, Nepal never tipped over into a humanitarian crisis, although the potential was clearly there. Engaging in careful negotiations across different levels and with different groups at least ensured that access was maintained and that many humanitarian agencies could continue operating in the midst of an escalating civil conflict without losing the confidence of donors, beneficiaries, implementing partners or the parties to the conflict.

It can take many years for a peace process to find a way through to a durable solution. Meanwhile, those humanitarian diplomats who seek to assist and often involuntarily assume the role of "go-between" should continue to support any effort that inspires reconciliation and helps tackle the root causes of the conflict without harming the structures and mechanisms by which the population manages to survive and without undermining the basic principles of humanitarian work.

Notes

1. *Country Report Nepal*, London: Economist Intelligent Unit, May 2004.
2. Figures published by the Informal Sector Service Center (INSEC), Kathmandu, Nepal.
3. *United Nations Agencies Guiding Principles*, Kathmandu: United Nations, 7 January 2004, available at ⟨http://www.un.org.np/basic1.php⟩ (accessed 25 April 2006), and *United Nations Agencies Basic Operating Guidelines*, Kathmandu: United Nations, 16 January 2004, available at ⟨http://www.un.org.np/basic.php⟩ (accessed 25 April 2006).
4. Kul C. Gautam (Deputy Executive Director, UNICEF, and Assistant Secretary-General of the United Nations), "Cambodia 1974, Nepal 2004: How to Avoid Nepal's Descent towards a Failed State?", 5 April 2004, ⟨http://kulgautam.org/website/index.php?option =com_content&task=view&id=33&Itemid=62⟩ (accessed 25 April 2006).
5. United Nations Country Team, Written Statement to the Nepal Development Forum 2004, Kathmandu, 4–6 May 2004, available at ⟨http://www.ndf2004.gov.np/pdf/chairmanreport.pdf⟩ (accessed 2 May 2006).

Part IV
Africa

11

Nurturing humanitarian space in Sudan

Masood Hyder

Context

In the closing years of the twentieth century, the international community became familiar with a new term, "complex emergency", used to describe the combined effects of civil strife, displacement and drought on countries in turmoil. It discovered that, in those circumstances, reaching people in need was not a simple matter. It required negotiation, communication and an unprecedented degree of coordination. In the front-line of this action were humanitarian workers, not diplomats, though they were engaged in an activity reminiscent of diplomacy, here termed "humanitarian diplomacy". This chapter focuses on operations in the Republic of Sudan during 2000–2002, with particular reference to the World Food Programme's large-scale interventions and the role of humanitarian diplomacy in the pursuit of operational humanitarian objectives in that troubled country.

Sudan's independence from British and Egyptian rule in 1956 brought with it neither peace nor prosperity but heralded a turbulent phase in the country's history that has lasted to the present day. The post-independence period was marked by short intervals of ineffective parliamentary government, followed by longer periods of military rule. Worse, there were repeated instances of large-scale civil conflict, as the Muslim majority in the north unsuccessfully tried to assert the authority of the central government on the non-Muslim south. The latter responded with rebellion from 1963 to 1971, and again from the mid-1980s to the present.

In such circumstances, economic development could hardly take place, and Sudan, once the breadbasket of the region, fell prey to repeated bouts of famine, drought and displacement. By 2000, a succession of disasters had led to 2 million dead and 4 million displaced.

In 2004, just as a peace settlement was being concluded between the north and the south, war broke out in the western province of Darfur, when a rebel insurrection, frustrated by what it called the Sudan government's marginalization of Darfur, revived longstanding demands for economic and political reforms. The government struck back through Arab militias. The resulting violence killed tens of thousands and displaced almost 2 million people. Thus, even as the civil war appeared to be ending, the heritage of violence continued to take its toll.

It had become clear for some time that a major crisis was unfolding in Sudan and that people caught up in the turmoil needed assistance. In 1989, Operation Lifeline Sudan (OLS) was created to facilitate humanitarian access into southern Sudan. It was an arrangement between the belligerents (the government of Sudan and the opposition Sudan People's Liberation Army/Movement (SPLA/M)) and the international community.[1] It evolved during subsequent years, but basically comprised a set of formal agreements, developed over time, that facilitated humanitarian access into southern Sudan and helped provide assistance (and, to a certain extent, protection) to millions of people affected by the conflict.[2] OLS enshrined the idea of "unimpeded access" for member humanitarian agencies, including many non-governmental organizations (NGOs), to individuals in need in southern Sudan and parts of government-held territory affected by war.

Despite the existence of an impressive array of written protocols, however, access could not be taken for granted on a day-to-day basis. Instead, "humanitarian space" – that is, the scope for humanitarian action – widened or narrowed depending on a number of factors, including political, military and administrative considerations.[3] Nurturing humanitarian space is the essence of humanitarian diplomacy. Its objective is to save lives, to alleviate suffering and to uphold humanitarian principles. In order to achieve that, it must deal with operational constraints as they arise.

Operational issues

Operational constraints refer to the existence of real, immediate and serious impediments to the delivery or sustainability of humanitarian assistance. Notable among these are: access – how to reach those in need; compliance – how to ensure delivery without the use or threat of force; coordination – how to function in conditions of uncertain political support; and explication – how to defend or justify aid, especially in protracted operations. These and other constraints constitute a sort of resistant medium whose effects humanitarian diplomacy is engaged in overcoming.

In the case of the World Food Programme (WFP) in Sudan, the main operational issue concerns access, or reaching the people in need of assistance. WFP's job is not done when a donor is found, or a vessel engaged or even when the food arrives in port; that is in fact often the beginning of the difficulties. Humanitarian intervention begins at the point where it becomes clear there are urgent needs that are not going to be met unless outside agencies take action. But such intervention encounters the same obstacles that deprived the local population of food in the first place. Access too is an entitlement issue, as much as the more familiar topics concerning the political economy of hunger. If anything, it is a reminder that the contending principles of humanitarian intervention and non-interference in the internal affairs of sovereign states are not easily reconciled.[4]

The second operational issue concerns compliance: how to execute policy without the use or threat of force. Humanitarian diplomacy as practised by WFP and its sister UN aid agencies is conducted in the absence of the ultimate sanction of force. Nor does the promise of assistance delivered free of charge guarantee an unconditional welcome. The host government, although generally anxious to receive assistance, has other, justifiable, considerations to weigh in the balance, not least of which is security (in the sense of exercising control over its territory, people, administration and policy, as well as ensuring the safety of expatriate staff). For these and other reasons, the humanitarian community often appears more anxious to render assistance than are the national authorities to receive it. Therefore any moral or diplomatic advantage that may be assumed to come from being a donor is diluted or lost. Assistance does not provide the leverage that one might imagine, commensurate with the value of the commodities involved or the urgency of need. The humanitarian community can, of course, resort to withdrawal or suspension of operations but that is, in a sense, self-defeating.

The third operational issue is how to function in the virtual absence of political support. Humanitarian diplomacy needs, but often does not obtain, political backing. For the UN Representative in the field, the Department of Political Affairs, the Secretary-General's Office in New York, or the Security Council are very remote institutions. In theory, there is a two-way channel of communication between New York and the field; in practice, the political initiative lies with New York and often stays there. Although not unaware of what is transpiring in the field, UN secretariat officials with political portfolios often keep their own counsel.

The fourth operational constraint for the period under review in Sudan concerns the articulation of the role of food aid in a complex emergency. Welcomed initially, WFP's role came under critical scrutiny as time passed. Why could it not achieve unimpeded access? Why was monitoring so poor? Was food being diverted to the rebels? Was food aid prolonging the conflict? These are donor concerns.[5] The host authorities also develop concerns over time, which have to do with the risks of dependency that external assistance represents, of penetration by foreign interests, and generally reflecting their ambivalence about food assistance. No one likes accepting food; unlike financial or technical assistance, the receipt of food assistance suggests a level of impoverishment that no state likes to admit.

Obstacles and opportunities

Given the operational constraints, negotiating for humanitarian space is a constant, unremitting struggle. It will be argued here that humanitarian diplomacy may be considered as a type of policy implementation activity, undertaken in an adverse political and physical environment. The usual limits to successful implementation apply, but with greater force. Three points emerge. First, the humanitarian imperative may be paramount in theory, but the process is subject to competitive and contending political forces. Second, the process of maintaining humanitarian space is compromised by structural weaknesses both in the government machinery (weak administration, poor communication) and in the humanitarian community (absence of consensus, lack of support from headquarters). Third, contradictions in the design of humanitarian policy emerge, eventually, as a major limiting factor. If the policy is designed to save lives but not to restore livelihoods, then the objective of transiting out of crisis will not be achieved.

A number of reasons may be offered for the intractability of humanitarian affairs as experienced in complex emergencies. The insights come from policy implementation studies. Nurturing humanitarian space may legitimately be regarded as a particular type of implementation problem, concerned with securing compliance in a hostile environment. Although, traditionally, policy implementation deals with a single bureaucracy, regarded as a rational form of human organization,[6] the present study represents a case of implementation across national boundaries,[7] or rather the attempt to carry out a special type of agreement, one that permits the United Nations and its NGO partners to operate in the middle of a civil war. Three approaches originally developed in the policy implementation literature apply. It can be studied in terms of a political process, where multiple or ambiguous political objectives "prevent administrative success";[8] or as an inter-organizational process of bargaining, interpretation and negotiation;[9] or in terms of "administrative limits", which reminds us that bureaucracies, though rational, are not perfect instruments of policy.[10] The analytical lens of policy implementation studies provides a focus to our observations.

First, humanitarian diplomacy operates in an environment characterized by multiple or ambiguous political objectives. In Sudan, the government's other preoccupations determined the priority accorded to humanitarian work, and the exigencies of the civil war asserted primacy over humanitarian concerns. (The same observations apply to the opposition SPLA/M, which is also political, faction-ridden and operating in the real world.)[11] In the middle of conducting its campaigns, the military (on either side) would not have its hands tied, and it clearly resisted having humanitarian concerns stand in its way. There exists therefore a hierarchy of intent, and humanitarian concerns are seldom at the top. Indeed, OLS was often blamed by either side in the war for being the cause of any reversals that they might have suffered.

The government's internal structure (and that of the opposition) determines its responsiveness to humanitarian concerns. The administration often appeared to consist of a loose coalition of interests and factions, only some of which conceded any degree of priority to humanitarian interests, especially if these concerned the welfare of groups alienated from the ruling élites or not considered sufficiently important by them. The province of Darfur is a case in point: it has always been regarded as ethnically distinct from the Arabized north; it was not even part of Sudan until 1916, and has suffered neglect since, which accounts for the history of political protest going back to the mid-1960s. For all these reasons therefore, Darfur's needs did not receive a sympathetic hearing at the centre in Khartoum.

Darfur, long subject to drought, also suffered from the tendency to hide failures and setbacks. The current administration in Sudan was fervent about basic self-sufficiency, especially in terms of food. To admit therefore that it could not feed itself and to ask for international assistance for this purpose (even following a drought) went against that image of self-sufficiency. The authorities would rather deny need than ask for help. There existed a striking similarity to the North Korean ambivalence to food aid, as described in Chapter 9 by David Morton. In both cases, the political and administrative culture determined the priority given to humanitarian concerns.

The government of Sudan also displayed a sort of fatalistic acceptance of suffering. The people have always faced drought; they have always moved when disaster strikes; they cope, somehow; and there is not much that can be done. This passive attitude towards suffering was very much at odds with the activist, interventionist approach of the international community. Indeed, the latter derives its humanitarian imperatives largely from the post-modern state, but applies them in rather more traditional settings.[12]

The second set of issues concerns structural problems. The most fundamental of these arose from the fact that Sudan was divided and poorly administered: the government's writ ran over only half the country; the other half was in rebellion. The administrative machinery was weak and ill-equipped, and basic physical infrastructure was lacking. Notable amongst the weaknesses was the inability of the periphery to communicate with the centre. This was owing to poor physical lines of communication, a lack of effective communications between the civil and military authorities, and a failure to assign responsibility at the provincial level for reporting on humanitarian disasters.

Normally, a robust, independent press and other news media would expose those weaknesses. But the local news media were weak and unable to act as an effective, independent force. The international media, on the other hand, operated from Nairobi, and were therefore in closer touch with the Sudanese opposition, also based in Nairobi; they had virtually no impact internally in Sudan.

Commercial interests, on the other hand, had undeniable reach and impact on the administration. The large farmers, grain merchants, commercial transporters and the like could be very influential. Often their interests seemed to prevail. The government's attempts to create and operate a strategic food stock reserve, to make timely purchases of food, to exert a stabilizing influence on the grain market, to facilitate the transportation of humanitarian assistance were all influenced as much if not more by commercial as by humanitarian interests.

The weaknesses affecting policy initiatives were not all on the Sudanese side. The humanitarian community's bargaining position was, in later years, compromised by the unwillingness of OLS to police non-OLS flights. OLS had struggled to run its operations as correctly as possible, flying only to agreed destinations, scrupulously limiting itself to the transportation of humanitarian cargo, and generally abiding by OLS rules and agreements. However, non-OLS flights (also taking place from Lokichoggio, or "Loki," in northern Kenya) had been free from any such restraint. Thus unauthorized flights entered Sudanese air space without government clearance. They had nothing to do with the United Nations or OLS, but shadowed OLS flights in order to escape government of

Sudan surveillance and to fly to opposition-held destinations. It is impossible to judge how effective these flights were in providing either humanitarian assistance to denied locations or other forms of assistance to opposition forces, but this proved to be an enormous irritant to the government of Sudan, which usually retaliated by imposing restrictions on OLS.

This was clearly a case where the humanitarian community did not act as one. Other examples exist. The split between the needs-based and the rights-based approaches (as described in the Bieh incident below) was a major factor in weakening the humanitarian community's negotiating position.

There is a temptation to interpret the problem of negotiating humanitarian space solely in terms of intractable partners on the ground, such as the government or the opposition, military factions, and so on. The practitioner has in fact to lavish almost equal care and attention to maintain a consensus at headquarters level, especially in a crisis. Do the UN agencies support the policy being proposed? Is the United Nations Office of Security Coordination (UNSECOORD) in New York in agreement? Are the major donors and NGOs behind the UN Humanitarian Coordinator's line? The cases presented in the next section of this study make this point clear. Headquarters-level support and consensus are crucial in the implementation of policy across national boundaries.

The third set of issues raises concerns about the effectiveness of humanitarian policy itself. In many countries in turmoil, including Sudan, the donor community is willing to provide emergency humanitarian assistance but it is not willing to move forward into reconstruction and development. This circumspect approach can have disastrous results. The drought of 2001 hit Darfur and Kordofan so hard because there had been no follow-up after the previous emergency. The water sources had not been maintained; the pumps were not working; the dams had silted up. More importantly, humanitarian action in previous droughts had saved lives but not livelihoods. The people had survived but had not been able to get back on their feet. The failure to build up local capacity, to maintain water sources or to restore livelihoods was essentially a failure to do any sort of development work. The humanitarian community was condemned, as a consequence, repeatedly to address the crises that ensued. Humanitarian action is, eventually, self-defeating if it is not followed up by development at the appropriate time. Thus, even perfect implementation of a purely humanitarian policy achieves only part of what is required.

I have looked at obstacles – what of opportunities? In negotiating for humanitarian space, the practitioner is more conscious of obstacles than of opportunities; there is a fundamental intractability attending humanitarian action. Even those parts of the recipient authority designed to liaise with humanitarian agencies and to expedite their work end up controlling rather than facilitating. There is no reason therefore to look for a dialectical balance here: we need not imagine that, if there are constraints, there must be opportunities also. The game of humanitarian diplomacy does not take place on a level playing field.

Negotiations

Negotiations are required at all stages of a humanitarian operation, but not all negotiations are diplomatic in character. Settling barge rates for transporting food up-river or haggling over office rents do not constitute humanitarian diplomacy, although they may have implications for the effectiveness of humanitarian operations. Humanitarian operations involve transactions of a higher order. A clear humanitarian objective is involved and the action takes place in a political setting, as in the two case studies presented here. One involves the challenge of negotiating minimum access arrangements to the region of Bieh in Western Upper Nile province in early 2002, an area contested by the government and the SPLA. The other involves the suspension of operations as an instance of hard negotiation.

Bieh: Negotiating minimum access requirements

By 2002, the conflict in southern Sudan had been going on for so long that it was possible to discern a pattern in the violence: every spring, the conflict would intensify, and then continue through the summer until the rains arrived, when military operations became more difficult to execute. It was, generally speaking, a very "civilized" form of war, in that it had a direct impact on the civilian population, and was conducted at varying levels of intensity. There were, of course, army-against-army confrontations between the forces of the government and the opposition. More frequently, however, there were clashes between the militias associated with either side. Even more commonplace were the actions of the militias against the civilian population, which were undertaken as a means of retaliation and harassment and were intended to demoralize the enemy; they resulted in the displacement of populations and caused various forms of distress. Further down the scale of violence, but more frequent in occurrence, were inter-tribal, inter-ethnic clashes, raids and fights, down to episodes of cattle-rustling and crop-burning that had more to do with a traditional way of life than the conduct of politics by other means.

Spring 2002 was no different, except that the sequence of events seemed to start a little early, and included a number of attacks against civilians at or near food distribution points and the looting of humanitarian facilities. On 2 February, offices of Médicins Sans Frontières (MSF) at Nimne were looted and its laboratory destroyed. On 9 February, Nimne was bombed by a government aircraft, which resulted in the death of five civilians, including one MSF relief worker. On 10 February, two people died and a dozen more were injured when a military aircraft dropped bombs at a site in Akuem where the WFP had just finished food distribution. But the worst incident occurred on 20 February 2002, when a WFP food distribution site in Bieh, Western Upper Nile, was attacked by a government helicopter gunship shortly after a food distribution, and 24 civilians were killed.

The United Nations strongly condemned the action. The donor community also reacted vigorously to the attack. On 23 February, after a reception at the presidential palace in connection with the Muslim New Year, the president, General Omar Bashir, invited the representatives of the United States, France, the United Kingdom, Germany and Switzerland to stay behind, in order to explain to them the government's position on the incident. He said he hoped that the incident would have no negative impact on the ongoing peace process, and that what had happened was a mistake by a local commander who had been misled by information planted by the SPLA about non-UN aircraft dropping weapons and ammunition at Bieh. Henceforth, areas in which humanitarian operations had been authorized would be declared no-combat zones, and any military action there would have to be authorized at the highest level in Khartoum. Coordination between the military and humanitarian arms of the government would be reinforced with the appointment of a brigadier-general in place of the captain who currently headed the coordination unit. Lastly, the president assured his guests, a full investigation of the incident was under way.

In the days that followed the attack on Bieh, both the humanitarian community and the government authorities acted in predictable ways. Humanitarian activities continued, with the adoption of increased security precautions. The administrative authorities invited the United Nations to work with them in order to put in place improved procedures, while themselves clearly operating under pressure from the military and intelligence services to restrict access.

Thus, the scene was set for what the Secretary-General's Special Envoy to Sudan was to later describe as the most serious humanitarian crisis to befall Sudan since the Bahr el Ghazal famine of 1998. The crisis concerned access and at its height endangered the lives of well over 1 million people in southern Sudan. In large part, access to most places in southern Sudan is achieved by air, because surface transportation either does not exist or is too dangerous to undertake. In 2001, WFP alone flew about 40,000 tons of food into southern Sudan; other OLS partners transported additional quantities of medical and other supplies.

This is the context in which, every month, an elaborate game of wits was conducted. OLS would request air access to about 200 locations, while intending to fly to about 100 locations in the course of the month, thereby giving itself room for manoeuvre. The government would approve access to over 90 per cent of the locations requested, but a great hue and cry would be raised both by the United Nations and by the NGO community about the 17 or so locations normally denied. Most of the locations denied could in fact be accessed by road (flight denial does not mean the location cannot be reached by other means); some of the denied locations might not be in need of humanitarian assistance; and some might indeed be too dangerous to access. If all this was taken into account, real denials were much lower than the 17 or so locations refused by the government.

From March 2002, however, access was seriously curtailed. Growing prospects for peace seemed only to intensify the conflict, especially in Western Upper Nile and Bahr el Ghazal. As the conflict intensified, the government employed several means to interrupt humanitarian assistance. First, denials to specific destinations increased, from the usual 17 locations to about 45. Secondly, the government resorted to blanket denial covering large parts of Western Upper Nile. Thirdly, it issued advisories stating that parts of Bahr el Ghazal and Western Upper Nile were not safe owing to SPLA activity and that the government advised the humanitarian community not to proceed to those areas. Fourthly, it requested clarification about a large number of requested locations, stating that they were not known to the government, which therefore found itself unable to authorize access until precise coordinates were supplied.

By April 2002 it was becoming clear that the government was not likely to back down on flight clearances. The monthly clearance for April was forwarded to the United Nations very late and once again denied clearance for large parts of southern Sudan. This was now becoming truly worrying. With the return of the dry season, the hunger period begins in earnest and the need for food aid becomes urgent between April and September. It was calculated that over 1 million people in need were being affected by the denials and that their situation would soon become serious, leading to malnutrition, perhaps thousands of deaths and even the repetition of the 1998 Bahr el Ghazal famine.

From April 2002, the United Nations in Sudan began advising UN Headquarters in New York (and the major UN agencies based in Rome and New York) that the situation required high-level intervention. UN

Khartoum suggested that, among the donors, the United States could be most helpful, and that on the UN side two options should be considered: either to brief the Security Council or to bring in the Secretary-General, Kofi Annan. After further consultations, New York decided to send the Secretary-General's Special Envoy for Humanitarian Affairs for Sudan, Ambassador Tom Eric Vraalsen of Norway, to Khartoum. After some delay over dates, he arrived in Khartoum on 25 May 2002 for three days of hard, even grim negotiations.

At this point the government introduced a new (though not unfamiliar) issue – the closure of Lokichoggio. For the purpose of supplying humanitarian assistance in southern Sudan, WFP (the air arm of OLS) was deploying 19 aircraft from two airfields, Loki in Kenya and El Obeid in government-held Sudan. These are the two main points of entry into OLS territory. Both were important not only from a logistical point of view but also politically: the government would have liked all operations to take place from El Obeid; the opposition would have liked them to take place from Loki. At the time, a delicate balance existed, with equal quantities of supplies transiting from either point of entry. This was the framework within which WFP and its OLS partners negotiated access. But some NGOs working outside the context of OLS chose to enter Sudan without government clearance. They operated from Loki, and this was one of the primary reasons for the government's unease about operations from Loki.

The negotiations with Vraalsen went badly, and it rapidly became clear that the government was not interested in instituting a humanitarian cease-fire (in order to resume deliveries of assistance). Nor would it offer any realistic assurance of easing up on flight denials. At the end of the negotiations, First Vice President Taha, speaking for the government, told the Envoy categorically that Loki was to be closed.

This was a major blow. If Loki was to be closed, the SPLA/M would not allow assistance to come from El Obeid either. The impasse would have meant the end of UN humanitarian operations and most likely the end of OLS; famine and death on a large scale would most certainly follow in southern Sudan. Knowing this, Vraalsen spent his last hours in Khartoum obtaining a deal for which he was later criticized. Under this agreement, humanitarian assistance would resume right away and Loki would remain open. But, for the next four or five weeks, all humanitarian assistance to Unity State would go from El Obeid and not from Loki.

From the UN negotiator's perspective in Khartoum, there was little wrong with this arrangement: it allowed humanitarian assistance to continue; it did not violate the underlying principles of OLS work (under which points of access cannot be shut down unilaterally) as Loki remained open. It did give in to government insistence that nothing should come from Loki to Unity (Western Upper Nile), but only on a temporary basis. If Vraalsen had not agreed to that, then Loki would have been closed down altogether and no assistance would have been possible for any part of southern Sudan. Although not perfect, it was the best deal possible. All donors in Khartoum supported the deal, including the US representative. In practical terms, too, it worked. WFP was capable of providing food assistance from El Obied to Unity; it already did that to some extent. There were no practical constraints to the arrangement. The constraints were political.

The SPLA/M did not like the idea of conceding to the government's insistence that aid should go, even on a temporary basis, from a northern point of entry. The NGOs disliked the idea too, especially the ones that undertook unauthorized flights from Loki into Western Upper Nile and elsewhere. If the United Nations did not fly from Loki, these NGOs would not have "cover" to fly themselves. But depriving the NGOs of access for four weeks would not have had any serious consequences. For the Envoy, reaching the people was the main goal; for others, he had conceded too much or he had given in to blackmail.

In Sudan, the humanitarian community often has to deal with the real authorities only at second hand. Behind the hard men negotiating with the United Nations are harder men pulling the strings. Negotiations take place at one remove, and the government interlocutors are themselves caught between the outside world, represented by the United Nations, and the hard-liners at home. Of course, this handicap can be turned to the government's advantage when its negotiators imply that their hands are tied. So when, on the evening of 28 May 2002, a senior official of the government called Vraalsen to the ministry of foreign affairs and assured him that the military wanted to close down Loki, and that the best compromise was to fly from El Obeid to Western Upper Nile, was it a bluff or was it sincerely meant? If the latter, was it acceptable? The critics would have preferred a breakdown of negotiations rather than a compromise on principle, but then the crisis would have dragged on. Vraalsen, an experienced negotiator, chose the humanitarian option.

In the end, the Envoy's compromise was not totally rejected. But it brought into sharp focus the two competing approaches to humanitarian assistance that have still to be reconciled in Sudan. From a rights-based perspective, access to victims of a humanitarian disaster is not an end in itself. It demands rather that all humanitarian aid be judged on how it contributes to the protection and promotion of human rights. But, according to the needs-based approach, humanitarian assistance must not be denied to people in need, in pursuit of other objectives. Humanitarian response is above all about meeting urgent needs; the rights-based approach risks missing this point. For the Envoy, reaching the people in need was the main goal.

This is not a theoretical question in the Sudan context, and it is possible to cite other examples. Should food assistance be denied to the people of Nasir because of their association with Commander Gordon Kong, a militia commander working with the government who in the past has, on more than one occasion, held humanitarian workers hostage? Should thousands of people go without assistance, which could otherwise be supplied to them, in order to punish one man? Should assistance be denied to government-held Nuba if it cannot be supplied to opposition-held Nuba? Should assistance be held back because, as a consequence of giving it, there might be a shift of population in that contested region? Might the government or opposition manipulate humanitarian aid in this way as a matter of tactics? In providing humanitarian assistance in a highly politicized environment, can practitioners realistically keep this assistance out of politics? In other words, humanitarian space can come under pressure not only from the combatants but also from the wide-ranging and divergent concerns of the humanitarian community itself. The next case touches on this point too, in emphasizing the importance of consensus-building at headquarters level.

Suspension of operations

In early July 2000, in the course of the annual bout of summer fighting, the SPLA took Gogrial, a government-held town in the Bahr el Ghazal region of southern Sudan, despite a cease-fire that was then in place. Soon after Gogrial changed hands, the foreign minister summoned the diplomatic community in Khartoum to lodge a protest. He specifically asked the UN Humanitarian Coordinator to convey to New York the government of Sudan's expectation that the United Nations would condemn the taking of Gogrial.[13] The message was duly passed on by the UN Humanitarian Coordinator, emphasizing the desirability of a more proactive engagement in Sudan by the political arm of the United Nations. When the United Nations remained silent on Gogrial, Sudanese frustrations were vented in other ways.

On 23 July 2000, the Khartoum newspapers carried dramatic reports of the president's denunciation of OLS in a speech the previous evening. He was reported to have called it "Operation Bloodline" and to have implied that OLS was facilitating the supply of arms to the opposition. The United Nations immediately contacted the foreign ministry, which assured the UN Humanitarian Coordinator that it was not aware of any change of policy or approach towards OLS or the United Nations.

On 24 July, the UN Humanitarian Coordinator met the state minister for foreign affairs, who said that OLS was not being accused but that there was dissatisfaction about other non-OLS flights taking place "in the shadow of OLS" or taking advantage of OLS and hinting that a review of OLS management might be necessary. The overall tone, however, was placatory.

But evidently the military interpreted the speech differently, and attacks on humanitarian flights and personnel increased in frequency. On 27 July 2000, a UNICEF vaccination team on the Sobat River near Malakal was shot at by unknown gunmen and a member of the medical team was injured, though not fatally. Also on 27 July, a Red Cross plane was bombed in Billing, Lake State. On 28 July, two WFP aircraft carrying humanitarian staff and supplies on a mission of which the government had been previously notified were attacked when they landed in Bahr el Ghazal. The government Antonov flew overhead and dropped bombs. The bombs fell very close to the aircraft and the blast from the explosion nearly upturned one UN aircraft as it taxied for emergency take-off. Both aircraft were able to return to base unharmed. The incident was serious enough to alert the UN Special Envoy, Ambassador Vraalsen (concurrently Norway's ambassador in Washington), who contacted the foreign minister of Sudan by telephone from Washington and subsequently instructed UN Khartoum to provide the foreign minister with details of the incident. This was done on 29 July 2000.

At this point, the UN Humanitarian Coordinator came under some pressure from colleagues to stop all humanitarian flights. But he decided to continue in view of several considerations. First, a high-level protest had been lodged by Ambassador Vraalsen. Secondly, flights would be easy to stop but difficult to resume. Thirdly, stopping would be perceived as giving in to government/military pressure: the hard-line elements in the government would be only too pleased if OLS supplies to the south ceased altogether. Fourthly, stoppage would give the government an excuse to reject the monthly flight clearance (if OLS was not flying, it would not need flight clearance).

On the other hand, flying was indeed becoming more dangerous. The Humanitarian Coordinator therefore gave instructions on 29 July that airdrops should continue but airlifts should be suspended. That way, OLS could remain operational but, if its aircraft did not land, they could not be attacked. At that time, the government's method of attack was somewhat basic and consisted in rolling bombs from the rear of Antonov cargo planes at targets on the ground; they did not have the capacity to engage in air-to-air attack. As a short-term strategy, confining operations to airdrops worked well, though it was untenable over a longer period. Thus, the Humanitarian Coordinator did everything possible to avoid bringing the situation to crisis point: humanitarian space had to be preserved.

On 31 July 2000, clearance was received for OLS flights for the month of August. On 2 August, the foreign minister wrote to Vraalsen, affirming that no further attacks would take place. In the meantime, a brief mission by the United Nations Office for the Coordination of Humanitarian Affairs (OCHA) had stopped over in Khartoum during 29–31 July. Ross Mountain, a senior official of OCHA, and Nils Kastberg, Head of Emergency Operations, UNICEF, came to Khartoum in an attempt to defuse the situation. The press, waiting for an opportunity to entrap a UN official, systematically misquoted Mr Mountain on various issues, implying that the United Nations had conceded on all points raised by the government of Sudan concerning Gogrial and OLS. Back in Geneva, Mountain had to engage in a vigorous rearguard action to correct the record. The feeling therefore persisted that, despite the assurances from the foreign minister, the crisis was not over and that various parts of the government still remained highly dissatisfied with the United Nations. In short, the capture of Gogrial despite the cease-fire was still affecting the political climate in Khartoum, to the detriment of humanitarian operations. The possibility remained that, despite the foreign minister's assurances, attacks on OLS flights might continue.

In the meantime, the Humanitarian Coordinator did everything possible to ensure that OLS flights continued to follow proper procedure and that nothing untoward would happen that would worsen an already difficult situation. Accordingly, steps were taken to tighten flight procedures in Loki. A senior WFP officer was sent from Nairobi to take charge of flight operations in Loki. Despite these precautions, a security flight (intended to clear locations in advance of humanitarian operations) took off on 3 August headed for a location that was on the current "denied list". The OLS security officers landed in Nialdhu, assuming it was in opposition hands, and found themselves detained by a militia leader allied to the government. A potential hostage situation ensued that was resolved only 24 hours later. The government could have made much of "unauthorized OLS flights", but, like the Humanitarian Coordinator, probably did not wish to further disturb an already delicate situation. Practitioners engaged in opening up humanitarian space not only have to struggle with their government counterparts but also have to spend a lot of energy ensuring that their own side is not undoing their efforts.

This incident was soon overshadowed by news on 7 August 2000 from Mapel, Bahr el Ghazal, that a WFP/OLS aircraft had been attacked. The bombs missed the aircraft, but the resumption of attacks was bad news indeed. Attacks were evidently continuing, despite written assurances from the foreign minister. And Mapel was such an unexpected target that it challenged previous assumptions about areas of vulnerability. After Mapel, all of southern Sudan seemed vulnerable. The time had come seriously to consider suspension of OLS flights. The Humanitarian Coordinator issued instructions that the number of OLS flights be immediately restricted. But he did not cancel all flights. The office of the UN Security Coordinator in New York contacted him to assure him that cancellation was "his call", and UNSECOORD would support him whatever he decided.

Still, the Humanitarian Coordinator refrained from taking the decision. Although he knew that suspension was "his call", he felt that he must first ensure that his decision would be supported by the major operational agencies – UNICEF and WFP. In order to be certain of such support, he postponed the decision to suspend by 24 hours, until 4 pm the following day (8 August). And, in order to ensure that no OLS aircraft came under attack in the meantime, he cut back drastically on OLS flights for 8 August. In the end, near midnight of 7 August, he was left with three scheduled OLS flights for the following day, all (he was assured) flying to safe destinations. Technically, OLS was still flying, but with minimum risk. The following morning, 8 August 2000, he received the assurances from the UN agencies that he was seeking. At 4 pm Khartoum time, just as UN New York opened for business, he formally recommended suspension of all OLS flights.

This careful consensus-building ensured that the decision was taken seriously in New York and supported there (and by WFP in Rome). The Humanitarian Coordinator's recommendation to suspend was backed by UNSECOORD and approved without delay by the UN Secretary-General.

The meticulous preparation paid off. On 8 August itself, the Secretary-General wrote to the president of Sudan expressing his concern about the humanitarian situation, explaining the reason why he had suspended operations, and urging the president to take the necessary steps that would permit their resumption. The president replied promptly, on 10 August, offering his regrets for the attacks, confirming his support for OLS and expressing the hope that humanitarian flights could resume at the earliest possible moment.

The crisis was over. The Humanitarian Coordinator approached the foreign minister on 12 August and requested him to ascertain how long it would take the military to issue instructions to its personnel on the front-lines that would ensure the safety of the OLS flights. The foreign minister came back suggesting 72 hours. OLS flights resumed on 16 August 2000.

The decision to suspend was taken with due care, with importance given to the manner in which it was taken. The reasons for stopping were clearly spelled out: action had been taken for ensuring the security of staff. The implications were explained: flights had been suspended, but humanitarian work on the ground could continue. The Humanitarian Coordinator remained deliberately circumspect about assigning blame; he left that to the different headquarters. He avoided all vituperation. As a consequence of his restraint, it was easy subsequently for the United Nations in Khartoum to resume normal relations with the government as the crisis blew over. If anything, the stock of the United Nations rose in Khartoum. Never before in the 11-year history of OLS, despite comparable provocation, had the United Nations suspended flights. Humanitarian space had been closed temporarily in order to preserve it in the long run. The decision quite probably increased respect for the humanitarian principles upon which the programme was based.

It had all begun with the capture of Gogrial during a cease-fire and with the perceived failure of the political arm of the United Nations to condemn the action with sufficient vigour, which could have defused the situation. The balance between too much political intervention in humanitarian work and too little is hard to maintain. But, in Sudan, the tendency of the political arm of the United Nations had been to keep its distance, resulting in some additional strain on humanitarian work.

Wider implications

The term "humanitarian diplomacy" has been used in this chapter to describe the process of nurturing or maintaining access to those in need, in difficult physical and political circumstances. Four points have been highlighted: the intractability of humanitarian affairs, the centrality of negotiation to humanitarian diplomacy, the importance of communication, and the relative neglect in the UN system of a fourth essential component of humanitarian diplomacy, namely coordination.

The formula for coordination varies according to the type of humanitarian crisis confronting the UN system. It is possible to distinguish three varieties of coordination. The first involves consensus-building at the country level. One-off emergencies, such as a cyclone or earthquake, are dealt with by field-based agencies, which might get together to constitute a Disaster Management Team under the UN Resident Coordinator. The latter, who is normally the United Nations Development Programme's Resident Representative, has to build consensus and provide leadership to UN funds, programmes and agencies in the field, whose representatives are ultimately answerable to their respective headquarters and not to the Resident Coordinator.

In the second case, coordination has to do with the challenge of co-opting the political side of the United Nations in the humanitarian enterprise. Complex emergencies in the 16 or so countries where a Humanitarian Coordinator is already in place involve OCHA and, through OCHA, the United Nations Department of Political Affairs (DPA). The difficulty here is that the crucial political dimension has to pass through too many channels. The links between the DPA and the Humanitarian Coordinator are tenuous at best and often non-existent. The DPA's headquarters-oriented culture makes communication with the field difficult. There are other constraints. The major operational agencies are relatively inactive in the Executive Committee on Peace and Security (chaired by the Under-Secretary-General of the DPA). They report at infrequent intervals to the Security Council. They have no say in the selection or day-to-day work of the Special Representatives of the Secretary-General or the variety of Special Envoys employed by the Secretary-General's office. These are serious drawbacks. As we have seen in this chapter, humanitarian diplomacy cannot reach its potential unless it is better served by the political side of the United Nations.

In the third case, coordination is a multidimensional enterprise, occurring in post-conflict situations such as those prevailing currently (2004) in Sierra Leone, Afghanistan, Sudan or Liberia. It involves the Department of Peace-Keeping Operations (DPKO), in addition to the usual headquarters- and field-based offices, funds, programmes and agencies. It covers a wider range of post-conflict activities, including elements of the rule of law, human rights, civil administration, governance and reconstruction. These are areas where the potential for confusion, overlap and lack of coordination is greatest. The UN funds and programmes have considerable expertise in these subjects, and their activities are likely to both precede and continue once the mandate of the peacekeeping mission expires. Thus coordination in this instance means accommodating the temporary presence of a resource-rich, well-staffed UN department, the DPKO, and learning to work with it under the overall guidance of the Special Representative of the Secretary-General.

The relationship between the funds and programmes and DPKO and what roles the funds and programmes should play in the civilian component of the peacekeeping operations are only now being systematically addressed by the UN system. Integrated missions may yet show the way for the coordination of other complex emergencies. The fear has been expressed, in the case of integrated missions, that they would inadvertently choke off humanitarian space. This may be a legitimate concern but, in the cases presented in this chapter, we have seen the opposite: absent the political dimension, the humanitarian mission can be jeopardized.

Notes

1. Larry Minear, *Humanitarianism under Siege: A Critical Review of Operation Lifeline Sudan*, Trenton, NJ: Red Sea Press, 1991.
2. United Nations Office for the Coordination of Humanitarian Affairs, United Nations Technical Committee on Humanitarian Assistance, *Protocols Signed between the Government of the People's Republic of Sudan, the Sudan People's Liberation Movement, and the United Nations*, New York: OCHA, 1998.
3. Cristina Eguizábal, David Lewis, Larry Minear, Peter Sollis and Thomas G. Weiss, "Humanitarian Challenges in Central America: Lessons from Recent Armed Conflicts", Occasional Paper No. 14, Institute for International Studies, Brown University, 1993.
4. Amartya Sen, *Poverty and Famines: An Essay on Entitlement and Deprivation*, Oxford and New York: Oxford University Press, 1981.
5. Larry Minear, *The Humanitarian Enterprise: Dilemmas and Discoveries*, Bloomfield, CT: Kumarian Press, 2002.
6. Max Weber, *On the Methodology of the Social Sciences*, Glencoe, IL: Free Press, 1949.
7. David Lewis and Helen Wallace, eds, *Policies into Practice: National and International Case Studies in Implementation*, London: Heinemann, 1984.
8. Christopher C. Hood, *The Limits of Administration*, London: Wiley, 1976.
9. Aaron Wildavsky, *The Art and Craft of Policy Analysis*, London: Macmillan, 1979.
10. Andrew Dunsire, *Implementation in a Bureaucracy: The Execution Process*, Oxford: Martin Robertson, Vol. 1, 1978.
11. The present narrative is based on my own experience in Khartoum, and therefore focuses more attention on the government than on the opposition.
12. Shaun Riordan, *The New Diplomacy*, Oxford: Polity Press, 2003.
13. Normally, the UN Resident Coordinator is also the UN Humanitarian Coordinator. During his absence (in the crisis described here), the WFP Representative was in fact Acting Humanitarian Coordinator.

12

"Military humanitarianism" in Liberia

'Funmi Olonisakin

This chapter argues that, in Liberia, humanitarian actors were not always the traditionally accepted ones. At critical moments, the regional peace force ECOMOG – the Cease-fire Monitoring Group of the Economic Community of West African States (ECOWAS) – was the only serious humanitarian actor on the ground in Liberia. The experience of ECOMOG in Liberia demonstrated that, by its very nature and orientation, the military is unsuited for humanitarian diplomacy, but it was the only actor on the scene at crucial stages and it was compelled to respond to humanitarian needs notwithstanding its rough edges. The chapter concludes that, even though humanitarian actors often have superior knowledge of their operational environments, they do not always make good diplomats, given their narrow focus and objectives in conflict areas. The focus of this chapter is on the period of the first war in Liberia, which lasted from 1989 to 1997.

Context

The way in which the Liberian war was conducted made it virtually impossible for humanitarian actors to operate in the country. This section provides a brief background on the war and highlights key elements that made the Liberian operational environment particularly unsuited to traditional humanitarian actors at critical periods.

The Liberian conflict was among the first to reveal the nature of post–

Cold War conflicts and the complex environment in which those responding to conflict and humanitarian crises will have to operate. The conflict has its roots in the separatist policies of successive regimes since 1847, when independence was declared under a regime formed by freed slaves settled in Liberia from 1821. Successive settler regimes suppressed indigenous Liberians for a period of 133 years until Samuel Doe's rise to power via a military coup in 1980. Doe's regime did not fare better than the previous ones because its patrimonial rule served to exclude indigenous Liberians who were not from his Krahn ethnic group or their Mandingo allies, further widening the cracks among Liberians. The rebellion led by Charles Taylor on Christmas Eve in 1989 was one of several attempts to oust Samuel Doe since 1985. Unlike previous attempts, the rebellion quickly spread around the countryside and escalated into a full-scale war between the Armed Forces of Liberia (AFL) and the National Patriotic Front of Liberia (NPFL) led by Charles Taylor. The emergence in the summer of 1990 of the Independent NPFL (INPFL), a splinter group of the NPFL led by Prince Yomie Johnson, began the proliferation of armed groups that became a prominent feature of the war. The armed groups in Liberia numbered up to eight by August 1996, when the Abuja II Agreement paved the way for elections in Liberia.

The Liberian conflict spanned a period of 14 years from December 1989 to August 2003 and can be divided into two distinct periods: the first war, from 1989 to 1997; and the second war, from 1999 until 2003. Several factors distinguish the two periods. The period of the first war began with a rebellion that rapidly escalated and resulted in the complete collapse of the Liberian state; it involved at least eight armed factions and attracted regional and UN peacekeeping from 1990 to 1997. The second war was waged with an elected regime led by Charles Taylor, and without an international peacekeeping presence, until the resignation of President Taylor in August 2003. The first war lasted seven years, with four distinct phases separated by key events. The first phase lasted from December 1989 until November 1990, when the first cease-fire agreement was secured. The second phase occurred between then and October 1992, when the NPFL launched an attack on Monrovia in an operation code-named "Octopus". Phase three lasted from Operation Octopus until the signing of the Cotonou Accord in July 1993, which resulted in the deployment of a UN Observer Mission alongside the regional force, ECOMOG, which had been present in Liberia since August 1990. Phase four began with the Cotonou Accord and lasted until elections in 1997. The second war, on the other hand, started as a relatively low-key rebellion against the Taylor regime. The rebellion increasingly gained momentum and was assisted by international pressure on Taylor, which led to his resignation in August 2003.

The differences between the two periods of war are also marked by the nature of the Liberian operational environment. There was a total collapse of the Doe regime and of the Liberian state during the first war and a complete dependence on a regional peace force for the provision and maintenance of security, upon which humanitarian actors depended for their security. With Taylor's landslide victory in the 1997 elections, there was some semblance of order; the humanitarian community was largely present in Liberia and there was a general consensus that an elected (even if illegitimate) government existed in the country. The conflicting parties were also clearly identifiable: the Taylor-led government was pitched against two armed groups – Liberians United for Reconstruction and Democracy (LURD) and the Movement for Democracy in Liberia (MODEL) – in contrast to the eight factions struggling to control the seat of power during the period of the first war. For a large part of the second war, the violence occurred within one part of the country – Lofa County – in contrast to the rapid spread from Nimba County to Monrovia that occurred in 1990. And, for a sustained period, it was possible to contain the violence within this area. Things deteriorated rapidly, however, when the rebel forces arrived within firing range of Monrovia.

Additionally, humanitarian actors operated within two distinct contexts during the two wars. The first war occurred without much precedent in the sub-region, and indeed the entire continent, for responding to the level of humanitarian tragedy that unfolded in Liberia. The crises that had occupied the attention of Africans and the United Nations were largely wars of an inter-state nature and the liberation wars in southern Africa, with exceptions being the Congo crisis from 1960 to 1964. With the ending of the Cold War, and the removal of the restraining danger of superpower confrontation, came a surge of vicious conflicts that resulted from longstanding, unresolved internal conflicts that had not found space for expression in a Cold War environment. Liberia was the first of such conflicts to erupt into a bitter armed struggle.

This chapter focuses largely on the period of the first war in Liberia. The conflict that was played out in Liberia following the incursion of Charles Taylor's NPFL in December 1989 had several elements, which influenced the operational environment in which those responding to the crisis had to work. First, the conflicting parties and their methods and conduct of the war created a humanitarian tragedy that surpassed the capacity of the humanitarian community in Liberia, such that traditional humanitarian actors had to be evacuated from the country at the height of the crisis in 1990. The initial parties to the conflict, the AFL and the NPFL, were locked in a bitter struggle in which all the rules of war were abandoned. Innocent civilians paid the price; they were the focus of vio-

lence and they were pursued by warring parties even into previously recognized sanctuaries such as churches and places of worship.

Second, humanitarian actors had to adjust to a fluid operational environment in which conflicting parties constantly multiplied amid divergent
interests and strategies. This had a corresponding impact on those responding to the crisis, who had to adopt different approaches in responding to the situation on the ground. The proliferation of warring factions,
which began in July 1990 with the breakaway of the Johnson-led Independent National Patriotic Front of Liberia (INPFL) from the NPFL,
exacerbated the situation in Liberia. It created an unstable environment
in which leading actors and the territories under their control were constantly changing, further complicating the work of peacemakers and humanitarian actors. By July 1996, eight factions signed the second Abuja
Peace Agreement.[1] In such an atmosphere, where parties to the conflict
multiplied at regular intervals, it was difficult to negotiate or reach an
agreement that could be successfully monitored.

Under the prevailing conditions, it was difficult, if not impossible, for
traditional humanitarian actors to operate in Liberia. With the indiscriminate killings, Liberians and foreigners alike were fleeing the country. At
critical periods, particularly during enforcement phases, most of the representatives of international agencies in charge of humanitarian operations were evacuated from Liberia. The only actor able to operate under
these conditions was the ECOMOG force. It was left to this force, and
the few traditional humanitarian actors that remained, to address the crisis in Liberia. Focusing largely on the period of the first war, this chapter
discusses the role of ECOMOG as a humanitarian actor and the challenges that confronted this force as it attempted to combine this role
with the primary military functions that it was mandated to perform in
Liberia.

During this period, the Liberian war presented a number of obstacles
for those responding to the humanitarian crises on the ground. These included the method of war that was employed by the warring factions; the
proliferation of actors and factions; the problem of access to communities
in need; the faction leaders' lack of commitment to the peace agreements
they signed; and the lack of long-term planning for reconstruction. In the
environment of breakdown in law and order that ensued, ECOMOG was
the only serious humanitarian actor able to address the immediate crisis
on the ground.

Instability and a breakdown in law and order

During the first phase of the first war, there was a total breakdown of law
and order as power devolved down into the hands of warlords (the state

having previously had limited capacity and its undisciplined army having lost control and contributed to the mayhem that ensued). The state of Liberia had collapsed and this was most visibly illustrated by the collapse of social order and the mass movement of people fleeing the horrors and misery of the war. Monrovia, the capital city, contained at least half of the country's population of more than 3 million, while tens of thousands sought refuge in neighbouring West African states, particularly Guinea, Sierra Leone and Côte d'Ivoire. By July 1990, foreigners and thousands of Liberians were evacuated from the country. By October 1990, refugees in neighbouring states numbered more than 600,000.[2]

The second phase was a period of relative stability from November 1990 until October 1992, when the main warring faction, the NPFL, launched a major attack against ECOMOG and Monrovia (known as Operation Octopus). But it was also in this phase that another faction, the United Liberation Movement for Democracy in Liberia (ULIMO), emerged.

Operation Octopus, which marked the beginning of the third phase, was characterized by active combat between ECOMOG and the NPFL, lasting from October 1992 until July 1993. ECOMOG had once again to embark on enforcement action to subdue the forces of the NPFL. After resisting the NPFL attacks and successfully driving the force out of Monrovia, it went on the counter-offensive, seizing strategic locations such as the ports of Greenville, Harper and Buchanan from the NPFL. This counter-offensive was brought to an end with the negotiation of the Cotonou Agreement in July 1993. The phase that followed was largely a period of attempted reintegration and reconstruction, but it was, once again, interrupted by the 6 April 1996 crisis in Monrovia.

The impossibility of conventional humanitarianism

There were very few humanitarian actors in Liberia during the early phase of the Taylor war. Humanitarian activities were extremely difficult to undertake in an environment where conflicting parties completely disregarded the rules of war and preyed on innocent civilians. Thus those who were engaged in humanitarian activities were themselves forced to flee that scene. Although the UN involvement during the first two years of the war was strictly in a humanitarian role, the organization was hardly present during the first 11 months of the war. The United Nations Disaster Relief Organization (UNDRO)[3] led an assessment mission in February 1990, and this was followed by an effort to distribute food and medicine in Liberia from March 1990, in collaboration with Médecins Sans Frontières (MSF) and Catholic Relief Services (CRS). By May 1990, UNDRO and other UN staff were evacuated from Liberia. In July 1990, the

United Nations Special Coordinating Office for Liberia (UNSCOL) was established by the UN Secretary-General to coordinate operations of UN humanitarian agencies, which were at the time operating from Guinea and Sierra Leone – these included the World Food Programme (WFP), the United Nations Children's Fund (UNICEF), the World Health Organization and the United Nations High Commissioner for Refugees. Only MSF Belgium and the International Committee of the Red Cross (ICRC) maintained a continuous presence in Liberia.

During the second phase, a UN security and relief assessment mission was conducted in October 1990, as a result of which critical humanitarian needs were highlighted, and it paved the way for UN agencies to return to Liberia to work side by side with ECOMOG. Following an assessment report by UNSCOL in November 1990, a core team was on the ground in Monrovia. The United Nations Development Programme was the hub of UN operations after the agencies returned to Monrovia. It served as a base for UNSCOL. UNICEF was the largest UN humanitarian agency in Liberia, its operation spanning health, social welfare and water sectors. WFP coordinated all food aid. International non-governmental organizations (NGOs) were also active in Liberia during this phase. MSF Belgium was the largest international NGO focusing on relief services, with input from its French and Dutch counterparts. The Lutheran World Service (LWS) also operated in Liberia from October 1990, and Save the Children Fund (UK) became active in the country from 1991. Additionally, a joint Nordic initiative, known as Swede relief, established a field hospital in Monrovia.

However, ECOMOG remained critical to the work of the traditional humanitarian agencies, given its central role in providing security. The greatest obstacle confronting the humanitarian community during this phase was restricted access to the Liberian hinterland. Their operations were limited largely to Monrovia and its environs (often referred to as Greater Monrovia) or, in most cases, humanitarian agencies deployed in areas where ECOMOG provided security. Charles Taylor and the NPFL maintained tight control over Greater Liberia, where a rival government, the National Reconstruction Assembly (NIPRAG), operated from Gbarnga. This problem was, however, more apparent with the United Nations, which failed to deploy outside of the areas where ECOMOG was based. UN agencies operated only in Greater Monrovia, whereas NGOs such as the CRS, ICRC, LWS and MSF operated outside of this limited area despite the security risk. Nonetheless, the United Nations achieved a fairly effective coordination of humanitarian activities in Liberia. UNSCOL held weekly and a few ad hoc coordination meetings with UN agencies and NGOs, and the Interim Government was sometimes represented.

The third phase witnessed a more complicated relationship between the NGO community, the United Nations and ECOMOG. There were disagreements over access routes across Liberia's border with Côte d'Ivoire. Coordination in the humanitarian community was also drastically reduced.

After the signing of the Cotonou Peace Accord in July 1993, a Special Representative of the UN Secretary-General was appointed for Liberia, and this phase saw the departure of the head of UNSCOL and a reduced role for that office in Liberia. A United Nations Mission in Liberia was established with a mandate for up to 400 military observers to work alongside ECOMOG in the implementation of the Cotonou Accord. A Liberian National Transitional Government was also installed as part of the provisions of the peace agreement. The humanitarian community did not benefit much from these developments because major obstacles such as restrictions on access remained. Indeed, humanitarian access became more complicated with the presence of multiple political actors and a proliferation of armed groups and parties to the Liberian conflict.[4]

The salience of ECOMOG as a humanitarian actor

In the absence of humanitarian actors, ECOMOG, which was deployed to restore law and order in Liberia, was compelled to take on humanitarian functions. ECOMOG would not only play the role of peacekeeper and enforcer but also serve as one of the few humanitarian actors on the ground in the early phase of the conflict. In the vacuum created by the crisis and the resulting evacuation of civilians, including humanitarian workers and diplomats, ECOMOG commanders were left to play roles for which they were ill prepared. They were forced to attend to humanitarian issues as well as perform crucial political and diplomatic functions, including negotiating with various actors, particularly the conflicting parties – the AFL, the NPFL and the INPFL.

The need to take on humanitarian concerns, even if in a limited way, was obvious upon ECOMOG's landing in Monrovia. The force confronted the harsh reality of this war environment as troops were mobbed at the Freeport of Monrovia by thousands of displaced people fleeing the conflict, full of hope that ECOMOG would not only rescue them but provide desperately needed relief aid. This was not anticipated by ECOMOG's planners, even though the whole rationale for deploying the force in Liberia was hinged on humanitarian concerns.[5] The force was ill prepared for its mission, initially conceived as one of peacekeeping rather than as an enforcement mission, and immediately faced the challenge of having to provide meagre humanitarian assistance. ECOMOG soldiers shared their rations with hungry displaced people at the Port of

Monrovia. Indeed, the ECOMOG High Command had expectations that the United Nations would deploy a humanitarian taskforce to operate alongside the ECOMOG mission rather than leave the force to cope with challenges emanating from the humanitarian situation on the ground.[6]

In addition to this, ECOMOG commanders were in the unique and perhaps unfortunate position of having to perform political functions in addition to their already difficult military tasks. Without any political office on the ground, ECOMOG commanders had to negotiate directly with the civilian authorities (which were almost non-existent at the time), as well as with the warring parties. The ECOMOG mission had no civilian component and as such no parallel political office to perform the task of negotiating with critical actors on the ground in Liberia. Although the ECOMOG organizational plan provided for the positions of Political and Legal Officers, these posts were left unoccupied for several years owing to a lack of funds. A Special Representative of the Executive Secretary of ECOWAS was not appointed until 1995, five years after the deployment of ECOMOG in Liberia. This has been identified as one of the main weaknesses of the ECOMOG operations because it exposed commanders to political situations for which they had received no prior training.

The role of ECOMOG altered with the changing circumstances on the ground in Liberia. Its role as a humanitarian actor was more prominent during certain phases of the first war. In the first phase, ECOMOG had to switch from a peacekeeping role to one of enforcement in order to restore a measure of order in the Liberian capital. Having prepared for a peacekeeping role, the force was met by a hostile NPFL force. ECOMOG's mandate was subsequently changed to one of enforcement in September 1990, enabling it to push the rebels back outside of firing range of Monrovia.[7] The single most important benefit of ECOMOG's enforcement action during this phase was that it led to the signing of a cease-fire agreement in November 1990 and created a relatively stable environment in Monrovia in which basic humanitarian activities could take place. And if ECOMOG could lay claim to having performed an effective humanitarian role in the war, it would be that it managed to reduce the carnage and to create a measure of order in Greater Monrovia, which served as a safe heaven for a significant percentage of the Liberian population for several years, albeit with interruptions in 1992 and in April 1996. By protecting key sites and installations, including Roberts-field airport, it was possible for relief convoys to operate with reduced threat to personnel.

However, the signing of the cease-fire agreement in November 1990 did not lead to sustained stability in the country. It was to be the end of the first of several phases in this conflict, which proved to be a mediator's and a negotiator's nightmare. It was assumed that political actors in ECOWAS would be able to build on the cease-fire by negotiating a lasting settlement to the conflict. This was not possible despite a number of peace conferences and agreements.[8] Between November 1990 and July 1996, 12 agreements were signed by parties to the Liberian conflict. All of them were reneged upon until the August 1996 Abuja II Agreement, which led to the staging of elections in Liberia.

ECOMOG played less of a humanitarian role during the second phase because conventional humanitarian actors were able to return to a relatively stable environment in the capital. Although humanitarian operations had fully resumed, they were largely restricted to the capital and the suburbs. The dependence of these agencies on ECOMOG for their movement and for their security demonstrates the importance of ECO-MOG's presence on the ground.

Operational issues

This section provides an overview of the operational issues around which ECOMOG was compelled to negotiate during the first war in Liberia. The operational issues that ECOMOG negotiated directly or alongside other actors in this period included cease-fires with warring factions; access to strategic locations, such as ports and other routes; and access to populations in need. ECOMOG's experience here revealed the complexities of the military acting as humanitarians. From conducting negotiations for humanitarian purposes during one phase, ECOMOG became the party with whom other humanitarian actors had to negotiate during other phases. ECOMOG thus served as both an enabler of humanitarian work as well an obstacle to humanitarian activities in Liberia.

ECOMOG played a dominant role during the first phase of the first war, because humanitarian agencies were largely operating outside of Liberia. The operational issues negotiated by ECOMOG during the first war varied according to the situation on the ground during each phase. The problem of access to affected communities remained a constant issue. The major negotiating task that confronted the ECOMOG field commander during the first phase of this war was to bring all conflicting parties to the table to negotiate a cease-fire and ensure access to the countryside.

Other operational issues that ECOMOG sought to negotiate during this phase concerned access to strategic locations such as Robertsfield airport (in part to ensure the provision of supplies and the movement of personnel); and access to Monrovia and beyond in order to restore order throughout the country. But, in order to achieve this, ECOMOG had to negotiate a truce with key players – the embattled government of Samuel Doe; Prince Yomie Johnson of the INPFL; and the NPFL, led by Charles Taylor. It also meant that ECOMOG commanders needed to facilitate Doe's resignation, which was the objective of ECOWAS leaders prior to ECOMOG's deployment. The most conciliatory of the warring factions was the INPFL – it provided much-needed logistical support and local intelligence, which later allowed the force to venture beyond Monrovia's Freeport. This would later dent ECOMOG's credibility with other warring factions, as discussed further below. The task of bringing all warring factions together to negotiate a cease-fire and to clarify ECOMOG's role to all concerned was the force's first real test and it led to the kidnap and eventual death of President Doe.

The second phase, from November 1990 to October 1992, was one in which humanitarian organizations were relatively autonomous and were able to carry out their operations. However, the main issue to be negotiated by humanitarian actors was the lack of access to populations in Greater Liberia. During this period, negotiations for access to civilian populations in government-controlled areas and some rebel-held territories were conducted by UNSCOL on behalf of the humanitarian community, the United Nations and NGOs alike.

In the third phase, during and immediately after Operation Octopus, a number of factors changed the way in which the humanitarian activities were coordinated and the extent to which actors were successful in negotiating. ECOMOG had switched to enforcement rather than the policing duties it performed in the preceding phase. The United Nations assumed greater political involvement with the appointment of a Special Representative of the Secretary-General in October, and this served to complicate the role of humanitarian actors in ways that are discussed below. ECOMOG's enforcement operations, which were aimed at pushing the NPFL out of the capital, Monrovia, and its counter-offensive aimed at seizing control of strategic locations from the rebels had the effect of creating its own humanitarian crisis. ECOMOG's air raids against NPFL targets resulted in what the force described as collateral damage. But the reality of this damage was that it was civilian and aid installations that were hit, including medical facilities.[9] The ECOMOG action also created insecurity for humanitarian personnel, who did not have freedom of movement. Thus, access to affected populations, security and freedom of movement for humanitarian personnel were the main issues to be negotiated by the NGOs in particular.

ECOMOG found itself on the other side of the humanitarian divide and had become one of the actors with whom the humanitarian community had to negotiate. Indeed, humanitarian organizations experienced a major setback during this phase, as ECOMOG, with the UN Special

Representative's acquiescence, prohibited cross-border aid from Côte d'Ivoire to populations in NPFL-held territory, arguing that some NGOs were smuggling arms to the NPFL under the pretext of humanitarian relief supplies. The need to reverse this decision was one of the key issues to be negotiated during this phase.

Although the signing of the Cotonou Agreement marked the end of Operation Octopus, and increased prospects for peace negotiations, humanitarian actors still had to operate in an insecure environment, in addition to the same old problem of access to the civilian community in need of aid. Issues to be negotiated included their own protection as well as access to rebel-held areas. As the United Nations was itself a new actor on the political scene, and with the entry of new factions into the war, the numbers of actors with whom NGOs had to negotiate access had increased dramatically. UN agencies also had to negotiate their own access separately, further indicating a lack of coordination, a role previously performed by UNSCOL.

Underpinning all of the negotiations for access by humanitarian actors, including UN agencies, UN observers and NGOs, was that they all depended on ECOMOG for their security and safe passage in some of the areas where they had to operate, particularly when there was no clarity over rebel control of those areas.

Obstacles and opportunities

This section focuses on the obstacles confronting ECOMOG as a humanitarian actor during the first war. These obstacles resulted from five main issues. The first concerned the multiple roles of ECOMOG and the nature of the force's interaction with the warring parties. Second was the proliferation of armed factions, which served to complicate both the humanitarian and the political efforts on the ground. The third concerned the combat operations launched by armed factions such as in Operation Octopus and subsequent counter-attacks by ECOMOG. The fourth was the late political involvement of the United Nations and the lack of West African political presence on the ground. The last issue was the negative perception of ECOMOG in terms of its low level of respect for human rights, particularly during enforcement periods.

For a force that initially had a peacekeeping mandate and was required to maintain law and order throughout Liberia, the lack of cooperation from the largest warring faction and resulting attacks presented a major setback, particularly during the first phase of the war. ECOMOG was initially unable to move beyond the Freeport of Monrovia, let alone gain access to the hinterland. In addition, ECOMOG had to deal with a large concentration of civilians in an environment in which it had to return fire if not engage in major combat against one of the parties. The force commander was faced with the task of negotiating with the armed factions, or at least with the INPFL, for access and of persuading an unpopular and besieged president, Samuel Doe, to step down from power. It was a difficult humanitarian and political environment.

In the absence of political and humanitarian offices, ECOMOG encountered several obstacles that affected the overall humanitarian and political situation on the ground. Perhaps the greatest challenge it faced was that it had to negotiate directly with the warring factions. Its encounter with the Johnson-led INPFL had some disastrous results. ECOMOG, particularly the Nigerian contingent, was equipped with inadequate uniforms and boots and was compelled to accept gifts of boots and uniforms from Prince Yomie Johnson of the INPFL, a situation that served to compromise the force's neutrality. The INPFL later lured ECOMOG commanders into a false sense of confidence when it captured Samuel Doe in ECOMOG's headquarters during an attempt to negotiate a cease-fire and subsequently executed him. This occurrence haunted the ECOMOG leadership for several years. ECOMOG was criticized by all parties to the conflict. Whereas the AFL criticized it for allowing the capture of President Doe, the NPFL accused it of taking sides with the AFL and the INPFL and of not providing desperately needed humanitarian aid to Liberians. The INPFL also accused the force of failing to go on the offensive against the NPFL.

The continuing proliferation of warring parties was a major obstacle confronting ECOMOG and indeed the political and humanitarian community in Liberia. ULIMO had entered the conflict in 1991, thus complicating negotiation processes and contributing to a more difficult operational environment. Further proliferation occurred with ULIMO's split into two camps – ULIMO-K, led by Alhaji Koroma, and ULIMO-J, led by Roosevelt Johnson. The Liberian Peace Council had also emerged, as well as the Central Revolutionary Council, which broke away from the NPFL, as well as the Lofa Defence Force and the Liberian National Council.[11]

This proliferation was compounded by the fact that the warring parties' objectives differed significantly from those of the international actors that were responding to the crisis, whose overriding objective was the restoration of law and order. Apart from the NPFL, whose leader saw the presidency of Liberia as his manifest destiny, many of his men, and indeed all other factions, sought more immediate objectives, such as seizing control of territory largely for personal advantage.

The failure of the United Nations to engage politically with Liberia was another obstacle, making a more productive involvement by the

United Nations impossible to achieve. Some observers argued that earlier involvement by the United Nations might have brought the NPFL into an overall peace plan earlier, thus opening up the rest of the country for humanitarian support.[11] Additionally, ECOWAS did not have any political presence on the ground for much of the period of the first war, leaving ECOMOG commanders to serve both political and military functions.

A further major obstacle to the achievement of operational objectives by ECOMOG as well as other humanitarian actors in Liberia was the launch of Operation Octopus, which exacerbated the humanitarian crisis in the country and created thousands of additional refugees and internally displaced people. It also changed the focus of humanitarian personnel, who were advised to evacuate during the attack on Monrovia. ECOMOG was thus forced to shift its operational focus as it once again adopted an enforcement strategy and embarked on counter-insurgency operations. As a result, there were major disruptions to the work of humanitarian actors, who were themselves not secure from the ECOMOG bombardments targeted at NPFL locations, which hit humanitarian sites at times. This was the first time that ECOMOG's objectives appeared largely incompatible with the immediate objectives of the humanitarian actors.

The situation between ECOMOG and humanitarian personnel was worsened by the stopping of cross-border aid from Côte d'Ivoire, which further complicated the work of humanitarian personnel. Perhaps most damaging for the humanitarian community was the resulting split between the United Nations and the NGOs, which occurred when the United Nations allowed ECOMOG to close the cross-border aid routes from Côte d'Ivoire. As a result, the United Nations was no longer acting on behalf of the entire humanitarian community. NGOs preferred to enter into negotiations with the various parties on their own, having fallen out with the UN political side over its apparent support for the ECOMOG blockage of cross-border access. The United Nations' support of this move by ECOMOG created a lack of confidence in its negotiation and coordination efforts. It was also clear that UN political considerations had overshadowed humanitarian considerations, owing in part to the late political involvement of the United Nations, which was forced to take its cue from ECOMOG and ECOWAS in many cases.

Negotiations

The negotiations that took place, particularly during periods of active combat or general insecurity in Liberia, reveal the limited objectives and narrow interests of the humanitarian actors. Two main issues took precedence – the security of humanitarian actors and their access to the communities to whom they provided assistance. Other issues, such as the broader governance environment and the conduct of warring parties and the peace force, did not rise to the fore of their agenda. This is however understandable, given that they were operating in a dangerous environment in which their security as well as the security of their target populations could be compromised in an attempt to pursue broader objectives.

This section deals with specific negotiations that ECOMOG undertook during the first war. Two categories of negotiations are highlighted here: those that ECOMOG undertook as a humanitarian actor for the benefit of the humanitarian community or on humanitarian grounds; and negotiations in which ECOMOG was regarded as a potential obstacle to humanitarian work.

ECOMOG and the INPFL

Given the circumstances in which ECOMOG landed in Liberia during the first war and the obstacles that stood in the way of achieving its stated objectives, its commanders were only too ready to negotiate with the one seemingly friendly faction, the INPFL. ECOMOG arrived at the Liberia Freeport to realize that it was ill prepared for the mission. The expectation of its planners that ECOMOG's arrival on the scene would put fear into the rebel camps was not realized. The only reality that confronted the force was vicious attacks from an NPFL faction that saw ECOMOG's presence as an intrusion and a major obstacle to the realization of its own objective. ECOMOG did not have the logistical capacity to deal with this immediate challenge. Some of the contingents sent by some troop-contributing countries were unarmed and from a customs and immigration background or, in some cases, were not physically fit enough to perform enforcement or combat operations.[12]

Thus, at the earliest opportunity, ECOMOG met with the INPFL to negotiate access to INPFL-controlled areas and for the provision of information on local routes by the INPFL, as well as local intelligence, including the location of other rebel forces, including the NPFL. ECOMOG commanders achieved all of this and this enabled the force to begin to venture beyond the Freeport of Monrovia, where it had been confined. However, ECOMOG commanders compromised the purported neutrality of the force by accepting gifts from the INPFL. Troops from the Nigerian contingent did not all have the necessary logistical support such as uniforms and boots. As such, in the friendly atmosphere following their negotiations with the INPFL, they accepted Prince Yomie Johnson's offer of uniforms and boots. As discussed below, this proved costly for the mission.

Negotiations with warring factions

In September 1990, following the apparent success of the initial meetings with Prince Yomie Johnson, ECOMOG commanders sought to bring the warring factions (which numbered only three at the time – AFL, NPFL and INPFL) together to negotiate a cease-fire, the resignation of President Samuel Doe and a plan for implementation of the cease-fire. This would lead, among other things, to access to the Liberian hinterland, in order for ECOMOG to provide security and maintain order throughout Monrovia. The NPFL, which was fiercely opposed to the ECOMOG presence in Liberia, declined to participate in the negotiations. Prince Johnson and President Doe, who favoured the presence of the force and who seemed assured of its protection during the negotiations, agreed to be present. The location of the meeting was the ECOMOG base in the Freeport of Monrovia. The INPFL, under Prince Johnson's leadership, took advantage of its superior knowledge of the location and the camaraderie with ECOMOG to kidnap President Doe, who later died in Johnson's custody. ECOMOG suffered a serious loss of credibility as a result of this event, with all sides doubting its claim to neutrality and impartiality. ECOMOG learned difficult lessons from this experience. For a force seeking to act as an impartial arbiter, its close association with the INPFL, compounded by ill-preparedness for the mission, reduced its chances of success from the start.

NGOs and ECOMOG

A key challenge for humanitarian actors during the third phase of the first war was that, although ECOMOG's offensive and its bombing raids on rebel locations were aimed ultimately at creating some stability, they disrupted humanitarian operations. Thus humanitarian organizations, particularly NGOs, requested in their negotiations with ECOMOG that the force inform them in advance of such bombardments so that they could subsequently avoid those locations. ECOMOG argued that it was not possible to do this because its commanders felt that this would endanger their troops and give away information on planned operations to the rebels, thus endangering the mission as well as the troops.[13] Although ECOMOG did not share information with NGOs on planned operations, it did agree in exceptional cases to offer protection to convoys. However, it did not do this readily until the fourth phase, during implementation of the Cotonou Agreement.

One issue on which ECOMOG and NGOs disagreed and to which they did not find a solution was ECOMOG's ban on cross-border aid from Côte d'Ivoire to NPFL-held territory. During several negotiations, NGOs argued that this was the most effective route, but ECOMOG accused some NGOs, particularly MSF, of smuggling arms to the NPFL alongside relief materials.[14] In the end, NGOs were not successful in operating in NPFL areas and their relationships with both the United Nations and ECOMOG were soured for a long period as a result of disagreements over the cross-border aid ban.

Wider implications

The Liberia experience illustrates the complications that can arise when the United Nations fails to take decisive steps to address a crisis at an early stage. Although the ECOWAS efforts in Liberia received implicit support from the United Nations, the latter's political engagement in that crisis came two years after ECOMOG's deployment, following Operation Octopus. By this time, ECOMOG had assumed control of the operational environment and, by implication, political authority over the mission rested with ECOWAS. Even when a UN Observer Mission was eventually deployed, its troops, like the humanitarian community on the ground, depended on the regional body for their security. In the absence of a secure environment, humanitarian actors could not hope to reach the communities they were there to serve.

This underscores an important factor – that the humanitarian cannot be detached from the political. It is indeed more rewarding to give political backing to humanitarian processes at an early stage and to ensure a balance between the humanitarian and the political. Without the much-needed "teeth" that political authority can offer, humanitarian efforts on their own have less chance of success. The United Nations has struggled to deal with the political and humanitarian imbalance, but has nonetheless adopted some strategies to deal with this. For example, Resident Coordinators and their Deputies serve as overall coordinators of the UN presence in target countries; and they relate to the Special Representative where this role is required, particularly when peacekeeping missions are present.

The Liberian experience highlights the limits of the effectiveness of humanitarians as diplomats. Humanitarians are not always the best diplomats and often have limited objectives in operational environments. In Liberia, the agenda of the traditional humanitarian actors was often restricted to the pursuit of their own security and the securing of access to their target populations. It was unusual for them to pursue broader political goals in support of this agenda. But, although humanitarian actors rarely achieve unity of purpose, Liberia was one of the few cases in which this occurred at certain critical periods. One unifying factor was the total lack of security and public safety, which prevented humanitarian actors from gaining access amid heightened insecurity during certain phases. This forged a collective negotiation process in which the United Nations acted on behalf of the entire humanitarian community in dealing with the warring factions. Even so, this did not last long. Despite this flaw, however, humanitarian actors are the best on offer because they often possess excellent knowledge of the local environment, an attribute that is crucial for the success of negotiations in target locations.

Nonetheless, as the experience in Liberia has indicated, utilizing humanitarian actors for political and diplomatic roles can ultimately compromise their role in that environment if the process is not properly managed. This is particularly true for unusual humanitarian actors such as ECOMOG. Even when ECOMOG commanders sought to respond spontaneously to the humanitarian crises that they met on the ground in Liberia – for which they were not prepared – they were severely limited by their fundamentally military approaches. This was compounded by the sheer weight of the task at hand. At crucial moments, ECOMOG was responding to a combination of political, humanitarian and military issues in Liberia in the absence of political leaders and traditional humanitarian actors. In the initial stages, given the poor provision of logistics, it was ill equipped for its own traditional military operations, let alone for the humanitarian and political functions it was compelled to perform. In normal situations, military actors are not often suited to non-military roles. The very nature of their mandates and objectives – the use of force or the threat of the use of force – contradicts the regular role of humanitarians. Liberia illustrated the conflicting goals and roles that occur when the military attempts to take on traditional humanitarian roles.

Notes

1. The war, which was initially between Doe's government and Taylor's NPFL, became a peacemaker's nightmare with the proliferation of warring factions. In 1995, there were eight recognized parties to the conflict. Those that signed the Abuja Agreement of 1995 were the Armed Forces of Liberia; the National Patriotic Front of Liberia, the largest rebel group; the Central Revolutionary Council, a splinter group from the NPFL; the Liberian Peace Council; the Lofa Defence Force; the Liberia National Conference; and the United Liberation Movement for Democracy in Liberia (ULIMO), which was split into two camps – ULIMO-K and ULIMO-J.
2. Figures reported by the United Nations High Commissioner for Refugees in Côte d'Ivoire. See *Africa Research Bulletin*, 1–31 October 1990, p. 9873.

3. UNDRO was later collapsed into a new Department of Humanitarian Affairs in April 1992.

4. UNOMIL, for example, insisted on security clearances – this was in addition to existing arrangements with ECOMOG and the Interim Government of National Unity.

5. An ECOWAS Communiqué on 7 August 1990 indicated that ECOWAS was intervening in the Liberian conflict on humanitarian grounds.

6. Interviews conducted in Nigeria and Liberia in 1993 and 1994. See also Colin Scott et al., "Humanitarian Action and Security in Liberia 1989–1994", Occasional Paper No. 20, Thomas J. Watson Institute, Brown University, 1995, p. 15.

7. Lt. Col. A. Olaiya, "ECOMOG Mission and Mandate", *The Peacemaker*, No. 1, September 1991–March 1992, p. 11.

8. For a detailed analysis of these peace agreements and the peace negotiations between November 1990 and October 1992, see M. A. Vogt, ed., *The Liberian Crisis and ECO-MOG: A Bold Attempt at Regional Peacekeeping*, Lagos: Gabumo Publishers, 1992. See also W. Ofuatey-Kodjoe, "Regional Organizations and the Resolution of Internal Conflict: The ECOWAS Intervention in Liberia", *International Peacekeeping*, Vol. 1, No. 3, Autumn 1994, pp. 261–302, for a detailed discussion of the background and politics of the ECOWAS intervention.

9. See, for example, Africa Watch, *Waging War to Keep the Peace: The ECOMOG Intervention and Human Rights*, New York: Human Rights Watch, 1993.

10. It should be noted that the INPFL had by now fizzled out, having been neutralized by ECOMOG when its leader, Yomie Johnson, was taken to Nigeria. Furthermore, the parties had varying military capabilities. For example, the Central Revolutionary Council had no recognized military presence on the ground. The other factions divided the country among themselves in varying proportions, although the NPFL remained the largest warring faction.

11. See Colin Scott et al., "Humanitarian Action and Security in Liberia 1989–1994", p. 10.

12. See General C. Y. Iweze's account "Nigeria in Liberia: The Military Operations of ECOMOG", in M. Vogt and E. E. Ekoko, eds, *Nigeria in International Peacekeeping 1960–1992*, Oxford: Malthouse Press, 1993.

13. Ibid., and personal interviews with ECOMOG commanders in summer 1994.

14. *Africa Research Bulletin*, June 1993, and interviews in Liberia, June 1994.

13

Negotiating the release and rehabilitation of child soldiers in Sierra Leone

Omawale Omawale

The recent war in Sierra Leone raged on for a decade during which the atrocities committed against non-combatants attracted international attention, as did the efforts to rehabilitate thousands of child soldiers caught up in the fray. This chapter will give an example of how humanitarian workers can engage in significant diplomacy. It will explore how the earliest negotiation for the release and rehabilitation of Sierra Leone's child soldiers, led by the United Nations Children's Fund (UNICEF) in 1993, overcame challenges such as the difficulty in accessing information on child soldiers, the lack of mass media, the tendency for officials to deny or justify the existence of child soldiers, and the attractiveness to the military of using children for strategic advantage in the war. This case study will argue that UNICEF was well placed to lead the negotiation because of its international reputation, its child protection mission and its previous record of humanitarian assistance in the country. It will also show that the negotiation was successful and important not only because it secured the identification and release of child soldiers by military rulers who were still conducting war, but also because it energized a largely dormant civil society.

Context

This section sets the context for the analysis. I discuss the antecedent impact of the Liberian civil war, the internal instability in Sierra Leone and the emergence of an untrained army, which precipitated the 1991 coup.

276

Next, I explain the delayed international response to the emergency and the UN response, focusing particularly on UNICEF's role and its identification of the problem of child soldiers.

Impact of the Liberian civil war

An important antecedent of the conflict in Sierra Leone was the Liberian civil war, which started in December 1989. At this point Sierra Leone was peaceful by comparison with neighbouring Liberia. The population of 4.25 million was mostly poor, although the country was fortunate (some now say cursed) to have significant deposits of rutile (a major ore of titanium), bauxite, iron ore and easily mined diamonds. Sierra Leone had earlier experienced several military coups and attempted coups, but there had been civilian government for two decades and, although there were tribal rivalry and jokes about corruption, crime was petty, the streets were safe and there was hardly any sense of instability. The military was small and poorly armed, probably as a deliberate strategy to limit the possibility of a successful coup. However, the civil war in Liberia soon sent a flood of refugees across the borders into Sierra Leone, Guinea and Côte d'Ivoire. UNICEF responded rapidly by establishing an emergency programme for humanitarian assistance in Sierra Leone.

Further, in March 1991 the Liberian conflict spilled over into Sierra Leone, followed by the emergence of the Revolutionary United Force (RUF), a Sierra Leonean rebel group backed by Charles Taylor of Liberia and his National Patriotic Front of Liberia (NPFL).[1] Taylor is believed to have engineered the RUF-led attacks because, in an interview with the BBC, he threatened to teach Sierra Leone a lesson for allowing the Cease-Fire Monitoring Group of the Economic Community of West African States (ECOMOG) to use its facilities to attack NPFL forces in Liberia.[2] By April 1991, Foday Sankoh – a former corporal in the national army of Sierra Leone who had been jailed for seven years for his part in a plot to overthrow the government in 1971 – declared that he was the leader of the RUF. He announced that his objective was to bring to an end the one-party system presided over by President Joseph Momoh and his All People's Congress (APC), which had ruled the country for 23 years.

Internal instability

Economic and internal ethnic sensitivities in Sierra Leone comprised a second set of factors that were also significant contributors to the civil war. These can be conveniently linked to Joseph Momoh's appointment as head of state by the powerful Siaka Stevens, who resigned the position in September 1985. Probably sensing the unpopularity of his patron, President Momoh seemed to distance himself from Stevens' policies through what he called his New Order Administration. In November 1986, President Momoh concluded a long-term structural adjustment facility with the International Monetary Fund (IMF), as part of the new economic recovery programme. The loan agreement required macro-economic conditionalities such as devaluation, a reduction in the size of the public service, removal of subsidies on essential commodities, such as rice and petroleum, deregulation of rice importation, and deregulation of internal and external trade and the exchange rate.[3]

In 1987, President Momoh declared a State of Economic Emergency under which the government assumed wide powers to crack down on corruption, gold and diamond smuggling, and the hoarding of essential commodities and the local currency, the leone. The aim of these policies was to counter the thriving parallel market, to which the formal banking sector had lost millions of leones. The president went further by applying the conditionalities even after the IMF terminated the agreement in 1990, because the government was unable to pay arrears on the loan. He initiated his own austerity programme without the IMF funds to cushion the worst effects. Soon these policies began taking their toll, as prices of basic commodities soared and inflation consumed savings and wages.

President Momoh's position in the APC was never as powerful as Siaka Stevens' because he was in effect an imposed candidate for the presidency and leadership of the party in which he did not have any solid political base. Many considered President Momoh too phlegmatic and "a very indecisive, weak leader allowing ministers free rein to be corrupt".[4] Others regarded him as an ethnic upstart (he was from the minority northern Limba tribe). Among these was his deputy, Francis Minah, who allegedly seized upon President Momoh's growing unpopularity to organize a coup. Minah was executed for high treason and it is important to note that he had his roots in Pujehun District, one of the areas that became the civil war front-line. Minah had also been involved in "a rural rebellion in the mid-1980s against the APC Government of Siaka Stevens".[5]

Minah's execution incensed many people from his native Pujehun District, who felt that it was part of a plot by northerners to deprive them of power, since Minah was expected to succeed Momoh to the presidency. Simultaneously, President Momoh alienated two of Sierra Leone's most powerful ethnic groups, the Temne from the northern and central areas and the Mende from the south. Together, these two groups constituted over 60 per cent of the total population. The president further aggravated the situation by calling for "ethnic corporatism" – essentially the formation of ethnic cliques – in a speech in 1990 to the Akutay annual convention at Binkolo, Bombali District, which was broadcast on Sierra Leone Broadcasting Service radio. This broadcast confirmed the popular view that power had shifted from parliament and the cabinet to the Akutay,[6] an exclusive group of Limba politicians, businessmen and intelligentsia aligned with President Momoh. The Akutay was in effect Momoh's kitchen cabinet, which made decisions that constitutionally should have been the preserve of the official cabinet and parliament.

The consequence of the growing influence of the Akutay in the affairs of state was the further worsening of ethnic relations and the acceleration of economic decline. By 1991, the United Nations Development Programme's *Human Development Report* put Sierra Leone last among the 175 countries analysed.[7] President Momoh's control of state affairs began to slip and the Eastern Province, Kono District in particular, gained "notoriety as the 'Wild West of West Africa', with a semi-permanent lawlessness in the diamond mining areas".[8] By the early 1990s, donors had been demanding a return to democratic multi-party politics in Africa as a condition for official loans. However, President Momoh resisted demands for democratic pluralism led by the Sierra Leone Bar Association and the university community, as well as school children and the unemployed – all key actors in the subsequent civil war. The president's response to demands for multi-party elections was to send the Secretary-General of the APC, E. T. Kamara, to warn people in the Southern and Eastern Provinces that talk of multi-party democracy would be met with the full force of the law, since such discussions were illegal under the one-party state. The scene was thus set for a revolt.[9]

Precipitation of the coup

The March 1991 RUF attack caught the national army, the Republic of Sierra Leone Military Force (RSLMF), unprepared: it was ill equipped, badly trained and highly politicized. A few months after the first attack, the RUF controlled one-fifth of the country in the south-east region. In a counter-offensive, the RSLMF hastily conscripted hundreds of recruits and its numbers rose from 3,000 to 10,000 in the first two years of the conflict.[10] The new recruits were rushed to the war front, inadequately trained, poorly equipped and often highly undisciplined.

The economy continued its decline and the war continued to take its toll on the population. By early 1992, some 10,000 people had been killed, over 300,000 were displaced, 400,000 were behind rebel lines and another 200,000 crowded refugee camps in Guinea. The ill-equipped army faced humiliation on the war front. As casualties mounted, a group of young officers entered Freetown in April 1992 and ousted President Momoh's regime, accusing it of incompetence and promising to bring the war to a speedy end. The leader of the ruling junta, calling itself the National Provisional Revolutionary Council (NPRC), was a charismatic 27-year-old army captain, Valentine Strasser.

Delayed international emergency response

At first, most refugees in Freetown were affluent Lebanese who took up residence with friends and in local hotels. But the situation nearer the Liberian border was different. There, the refugees were typically poor people who were originally welcomed by compassionate local villagers, many of whom were unrelated to their new guests. However, the refugee population in many villages soon outnumbered the local population several times over. The fact that most refugees were accommodated either in Freetown or in village homes tended to obscure the extent of the growing emergency and delayed an appropriate international response. However, the Sierra Leone village hosts eventually became totally impoverished, the environment was rapidly degraded and the waves of homeless refugees and internally displaced persons increased.

The UN emergency response

Because the international response was delayed, most initial assistance came from the few UN agencies that had already been doing development work in Sierra Leone. However, the United Nations High Commissioner for Refugees (UNHCR) soon secured funding and provided shelter and basic necessities for the refugees. Even though the constraints of its mandate made it difficult formally to assist the internally displaced nationals, the UNHCR programme grew rapidly and became a major provider of humanitarian assistance, some of which inevitably benefited nationals. The World Food Programme (WFP) also began to make significant contributions through food aid without which both the refugees and the internally displaced population would have suffered even more than they did.

The United Nations Development Programme (UNDP), which had long supported development activities in Sierra Leone, now provided emergency assistance primarily through the specialized agency of the Food and Agriculture Organization (FAO). The FAO helped both refugees and internally displaced populations establish food production. UNDP also administered a programme of UN Volunteers – professionals who worked in the field with other UN agencies, government and civil society partners. During the first year of the emergency, there were several partners in health sector assistance, the biggest contributor being

UNICEF. Other partners included the United Nations Population Fund, which supported reproductive education, and the World Health Organization, which primarily provided technical assistance. In addition, there were a few healthcare non-governmental organizations (Africare, CARE, Concern Worldwide and Catholic Relief Services), which also provided field workers. Shortly after the war commenced, the International Committee of the Red Cross (ICRC) became actively engaged in efforts to protect the rights of prisoners of war. Unfortunately, its mandate and customary method of work prevented it from sharing significant information on human rights abuses with other agencies.

UNICEF in Sierra Leone

UNICEF, like UNDP, already had a long-established programme of cooperation in Sierra Leone. The Country Programme of Cooperation provided US$11 million of assistance in basic health, education, water and sanitation during the 1991–1995 period. The objectives of that programme were to "create a sustainable community structure through which vulnerable groups could be motivated to participate in social and economic development; to achieve universal access to maternal and child health services by 1995; to design services to enable young school-leavers to attain minimum life skills; and to make rural primary education more relevant".[11] The programme was rapidly adapted in 1991 to respond to the crisis caused by the refugee influx and the emerging civil war.

By the time the emergency had escalated in 1992, UNICEF was probably the best-known international agency in the country, partly because it had the largest contingent of field staff, three-quarters of whom were Sierra Leone nationals. The organization had a close working relationship with the government and successfully advocated for a delegation, led by President Momoh, to attend the 1990 World Summit for Children (WSC). UNICEF advocacy also resulted in Sierra Leone being one of the first countries to ratify the 1990 Convention on the Rights of the Child (CRC). The organization had a clearly assigned role to follow up on the implementation of the WSC and a specially assigned role in relation to the CRC. Consequently, UNICEF organized a national event in April 1991, attended by President Momoh. This was designed to encourage follow-up actions in keeping with the Declaration of the WSC, which the President had signed the previous September in New York.

By 1990, in accordance with the UN Secretary-General's reform measures, a UN Country Team, led by the UNDP Resident Representative, had been established to coordinate cooperation with the Sierra Leone government. The team, consisting of the local agency heads, held monthly inter-agency meetings, which became a useful mechanism and were held more frequently when the emergency broke out. The UNDP Resident Representative was also the UN Resident Coordinator and the designated official for emergency coordination. In his absence, the UNICEF Representative performed those functions, a reflection of the size and significance of the organization's programme. In November 1991, the government established the National Rehabilitation Committee (NARICOM) to coordinate relief and rehabilitation assistance for internally displaced persons. Because the UN Country Team felt it important to help the government develop the capacity of NARICOM for emergency coordination, a sub-group consisting of the heads of UNHCR, UNICEF and WFP was assigned this task. Coordination with the few non-UN agencies assisting in the country in the early stages of the emergency was done more informally.

Identification of the child soldier problem

From the inception of the insurgency, the UNICEF Freetown office received verbal reports that children were engaged in the hostilities on both the rebel and the government sides. Such activity contravened Article 38 of the CRC (see the boxed text), which the government had ratified in 1990. However, when the UNICEF Representative brought these reports to the government's attention, the government initially denied the use of children and later argued that such use was legitimate. The government's position clearly emerged during the April 1991 public meeting organized by UNICEF. The event included a mock children's debate during which a member of one team accused the opposing side (representing the government) of using child soldiers to fight the rebels. At that point President Momoh, who was seated next to the UNICEF Representative, jovially commented in Krio, "Defence, Bo" ("necessary for defence, my brother" – a justification for having children bear arms in the villages).

In contrast, the National Provisional Revolutionary Council was more concerned about the country's international image and seemed interested in social change. Chairman Strasser and the other leaders of the NPRC were all young and inexperienced in civilian administration, but they quickly espoused a populist agenda of anti-corruption, civic pride and national renewal. One of the activities flowing from this agenda was a weekly clean-up day. On that day all citizens were expected to follow the lead of the NPRC in dramatic efforts to clean up the city, which had become littered with piles of refuse and sewage-filled drains in many places. The military leaders soon embraced a few civilians who had more administrative experience and sought international recognition of their administration, which they claimed to be an interim government.

The Convention on the Rights of the Child

The Convention on the Rights of the Child (CRC) was adopted by the General Assembly of the United Nations on 20 November 1989 and came into force on 2 September 1990 when over 20 countries had ratified it. Only two countries have not yet ratified: the United States and Somalia, which have signalled their intention to ratify by formally signing the Convention. The Convention contains 54 articles that legally bind ratifying States Parties. Significantly, Articles 38 and 39 state:

Article 38

1. States Parties undertake to respect and to ensure respect for rules of international humanitarian law applicable to them in armed conflicts which are relevant to the child.
2. States Parties shall take all feasible measures to ensure that persons who have not attained the age of fifteen years do not take a direct part in hostilities.
3. States Parties shall refrain from recruiting any person who has not attained the age of fifteen years into their armed forces. In recruiting among those persons who have attained the age of fifteen years but who have not attained the age of eighteen years, States Parties shall endeavour to give priority to those who are oldest.
4. In accordance with their obligations under international humanitarian law to protect the civilian population in armed conflicts, States Parties shall take all feasible measures to ensure protection and care of children who are affected by armed conflict.

Article 39

States Parties shall take all appropriate measures to promote physical and psychological recovery and social reintegration of a child victim of: any form of neglect, exploitation, or abuse; torture or any other form of cruel, inhuman or degrading treatment or punishment; or armed conflicts. Such recovery and reintegration shall take place in an environment which fosters the health, self-respect and dignity of the child.

The World Summit for Children

At the World Summit for Children, held in New York on 29–30 September 1990, 71 heads of state and government and 88 other senior officials, mostly at ministerial level, strongly endorsed the CRC and adopted a Declaration on the Survival, Protection and Development of Children and a Plan of Action for implementing the Declaration in the 1990s. The Plan has 7 major and 26 supporting goals in health, nutrition, education, water, sanitation, and children in difficult circumstances.

UNICEF in Sierra Leone regarded this as an opportunity to raise the child soldier issue again.

These events were shortly followed by another opportunity for advocacy to end the government's use of child soldiers. One day in January 1993, while on board a river ferry on its way to Freetown, the UNICEF Representative observed two young boys wearing military uniform and carrying weapons. He engaged the boys in conversation and they revealed themselves to be orphans, aged 9 and 13, but proud combatants heading to the official residence of the chairman of the NPRC, where they would be fed and accommodated while in town. During this initial contact the UNICEF Representative persuaded the boys to visit his office. This they did the following day and on two subsequent occasions during which they were interviewed. Both boys said that they started travelling with the government soldiers after their parents were killed by rebels who had attacked their village. This first-hand information about the involvement of child soldiers and their association with the new rulers was used in negotiations to end the practice.

Operational issues

In January 1993, the UN Country Team agreed that the UNICEF Representative should pursue four issues for negotiation. These were the Sierra Leone army's release of child soldiers into UNICEF's custody, the military's identification of the children to be so demobilized, government's partnership in providing services and facilities for rehabilitation of the children, and the partnership of civil society in the counselling and management of the children to be rehabilitated.

One significant omission from the negotiations was any effort to secure the release of child soldiers under rebel control. This was because the RUF leadership remained very much in the shadows. Thus, although Foday Sankoh identified himself as the leader of the RUF in 1991, two years later he still was not readily accessible to the international media. It is true that he did have support from Charles Taylor's NPFL, through which it might have been theoretically possible to arrange a meeting. However, at the time of these negotiations, the UN Country Team had no ready access to the NPFL either and it was decided to concentrate initial efforts on the NPRC.

The basis for UNICEF's role and negotiating position

The proposed negotiation was regarded as an important part of the UNICEF Representative's responsibility, in keeping with the organization's role assigned by the WSC and the CRC.[12]

UNICEF's role was deduced from Sections II and III of the 1990 WSC Declaration. Section II (Specific Actions for Child Survival, Protection and Development), paragraph 25, states as follows:

Protection of children during armed conflicts
Children need special protection in situations of armed conflict.... Resolution of a conflict need not be a prerequisite for measures explicitly to protect children and their families to ensure their continuing access to food, medical care and basic services, to deal with trauma resulting from violence and to exempt them from other direct consequences of violence and hostilities. To build the foundation for a peaceful world where violence and war will cease to be acceptable means of settling disputes and conflicts, children's education should inculcate the values of peace, tolerance, understanding and dialogue.

The Declaration, in Section III (Follow-up Actions and Monitoring), paragraph 35, also states as follows:

Action at the international level
Action at the community and national levels is, of course, of critical importance in meeting the goals and aspirations for children and development. However, many developing countries, particularly the least developed and the most indebted ones, will need substantial international co-operation to enable them to participate effectively in the world-wide effort for child survival, protection and development.

The UNICEF Freetown Country Management Team (CMT) identified a responsibility to provide the assistance envisaged in the above-cited paragraphs within the 1991–1995 Sierra Leone Country Programme of Cooperation (CPC). It also identified responsibility under the provisions of the CRC, Article 43 of which provides for the establishment of an international Committee on the Rights of the Child, and Article 44 of which requires States Parties "to submit to the Committee, through the Secretary-General of the United Nations, reports on the measures they have adopted which give effect to the rights recognized herein and on the progress made on the enjoyment of those rights".
Further, Article 45 states that,

In order to foster the effective implementation of the Convention and to encourage international co-operation in the field covered by the Convention:
(a) The specialized agencies, the United Nations Children's Fund, and other United Nations organs shall be entitled to be represented at the consideration of the implementation of such provisions of the present Convention as fall within the scope of their mandate.

Consequently, the UNICEF Representative recognized that negotiating the release and rehabilitation of child soldiers did not require authorization by UNICEF headquarters, which however endorsed the initiative when informed.

Agreement to release the children

The release of the children required an official acknowledgement that they existed and a clear policy decision to end the practice. For a military government without diplomatic experience this was a significant hurdle. However, it was one that had to be negotiated since, without it, UNICEF could not make the army's field commanders receptive to protecting children from any exposure to combat then and in the future. It should be noted that, although the CRC permitted recruitment of children under 18 years of age but older than 14 years, it urged that preference be given to the older children in this age group. Nevertheless, the CMT decided that UNICEF would negotiate the demobilization of all children, i.e. all persons under 18 years of age. It should be noted, in passing, that Sierra Leone subsequently enacted legislation to prohibit military service before 18 years of age.

Implementing the agreement

As noted above, UNICEF felt that identification of the child soldiers required full cooperation from all ranks of the army because it presaged relinquishing what appeared to be a powerful asset in the military arsenal. The information from the two interviewed child soldiers was that girls were mainly cooks and maids for the troops, although some were engaged in sex with the soldiers. They reported that some boys helped carry equipment for the troops, but their most effective use was for reconnoitring. Apparently, because of their youth, they could dress in civilian clothes and wander unsuspected among the population to gain information about the activities of the enemy through observation and discussion. This information would enable their units to stage surprise raids or avoid enemy ambush.

However, the interviewed informants also said that some boys were actually trained and employed as armed combatants. Typically they would first be fed stimulants, including gunpowder mixed into meals, and made to perform some atrocious, cold-blooded murder to establish loyalty and worthiness. After this initiation they became regular combatants carrying and using arms on missions alongside adult soldiers. One of the informants drew attention to a scar on his leg and claimed that it was a bullet wound he never felt because he was "high" when shot. Both boys told of having nightmares about killings, including seeing the faces of people they shot in cold blood. They exhibited a degree of ambivalence about being child soldiers and UNICEF felt these mixed emotions gave credibility to their accounts and would be typical of most of their peers. On the one hand, they told of feeling powerful and respected by adults when armed and in uniform, as evidenced, for example, by being given free passage on the river ferry. On the other hand, they said that they missed their families and longed to do childhood things, including going to school.

Negotiating facilities and partners for rehabilitation

As much as the CMT wanted the children to be released immediately from the army, it was evident that the responsibility of caring for them would be beyond the existing technical and administrative capacity of UNICEF on its own. Consequently, it was necessary to identify collaborators and persuade them to become partners. Physical facilities would be needed to house the estimated hundreds of children, and people with psychiatric, psychological, social and administrative skills would be needed to supplement UNICEF's existing human resources.

The CMT felt that, for the negotiation to succeed, the hurdle of NPRC acceptance had to be approached by people and/or organizations with some existing leverage. Apart from its UN mandate to protect and pursue the interests of children, reinforced by the WSC Declaration and the CRC, UNICEF's longstanding presence and good reputation in the country and the substantial cadre of nationals on its staff seemed to place it in the best position to undertake this task. The negotiations were thus undertaken by the UNICEF Representative, with the full backing of UNICEF headquarters and the Sierra Leone UN Country Team.

Obstacles and opportunities

Two major challenges lay in the way of successful negotiations: the difficulty of accessing reliable information to support negotiation and the paucity of public media through which to communicate. However, the credibility of UNICEF and national goodwill towards the organization were countervailing assets that could be seized as opportunities during negotiations.

The information challenge arose in the context of denial and justification by the previous civilian administration. At first the CMT reasoned that, if a civilian administration with years of diplomatic experience and international relations could justify the use of children "in defence", a military junta might hardly consider use of child soldiers a matter to be debated when the insurgency had escalated and soldiers were being killed in increasing numbers. UNICEF would have to bring convincing information about the existence of child soldiers and offer a compelling reason for the NPRC to relinquish what it apparently regarded as an asset. Meanwhile, it had come to the organization's attention that the ICRC had access to prisoners of war and might thus be a source of information about child soldier prisoners. However, the ICRC delegate advised the UNICEF Representative that, in accordance with longstanding policy and operating procedures, information obtained from visits to prisoners could not be shared with a third party such as UNICEF, lest this jeopardized future access to the prisoners. Still, the ICRC did undertake to visit and seek the protection of any child soldiers who might have been taken prisoner. Consequently, the only information UNICEF could present to the NPRC was based on the interviews with the UNICEF Representative's two child soldier contacts.

The challenge of poor communications arose because of the disrepair into which the country's infrastructure had fallen. Telecommunications were weak and short-wave radio transmission, previously and extensively used by UNICEF, was severely restricted because of the NPRC's security concerns, as well as the fact that some of the equipment had been seized by rebels. There was no television service and the radio operated only on a very limited daily schedule because of electricity shortages and lack of equipment. Daily newspapers did not exist either, so the army and the population at large could not be readily reached by common mass communication methods.

The major compensatory asset was UNICEF's longstanding relation with the population, which had been mobilized in previous years to immunize virtually the entire population under the age of 5 years. This mobilization involved faith-based organizations, both Christian and Muslim, as well as the government, particularly the ministry of health. Because of its clear humanitarian mandate, UNICEF also began to work with the new NPRC administration immediately it was established in May 1992. UNICEF's flexibility and rapid emergency response capability were particular advantages that made it attractive to the administration. Further, the national staff employed by UNICEF provided contacts with a wide cross-section of the Sierra Leone population. Thus these nationals were an important source of information and a conduit for pre-negotiation exploration.

Negotiations

Developing the negotiation strategy

The actual negotiations were based on a strategy developed by the CMT that bore in mind the challenges and opportunities outlined above. As suggested above, there were two main parties with which UNICEF had to negotiate. The negotiation with the NPRC administration was of the utmost importance in order to persuade it to acknowledge the existence of child soldiers, formally indicate its adherence to the CRC, renounce the practice of using child soldiers, and release existing child soldiers into UNICEF's custody. In support of this negotiating issue, UNICEF would remind the NPRC that the predecessor civilian government was an enthusiastic signatory of the 1990 WSC Declaration and that Sierra Leone had the honour to be one of the earliest ratifiers of the CRC. The second aspect of negotiation was the involvement of partners to deal with the logistics of receiving, housing and rehabilitating the children. This appeared no less challenging than the first, given the paucity of local not-for-profit organizations, the huge decline in civic-mindedness and the overall degeneration of Sierra Leone society and physical infra-structure consistent with being last in the world according to the UNDP's Human Development Index.[13] UNICEF was able to draw on established contacts to reach psychiatrists, local volunteers and an experienced youth project manager to help with the children's rehabilitation.

The negotiating strategy was developed by the CMT in a series of meetings over a one-week period in January 1993. The team realized that, because of previous experience with the recently deposed civilian administration, any negotiator would have to present some hard evidence to get the NPRC to concede that the army had children engaged in the war. Then it would be necessary somehow to persuade the junta that desisting from the use of child soldiers would be in its interest. Since UNICEF already knew that the children were considered very useful military assets, some other interest had to be identified and leveraged. A win–win scenario needed to be proposed and the style of negotiation was to be cooperative rather than adversarial.

In the months following its April 1992 takeover, the NPRC engaged in increasingly strenuous efforts to justify the military coup to the Sierra Le-one population and to the world at large via the diplomatic community. The leadership was also presenting itself as being against corruption and in favour of popular justice in order to obtain national and international recognition. UNICEF identified this need for recognition as a key inter-est to which the organization could appeal. The proposition to the NPRC would be that a policy decision to forswear the use of children in combat could be made in the context of Sierra Leone's commitment to the CRC. This would then permit UNICEF publicly to compliment the government on its laudable action for children. And, given UNICEF's stature in the international community, relations with foreign states could be expected to be opened and to improve.

The CMT's first thought in preparing for the negotiation was the importance of identifying a potentially strategic ally as an entry point to the NPRC. This would create space for discussion and prevent a reflex and outright public denial of the existence of child soldiers. It would be difficult to persuade the junta to retreat from such a denial once it was made public. In this regard, UNICEF identified the Public Relations Officer of the NPRC, Captain Karifa Kargbo, as such a potentially strategic ally and interlocutor. First, he appeared to be more sophisticated than his fellow officers, which probably explains his appointment to the sensitive post of Public Relations Officer. For this reason the CMT felt that he would appreciate the significance of adhering to the CRC, and with it the opportunity to advance the quest for diplomatic recognition rather than simply expecting foreign states to accept the NPRC's de facto power. Second, he was a former university acquaintance of a UNICEF national staff member, who could thus be an informal communication channel. Third, he happened to be the son of the former minister of health, with whom UNICEF had worked for several years and with whom the UNICEF Representative had earlier established a very cordial personal relationship.

Initiation of the negotiations

Time line of negotiation, January–May 1993

January   UNICEF Representative first sees and interviews boy soldiers and decides to negotiate their release UN partners endorse UNICEF as lead negotiator; CMT develops negotiation strategy

February   Fr Hickey contacts UNICEF about youth workshop; UNICEF initiates negotiations with NPRC

March   UNICEF Representative advances negotiation with NPRC; Sierra Leone First Lady mobilized in support of children

April   NPRC announces intention to release child soldiers

May   Civil society mobilized for rehabilitation; facilities and services established for rehabilitation; Child soldiers released and rehabilitation initiated

---

In February 1993, the UNICEF Communications Officer made formal contact with the Public Relations Officer. As expected, Captain Kargbo readily seized the significance of the NPRC's recognizing the CRC and making a public statement against the use of child soldiers. However, his challenge was how to "save face" for his administration. This was indicated by his initial position denying knowledge of the NPRC's use of child soldiers and suggesting that the rebels were the ones using them, evidenced by the fact that some had been taken prisoner by the military. He volunteered that those prisoners could possibly be released to UNICEF. Nevertheless, he did agree to arrange for the UNICEF Representative to make a courtesy call on Chairman Strasser of the NPRC, subsequent to which the matter of child soldiers could be discussed. This he promptly did.

During the first meeting with the UNICEF Representative, the NPRC chairman appeared to be well briefed and expressed gratitude for UNICEF's work in Sierra Leone. He also mentioned that he had been told of the population's warm feeling towards the UNICEF Representative, who had been observed to quickly learn Krio, the local working language in Freetown. The UNICEF Representative exploited this welcome and referred the chairman to Sierra Leone's commitment to the WSC Declaration, made by the former government. He stressed the importance of endorsing both this commitment and the CRC, which Sierra Leone was one of the first countries to ratify. Without conceding that the army was using child soldiers, the chairman endorsed the view that children should not be engaged in combat. The cordiality of the meeting led to an invitation for further discussions, a week later, at the chairman's official residence.

Meanwhile, UNICEF learned that the chairman's spouse was expecting a baby and thought this presented an opportunity to open a second front of negotiation. The idea was to use this personal event to seek the NPRC leadership's embrace of exclusive breastfeeding, one of the hallmarks of UNICEF advocacy for children and women. This was in keeping with the longstanding UNICEF social mobilization strategy of using leaders to endorse the children's cause and to set examples for national emulation. Thus, in early March 1993 the UNICEF Nutrition Officer and the Representative's spouse, who was also a graduate nutritionist, were dispatched to meet the new First Lady and persuade her to endorse exclusive breastfeeding and lead by her personal example. Since this was her first child, a period of preparation, including follow-up visits, was undertaken over a two-week period. The approach was successful and, with Mrs Strasser's agreement, the UNICEF Freetown monthly magazine featured her in an article on breastfeeding, including a picture of her feeding her baby.[14]

The government response

Within a month of their first meeting, the relationship between the UNICEF Representative and the chairman and his family had warmed. At

this point the UNICEF Representative met the head of state at his official residence and shared the information obtained from earlier discussions with the two child soldiers. The chairman conceded that he had
heard about children associated with the military, but he suggested that
they had actually been "rescued" by the army. He contended that these
children had been either orphans of rebel atrocities or separated from
their parents after taking flight in the face of rebel assaults on their villages. He said that the government soldiers took these children under
their protection out of compassion and this explained why they were in
the company of the military. The meeting ended cordially and a week
later, in April 1993, a public announcement was made that the NPRC
had decided to release the children to UNICEF's care. However, UNI-
CEF was asked to refer to the children not as soldiers but as Children
Associated with the War. The UNICEF Representative quickly responded by complimenting the NPRC's action in radio interviews with
the BBC and other international media.

The army's response

During the next operational step the UNICEF Representative met with
the head of the army, by arrangement with the NPRC chairman, in order
to work out details of the army's facilitation. It is instructive that the
military head insisted that, although a few child prisoners might probably
be identified, child combatants with the army were unlikely to exist.
However, he assigned a female officer, Captain Samba, to head a unit
for rehabilitation of the affected children. Her involvement was crucial
to the success of the project because she travelled extensively to the
many military unit locations, making the army aware of the child soldier
issue, identifying affected children and arranging for them to be brought
to Freetown. UNICEF noted that there was only one female in the first
batch of child soldiers brought to Freetown and urged Captain Samba to
ensure that girls not be excluded. As a consequence, more girls were
among the subsequent batches arriving in Freetown.

Mobilization of project partners

Within two weeks of Captain Samba's assumption of duties, the army reported that it had identified 370 boys and girls who would be delivered to
UNICEF's care. Based on experience in other countries and the stories
from the two informants, UNICEF expected some of the children to be
suffering from post-traumatic stress disorders. Consequently, UNICEF
needed to identify local professional assistance in addition to the sole
government psychiatrist, Dr Edward Naim, who worked at the govern-

ment hospital in Freetown. Dr Naim willingly agreed to assist with the assessment and rehabilitation, but it was clear from the start that he could not carry his current workload and take care of this prospective new caseload on his own. After a week of enquiries, UNICEF located the only other trained psychiatrist, Dr Mathurin, who had long retired but was part of the local Catholic network and now lived in the rural town of Bo. UNICEF made contact with him and he willingly agreed to participate in the anticipated rehabilitation of the children.

This still left the task of locating physical facilities to house the children and adults to provide other critical services they needed. The UNICEF Health Officer held discussions with his ministry of health counterpart, who managed to secure the temporary use of the prison officers' training school complex, which was conveniently located opposite the UNICEF Freetown office. Not only was space made for the first batch of children to be housed and schooled but an outdoor area was cleared for them to play soccer. The ministry of health arranged for each child to be given a health check and any care that was subsequently indicated. A second temporary facility for the children's rehabilitation was secured through the help of a restaurant owner, Joy Samake, who was approached by the UNICEF Representative. A youth facility provided land, the army supplied tents and Ms Samake persuaded a local architectural and engineering firm to provide technical support for the design and establishment of the rehabilitation facilities. Ms Samake was also instrumental in mobilizing other civil society members to contribute cash, services and food to help with the children's housing, education and recreation. Given the malaise into which the society had fallen up to the time of the 1992 coup, the civil society response led by Ms Samake was admirable.

Fortuitously, in January 1993, Fr Hickey, a Catholic priest, had approached UNICEF for financial support for a youth workshop he was organizing, and a good relationship had developed from this initial contact. Consequently, when the need arose three months later, the organization was able to persuade him to contribute his services. Fr Hickey had had ample experience with running facilities for young people and, after meeting the UNICEF Representative, he agreed to be the administrator of a project to rehabilitate the children. However, it took several weeks and many further meetings before the details were settled. Fr Hickey had two concerns: he wanted total control, including control over funds earmarked for other implementing partners, if he were to accept overall responsibility for the rehabilitation activity; he also wanted a direct relationship with the highest UNICEF authority. Consequently, even after he assumed responsibility on the basis of a verbal agreement with the UNICEF Representative, he was reluctant to deal on a day-to-day basis with less senior UNICEF staff. He even wrote a letter to the UNICEF

Executive Director at the New York headquarters seeking to report directly to her. Fortunately, the UNICEF Representative eventually persuaded him to work with the country office in the manner normal for all UNICEF-supported projects.

Because of UNICEF's flexible and rapid response to emergencies, the Representative in Freetown was able to reallocate available resources from the regular country programme to meet the immediate needs of the Sierra Leone emergency. This was simply done by agreement with the government and received UNICEF headquarters endorsement. In this context, once a preliminary plan for rehabilitation of the 370 children was drawn up by the UNICEF Freetown office, virtually all of the initial costs were readily met from already available UNICEF resources, and approaches to external donors for project support started only after implementation of the project had already commenced and a more detailed project was developed.

Reasons for success

The success of this set of negotiations can be attributed to measures taken to overcome the two types of challenges earlier envisaged and to the immediate seizure of the opportunity identified. UNICEF was able to overcome the information challenge by presenting incontrovertible evidence of the existence of child soldiers, obtained directly from the testimony of two affected children. The anticipated reluctance of the military to relinquish use of child soldiers was partly overcome by appealing to the NPRC chairman's sense of obligation to adhere to the ratified CRC. This was reinforced by presenting the leadership with a win–win situation – almost an offer they could not refuse: releasing the children in the context of meeting CRC obligations raised the prospect of international respectability, and would contribute to the legitimacy of an administration that was not elected. The NPRC's Public Relations Officer, given his task of burnishing the junta's image, seemed to grasp this readily and was probably influential in persuading his less aware colleagues, such as the head of the army, who might otherwise have ignored the international implications.

UNICEF's stature in the international and local community made it possible for the NPRC leadership to have confidence in the negotiation proposition. This confidence was bolstered by the subsequent series of one-to-one meetings between Chairman Strasser and the UNICEF Representative, the principal negotiators who had no previous knowledge of each other. Further, the project was presented to the NPRC as a collaborative activity that included civil society partnership, a fact reinforced by the involvement of respected citizens such as Fr Hickey, Dr Mathurin and Ms Samake. It helped that UNICEF not only identified a problem for the NPRC to address – ending the use of child soldiers – but offered a solution in the form of a project for the rehabilitation and reintegration of the children. The negotiation was further supported by UNICEF's proposal for NPRC partnership in the project, and the army even established a unit for rehabilitation of the affected children. Finally, UNICEF's promotion of gender awareness during the negotiations resulted in the release and rehabilitation of several girls who would otherwise not have been included in the project.

Limitations of the exercise

Although the child soldiers under government control were identified and released for rehabilitation, other children engaged in the conflict on the side of the rebels were not covered by this project, for reasons mentioned earlier. Further, remobilization of some of the released children was a danger in the absence of an environment that provided them with an attractive alternative. A resolution of the civil conflict would be required to significantly reduce the opportunities for remobilization. Moreover, the children would need supportive family environments as well as livelihood opportunities and socialization to help them find fulfilment in peaceful pursuits, replacing the adult-like status and respect they enjoyed while carrying arms. Unfortunately, the families of some of the children could not be located and the project on its own could not provide the enabling environment required for peaceful fulfilment of all of the children's ambitions.

Wider implications

This chapter set out to give an example of how humanitarian workers can engage in significant diplomacy. The case demonstrated how the widely accepted humanitarian mission of UNICEF to protect children, along with its track record of service in Sierra Leone, was used to influence military rulers who were conducting a war that employed children. The junta's interest in international recognition was leveraged to secure its acknowledgement of the existence of child soldiers, its endorsement of the CRC, which prohibits such use of children, and its cooperation in releasing and rehabilitating the children in exchange for UNICEF's public acknowledgement of this action. The mobilization of civil society to collaborate in the rehabilitation of the boys and girls was also significant because of the previous decline in civic social activity.

It must be conceded that the subsequent barbarity of rebel activities against the Sierra Leone army and the population at large would have made a similar negotiation much more difficult. Thus remobilization and recruitment on a larger scale followed by demobilization of child soldiers occurred on and off as the conflict raged, even after a 1999 cease-fire and peace accord. Eventually, persistent advocacy led to the signing in May 2002 of a significant optional protocol to the CRC by all parties. That protocol forbade recruitment and involvement in armed conflict of children under 18 years of age. By 2003, it was estimated that as many as 7,000 child soldiers had been used by all sides in the decade-long conflict in Sierra Leone.

Nevertheless, although it is true that the negotiations described in this chapter exploited favourable conditions at a particular juncture in Sierra Leone, virtually all of the enabling factors are of general relevance. Further, identifying favourable conditions and exploiting them are quite important factors in any negotiation.

This experience suggests that state diplomats might find it useful to embrace humanitarian diplomacy as a type of third channel for conflict resolution. The use of third channel diplomacy is well established but usually involves nationals in close collaboration with their foreign ministry, even when their activities are informal or the link is such as to offer plausible deniability by the state. A well-known example of third channel diplomacy is former US President Carter's negotiation with the DPRK's Kim Il Sung, undertaken with the full knowledge and backing of the US administration of the day. In the case of UNICEF and other children's organizations, the concept of children as a zone of peace is a potentially powerful one that might even be a leading edge in many negotiations for conflict resolution.

The late James P. Grant, a former UNICEF Executive Director, was probably the first person to advance the idea of "children as a zone of peace". Under this banner, he negotiated cease-fires in several countries to permit secure humanitarian activities for children. Notable examples were immunization during the civil war in El Salvador, food and medical aid to battle areas in Sudan, and convoys of humanitarian assistance into war-torn Afghanistan. James Grant further advocated top priority for children. He persuaded many world leaders of varying political persuasions to endorse this ethic of "Children First". He also persuaded political opponents to subscribe to this paradigm. In his words, he was making advocacy for children's issues "good politics". Thus it is conceivable that, if warring parties could agree to temporary cease-fires for the sake of children, in some cases they might be persuaded to agree to full cessation in order to put "Children First". That might then create the breathing space for state diplomats to engage in dialogue towards conflict resolution.

Conclusion

Humanitarian diplomacy is most likely to succeed if it employs reliable and incontrovertible information; is based on some established international convention to which the negotiating parties subscribe, or on relevant national law; identifies some key interest of the other negotiating party that can be satisfied by the negotiation – a win–win proposition; identifies a strategic ally either as an entry point or as a supportive resource during negotiation; uses a lead negotiator who brings to the table some credit or credibility with the other negotiating party; involves other like-minded entities or individuals as parties to the negotiation wherever possible; proposes solutions to any problems the other negotiating party has to acknowledge; and engages in a collaborative negotiation whenever possible.

Notes

1. Richard Carver, "Sierra Leone: From Cease-Fire to Lasting Peace", *Writenet*, 1 January 1997, reported in *Refworld* at ⟨http://www.unhcr.org/⟩, Geneva: United Nations High Commissioner for Refugees, Centre for Documentation on Refugees (UNHCR/CDR).
2. Abbas Bundu, *Democracy by Force? A Study of International Military Intervention in the Conflict in Sierra Leone from 1991–2000*, Boca Raton, FL: Universal Publishers, 2001.
3. A. B. Zack-Williams, "Sierra Leone: Crisis and Despair", *Review of African Political Economy*, No. 49, Winter 1990, p. 29.
4. Derek Partridge, quoted in Jane Knight, "Sierra Leone: Will Hope Triumph Over Experience?" *One World Link Newsletter*, June 1996, p. 7.
5. S. Riley and A. Max-Sesay, "Sierra Leone: The Coming Anarchy?" *Review of African Political Economy*, No. 63, 1995, p. 122.
6. A. B. Zack-Williams, "The Politics of Crisis and Ethnicity in Sierra Leone", paper presented at the Centre for African Studies, University of Liverpool, February 1991.
7. United Nations Development Programme, *Human Development Report 1991*, New York: United Nations, 1991.
8. Riley and Max-Sesay, "Sierra Leone: The Coming Anarchy?", p. 122.
9. Ibid.
10. *The New Republic*, Vol. 212, No. 15, 10 April 1995, p. 10.
11. United Nations Children's Fund, "Recommendation for Funding for Short-duration Country Programmes and for Additional General Resources and Supplementary Funding to Fund Approved Country Programmes in West and Central Africa Region", Executive Board document, E/ICEF/1995/P/L.28, New York, 13 March 1995.
12. United Nations Children's Fund, *FIRST CALL FOR CHILDREN: World Declaration and Plan of Action from the World Summit for Children. Convention on the Rights of the Child*, New York: UNICEF, 1990.
13. UNDP, *Human Development Report 1991*.
14. Bertha Jackson and Joan McLeod-Omawale, "First Baby in Safe Hands", *Keeping the Promise*, No. 5, June 1993, p. 7.

14

Blurring of mandates in Somalia

Karin von Hippel

Somalia is normally described by pundits as a "failed state" or "anarchic", because the country has been without a central government since January 1991.[1] At the close of 2004, Somalia could lay claim to the title of the most protracted example of state collapse since the end of the Cold War, if not in the post-colonial period (even taking into account the new Transitional Federal Government, which at the time of writing had yet to relocate from Kenya into Somalia). The mere mention of Somalia invokes images of warlords and child soldiers pillaging this East African version of the "Wild West". The country has allegedly been colonized by Osama bin Laden's henchmen, who are supposedly turning vast swathes of Somalia into a new Afghanistan, complete with training camps. In humanitarian and development terms, official indicators place Somalia at the bottom of all development indices – that is, life expectancy, adult literacy, school enrolment, infant mortality, per capita income, malnutrition, and a host of others.[2] Although these perceptions may contain some partial truths, the reality is far more complex.

Indeed, Somalia today is a country of sharp contrasts. On the one hand, there is an extremely dynamic image few outsiders appreciate. In many parts of Somalia, electricity lights up the streets at night (a service sadly lacking in most of neighbouring Kenya), and the mobile telephone network in Somalia is the cheapest in East Africa and possibly the second cheapest in all of Africa. Somalis from the diaspora remit funds into Somalia at a lower cost and faster rate than most other money transfer services worldwide – both formal and informal. Fatuma's US$250 sent from

Minneapolis on Tuesday evening will arrive at the door of her mother's house in Galkaayo early morning on Wednesday, 12 hours later, and the transfer fee will be lower than that charged by Western Union or Citibank. Mogadishu has a number of schools providing elementary, secondary and even tertiary education, as well as television stations, hospitals and medical clinics. Hargeisa has car insurance, internet cafés, hotels and restaurants, and several Somali airlines operate scheduled services throughout the country. All are private, Somali-run businesses.

In some regions, such as in Somaliland in the north-west or Puntland in the north-east, local and regional administrations function with traditional and religious authorities acting as legislative and constitutional assemblies that legitimize their authority. In many respects, therefore, it could be argued that Somalia without a central government may be better off and more accountable than many so-called "intact" states, and certainly more so than a centralized, non-representative Somali government. As for terrorism, there is little evidence that Somalia has been used as a breeding ground, but it has been used by a limited number of terrorists seeking sanctuary after attacks elsewhere and for transhipment activity.[3] In other words, the picture is far from straightforward.

There is also a static and more depressing Somalia, one in which large pockets of the population live in extreme poverty. The United Nations estimates that far too many Somalis suffer from grave human rights violations, chronic drought, food insecurity and sporadic violence, all of which inhibits development and prevents international aid workers from accessing many parts of the country. According to the United Nations, 750,000 Somalis are "chronically vulnerable",[4] out of an estimated population of 7 million (or 7.5 million or 8 million or 9.6 million, depending on the source[5]). It is in fact these unreliable figures that are themselves part of the problem.

Since the state collapsed, statistics have been difficult to accrue given the insecurities on the ground and the lack of regular and reliable data collection, and because up to half of the population is nomadic. In fact, owing to this problem, Somalia has not been included in the United Nations Development Programme's (UNDP) global Human Development Index since 1997, even though, in recent years, data collection in some sectors has improved.[6] Thus rankings for Somalia are mostly estimates.[7]

Different organizations – both Somali and international – gather data in different ways, with no agreed methodology or reliable means for accumulating information over time. Not only do population estimates vary considerably, but so too do figures for the Somali diaspora, as well as for how much money is remitted into the country annually. Estimates of the size of remittances going into Somalia on an annual basis range from

US$500 million to US$1 billion. How can appropriate needs assessments be made when family coping mechanisms are so poorly understood?

Even given the lack of reliable statistical information, one assumption I make, which underpins this chapter, is that Somalia has not fallen into the abyss since the state collapsed, primarily because of the efforts of Somalis themselves – both in the diaspora and in Somalia. The tight Somali social networks, based on close ties of clan and kinship, have been critical to the survival of Somalis and Somalia. But again, this is really only an informed opinion, since the data to back this claim are also unreliable.

This is to argue not that the efforts of the international community have been wasted or well-meaning, but rather that the international community has yet to develop a consistent response to overcome the complexities caused by the protracted collapse of central authority. It may in fact be this inconsistent international behaviour that forced Somalis to rely on their own social networks, even more than they had in the past. Thus the discussion of humanitarian diplomacy in Somalia, as conducted by the international community since 1991, needs to be considered in juxtaposition to this fairly fluid, often opaque picture.

In fact, circumstances in Somalia since 1991 have forced a fundamental rethink of several basic concepts of humanitarianism – particularly the core issues of neutrality and impartiality. The lack of effective governance in Somalia has meant that *all* international actors in Somalia – whether humanitarian, development, political or even military – inevitably act as diplomats and inevitably become embroiled in politics, even when this falls outside their individual mandates. There has been a blurring of the lines in Somalia. This chapter will therefore not focus exclusively on humanitarian action; rather, it will also discuss the political process, development modalities and, during the intervention, the involvement of the military.

I consider "humanitarian diplomacy" in Somalia throughout the period of state collapse, that is, from 1991 to 2004. This time frame in turn will be divided into two distinct periods, to reflect the country's lurch from one extreme to another. The first period covers 1991–1995, when Somalia was in the international media spotlight because of state disintegration, famine and the consequent UN peace support operations. The second period covers Somalia from mid-1995 to 2004, after the soldiers and journalists had moved on to the next crisis, when Somalia became yet another forgotten emergency. In the first period, international assistance reached nearly US$1 billion per year at its peak, whereas in the second the average was US$50 million per year.[8] Yet neither the highs nor the lows were sufficient to help Somalis overcome the centripetal forces that caused the state to implode.

I analyse humanitarian diplomacy in Somalia in five sections: the first provides a historical outline of the crisis, the second examines operational issues, the third focuses on obstacles encountered throughout, the fourth discusses the negotiations that attempted to bypass or overcome the obstacles, and the chapter concludes with an examination of the wider implications of the crisis. In each of the five sections, the issues will be considered over the two time periods noted above.

Context

The antecedents of the conflict can be traced back to 1960, when the United Kingdom and Italy departed from their colonial outposts: the United Kingdom from the north-west (the British Somaliland Protectorate) and Italy from the southern trusteeship territory. The two parts joined to form the Somali Republic. Although the new country established a multi-party democracy, this disintegrated fairly soon owing to immense political and social fragmentation and administrative and financial mismanagement. Just nine years after independence, General Mohamed Siad Barre took over the Somali Republic in a military coup.

Siad Barre was to rule this country for over 20 years through shrewd manipulation of clan politics and rivalries, military coercion and the exploitation of state resources and foreign assistance. Formally, he proclaimed that the clan structure that permeated Somalia would no longer dominate. In reality, however, for all important public posts he favoured the Darod clan-family (of six major clan-families), especially his own Marehan clan, his mother's clan (Ogaden), and the clan of his son-in-law (Dulbahante).[9]

During the Cold War, the Soviet Union supported Somalia and, from 1974, Ethiopia as well. The war between Somalia and Ethiopia (1977–1978) forced the Soviet Union to choose between its two allies, and it chose Ethiopia. This exchange, coupled with Somalia's defeat in that war, thereafter placed Somalia under the patronage of the United States, and the country then became dependent on Western foreign aid and remittances from Somalis in the Gulf to sustain its economy. Peace with Ethiopia was not formalized until 1988, but by then the Somali economy had all but collapsed as a result of widespread corruption, erratic economic policies, a financially draining civil war that pitted the government in Mogadishu against the majority clan (Isaq) in north-west Somalia, and the massive influx of ethnic Somali refugees from the Ogaden region of Ethiopia. A nationwide civil war ensued.

In January 1991, after various rebel groups had parcelled up most of Somalia, President Siad Barre finally fled Mogadishu. Four months later, the north-west region of Somalia declared its independence from the rump state as the "Somaliland Republic" (it has yet to be recognized by a single member of the United Nations). The civil war had caused immense devastation, with enormous numbers of refugees (at least 500,000 going to neighbouring Kenya, Ethiopia and Djibouti), internally displaced persons (IDPs – another 500,000) and civilian deaths, most of which were famine related (estimated at 350,000). The grain-growing region between the Shebelle and Juba rivers in the south was particularly ravaged, and famine thus spread rapidly throughout the country.

By the early 1990s, foreign food aid could no longer get through to affected Somalis. Instead, warlords plundered relief supplies to feed their militias and exchange the aid for more weapons. The humanitarian relief agencies remaining in Somalia were forced to hire thug Somalis to protect them and their work (usually from the self-proclaimed protectors). Relief workers watched helplessly while most of their food aid filtered through this corrupt system, in the vain hope that some of it would trickle down. The aid only enhanced the role and strength of the militias, and the population at large continued to starve.

The UN Security Council, indecisive and hesitant in its response to the looming disaster, passed Resolution 733 on 23 January 1992, which called for a total arms embargo and the establishment of an immediate cease-fire. By February, the parties to the conflict agreed to the cease-fire, mediated through the coordinated efforts of the United Nations, the League of Arab States, the Organization of African Unity and the Organization of the Islamic Conference. Yet the situation on the ground remained conflictual.

International intervention soon crystallized as the number of refugees, IDPs and deaths from hunger ballooned: approximately 23 per cent of the population were directly affected by the famine, and up to 70 per cent were reportedly in the queue. Moreover, extensive media coverage of emaciated Somalis ensured a suitable international outcry (the "Do Something" response), although some have since argued that the state of emergency was vastly exaggerated by the media.[10] The media were greatly assisted in this effort by the relief agencies which, together with interested members of the US Congress, launched one of the more successful public relations campaigns with the hope of raising funds for their work and putting a stop to the famine.[11] This alliance left the international community with relatively few options.

For US President George Bush (Senior), still heady from his victories in the Cold War and the Gulf War and hoping to realize a "New World Order", and UN Secretary-General Boutros Boutros-Ghali, eager to test the potential of an organization that had been in a superpower stranglehold since its inception, Somalia provided the perfect opportunity. The United Nations Operation in Somalia (UNOSOM) was thus conceived through Security Council Resolution 751 (24 April 1992) to facilitate the delivery of humanitarian assistance. The overwhelming endorsement at the United Nations for the intervention was garnered because the state imploded and the formal institutions of government disappeared, leaving the population unprotected from the ravages of the civil war, the resultant man-made (or warlord-inspired) famine and the local warlords themselves, who were committing human rights violations on a massive scale.

July witnessed the arrival of the first 50 military observers, who comprised the initial security force for UNOSOM, which grew to 500 by mid-September. It quickly became apparent, however, that the provision of widespread relief needed a much larger organization than UNOSOM to secure food delivery. Hence, in December 1992, the United States initiated the Unified Task Force (UNITAF), also known as Operation Restore Hope, transporting 37,000 troops to the African continent to do just that. Because of fears of "mission creep", UNITAF was to last only five months, with its primary aim the protection of food relief. A handover to a multinational, peace enforcement operation – UNOSOM II – was therefore arranged for May 1993, with the United States providing some troops and the new Special Representative of the Secretary-General (SRSG). Security Council Resolution 814 (March 1993) also tasked UNOSOM II to assume responsibility for a comprehensive "nation-building" exercise in Somalia, setting a precedent for the United Nations.

On 5 June 1993, General Mohamed Farah Aideed's men ambushed a contingent of Pakistani soldiers, killing 24 and wounding many more.[12] From that day forward, the operation veered off course and soon came to a crashing halt. The next day, the Security Council passed Resolution 837, which explicitly called for the detention and trial of those responsible. What started out as an impartial peacekeeping operation to feed the starving soon turned into an unsuccessful, all-out man-hunt in pursuit of Aideed, culminating on the night of 3 October when 18 US Army Rangers were killed and 77 wounded after an attack on an Aideed meeting place in Mogadishu. The Somali casualty list was even higher: an estimated 300 were killed and another 700 wounded, with up to 30 per cent of the victims women and children. This was the bloodiest confrontation of any UN operation.

Americans once again reacted strongly to media coverage on CNN. This time it was not starving children but rather a dead US soldier dragged through the streets of Mogadishu by Aideed's men. The "Do Something" cries were rapidly replaced by a rousing chorus of "Get Out", because the US public could not understand why Somalis were killing their troops – troops who were sent to Somalia purely on a humanitarian mission. President Clinton promised to have all US soldiers out by March 1994.[13]

In early January 1994, Boutros-Ghali recommended scaling back the mission and, the following November, the UN Security Council set March 1995 as the final date of operation for UNOSOM II. The operation stumbled on until its termination, on schedule, without accomplishing political reconstruction, disarmament of the factions or a resolution of the conflict – all of which were stated aims of the intervention. The human cost was 156 peacekeepers and several thousand Somali civilians. The three UN operations – which lasted from April 1992 to March 1995 – did, however, put a stop to the famine: an estimated 100,000 lives were saved by the intervention.

Immediately after the United Nations terminated the operation, much of Somalia slipped back into the situation of sporadic lawlessness that had prevailed before foreign troops arrived, despite the enormous infusion of funds during the three operations (US$2.3 billion spent by the US government[14] and US$1.64 billion by the United Nations[15]) and the invasion of untold numbers of aid workers and foreign soldiers (close to 50,000 troops at its peak). The country was no longer in an emergency "famine" situation, but rather had moved into a situation that was very fluid, marked by occasionally erratic and inconsistent acts of violence and punctuated by irregular humanitarian crises in different parts of the country. This was set against a backdrop where all public social welfare services that had been provided by the state were now gone.

Operational issues

In neither the UN intervention phase nor the post-UN period has operating in Somalia been a straightforward affair for humanitarian and development organizations. Every aspect of working in Somalia has been affected by the absence of government.

The intervention period

If international support for the Somali intervention was garnered because the state had collapsed, an equally valid point is that many of the problems encountered by the international community were owing to the inability of a traditional peacekeeping operation to function in a society with no government.

Technically, UNOSOM was a small, traditional peacekeeping operation that was intended to separate the warring parties (which had already agreed to a cease-fire). UNITAF then took over as a US-led, UNendorsed peace enforcement operation to secure urgent humanitarian assistance. It was not a Blue Helmet operation precisely because of the flexibility it allowed a member state – in this case, the United States – to take certain actions to maintain or promote peace and security. The bulk of the financial costs of UNITAF were borne by the United States (approximately 75 per cent instead of the normal 27 per cent of peacekeeping) in exchange for a non-UN command and control operation.

The three objectives of UNITAF were: to secure the seaports, airstrips and food distribution points; to protect relief convoys and ensure the smooth operation of relief agencies; and to assist UN agencies and nongovernmental organizations (NGOs) in providing relief to the famine-stricken population. The provision of security also entailed voluntary disarmament and cantonment of weapons in exchange for money or food, and retraining Somalis for civilian employment. International military escorts were used so that Somali security guards, riding in "technicals",[16] could no longer profit.

What complicated the Somalia operation was the overt emphasis on "nation-building" in a situation of prolonged state collapse, officially tacked on after the operation began. UNITAF had managed to sidestep this issue, although the US government had been fully aware from the start that political reconstruction needed to be addressed in order to prevent a return to the *status quo ante*, i.e. internecine warfare and possibly another famine.[17] Initially, political reconstruction did not appear to be a very daunting task, because the very same warlords who had instigated the civil war had, since the start of the UN operation, signed various agreements that were to lead to the formation of new political structures. Yet none of these was successful, as will be discussed below.

Post-interventions

The public failures of the UN operations in Somalia, irrespective of who was to blame, discredited the United Nations – both inside Somalia and internationally. In fact, the establishment of rudimentary local and regional authorities in some parts of the country, along with the emergence of a robust private sector, occurred in areas where UNOSOM had not interfered (especially in the north-east, or Puntland, and in Somaliland).

In December 1993, at the Fourth Coordination Meeting on Humanitarian Assistance for Somalia, several important donors, in particular the United States, the United Kingdom, Sweden, Italy and the European Commission (EC), along with representatives of some UN agencies, met on the fringe to determine how to establish a new, independent mechanism to deliver aid, one that would be distinct from UN military and political structures because of the negative image UNOSOM then had, both in Somali eyes as well as to many others. At that time, the US government had already decided to withdraw from the UN operation in Somalia, but it remained committed to supporting the international – and particularly the humanitarian – efforts in the country. It was also not clear then if the UN peace support mission was going to be terminated; UNOSOM II still had a heavy military presence in Mogadishu.

Accordingly, in February 1994, these donors and some of the UN agencies established the Somalia Aid Coordination Body (SACB) to serve as a new coordination body for donors, UN agencies, NGOs and other international organizations. One year later, the SACB adopted a Code of Conduct for International Rehabilitation and Development Assistance to Somalia. This Code provided a framework for international involvement in Somalia, and was endorsed by Somali authorities in the different regional administrations (where they existed), which acted as legitimate repositories of Somali sovereignty.

Although the Code of Conduct permitted traditional EC and UN rehabilitation and development instruments to adapt to the realities of state collapse, the degree of acceptance and enforcement of the Code varied significantly from region to region, owing to the volatile political situation. Despite the problems encountered, the establishment of working practices within the SACB paved the way for some major donors to continue operating through NGO partners in Somalia, albeit at greatly reduced levels, while others, such as the World Bank or the International Monetary Fund, were unable to adapt.[18] After UNOSOM II departed, the SACB – which was located in Nairobi and not in Somalia for security reasons – became the only international forum where political, security and humanitarian questions were debated and policy adopted in a series of committees.

The SACB assumed the coordinating role normally provided by a UN agency. It was led from the start by the European Commission because it was then the largest donor in Somalia. The European Commission subsequently adopted three guiding principles for involvement in the country: (1) strict neutrality with respect to the fighting factions; (2) non-recognition of any government that is not broadly representative; and (3) no direct mediation role but rather encouragement and support for initiatives by the United Nations and the Organization of African Unity.[19] Whereas in theory the European Commission was to take a back seat politically (as noted in the third principle) and focus on its more traditional humanitarian and development roles, in practice the European Commission would become highly political because of an astute EC Special Envoy, Sigurd Illing, and an emasculated United Nations. By early 1996, Illing had succeeded in placing the European Commission (and, technically, the European Union) at the forefront of international involvement in the country.

In many respects, the SACB has proved to be a creative adaptation by the international community to state collapse, and it was unique in its composition because it brought together donors with NGOs and UN agencies. Yet, it also has been criticized for being overly bureaucratic and less relevant to affairs in Somalia because it is based in Nairobi. Many argue that the aid community spends far too much time in meetings in Kenya, rather than implementing agreed policies in the field.[20]

Moreover, despite Somali involvement on the ground in the different regions of Somalia and Somali involvement in the political process, not enough Somalis have been involved in the SACB coordinating bodies. Initially it was felt that it would be impossible to select appropriate and representative Somalis, and that their inclusion would empower some at the expense of others. Only at the end of the 1990s were modalities elaborated to bring more Somalis into the decision-making process but, even then, their participation remained marginal.

At the political level, as noted, the European Commission became active. The UN political office was anyway unable to provide effective leadership because it had been rendered powerless by UN headquarters – left with only a skeleton staff, given a restrictive mandate, and its work divorced from that of the UN humanitarian and development office. The European Commission was also the largest donor in Somalia, even if its funds had been drastically reduced because Somalia no longer benefited from the Lomé Conventions,[21] since the country had not ratified the Lomé IV before it collapsed. Funds left over from previous financial commitments to Somalia within earlier Lomé Conventions and other funds from the various autonomous EC budget lines (e.g. food aid, democratization) therefore had to be mobilized to overcome the legal and institutional constraints posed by these unique circumstances.

In 1995, the European Commission launched a conflict management and governance project, based on the conviction that the initiatives sponsored by the United Nations and Somali leaders between 1991 and 1995 had failed to reach a settlement of the Somali conflict because they hastily tried to reconstruct a central state without elaborating constitutional arrangements compatible with traditional "uncentralized" Somali culture.[22] Additionally, they concentrated primarily on the warlords at the expense of members of civil society.[23] Ken Menkhaus commented, "The ability to destroy had been confused with the ability to govern. The power to govern, it turned out, had devolved to a much more localized level."[24] The departure of the EC Special Envoy subsequently led to the termination of this project at the European Commission by his successor, who had his own ideas about how to resolve the Somali conflict. The lack of consistent application of policies plagues most conflict zones, particularly when there is no overall agreement on the political process (given that the European Commission was pushing this and not the United Nations).

Internal power struggles between the United Nations and the European Commission hindered development and humanitarian programmes in Somalia for several years in the late 1990s until UN headquarters became more involved. A new RSG (David Stephen) was appointed, who had a bigger profile than previous representatives, and soon thereafter a more competent UN Resident and Humanitarian Coordinator (Randolph Kent) joined the team in Nairobi. Both made an effort to coordinate the work of the two offices, while also regaining control over coordination mechanisms from the European Commission, which, in turn, became less political and reverted to its traditional donor role.

Obstacles and opportunities

Just as operations were confused and mandates blurred at the macro level because traditional humanitarian actors played an overt political role, so too did this occur at the micro levels, in both time periods discussed in this chapter.

The intervention period

Somalis bear the ultimate responsibility for the crisis that has undermined their society, albeit endeavours of the international community exacerbated the situation. Concerning the latter, a number of mistakes were made throughout the interventions, and even prior to them, when there was no joint planning between the military and the heads of relief organizations, even though the military was originally deployed to provide protection for these organizations.

The United Nations also played a principal role in the unfolding Somali tragedy in many ways, including – but not limited to – issues related to poor coordination (and turf wars) between New York and Mogadishu staff; over-concentration on Mogadishu at the expense of the rest of the country; frequent changes of the person acting as SRSG and of the Humanitarian Coordinators (five of each rotated through Somalia within a three-year time period); and unclear rules of engagement and rules on the use of force and for civil–military relations. An overview of these factors could subsume them under the umbrella of management problems, which can threaten and impede any peace support operation. Moreover, each new head of agency or mission inevitably would want to put his or her stamp on the operation, particularly when there was no overall strategic framework. Such disparities in leadership and inconsistency in policy implementation only served to undermine the mission, and, in this case, did not provide Somalis with any predictable policy direction.

There were further difficulties in regaining control over security in this heavily armed, faction-ridden society.[25] In addition, resource allocation proved inadequate to accomplish mission mandates. The mandates did not match the means: UNITAF's mandate was limited, and its budget constraints were few; on the other hand, UNOSOM II was supposed to operate throughout the entire country on restricted funding.

In addition to poor coordination and inadequate funding, which have plagued other peace support operations, the United Nations and the US government had been considering political reconstruction of the Somali state since UNOSOM, and unrealistically assumed that impartiality could be maintained. Yet the Americans were (understandably) unclear on the means to accomplish this task, and therefore tried to foist political reconstruction onto the United Nations, while publicly committing only to undertake the temporary, stop-gap assignment of securing food delivery. UNITAF became partial and involved in politics anyway by virtue of securing food deliveries and choosing representatives in villages to assist with the distribution. External involvement in political reconstruction is by definition controversial and complex.[26] Arguably, the United States and the United Nations erred in pressing solutions on Somalis without properly involving them at different stages of the process or assisting them to develop their own revenue-raising capacity to sustain these institutions.[27]

UNOSOM II gave Boutros-Ghali his first opportunity to execute his *Agenda for Peace*, with the "largest multinational force ever assembled under [his] direct control".[28] Yet experimentation, by definition, is a trial-and-error process. Political rehabilitation was ill coordinated and applied patchily in Somalia, without any overall sharing of information between UN agencies, the military and humanitarian and development agencies. What was expected of the United Nations, in any case, was without doubt beyond its reach owing to the lack of resources and experience in this area. The mad Aideed man-hunt also invalidated any residual pretensions of neutrality and impartiality, and instead boosted Aideed's image amongst Somalis.[29] Finally, as mentioned, any UN contact with the warlords inevitably conferred more legitimacy on them, which only served to wrest control from many of the elders who traditionally held more influence and potentially also the prestige to assist in reconstruction.

Post-interventions

As noted, immediately after the termination of UNOSOM II, the United Nations in general had lost credibility. Meanwhile, the rise in political influence of the European Commission (a traditional donor that normally did not play a political role), along with the European Commission's assumption of control over the mechanisms of the SACB, was perhaps unavoidable given the power vacuum that was created within the international community. The subsequent turf wars between the European Commission and the United Nations, which endured until the late 1990s, resulted in the international community becoming as fragmented as Somali society, and the situation was made even more complicated because the European Commission was one of the United Nations' major funders.

After UNOSOM, there was a dramatic reduction in funds dedicated to Somalia. The situation deteriorated even further towards the end of the 1990s. In 2002, Somalia received only US$41 million through the UN Consolidated Appeals Process, falling short by 50 per cent of the overall appeal. One year later, the total raised for Somalia was a mere US$37 million.

Not only were funds reduced, but budgets for humanitarian and development projects were too short term. Many projects were funded on three- to six-month cycles, owing to the difficulties donors had funding projects in Somalia at all. In general these projects carried on at the end of each cycle, but all too often it was easy to terminate them, again interfering with consistency.

Moreover, after the SACB became operational, most of the major donors lost interest in Somalia, even if they stayed nominally involved.[30] This meant that the personnel deployed to Somalia were not always star performers, and it also meant that a powerful personality could wield undue influence because of the lack of interest by major capitals. Country policy was thus skewed and dependent on the vagaries of a project cycle or a particular personality working for a particular NGO, donor or agency.

Somalis learned to wait out the tenure of a head of agency, and the occasional naming of that person as persona non grata became a powerful tool wielded by Somalis in hastening this process. In addition, new directors could easily disband projects if they felt like it, as occurred with the EC governance project mentioned above. Alternatively, the headquarters of the donor agency, multilateral organization or NGO could change policy in a similar fashion.

Small NGOs working inside Somalia also exercised undue influence, given that there were so few actors on the ground (the majority remained in Nairobi and would visit irregularly). Often an NGO would be the only international presence, and the only employer, in a village. This meant that, even if the mandate of the NGO was strictly humanitarian, it became intricately involved in local politics. Only a handful of humanitarian and development workers had the training and experience for this type of working environment.

By the very end of the 1990s, the United Nations had finally succeeded in re-establishing its authority in the coordinating bodies. Further, the UN political office and the development and humanitarian office had managed to establish a close working relationship. Even then, there was no formal linkage between the two. This only ensured that the political office could make vague promises of aid or expanded UN activity, tied to the peace process, but such assistance was never guaranteed because of politics at UN headquarters, and development and humanitarian actors continued to be involved in politics by the very act of carrying out their programmes in Somalia.

Negotiations

Since 1991, there have been numerous, often contradictory, attempts by members of the international community – politicians, diplomats and humanitarians – to resuscitate the state, and none has been successful. "Negotiations" in this section refer mostly to the macro attempts at political reconciliation, which were considered essential for allowing development and humanitarian work to expand in-country, rather than the numerous micro-level negotiations that ensured occasional access or co-operation in aid delivery in different parts of the country. The latter were ongoing and, because neither local political actors nor international staff were in place for very long, the process had to be repeated every time a new political leader (or warlord) assumed control at the local level or a new employee of a humanitarian agency arrived in theatre.

Political negotiations: The intervention period

Before the UN operation got under way, attempts at reconciliation had been made by various groups of Somali intellectuals, by Somali warlords or "politicians", by foreign governments and by regional states. These continued throughout the interventions and resulted in numerous peace agreements. Between 1991 and early 1995, 17 national-level and 20 local-level "reconciliation initiatives" were attempted in Somalia and in neighbouring states.[31] In all the agreements, satisfying the stipulations *and* the parties involved proved impossible.[32]

Despite the plethora of agreements on peace, national unity and the formation of a central government, they failed because they focused almost exclusively on a rapid revival of a central state – without the prior elaboration of constitutional arrangements that could have accommodated the centrifugal realities of Somali society and built confidence amongst the various actors in the peace process. The national-level agreements also foundered because they included more warlords than traditional leaders from civil society, and these warlords could not fully control their claimed constituencies.

Local-level agreements achieved more results, especially in Somaliland, through the organization of many small meetings. These gradually transformed, over the course of a year, into a regional conference. The Boroma "national" conference, held between February and May 1993, capped this process. Here, elders agreed on a National Peace Charter for the "Somaliland Republic", which assisted in resolving clan conflicts. Significantly, this process received very little external financial assistance.

Post-interventions

After UNOSOM, despite the elaboration of a Code of Conduct for aid delivery, on the political side there was no overall strategy for rebuilding the state. (Even today, state collapse has not yet been incorporated into the normative structure of the international system.[33]) It was thus left to the creativity, or whim, of individual heads of organizations to develop and implement their own. First, the European Commission launched its governance project, based on the belief that a decentralized model would be most appropriate for Somalia. The European Commission may have also been experimenting with the emerging concept of a Common Foreign and Security Policy. After the Special Envoy departed, Brussels decided that his successor should have a lower political ranking and profile and focus more on the development and humanitarian role. His successor soon decided to abort the governance project.

The SACB subsequently supported what was alternatively called the "building block" or the "peace dividend" approach, which complied with its Code of Conduct and with a number of UN resolutions.[34] The idea was to support areas that made "progress on political reconciliation and security", based on the belief that a national government could be realized only if it were built on strong, peaceful, regional foundations. Essentially, this meant that any regional authority that could maintain peace and security would receive aid, whereas the so-called "poor performers" would receive only humanitarian assistance (when security permitted), and even then such assistance was minimal owing to funding constraints.

By the late 1990s, the building block/peace dividend approach had been endorsed by the Inter-Governmental Authority on Development (IGAD) – the East African regional organization – which was chaired at the time by Ethiopia.[35] Somaliland was already receiving the bulk of international assistance, and in 1998 the north-east soon established a regional charter for Puntland. Together these two regions comprise approximately half of all the territory of the former Somali Republic. Other regions in southern Somalia were at times declared to be "building blocks" by inhabitants of at least part of these regions, including Hiraanland, Jubaland, Gedo region and the Benadir Administration. Of all these regional administrations, only Somaliland and Puntland were formed in a bottom-up fashion; the rest were hastily assembled from the top down, probably from pressure exerted by the international community, and consequently have either disintegrated or been far less stable.

The hope was that these regional authorities would eventually come together and form a loose (probably federal or confederal) state, and this method of coming together would help ensure that power remained decentralized. Although in theory this approach made the most sense, and complied with what many Somalis from civil society had been advocating for years, in practice it was undermined by the relative indifference of some of the major powers, particularly the United States and UN headquarters. Their lack of interest and their reluctance to support this building block approach in a meaningful way allowed regional actors to interfere with relative ease, to the detriment of the political and security situation inside the country, while poor performers continued to deteriorate. Had the US government and UN headquarters put their full diplomatic weight behind this effort and applied greater pressure on Somali regional authorities, as well as assisted in democratization efforts, potentially this policy might have succeeded in re-establishing an effective government.

Instead, since 1997, a regional Cold War intervened in Somalia. The competition was first between Kenya and Ethiopia for control of the peace process, then between Ethiopia and Egypt owing to their longstanding dispute over the Nile, with each country supporting different, opposed warlords in both northern and southern Somalia. Ethiopia and Egypt also had mutually exclusive ambitions for the type of government they wanted established in Somalia. Remembering its past war with Somalia, Ethiopia preferred a decentralized state, which would be viewed as less of a threat to its larger neighbour. Ethiopia thus utilized its lead position at the time in IGAD to promote the building block approach, which of course also found resonance amongst Western states. Egypt, on the other hand, itself a highly centralized state, advocated a model similar to its own, and probably also because it preferred Ethiopia's neighbour to be strong. The Egyptian view was that, if Somalia were encouraged to break into "entities", there would be more of a likelihood that each entity would attempt to declare independence, as had already occurred in Somaliland. If instead a central government were formed first, then it could be up to the central government to decide on the regions that would comprise the state. Egypt argued that it was committed to preserving Somalia's integrity.

Complicating the equation was the Eritrean–Ethiopian war, which fully erupted in early 1999 and was responsible for an upsurge in arms flows into Somalia. Yemen and Libya also entered the picture and were accused of supplying arms to different actors as well. All these states additionally continued the earlier damaging policy of negotiating possible settlements only with the warlords (giving them large sums of money to attend so-called "peace talks" and sign agreements that could not be implemented). Thus, whereas at one level the international community, through the SACB, was advocating a building block approach and a focus on civil society, the regional states were pushing a contrary policy that essentially kept Somalia in a political stalemate and continued to empower the warlords.

Things only deteriorated further with yet another regional peace initiative, this time sponsored by the Djibouti government. In August 2000, at the Somalia National Peace Conference in Arta, Djibouti, a Transitional National Government (TNG) was officially announced. The TNG moved to the capital, Mogadishu, in October 2000. It received some support from the United Nations and financial support from several Gulf and North African states, including Saudi Arabia, which allegedly donated US\$6 million to it. The form of government agreed at Arta was nearer to the Egyptian preference and it too soon faltered.[36]

Because the TNG never managed to control more than half of Mogadishu, further political discussions took place in Kenya in 2003 and 2004. At the time of writing, a new Transitional Federal Government, decided by clans, had been declared, although it had not yet moved from its base in Kenya into Somalia. Whether or not it will be sustainable is too difficult to predict at this stage.

At the micro level, humanitarian and development work was often impeded by security concerns or incidents such as threats, or even on occasion murder, against local or international staff. When this occurred, the SACB would declare that all work would cease in that particular area until those who committed the atrocity were brought to justice by the local authorities and it was considered safe to resume activities. This policy rarely succeeded and in many respects it seemed unfair to put so much pressure on local authorities that exerted only partial control over the territories they claimed. With no overall rule of law structure in most of

Somalia (excluding Somaliland), it was very rare that Somalis could not only locate the accused but then bring that person to justice.

Once all international staff had been evacuated, their return would have to be agreed by the SACB, then their re-entry re-negotiated, along with a new *modus vivendi*. There were often great divisions within the SACB about when it was deemed safe to return, and decisions were not always made on security grounds. Some agencies needed an on-the-ground presence for fund-raising purposes, while others were worried about the humanitarian situation deteriorating with no assistance being provided. At one meeting I attended, a representative of an NGO remarked, "If we don't return to [Somali village], we will have no presence in Somalia, and that is not acceptable to our headquarters." As the United Nations gradually took over the leadership of the SACB at the very end of the 1990s, this policy was altered so that important humanitarian and development work could continue except in extreme security situations.

Thus, throughout both the intervention and the post-intervention periods, neither the humanitarian, nor the development nor the political actors were able to implement a coherent plan to rebuild the state and hence allow for the safe and consistent delivery of international humanitarian and development aid. Too many individuals and states succumbed to hubris or self-serving political purposes, believing themselves to be the saviour of the Somali nation. There was never a direct linkage between humanitarian and development aid and the political process, but it was understood that funding and programmatic activity would increase significantly if there was a recognized government counterpart on the ground.

Wider implications

In Somalia, because international actors had been operating with no effective national counterpart for over a decade, politics became integral to the development/humanitarian offices, and certainly to a greater extent than the mandates of many agencies dictated. Indeed, in the first period analysed, politics caused the famine that was to become an international humanitarian issue in 1992; thereafter, food plundering sustained the war economy. As Clarke and Herbst explained, "Where famine is man-made, stopping the famine means rebuilding political institutions to create order".[37] Not only did international actors exacerbate the famine and the civil war by sending in food aid (most of which was subsequently stolen), but they then became involved in clan politics during the intervention, which contributed to further political disintegration. These were clear examples of well-intended diplomacy gone awry and of the blurring of the lines between the humanitarian and the political. It was nearly impossible to respect ideals of neutrality and impartiality.

During the first period, Somalia was inundated with high-ranking envoys, diplomats and senior UN humanitarian representatives, although none stayed for very long and therefore policy was inconsistently applied. Funding for the mission was also generous. Throughout the second period, in contrast, international representatives were not so senior and were often inexperienced, and funding was reduced dramatically. Political fragmentation and the accompanying security problems on the ground ensured that humanitarian and development aid could be delivered only in an ad hoc fashion (except in Somaliland). At this time, the United Nations separated political efforts from humanitarian and development work, and the major donors established a new coordinating mechanism that was not directed by the United Nations, but led instead by the European Commission.

These changes have ensured an erratic and inconsistent narrative. The UN political office has had no carrot or stick to implement peace plans and has often been marginalized, whereas the development and humanitarian side has had some means and therefore often became involved in politics, sometimes to the detriment of the political process. Only from the latter half of 1999 did the United Nations regain momentum, but, even then, it was an informal decision by the two UN representatives rather than a decree from UN headquarters.

At the same time, as funds for development and humanitarian assistance decreased from the mid-1990s, so the influence of OECD donors declined accordingly. Regional states began playing a more critical – if at times obstructive – role, and Somalis from the diaspora have contributed substantially larger sums to Somalia than has the donor community, anywhere from 5 to 15 times the amount (depending on which total is endorsed). Even so, since international troops departed from Somalia, not enough Somalis have been brought into internationally led humanitarian and development activities, whether they be strategy formulation, coordination mechanisms, implementation or policy reviews. Somalis have, however, participated in political negotiations. Thus, just as UN political efforts were disconnected from the humanitarian and development work, on the Somali side there has been a similar disconnect.

Not only should Somalis be fully incorporated into SACB structures and programmes, but the diaspora too should be encouraged to work more closely with the international community. Given the huge disparity in contributions, the diaspora should be playing a far more significant role. The contributions of the diaspora – even when they take the form of collective remittances – are not factored into the UN Consolidated

Appeals for Somalia, which means that needs assessments are already distorted, despite recent attempts by some agencies to improve their understanding of remittances. The same applies to the work of Islamic NGOs in Somalia: they too should be brought into the SACB structures. Only a very small number of Islamic NGOs participate in the SACB and given that many Islamic NGOs are implementing projects in the country – building mosques, schools, hospitals – their exclusion (whether by choice or not) from the coordinating bodies does not allow for a complete picture to emerge.[38]

Lessons learned: Harmonizing the work of the United Nations

More than any other complex emergency in the 1990s, Somalia taught humanitarian workers that it is not always possible to remain neutral and impartial, and the deaths of several aid workers demonstrated that they were not always viewed as such by beneficiaries. In Somalia, given that the famine was man-made, it was inevitable that aid workers would become embroiled in politics. After the UN military interventions, there was finger-pointing from all sides: the US government blamed the United Nations, the United Nations blamed the US military, the NGOs blamed the United Nations and the US government, when, in fact, everyone and no one was to blame, given the overall lack of experience in dealing with a collapsed state.

Because the crisis in Somalia was fundamentally political, the formal separation of the political from the humanitarian work at the United Nations never made any sense either. Although there had been a de facto reunion of the two offices at the end of the 1990s, this had not been sanctioned at UN headquarters, and therefore they were not given the institutional support that would have been necessary to underpin the peace process in a meaningful way. This is not to argue that the work of the two should have been fully integrated, given that humanitarian work is supposed to be impartial and neutral and so many times in the past in Somalia it clearly was not. Rather, an enhanced, public degree of formal coordination and cooperation was necessary, because it would have prevented the humanitarian and development office from interfering in politics and given the political office some carrot to use for the implementation of peace plans.

Humanitarian delivery

International actors too have resolved some of the thornier issues impeding their work. For example, although many humanitarian agencies admitted that, during the famine, 90 per cent of food aid was stolen, by the end of the 1990s the World Food Programme (WFP) had developed a new modus operandi to overcome these delivery problems.[39] Other agencies involved in providing emergency assistance to children also utilize creative methods. For example, in some areas, food security agencies have stopped conducting nutritional assessments to determine whether children are malnourished. These assessments had attracted too much attention, raised expectations within communities, and also caught the eye of bandits. Instead, they use local staff to monitor the prices of certain local products and wages. If these figures "indicate a serious deterioration in food security, international staff carry out a very rapid assessment" and alter activity accordingly.[40]

And continued need

Despite these adaptations, state collapse has still left the majority of Somalia's citizens without consistent access to basic goods and services. Beyond assistance from family members abroad – for those lucky enough to have relatives in Germany or the United States or Australia – there is no social safety net in Somalia.[41] The attacks of 11 September 2001 in the United States have added a sense of urgency regarding "black holes", given that years of neglect in Afghanistan enabled Osama bin Laden to consolidate his lethal terror machine. Somalia thus once again reappeared on the radar screens of the US government owing to fears that the country had become a permissive environment for criminal and terrorist activity. New tools are still required to cope with the lack of government, tools that could improve the coordination of international agencies – both inside and outside the SACB – and, at the same time, harness the considerable energy of the diaspora and the dynamic Somali business community.

Notes

1. For more information about why the term "failed" is inappropriate, see Karin von Hippel, "The Proliferation of Collapsed States in the Post-Cold War World", in Michael Clarke, ed., *Brassey's Defence Yearbook 1997*, London: Brassey's, 1997.
2. See United Nations Development Programme (UNDP), *Human Development Report 2004: Cultural Liberty in Today's Diverse World*, ⟨http://hdr.undp.org/reports/global/2004/pdf/hdr04_complete.pdf⟩ (accessed 15 July 2004), for more information.
3. The Report of the Panel of Experts on Somalia to the Security Council described not only how Somalia harboured some of the terrorists who carried out attacks in Mombasa, but also how the territory was used to smuggle weapons into Kenya. See *Report of the Panel of Experts on Somalia Pursuant to Security Council Resolution 1474 (2003)*, UN Security Council, S/2003/1035, 4 November 2003.
4. See UN Office for the Coordination of Humanitarian Affairs, Consolidated Ap-

peals Process, *Humanitarian Appeal 2004: Somalia*, ⟨http://www.un.org/depts/ocha/cap/somalia.html⟩ for more information (accessed 20 July 2004).

5. See Somalia's country profile on ReliefWeb, ⟨http://www.reliefweb.int/rw/bkg.nsf/doc200?OpenForm&rc=1&cc=som&mode=cp⟩ for the range of figures.

6. In particular, see *Socio-Economic Survey 2002: Somalia. Report No. 1, Somalia Watching Brief, 2003*, UNDP with the World Bank.

7. According to UNDP, there is an absence of comprehensive baseline statistics. Information on population movement and displacement or seasonal migration patterns is weak. The informalization of the economy makes economic analysis particularly difficult and the extent of privatized services such as education is unknown. As data collection is dependent on the quality of access, there is a bias in the volume and quality of data collected to areas where there is better security. See UNDP, *Human Development Report: Somalia, 2001*, Nairobi: UNDP, p. 195.

8. See ⟨http://www.reliefweb.int/⟩ for more information on international assistance to Somalia.

9. For more details, see I. M. Lewis, *A Modern History of Somalia: Nation and State in the Horn of Africa*, Boulder, CO: Westview Press, 1988.

10. See Michael Maren, "Feeding a Famine", *ForbesMediaCritic*, Vol. 2, No. 1, Fall 1994.

11. For more information, see Warren P. Strobel, "The Media and US Policies Toward Intervention: A Closer Look at the 'CNN Effect'", in Chester Crocker, Fen Osler Hampson with Pamela Aall, eds, *Managing Global Chaos: Sources of and Responses to International Conflict*, Washington, DC: US Institute of Peace, 1996, pp. 360–366.

12. Aideed was one of the men responsible for the overthrow of Barre.

13. US troops briefly returned in March 1995 to provide protection off the coast during the final force withdrawal, Operation United Shield. Although US public opinion has been cited as the reason for withdrawing from Somalia, some researchers believe that the US government misread public opinion, which was in fact supportive of escalation despite (or because of) their outrage. See Steven Kull, I. M. Destler and Clay Ramsay, *The Foreign Policy Gap: How Policymakers Misread the Public*, College Park, MD: Center for International and Security Studies at Maryland, 1997, for more information.

14. John G. Sommer, "Hope Restored? Humanitarian Aid in Somalia, 1990–1994", Refugee Policy Group, November 1994, p. C-5.

15. UN Department of Public Information, accessed 1999.

16. A "technical" is a basic pick-up truck, mounted with a machine gun. They have been utilized by all faction leaders in Somalia, as well as by the international aid community. The term was coined by the non-governmental and intergovernmental organizations during the civil war because they were forced to hire Somali escorts to protect them, even though their constitutions did not allow them to do this. They thus justified their payments to these Somalis under the heading, "technical assistance".

17. See, for example, "Remarks by President Bill Clinton to the Congress from the White House Office of the Press Secretary, October 13, 1993"; or US-UN Press Release 37-(93), 26 March 1993.

18. The latter are restricted by their articles of agreement to working *only* with established governments.

19. See, for example, the speech by Ambassador Roberto di Leo, Embassy of Italy, Representing the EU Presidency, delivered to the participants at the "First Seminar on Decentralised Political Structures for Somalia", sponsored and organized by the European Commission, Lake Naivasha, Kenya, June 1996. For more information on the European Union's involvement in the Somali crisis, see Karin von Hippel and Alexandros Yannis, "The European Response to State Collapse in Somalia", in Knud Erik Joergensen, ed., *European Approaches to Crisis Management*, The Hague: Kluwer International, 1997.

20. See Nicola Reindorp and Anna Schmidt, "Coordinating Humanitarian Action: The Changing Role of Official Donors", HPG Briefing Paper No. 7, London: Overseas Development Institute, December 2002; and Joanna Macrae et al., "Uncertain Power: The Changing Role of Official Donors in Humanitarian Action", HPG Report 12, London: Overseas Development Institute, Humanitarian Policy Group, December 2002.

21. The first Lomé Convention was signed in Lomé, Togo, in 1975. The conventions, which are reviewed regularly, are essentially aid and trade agreements made by members of the European Union and are intended to promote development in 70 countries in Africa, the Caribbean and the Pacific (also known as the ACP states).

22. A group of academic consultants at the London School of Economics and Political Science (LSE) were commissioned by the European Commission to prepare "A Study of Decentralised Political Structures for Somalia: A Menu of Options" (August 1995), which outlined four models of decentralized government: three territorially based models (the confederation, federation and decentralized unitary state) and a community-based type of power-sharing known as consociation. Following publication of the study in 1996, the European Commission organized seminars in Kenya and, in 1997, several inside Somalia for members of civil society to provide the forum for these Somalis to deliberate the study in greater detail as well as contribute their expertise to the overall debate. I was the project manager for the LSE report and responsible for the seminars in Kenya and Somalia. See reports prepared by Karin von Hippel, entitled "First Seminar on Decentralised Political Structures for Somalia", Lake Naivasha, Kenya, June 1996; and "Second Seminar on Decentralised Political Structures for Somalia", Lake Nakuru, Kenya, 16–18 November 1996.

23. Security Council Resolution 814 made specific reference to support for civil society, but in practice this was not undertaken to a significant degree.

24. Ken Menkhaus, "Stateless Somalia", draft article; later published as "Somalia: The Political Order of a Stateless Society", *Current History*, Vol. 97, May 1998, pp. 220–224.

25. Boutros-Ghali sought to disarm the Somalis from the beginning of the operation, using whatever force necessary, yet he was unable to incorporate this aim until Security Council Resolution 814 was passed in March 1993. His aspiration was never realized owing to the US military, which did not want to participate in a door-to-door disarmament campaign because it was guaranteed to be bloody. Although a thorough disarmament programme could feasibly have helped lay the foundation for implementing political reforms – and Somalis today say that the failure to do so initially was a missed opportunity because most Somalis were willing to disarm at the start of the operation – US planners believed it would transform the mission of their troops from providing an impartial food security service to participating directly in the conflict. Ironically, this occurred anyhow. The little disarming that did take place was sporadic and voluntary, and eventually most of the weapons were stolen from the cantonment sites.

26. For a full analysis of political reconstruction after military intervention, see Karin von Hippel, *Democracy by Force*, Cambridge: Cambridge University Press, 2000.

27. Even the programmes that were considered more successful, such as the establishment of local and regional councils, did not prove viable, primarily because there was no overarching authority in place. See UNOSOM II documents, "Governance: District and Regional Councils, their Legitimacy, Effectiveness and Role in Reconciliation and Development", 22–24 June 1994, UN orientation seminar for newly arrived UN Volunteer specialists; "Meeting on Workshop for District Councillors in Somalia" and "UNOSOM II: District Councillors' Workshops", 10–11 August 1993.

28. Clement Adibe, *Managing Arms in Peace Processes: Somalia*, Geneva: United Nations Institute for Disarmament Research, 1995, p. 64.

29. It is unclear what other options were available to the United Nations. Obviously the

United Nations could not let troops be killed without reprisals. Many suggestions have since been made, albeit none very satisfactory. For one alternative, see Ameen Jan, "Peacebuilding in Somalia", IPA Policy Briefing Series, New York: International Peace Academy, July 1996.

30. The US Embassy in Nairobi assumed the Somalia portfolio, and for several years only one staff member followed events in the country. After he left, he was replaced by one person, who not only had the Somalia portfolio but was also responsible for the Great Lakes. Eventually, one person would be dedicated to each conflict zone, which was still insufficient.

31. Ken Menkhaus, "International Peacebuilding and the Dynamics of Local and National Reconciliation in Somalia", *International Peacekeeping*, Vol. 3, No. 1, Spring 1996, p. 43.

32. The precise demarcation of the regions was an insuperable obstacle, and the issue of self-determination for Somaliland was not broached.

33. "The situation in Somalia will continue to deteriorate until the political will exists among the parties to reach a peaceful solution to their dispute, or until the international community gives itself new instruments to address the phenomenon of a failed state" (United Nations, *The United Nations and Somalia (1992–1996)*, Blue Books Series, Vol. VIII, New York: Department of Public Information of the United Nations, 1996, p. 89).

34. As noted in UN Security Council Resolutions 886 and 897 (November 1993 and February 1994, respectively), and General Assembly Resolution 52/169 (December 1996).

35. A joint Ethiopia/Kenya letter of 31 January 1997, which referred to IGAD guidelines, noted the following: "We feel that United Nations assistance for the rehabilitation of Somalia in a well calibrated manner with a clear goal of strengthening constituencies for peace in the country is one of the most critical areas of support that the United Nations can provide for the regional effort for peace in Somalia."

36. As Matt Bryden explained, "The Arta conference effectively denied the existence of these [regional] authorities, and aimed instead at the formation of a government by a large group of hand-picked individuals, invited by the Djiboutian government. Since the leaders of the 'building blocks' declined to attend, the conference attracted their political rivals instead, and awarded them legitimacy and recognition under the rubric of a new 'Transitional National Government'. The consequences were dramatic: the administrations of Puntland and Bay/Bakool soon collapsed as pro- and anti-TNG groups struggled for power. Gedo region, which had been peaceful for several years, also erupted into inter-factional violence, and an alliance of pro-TNG militia from central Somalia assaulted and occupied the southern port of Kismayo." Matt Bryden, "No Quick Fixes: Coming to Terms with Terrorism, Islam and Statelessness in Somalia", *Journal of Conflict Studies*, Vol. 23, No. 2, Fall 2003, p. 44.

37. Walter Clarke and Jeffrey Herbst, *Somalia and the Future of Humanitarian Intervention*, Center of International Studies, Monograph Series, No. 9, Princeton University, 1995, p. 10.

38. There are additional worries that some of these Islamic NGOs are promoting a radical agenda through their aid. And, because Western international assistance is not significant in scale, the influence of some of the more extreme Islamist movements has increased. A recent International Crisis Group report noted that the fundamentalist movements inside Somalia "owe their rapid growth since 1990 less to genuine popularity than access to substantial external funding" (*Somalia: Countering Terrorism in a Failed State*, Africa Report No. 45, Nairobi/Brussels: International Crisis Group, 23 May 2002, p. 13).

39. Essentially, a Somali contractor would deposit a bond with the WFP that initially was equal to the cost of the delivery. The contractor would be responsible for all losses be-

tween the port and the "extended delivery point". This policy has dramatically reduced the theft of goods in transit (although losses after goods have been distributed are more difficult to ascertain). This process was clarified by Dr Simon Narbeth.

40. Susanne Jaspars, "Solidarity and Soup Kitchens: A Review of Principles and Practice for Food Distribution in Conflict", a joint project by NutritionWorks and the Overseas Development Institute with Nicholas Leader, HPG Report 7, London: Overseas Development Institute, August 2000, p. 8.

41. For example, in 2002 UNICEF reported that Somalia had "one of the lowest immunization rates in the world, only 18% of children were fully immunized with DTP". Over a decade earlier, more than double that number of children had been immunized. From *State of the World's Vaccines and Immunization*, jointly published by the World Health Organization, UNICEF and the World Bank, Geneva, October 2002, p. 3.

Part V

Europe and the Americas

15

Protection through diplomacy in Colombia

Lizzie Brock

Following an invitation by Colombian human rights workers to establish a project to protect lives against politically motivated attack, Peace Brigades International (PBI) established its Colombia Project in 1994, an initiative in which humanitarian diplomacy was integrated at every level. PBI Colombia's version of humanitarian diplomacy consists of maintaining an on-the-ground presence of international staff carrying out diplomatic activities in various regions of the country as well as internationally; obtaining reliable and detailed information and communicating it securely to contacts; and sustaining a clarity of mandate and consistency of message among the various branches of its international network. PBI Colombia's experience constitutes an important contribution to the thinking about humanitarian diplomacy in that, with limited resources and a relatively grassroots structure, it succeeded in protecting Colombian lives and human rights initiatives.

PBI Colombia's work offers unique perspectives with regard to the research questions presented in this volume. First, the project's accomplishments constitute evidence in favour of non-governmental organizations (NGOs) assuming the role of humanitarian diplomats and indeed their responsibility to do so. In addition, it shows that the humanitarian's role in negotiation differs from that associated with more traditional forms of diplomacy; in standing for the respect of internationally agreed upon principles, a human rights NGO may work within a more narrow scope of negotiation. In PBI's case, that negotiation occurred indirectly through third parties. PBI Colombia's work provides a particular recipe for the necessary ingredients for successful humanitarian diplomacy as well as strategies for how to address the political and logistical questions of conducting multi-level diplomacy with various interlocutors. The experience also shows how clarity of mission and consistency of action combined with the development of political support provide the foundation on which successful diplomatic activity can occur.

The aim of PBI was to protect human rights workers in Colombia. The methodical implementation of a multi-layered diplomatic strategy was essential to the success of PBI's activities. To this extent, the practice of humanitarian diplomacy constituted the modus operandi of PBI in Colombia. This chapter therefore explains PBI's methods of humanitarian diplomacy and shows to what extent they were successful in protecting human rights workers and resettled communities of internally displaced persons (IDPs).

In this chapter, I review PBI Colombia's activities between 1999 and 2003. After explaining the context in which PBI functioned, I show that PBI fulfilled its main objective of protecting human rights workers through its interlocution with the state. I then examine short-term emergency situations as concrete illustrations of diplomacy in action, and I analyse the causes of particular successes and failures. Finally, I reflect on PBI's experience in Colombia in terms of the larger discussion about humanitarian diplomacy.

Context

The arguments of this chapter are drawn from and reflect on Peace Brigades International's attempts to influence the grave and complex human rights crisis in Colombia and the varied but inadequate responses of the international human rights and humanitarian community. The political context contributed to shaping the development of the project's mandate with its specific methods of operation, which arguably constituted a unique model of humanitarian diplomacy.

The human rights crisis

During, but not exclusive to, the period in question, Colombia suffered the worst and longest-running situation of conflict and human rights abuse in the western hemisphere, with hundreds of political murders and dozens of massacres annually, and hundreds of thousands of new IDPs every year.[1] The contemporary armed conflict intensified during the years of a preliminary peace process between the administration of President Andrés Pastrana and the FARC (Revolutionary Armed Forces of Colombia) guerrillas, which fell apart in February 2002.

Time line of key events[2]	
1995	Paramilitary groups form a federation led by Carlos Castaño; violence and displacement of civilian populations in the countryside increase sharply
1997	United States enacts Leahy Amendment conditioning military aid to Colombia
6 April 1997	UNHCHR opens office in Bogotá
26 October 1997	Over 10 million Colombians vote for peace during national elections
June 1998	Conservative Andrés Pastrana wins presidential elections on platform of peace
August 1998	UNHCR establishes office in Bogotá
January 1999	Peace talks with the FARC begin and demilitarized zone ceded to FARC; United States increases military aid
February 1999	AUC kidnaps four human rights workers and declares Colombian human rights advocates military targets
March 1999	ELN hijacks a commercial airliner
April 1999	FARC kidnaps and kills three US activists; massacres of Peace Community members in Urabá
January 2000	Clinton administration proposes a US$1.6 billion military aid package
July 2000	Clinton signs into law H.R. 4425, with US$860.3 million for Colombia; Colombian government officials begin talks in Geneva with ELN
August 2000	Clinton waives all but one of the human rights conditions in the aid package and cash begins to flow
January 2001	AUC takes control of city of Barrancabermeja
February 2002	Peace process breaks down
August 2002	Independent candidate Uribe elected and takes power; war effort escalates
December 2002	US Special Forces arrive as part of US$98 million project to protect pipeline
2003	Public negotiations between government and paramilitary groups begin

Political and economic exclusion and repression of dissent, which led to the creation in the 1960s of the FARC and ELN (Army of National Liberation) guerrilla groups, continued alongside the armed conflict unabated into 2003. Reform politicians, union organizers and human rights and community leaders faced murder, harassment, disappearance and exile. However, in the past decade the Colombian state, formerly directly responsible for the majority of human rights violations, has shifted its strategy to collaborating with and outsourcing its dirty work to private armies of paramilitary organizations, in particular the Autodefensas Unidas de Colombia (AUC).

The paramilitary strategy came to dominate the landscape, but this was not new. The use of "irregular" or secret forces to carry out dirty-war operations, combined with elaborate political and propaganda schemes to evade state accountability, was a well-tested and fully documented counter-insurgency strategy, used by most Latin American militaries and at times explicitly recommended by United States advisers and trainers throughout the "Cold War" period of Latin American state terror regimes.

In addition, the strategic use of forced displacement by the right, as well as the fleeing of civilian populations from areas in dispute, produced an estimated 2 million internal refugees (in a country of 42 million) by 2002. Members of the élites employed the strategy of land expropriation and forced displacement in collusion with military and/or irregular forces and then instituted social control. Poor *campesinos* were then allowed to colonize new frontier territory, but, after they had opened the door and increased the value of the land, élites returned and took over landholdings – either buying the lands of the peasants under duress or expelling them by force.

Both domestically and internationally, government success at portraying the paramilitaries as an independent force yielded public debates regarding their "autonomy", with the state presenting itself as a victim and would-be arbiter between the paramilitaries and the guerrillas. Though the paramilitaries had their own leadership, composed of self-interested power seekers with their own motivations and ambitions, and a semi-autonomous command structure, they were nonetheless a strategy of the Colombian state, its army and the traditional economic élites.

Yet the paramilitaries were more than a strategic military tool of the army; they were also closely allied with and financed by a range of Colombia's economic élites. Paramilitaries directly implemented or facilitated their strategies and were deeply enmeshed in the drug industry. They collaborated on local and regional levels with large ranchers and kingpins of the mining industry as well as nationally with financiers and speculators. The business élite, facing rapid developments arising from globalization and international competition, were under increasing pressure to promote international investment and resource extraction, which increased the urgency of the paramilitary strategy in many areas.

These military demands and economic opportunities produced a paramilitary strategy with complex regional nuances. One analysis of their direct conflicts with guerrillas in many regions explained paramilitary activity as the need to control territory to corner more of the drug market. Elsewhere, they displaced communities in the name of clearing out support for guerrillas, but then facilitated the annexation of that land by allied ranchers. Or, again with an ideological defence, they destroyed unions that bothered local industrialists. The vigour with which they sought to eliminate the guerrilla presence in a given area was closely tied to the extent to which that guerrilla group had been extorting funds from their business allies or to the perceived profitability of the territory.

The civilian impact was generally worse in territory where paramilitaries disputed guerrilla control or supported a major push for economic exploitation. The paramilitaries used scorched earth tactics (massacres, assassinations, destruction of crops and houses, mass displacement, etc.), as well as more subtle tactics of bribery and co-optation. The FARC also participated in increased abuses against civilians. Both the FARC and ELN had long been willing to kidnap for profit and to kill suspected civilian collaborators with the enemy, but in earlier periods most of these abuses of civilians targeted only ranchers and other élites. In the period in question, the FARC often killed poor *campesinos* for collaborating with the enemy or to pressure a population.

Response of the international human rights and humanitarian community

From 1999 to 2003, Colombia hosted significant representation of the international community. European and North American countries fielded diplomatic missions to further their economic interests, in particular oil, minerals and biodiversity, as well as geo-strategic concerns resulting in large part from Colombia's proximity to the Amazon and Venezuela (the most oil-wealthy country in the hemisphere and the United States' largest hemispheric provider). The United States increased its military aid to the Colombian Armed Forces for coca eradication and interdiction as well as humanitarian aid through the United States Agency for International Development, much of both being part of the "Plan Colombia" initiative.

Whether because the Colombian government's propaganda apparatus met with great success in instilling doubt in the international community with respect to the nature of the paramilitaries or because North American and European business interests in the country outweighed their human rights agenda, the potential for political pressure in favour of human rights protection was largely neutralized. US pressure on President Andrés Pastrana to terminate peace talks with FARC guerrillas in favour of a military offensive (with large amounts of US aid and now trained and fortified armed forces) constituted one of the key factors leading to the breakdown of talks in February 2002. Colombia's President Uribe (elected in 2002) escalated the offensive and the militarization of the countryside with ample political support from both the United States and Europe – as well as from the majority of the voting middle-class population of Colombia.

The dramatic humanitarian crises caused by the irregular war on civilians, as well as the strategic importance of the country, facilitated the arrival of primarily European humanitarian agencies. The United Nations assigned a special delegate to Colombia, participated in the peace process with the FARC and fielded missions from the United Nations High Commissioner for Refugees (UNHCR) and High Commissioner for Human Rights (UNHCHR) as well as from other UN bodies. The European Commission's Humanitarian Aid department (ECHO) funded a number of initiatives, and other organizations funded projects or Colombian NGOs and/or fielded personnel in Colombia. By 2003, a number of international accompaniment groups had established small projects in particular areas of the country. UNHCHR, UNHCR, major European agencies (ECHO), the International Committee of the Red Cross (ICRC), foreign and international humanitarian organizations and, in some cases, Colombian NGO and church groups formed coordination groups, organized by topic or region to address particular aspects of the dynamic and to coordinate, and sometimes to pool, resources and diplomatic efforts. It was in this context that PBI operated its project of political protection for threatened human rights and community leaders.

Enter the PBI Colombia Project

The PBI Colombia Project, founded in 1994 at the behest of Colombian human rights leaders, consisted of a small group of foreign human rights observers split between Bogotá and the north-west regional city of Barrancabermeja. Between 1999 and 2003, the project expanded to a team of 40 field volunteers from 13 countries, making it the second-largest international humanitarian presence in the country (after the ICRC). By 2002, four teams in distinct regions of the country were accompanying at least 15 organizations and communities. The Bogotá team accompanied the leadership of seven primarily national organizations at their central offices and during their journeys to work and travelled with them in various regions of the country. These organizations included a lawyers' collective investigating cases of military impunity, organizations of victims, and groups supporting the work of local communities all over the country. In Barrancabermeja, a small regional city of 350,000, a team accompanied three organizations persecuted by the ongoing takeover of the area by right-wing paramilitary forces in both the city itself and the surrounding rural area. The Urabá team, based in a small coastal town, split its resources between two rural communities that had resettled in their original territories after forcible displacement by the military and its agents. By rotating its volunteers, PBI maintained a permanent presence in these outlying rural communities and accompanied the local NGOs that supported them, particularly on their trips by river and road. The Medellín team, based in the regional capital of the powerful Antioquia province, accompanied four leading regional human rights groups, including lawyers and political prisoners' rights leaders, both in the city and on their trips to the surrounding rural areas.

The PBI mandate and model: What does "accompaniment" mean?

"International protective accompaniment" is the physical accompaniment by international personnel of activists, organizations or communities who are threatened with politically motivated attacks. Accompaniment can take many forms. Some threatened activists receive 24-hour-a-day accompaniment. For others the presence is more sporadic. Sometimes team members spend all day at the premises of an office of a threatened organization. Sometimes they live in threatened rural villages in conflict zones. This accompaniment service has three simultaneous and mutually reinforcing impacts. First, the international presence protects threatened activists by raising the stakes of any attacks against them. Secondly, it encourages civil society activism by allowing threatened organizations more space and confidence to operate and by building links of solidarity with the international community. And, thirdly, it strengthens the international movement for peace and human rights by giving accompaniment volunteers a powerful first-hand experience, which becomes a sustained source of inspiration to themselves and others upon their return to their home country.

PBI adhered strictly to its interpretation of the principles of non-intervention and non-partisanship. It sought to promote respect for human rights and international humanitarian law, particularly the state's responsibility to fulfil its international obligations and protect the civilian population. It did this by appealing to the legitimate authorities for the guarantee of these rights. The organization's mission was to protect NGOs' security and the legitimacy of their role as human rights workers (not necessarily their particular tactics, political positions or analysis, but certainly their right to have and express them). PBI upheld the legitimacy of international presence for these ends, without seeking to replace the state in its primary obligation to guarantee the rights of its populace. The organization took a non-partisan view with regard to the armed actors in the conflict (legal and illegal), but stood firmly for the rights to protection under the law of the victims and the organizations that supported them.

PBI pioneered the use of a model to protect threatened human rights workers, organizations and communities against politically motivated attack. PBI's Colombia Project built on previous PBI experiences in Central America and Sri Lanka. The model is based on the premise that internationals can prevent attacks against human rights workers by positioning themselves as potential witnesses at their side. Yet successful prevention depends on the organization's capacity to alert the international community and generate a response. Thus, PBI's model of diplomacy depends on the simultaneous physical presence of its volunteers in many parts of Colombia and the world. In turn, this presence in the field depends on the use of diplomacy; the two activities are interdependent.

Methods of operation in Colombia

PBI's diplomatic activity ensured that each party was aware of PBI's communication with the other parties and the network served as a web of accountability. It kept the political costs visible to all. The necessary ingredients to prevent attack were thus: (1) the physical presence of a visible international witness with a threatened activist, (2) the witness's ability to communicate with a network of international allies, (3) allies with the will and ability to respond when notified, (4) a potential aggressor aware of points (1)–(3) and calculating the possible costs of action.

To identify themselves, PBI Colombia volunteers wore uniforms, travelled in clearly marked vehicles when in rural areas, visited only those zones where the organization had made contact with local authorities, and notified these authorities of their visits. They depended on constant email and phone communication, including cellular and satellite phones for trips and rural visits, with scheduled regular times for establishing contact.

The next step in increasing the safety of the accompanied human rights workers and communities was the communication of consistent and accurate information to targeted recipients. PBI published a number of reports on the Colombian situation, either based on information already made public by NGOs, the press and other international organizations or directly witnessed by members of PBI. The effect depended on the perceived reliability and legitimacy of the information published; by avoiding the role of source for political or legal accusations, PBI facilitated its reception as a non-partisan organization and promoted its legitimacy and, by extension, its clients' safety. PBI maintained regular dialogue with hundreds of contacts in the Colombian civilian government, the military hierarchy, local commanders, embassies, foreign governments, ministers and elected officials, UN offices and delegates, international funding agencies, humanitarian organizations and grassroots groups in countries all over the world. PBI used already scheduled meetings, coordination meetings, conferences, its regular publications, phone calls and diplomatic events all over Colombia and the world to carry out this ongoing communication and to keep diplomatic channels open. Having a team of 10–14 people in Bogotá, 8–10 in each regional team and another 8 or so distributed between London, Brussels, Ottawa, Madrid and Washington made this communication possible. Thus, the two most important aspects of PBI's communication strategy were that it derived from intimate simultaneous access to local and distant information and that the discourse was simple. PBI's message was basic: it reflected its mission and members said virtually the same thing everywhere.

Yet the physical presence of internationals and the provision of timely information to a network of recipients were systematically useful in protecting human rights workers only insofar as they could convince potential aggressors that costs would result from their aggressions. PBI understood costs as the possibility of political scandal, which could jeopardize funding sources, investment viability and political collaboration and threaten international legal action. One of the main functions of the publications and communication was to create and mobilize a virtual network of co-observation; each party knowing it was (or could be) monitored by the others and be observed observing. This phenomenon raised the costs of possible violation of human rights and even, to a certain extent, of the crime of omission or complicity.

PBI also requested contacts to apply pressure on each other in particular ways. PBI's action channelled and mobilized the communication between these actors as well and then – with its unique advantage of having so many people on the ground in various regions of Colombia and internationally, at the same time and in coordination – monitored and reported on the results. PBI ensured that the channels of diplomacy and information were always open, that a paper trail was always being laid, and that different actors knew PBI was in contact with their superiors and political competitors; this, more than the particular issues, was the key to how its model worked.

Operational issues

PBI's diplomatic methodology makes use of indirect negotiation. The Colombia Project participants saw themselves as observers who by their very presence promoted the safety of the population and embodied international concern for the respect of human rights principles. In short, although PBI was not literally negotiating, it was certainly communicating. PBI communicated in an indirect manner through third parties and directly through the presence of internationals, both of which communicated the issues at hand and the broader objectives (the safety of those accompanied). Via third parties, PBI made clear the potential costs of non-compliance. The project then dedicated considerable resources to analysing to what extent the authorities and allies felt pressured or swayed by its efforts. Insofar as PBI effectively developed and made use of a network of allies, its "messages" were heeded and responded to.

PBI had a number of issues it addressed through diplomatic activity. The first of these was the safety of the population, with a focus on those human rights groups and internally displaced populations whom PBI accompanied directly. The primary interlocutor for PBI was the Colombian state, the body responsible by virtue of its international human rights agreements and its own constitution for the safety of the population. Yet, given the complex context of political violence, PBI developed different sorts of diplomatic strategies towards the illegal armed groups.

Diplomatic objectives

PBI's principal objectives addressed by its diplomatic activity were to ensure the safety of the population, particularly but not exclusively those organizations and groups with which it had an explicit commitment to direct accompaniment, to promote the legitimacy of its work and to further the respect for human rights agreements (of which Colombia had signed many). To complete these overarching objectives, PBI's medium-term diplomatic goals included: the safety and access of its own personnel to various parts of the country, the respect for and legitimacy of the organization itself in the eyes of the different actors, and raising the visibility of particular situations. In the short term, PBI often acted in favour of the release of someone, for particular actions to be taken in response to threats for the protection of particular individuals and organizations, to press for an investigation, and so on.

PBI analysed the different actors' mandates, motivations and capacities in order to assign differing objectives, expectations, types of relationships and forms of interaction to these actors. PBI hoped to contribute to the formation of an interlocking web of preventative political pressure. PBI harnesses the various actors' concern to maintain their reputation as a major operating principle. The actors, their motivations and the PBI objectives are displayed in Table 15.1.

Table 15.1 Actors, motivations and PBI objectives

Actor with which PBI meets	Possible motivations	PBI's general objectives
Colombian government and current presidential administration	Avoid international scandal, guarantee international aid arrangements, provide strong business climate.	Take concrete steps for NGOs' security, publicly support and legitimize their work, facilitate access to influential contacts and decision makers. Refrain from policies and orders that violate rights of or endanger NGOs.
Colombian military hierarchy	Defeat the enemy. Increase standing and reputation of the military as effective and respectable within the country and internationally. Procure more funding.	Send orders to commanders in the field to respect human rights and comply with PBI's requests for access.
Local military commanders	Advance own career by completing military hierarchy's goals. Keep nose sufficiently clean.	Refrain from violations of human rights.
Foreign embassies	Advance government's economic interests, obtain information about political and economic situation.	Pressure Colombian government to protect the human rights of its citizens. Express support for NGOs and PBI.
Foreign parliamentarians, elected representatives	Appeal to constituency, weaken political opponents.	Same as embassies plus pressure embassies (and own government) to take a stand. Take on Colombia (or PBI or NGOs) as own cause.
Intergovernmental/United Nations	That international humanitarian law and agreements be respected. That its missions be allowed to continue, be funded, be protected.	Pressure or influence Colombian and other governments to fulfil international obligations. Actively support NGOs.
International non-governmental organizations	Complete projects, protect personnel and client organizations.	Actively promote NGOs' safety and support their work. Join PBI in facilitating their safety.
Base groups, member organizations, churches, affinity groups (outside of Colombia)	Protect environment, foster human rights, promote non-violence, develop international solidarity.	Take a stand for human rights and protection in own countries and Colombia. Develop further networks of personalized support. Strengthen direct connections with NGOs.
Press	Break the story.	Reflect an accurate picture of Colombia's situation, highlighting the pressure on NGOs.

The primary interlocutor: The Colombian state

Colombian politics did not allow for symmetry of diplomatic communication, owing to the fact that one party – the state – controlled PBI's legal ability to sustain a presence in the country and also prohibited communication with the guerrillas. The Bogotá team, however, was responsible for the bulk of communication with state authorities, including the top of the military hierarchy, and the majority of representatives of the diplomatic corps, the United Nations and international NGOs with personnel in the country. The regional teams maintained ongoing communication with local state authorities, regional military commanders and UN field offices.

Non-diplomacy with right-wing paramilitary groups

The central paradox to PBI Colombia's diplomacy was that it hoped to prevent attacks from paramilitary groups without explicitly seeking communication with them. Purposefully engaging in dialogue with paramilitary structures was prohibited by law in Colombia and considered politically dangerous and unnecessary by PBI Colombia. Dialogue was therefore avoided, although PBI personnel nevertheless encountered paramilitary agents regularly. In Table 15.1, paramilitary groups are therefore absent.

Paramilitary and military collusion and the ability of the state, the élite and the military to curb, control or, conversely, permit and even organize paramilitary actions were the central dynamics that both required the PBI presence and allowed the functioning of diplomatic activity without direct diplomacy. The relative success of PBI in preventing paramilitary attacks against human rights workers by right-wing paramilitary groups, such as the AUC and other less formal death squad conglomerations, provides suggestive evidence of the already well-documented collaboration between state and paramilitary organizations.

Just as the Colombian state was not monolithic, neither were the armed forces or the military/paramilitary organizations. Paramilitary organizations often possessed independent leaderships who sometimes engaged in armed conflict or power struggles with other groups and factions within the armed forces. PBI therefore needed to analyse these interrelationships. PBI also provided public evidence that there was indeed collaboration between death squads, paramilitaries or other private groups and the state itself. A concern of PBI was that if, despite often overwhelming evidence to the contrary, the state could assert that it had no connection to criminal acts, its agents could act with relative impunity.

Another factor was that, after the detention of former Chilean leader

Pinochet, AUC leader Carlos Castaño, a well-known public figure, became afraid of being captured and tried for violations of international humanitarian law. The result was that the AUC, a group created for the explicit purpose of doing the dirty work for the military, became concerned about its international image. On the surface, PBI's task of dissuading the AUC from attacking human rights workers seemed easier to carry out. However, collaboration with the AUC now became less effective because other, shadowy groups took over the dirty work and, as a consequence, the military and the AUC could deny responsibility.

Implicit deterrence with guerrilla groups

The great majority of human rights violations, particularly those committed against human rights workers, were the work of paramilitary groups. The guerrillas, however, also used repressive tactics against their political enemies and competitors. Their kidnapping of middle-class and wealthy Colombians for political and financial reasons is well known, but they also persecuted and assassinated peasants whom they regarded as civilian paramilitary or military collaborators. The communities that PBI accompanied in the Urabá region were victim to such pressures and, on occasion, attacks. Guerrilla groups also harassed and even killed members of international relief and humanitarian organizations. This was presumably when they perceived humanitarian organizations as a threat to their interests or contesting their hegemony and political influence, or humanitarian initiatives as serving the interests of foreign governments or the Colombian state or being manipulated by their political enemies.

PBI did not employ a proactive diplomatic strategy of direct communication with the FARC or ELN. Nevertheless, by accident and with the intent of the guerrillas, their fighters crossed paths with PBI volunteers. In these cases, PBI used a basic discourse about its role as an international human rights organization. Similarly, web and text editors made sure public information was consistent, and volunteers travelled in marked cars and wore uniforms so as not to surprise anyone. As usual, training for field volunteers placed emphasis on a strong understanding of PBI's role and limits and the ability to state them clearly.

Yet, although PBI did not explicitly pressure the guerrilla groups, it would be a mistake to think that its presence had no dissuasive effect on their behaviour. The typical foot soldier might not have had a strategic analysis about different international actors, but the hierarchy of the guerrilla organizations certainly had some concern about international opinion. Perhaps not much, according to some analyses, and certainly of a different kind from the state and the paramilitaries, but they were not indifferent to their image.

Obstacles and opportunities

Peace Brigades International's Colombia Project exists *because* of the country's human rights situation and political violence and the danger they create for PBI's clients – not in spite of them. Thus PBI regards the many instances of threat, attack or slander against these organizations not as obstacles but rather as the central reason for the presence of PBI in Colombia. In fact, obstacles can also represent opportunities. This section examines obstacles and opportunities by focusing on two emergency situations whose resolution depended on years of previous diplomatic work.

PBI prepares the teams for emergencies that are bound to arise and helps prevent them actually coming to pass. Emergency situations have sometimes resulted from PBI's errors in implementing its own model, such as failing to establish one of the vital links in the chain of communication. The system most often "failed", however, when aggressors were willing to assume the costs of attacks. At the same time, emergencies presented PBI with the possibility of mobilizing networks and sometimes had the effect of demonstrating PBI capacity and international support. On occasion, this show of strength increased PBI's political operating "space".

Emergencies differ from the ongoing maintenance and use of the network, in that they necessitate a particular series of rapid and finite decisions and actions, which are determined in the moment but nevertheless obey the same logic of analysis and mobilization of already existing relationships. There are three stages of emergencies: (a) a threat exists but nothing has happened yet; (b) an aggression has been committed but action can still prevent the situation from worsening, such as a disappearance or an armed incursion that is still going on; (c) an attack or assassination has occurred already.

Between 1999 and 2003, the PBI team lived and worked in a state described by situation (a). Many NGOs and communities they accompanied received constant serious threats. The team responded to this type of emergency on an ongoing basis. There were a number of weekends in 2000–2002, for instance, when signs pointed to possible paramilitary incursions in the rural communities. (The fact that threatened and actual attacks tended to occur on weekends when diplomatic contacts were harder to reach seems testament to the model's impact.) PBI notified a number of close contacts of its concerns and made sure it had a way to reach them over the weekend. PBI ensured that experienced members of the team were on call, as well as those outside Colombia.

If and when an act of aggression occurred, which happened sometimes without any clear warning, the entire network responded, based on previously determined procedures. The team at the site of the emergency, frequently one of the rural communities in Urabá, began by calling Bogotá and London and providing information. A short, factual message was usually easily crafted. All teams kept written records of who had spoken to whom at what time, what information was exchanged, and who required a follow-up call. Teams carried out exhaustive follow-up with contacts and recorded explanations, answers received and pledges of action. Often five languages were being spoken simultaneously in the Bogotá office as various volunteers called embassies, UN field offices and other humanitarian agencies on different cell phones and land-lines. Usually the request was simple: call contacts one–three, who usually comprised a local military official, a member of the national military command and a civilian official, and tell them to put a stop to activities. The local PBI team usually contacted local military commanders directly and the team in the capital contacted senior military personnel. Prior face-to-face contact between all of these targeted officials facilitated access.

When more time was available to verify information, the procedure was to analyse the situation, define objectives, determine messages and choose the most useful contacts to notify. One such example was the disappearance of a member of the Colombian human rights organization Justice and Peace on 11 November 1999 from a stretch of rural highway hotly contested by military and paramilitary groups and the FARC guerrillas. On the evening of the disappearance, community leaders notified Justice and Peace's head office in Bogotá by phone, which in turn notified PBI. PBI and Justice and Peace immediately began notifying allies and close contacts around the world, and Justice and Peace began seeking more information from its missionaries on the ground. A local radio station had broadcast that the missing woman had been detained and the reporter identified as his source the local army brigade. The brigade denied any knowledge of the events. That night Justice and Peace put together preliminary information, and the next morning PBI volunteers left with members of Justice and Peace for the site of the disappearance.

Witnesses told Justice and Peace that a truck with a woman in detention had passed through military checkpoints. Other PBI volunteers in the capital scheduled emergency meetings with embassies and cited the conflicting reports and possible military involvement. Later that afternoon, paramilitary commanders verified that they had her in their custody and would release her. They did so and she continued working in Colombia. The woman's release illustrates the possibility of success facilitated by PBI's ability concurrently to accompany and collaborate with local activists in outlying rural areas, visit multiple embassies in the capital, keep in touch with international human rights contacts and keep close logistical and diplomatic tabs on the local military.

In another case, PBI used an apparent emergency to its advantage. In 2001, as paramilitaries consolidated their control of the city of Barranca-bermeja, a paramilitary fighter confiscated a Swedish PBI volunteer's cell phone and passport, and told him in front of dozens of witnesses that he was a "military objective". PBI was able to mobilize international pressure and press coverage, not only about this event but also about the overall situation of assassinations and persecution of civilians by paramilitary groups right under the nose of the Colombian military. The next day, in an interview printed in the regional newspaper, the local paramilitary leader denied that it had been his soldier who threatened the international volunteer, which PBI took to mean that the threat in fact had been recanted. Nevertheless, as a precaution, PBI sent the volunteer in question to the capital for a few days, met with a number of embassies, and temporarily doubled the number of its volunteers in Barrancabermeja.

The mobilization of international attention drew attention to the human rights abuses in Barranca and the threats against local human rights groups struggling to protect the civilians of the city from assassination and forced displacement. Without the physical presence of an international staff member to "provoke" such an incident, PBI's diplomacy would have lacked a "hook" with which to generate attention. PBI demonstrated its international support and emerged strengthened from the emergency.

Negotiations

The ultimate "achievement" – for which PBI could never take more than a tiny fraction of the credit – would be to remove the necessity of a PBI presence in Colombia. In practice, PBI defined its achievements as small victories in assisting human rights organizations. PBI's diplomatic efforts and those of its allies did not transform the situation of human rights violations in Colombia but did represent some clear if limited successes, both in the short term and over the long term.[3] PBI failures sometimes derived from errors in implementing the PBI model of diplomacy, although the vast majority could be ascribed to the inadequacy of the model in the face of powerful actors.

Achievements

PBI's achievements were: to mitigate the effect of violent attacks and harassment on human rights organizations and activists; to facilitate and strengthen international information-sharing networks and thus knowledge about the human rights situation; and to help legitimize the human rights struggle. Successful strategies included: strengthening the viability of PBI as a tool in the protection of human rights defenders; gaining access to vulnerable regions; the complete prevention of attacks against PBI personnel; and supporting specialized support networks for particular initiatives. PBI did not succeed in protecting the lives of all the individuals it accompanied, particularly the thousands of internationally displaced persons involved in community protection campaigns. PBI was not helped by the fact that harassment and slanderous campaigns against human rights workers and organizations were common.

The continued survival of the rural internally displaced and resettled community of Cacarica, Chocó, provides an example of how intensive, multi-layered diplomatic work helped to prevent and diminish attacks and thus maintain the very existence of the settlement. The community organization, CAVIDA, was supported by a Mixed Verification Commission of government agencies and national and international NGOs (including PBI, which sat on the commission as an observer), which were mandated to verify government fulfilment of its agreements to provide protection, education, housing and health care. The commission met regularly from 1998. Diplomatic efforts by the commission in relation to its own military could not prevent paramilitary attacks on the community nor did it facilitate the implementation of the aid agreements. Yet the existence of the commission and its tightly knit web of diplomatic exchanges (a microcosm of the diplomacy I have described in this chapter) served as a deterrent. The Colombian government touted the Mixed Commission as a pilot project and as providing an example of the successful resettlement of IDPs.

When PBI and/or other NGOs received information indicating that paramilitaries seemed to be planning an attack, PBI and other NGOs contacted the civilian government authorities, which in turn notified the army. The army as a rule did not act to prevent the entry of paramilitaries into the community's territory. However, the NGOs considered that, because so many international organizations were observing the actions of both the civilian government and the military, the army did restrict somewhat the activity of the paramilitaries and attempted to protect its own image. PBI's presence in this commission alongside UN bodies and prestigious funding organizations strengthened PBI's own viability and thus the safety of its volunteers in the jungle. Conversely, the presence of PBI and the other international organizations validated the importance of the community's struggle to protect the rights of its inhabitants.

Failures

Failures were of three kinds: errors in implementing the model; the inadequacy of the model itself; and successful use of the model having opposite effects to those anticipated.

Sometimes, PBI failed to implement its own model of ensuring the connections between every "link in the chain" of communication. In December 2001, for example, PBI accompanied a high-profile human rights activist to an area in military dispute without verifying that the local authorities knew it was involved. A paramilitary incursion occurred in the town and, because it was not clear whether the paramilitaries or the local police commander knew who the PBI volunteers were, the client organization suggested that its and PBI's personnel leave the area without identifying themselves to the authorities. PBI was left in an insecure position in the middle of an armed action, hardly a moment to start scheduling meetings with the local police chief. The Colombian activist and PBI volunteers emerged unharmed, but the incident reinforced PBI's resolve to insist on verifying that faxes are sent, received, read and passed on by local commanders.

More frequently, the model itself was inadequate to a situation created by powerful political interests. In this case PBI may fail to protect the lives of human rights workers because aggressors are intent on carrying out their crimes. In Medellín in November 2001, for instance, two members of the Family Members of the Detained and Disappeared (ASFADDES) were "disappeared" after leaving their accompanying PBI volunteers. PBI mobilized a massive and rapid response but the two were never found. In the ensuing investigation, the authorities discovered that their own special unit on kidnapping, the GAULA, a joint venture of intelligence, police and military forces, had intercepted the phone lines of ASFADDES and other human rights organizations in Medellín. The obvious connection with the disappearance of the two activists created enough of a scandal to produce the dismissal of one member of the armed forces and transfer to the Colombian embassy in Chile for another. Although no one was ever prosecuted, the Medellín PBI team reported something of a honeymoon after the incident in the treatment it received from local armed forces. PBI analysis was that the impetus to attack the ASFADDES was so high, and its perceived strength so low, that the aggressors decided to assume the possible costs. The aggressors may have later perceived that they had miscalculated, but not until after the two activists were lost.

The issue that is more difficult to resolve is that successful implementation can have unforeseen side-effects and costs. PBI maintains that the safety of its volunteers in the field depends on the division of labour between accompaniment (with diplomacy) and direct denunciation and confrontation. PBI has discussed a future scenario in which staying in Colombia could imply complicity with violations of human rights – in this context PBI would leave and aim to create as much of an international scandal as it could. In the meantime, careful ongoing internal documentation of its work would allow for such future exposure if necessary.

One cost of the successful use of the PBI model is co-option by human rights violators as proof of their humanitarian behaviour – while they nevertheless continue to attack communities and activists. For instance, the Colombian administration used the "successful" initiative of the protection of the Cacarica community by international organizations as a "pilot project" to demonstrate their commitment to human rights. In addition, paramilitaries seized the opportunity to make use of the initiative's international reputation to showcase their even-handedness and good behaviour.

In 2001, during a high-profile, well-publicized visit by UNHCR, hundreds of paramilitary fighters occupied the area, arguing that they had given up their previous tactics and were now trying to engage in "friendly" dialogue. The population was terrified and the international officials wondered whether the benefits of their presence had outweighed the damage caused by the fact that the paramilitaries had taken the opportunity to show their strength and ostensible good intentions.

Another side-effect is that the privileged position of PBI as an international organization means that it competes for access with others, including local groups. PBI and its cautious discourse, along with that of other international organizations, can tend to frame the debate and capture resources, marginalizing other voices. By comparison, other Colombian and international initiatives may appear radical. Smaller, newer accompaniment groups have faced pressure not only from the Colombian state but from other internationals as well to "act more like PBI", and such uniformity could prevent the use of innovative tactics necessary to producing results.

Aggressors paid attention to the tactics employed by PBI and other organizations, learned from the experience and changed their own political tactics. By 2003, the military–paramilitary alliance operated more subtly than previously. Sometimes it appeared that PBI's method of response was taken into account and utilized by the aggressor. One particular paramilitary incursion in the community of San Jose de Apartadó in March 2001, for instance, was stopped when PBI alerted the Seventeenth Brigade and a group of soldiers appeared just after the paramilitary fighters had scattered. The army's swift action "saved the day" suspiciously easily and news of the "rescue" was on the desks of Colombian embassies in Europe the following day. In the short term, this was a success for PBI's protection strategy although, in the longer term, this public relations coup was used to support the Colombian army's claim that it was actively combating paramilitaries and defending human rights and therefore deserving of support and assistance.

An implicit trade-off into which PBI enters knowingly is that states that are violating human rights can use the fact of PBI's presence to indicate that they maintain a modicum of respect for human rights and international agreements. PBI's aim is to use the arrangement to the advantage of local threatened activists more than the state uses it for its own ends of continuing to use terror with negligible consequences. The danger, however, is that the balance might tip in the other direction.

Some have argued that the information in detailed reports on human rights violations prepared by a number of organizations, including PBI, prior to 2000 bolstered arguments in favour of Plan Colombia, which strengthened US influence over the Colombian armed forces and organized the fumigation of coca plants in the south of the country, the stronghold of the FARC. The legislation greatly increased the provision of US military aid, training and intelligence to the Colombian armed forces, who were responsible for the majority of violations, particularly via collaboration with paramilitary groups, with nothing more punitive than the removal of a few officers from their posts (without prosecution), some of whom began working more closely with paramilitary groups. In addition, human rights groups of all kinds reported on the devastating humanitarian consequences of the fumigation and the increased intensity of the war, which had always killed civilians at a much greater rate than combatants, not to mention the US legitimization of illegal tactics by an atrocity-committing army.

Wider implications

PBI activities in Colombia, a relatively modest operation compared with the majority of initiatives described in this book, nevertheless offer some interesting contributions to the discussion of humanitarian diplomacy. The PBI experience supports the importance of NGOs' assuming the role of humanitarian diplomats. PBI Colombia's work provides a particular recipe for successful humanitarian diplomacy as well as strategies for addressing the political and logistical questions of conducting multi-level diplomacy with various interlocutors.

NGOs will have of necessity to manage political pressures, often from many sides at once, which could endanger their mission and, more importantly, the safety of those they serve. NGOs therefore need to plan their activities. They need to engage in political preparation and analysis and establish criteria for action and a consistent discourse to all interlocutors.

The PBI recipe for successful humanitarian diplomacy, as well as strategies for managing multi-level challenges (global and local), incorporated effective political preparation as well as the logistical necessities of reliable information, communication, explicit training for humanitarian diplomats and the employment of a simple and agreed-upon discourse used at every level.

PBI presents a model in which humanitarian diplomats do not engage in direct negotiation but indirectly negotiate through third-party interlocutors. The idea is to publicize the PBI mandate and criteria for action to all parties. The physical presence of its international personnel embodies international attention to human rights abuses. PBI's range of negotiation is defined by its narrow role, which has given clarity and functioned as a strength rather than a deficiency. PBI's experience shows that a focus on political communication and the development of clear discourses and a network of allies can achieve successes even without direct negotiation with states or direct communication with other armed actors.

PBI is most effective when working in coordination with other initiatives and with organizations with other mandates and strategies. For example, PBI Colombia chose not to combine public denunciation with its role of physical accompaniment, considering that, in the particular Colombian context of the moment, denunciation might endanger the safety of its on-the-ground volunteers. Yet PBI Colombia sought at all times to facilitate the denunciation of violations by other organizations. The PBI perspective was that such denunciations furthered a common approach – of increasing political pressure on human rights violators in order to protect the population. Meanwhile, PBI's ability to maintain an international team in very dangerous areas allowed greater access to information for those organizations that could publicly denounce the violators.

PBI's model of diplomacy keeps people alive and organizations intact. It plays a key role in maintaining the existence of local structures for social change and human rights protection. The groups PBI accompanied assessed they would be worse off (exiled, weakened, dead or disbanded) without the PBI presence and protection.

In many conflict zones, players such as PBI, which operate with a primary protection mandate, are not present and instead international humanitarian non-governmental actors and church workers routinely find themselves forced into a "protection" role. This role can be accepted or avoided, depending on institutional and personal choices. The PBI experience may therefore be laying the groundwork for helping all kinds of field enterprises to find disciplined and modest ways to accept their ancillary duty of protection. Perhaps the PBI approach could contribute to creating discourses that will allow them to merge protection with their other missions.[4]

Although the so-called international "war on terrorism" has shrunk the operating space for human rights and humanitarian actors, the fear of the consequences of assuming the "protection" mandate – fear that protection is "too political" a role, will risk expulsion of the organization, or get in the way of the primary mission – may in some cases be exaggerated (and certainly cannot be of as much concern as the well-being of those served). We can seek creative ways to minimize risks while still integrating a protection discourse into humanitarian diplomacy on all levels. Long-term, sustainable changes in humanitarian and human rights conditions require tactics consistent with that end.

Notes

The concentration on the period specified in this chapter is a reflection of my own experience. It does not mean to imply that human rights abuses do not remain of grave concern in Colombia. PBI remains active in Colombia.

1. Liam Mahony, "Colombia's Political Background", unpublished draft, 2003. Mahony's research was based on the following reports by Human Rights Watch (Americas): *Colombia's Killer Networks: The Military–Paramilitary Partnership and the United States*, New York: Human Rights Watch, 1996; *The Ties that Bind: Colombia and the Military–Paramilitary Links*, New York: Human Rights Watch, February 2000; and *The "Sixth Division": Military–Paramilitary Ties and U.S. Policy in Colombia*, New York: Human Rights Watch, September 2001).
2. See Colombia Human Rights Network, ⟨http://colhrnet.igc.org/timeline.htm⟩.
3. Juan Ibañez, Lizzie Brock and Christiane Schwartz, "Evaluación de las Acciones Urgentes como Mecanismo para Frenar Violaciones a los Derechos Humanos", unpublished, Bogotá, 2003.
4. Enrique Eguren, "The Protection Gap: Policies and Strategies", *Humanitarian Practice Network*, 30 October 2000.

16

The Balkans: The limits of humanitarian action

Nicholas Morris

The humanitarian operation in the former Yugoslavia between 1991 and 1995 was one of the largest and most difficult in the history of the United Nations. The Office of the United Nations High Commissioner for Refugees (UNHCR) was the lead agency. UNHCR has considerable experience in negotiating with governments and other parties. This involves sensitive issues: refugees are non-nationals whose presence may be resented and a significant national burden and can affect bilateral relations. UNHCR's counterparts are as likely to be in or linked to ministries of interior and the state security apparatus as to ministries of foreign affairs. The conflicts in the Balkans and the breakup of the former Yugoslavia posed challenges outside the organization's experience.[1]

This chapter examines how these challenges were met.[2] It assesses the extent to which UNHCR was able to influence outcomes in wide-ranging negotiations. The humanitarian action had a high local and international profile and increasingly became a factor in the response of the international community. The level of both the involvement of UNHCR in diplomatic forums and the political and material support for UNHCR was unprecedented. In this sense, the operation involved humanitarian diplomacy writ large. Yet, as I shall show, the ability of UNHCR to influence events and ensure respect of humanitarian principles was limited.

The next section provides a brief description of the context: the course of the conflicts during the breakup of the former Yugoslavia;[3] their human cost; the organization of the humanitarian response; and the many actors involved. This is followed by reviews of the aim of the humanitarian operation, of the factors influencing its achievement, and of some actual negotiations. The reviews show why there was opposition to the humanitarian operation, and why it could not be overcome. After an assessment of the achievements during the conflict and a brief description of what happened next, lessons are drawn. The chapter illustrates why humanitarian action, however well supported, cannot substitute for political action to end a conflict. It concludes that, absent such action, a humanitarian operation is itself likely to face increasingly grave problems.

Context

The wars

The humanitarian operation took place in a complex political context, although it was clear at the time what made it necessary. Ruthless leaders went to war in the name of one ethnic group in order to extend or consolidate their power and control over areas with a significant and often majority pre-war population that was not of their group. The principal means to this end was forced population displacement – ethnic cleansing.

Conflict began in late June 1991, when the Federal Yugoslav Army (JNA) moved into Croatia and Slovenia immediately after they had declared independence. The war in Croatia lasted until January 1992 and left JNA-backed Croatian Serbs in control of three areas with a significant pre-war population of ethnic Serbs, later designated UN Protected Areas. The European Community (EC)[4] recognized the independence of Croatia and Slovenia on 15 January 1992.

A referendum on independence was held in Bosnia and Herzegovina (hereafter Bosnia) at the end of February 1992, against a background of rising violence from those opposed to independence: most ethnic Serbs boycotted the vote. Of a turnout of 63 per cent, 93 per cent voted for independence. The European Community recognized Bosnia on 6 April 1992. Violence intensified, spreading to Sarajevo. Many of the non-Serb inhabitants were driven from eastern Bosnia by local Serbs with support from Serbian paramilitaries and the JNA. Ethnic cleansing and conflict extended throughout Bosnia, and the JNA-equipped Bosnian Serb Army (BSA) besieged Sarajevo. In the spring of 1993, fighting began in central and western Bosnia between the Bosnian Croats, supported by the new Croatian army, and Bosnian government forces. This was formally ended by an agreement signed in Washington on 18 March 1994.

There were few major changes to the confrontation lines until early May 1995, when the Croatian army expelled local Serb forces from Western Slavonia. The enclave of Srebrenica fell to the BSA on 11 July. In

Time line of key events

27 June 1991	JNA forces move into Croatia and Slovenia
7 July 1991	War in Slovenia ends; conflict in Croatia continues to spread and intensify
14 November 1991	UN Secretary-General requests UNHCR to take the lead in coordinating humanitarian assistance
3 December 1991	UNHCR issues first appeal for funds, covering also UNICEF and WHO
11 December 1991	UN Secretary-General announces UNHCR's lead role (S/23280)
2 January 1992	Cease-fire in Croatia agreed
21 February 1992	Security Council Resolution 743 authorizes deployment of UNPROFOR in Croatia
20 March 1992	First large-scale forced displacement in northern Bosnia
11 April 1992	First distribution of UN relief food in Bosnia; conflict and ethnic cleansing becoming widespread
30 April 1992	UNHCR appeals to foreign ministers of 27 countries for funds to meet humanitarian needs
29 June 1992	Security Council Resolution 761 authorizes additional UNPROFOR elements to ensure security and functioning of Sarajevo airport; humanitarian airlift begins
29 July 1992	UNHCR convenes ministerial-level meeting in Geneva
26–27 August 1992	International Conference on the Former Yugoslavia in London
14 September 1992	Security Council Resolution 776 authorizes enlargement of UNPROFOR's mandate and strength in order to facilitate the delivery of humanitarian assistance in Bosnia
February 1993	Conflict breaks out between Bosnian Croat and government forces
16 April 1993	Security Council Resolution 819 designates Srebrenica as a safe area
6 May 1993	Security Council Resolution 824 declares that Sarajevo, Tuzla, Žepa, Goražde and Bihać should also be treated as safe areas

4 June 1993	Security Council Resolution 836 further expands mandate of UNPROFOR to include protection of the safe areas
18 November 1993	Political leaders of Bosnia meet with UNHCR in Geneva and sign commitment to facilitate delivery of humanitarian assistance
March 1994	Washington agreements end conflict between Bosnian Croat and government forces
April 1994	BSA offensive on Goražde; first NATO air action against BSA positions; retaliation against UNPROFOR; humanitarian convoys and airlift temporarily suspended
23 November 1994	NATO air strikes against BSA anti-aircraft sites
24 November 1994	BSA takes several hundred UNPROFOR troops temporarily hostage; humanitarian operation also disrupted
1–2 May 1995	Croatian forces reclaim Western Slavonia
11 July 1995	BSA forces take Srebrenica enclave
4–7 August 1995	Croatian forces reclaim remainder of territory except strip along border in Eastern Slavonia
30 August 1995	NATO begins large-scale air strikes on BSA positions
12–19 September 1995	Bosnian government and Croatian forces make major advances against BSA in northwest Bosnia
12 October 1995	Military action ceases in Bosnia
1 November 1995	Negotiations begin in Dayton, USA
21 November 1995	Agreement reached
14 December 1995	General Framework Agreement for Peace in Bosnia signed in Paris

early August, the Croatian army took the remainder of Serb-occupied territory in Croatia, with the exception of a strip in Eastern Slavonia, bordering Serbia. Air strikes by the North Atlantic Treaty Organization (NATO) against Bosnian Serb targets began on 30 August. Croatian and Bosnian government forces made significant advances against the BSA. The war in Bosnia formally ended in mid-October 1995.

The cost

These conflicts cost many lives and displaced 4 million people from their homes in Croatia and Bosnia. The majority remained within their country, in areas controlled by their ethnic group. Some fled to neighbouring countries: there were nearly 200,000 refugees from Bosnia in Croatia and about 650,000 from Bosnia and Croatia in Serbia. Others found refuge elsewhere in Europe: some 600,000 by the end of the war in Bosnia. Hundreds of thousands more were unable or unwilling to flee and found themselves surrounded by hostile forces. There was massive disruption in public services, the economy and the availability of basic supplies. Over half the population of Bosnia became largely dependent on outside assistance.

The humanitarian response

In early October 1991, the Federal Yugoslav authorities requested UNHCR's assistance in responding to population displacement in Croatia. Separate requests were made by Croatia and Slovenia. The High Commissioner, Sadako Ogata, consulted UN Secretary-General Pérez de Cuéllar, who requested her to lend her good offices to bring relief to internally displaced people and to coordinate humanitarian action in the region. The High Commissioner then consulted the International Committee of the Red Cross (ICRC) and the EC Presidency. Following their assurances of support, an assessment mission was fielded with the United Nations Children's Fund (UNICEF).

The mission's preliminary conclusion was that UNHCR should not become involved in a massive relief programme but rather should provide modest assistance to displaced families outside the war zones, to complement the ICRC's activities within them. The realities of the conflict and the international community's response dictated otherwise, but UNHCR's subsequent engagement was not simply reactive. Many of the rising number of displaced persons would become refugees when the Yugoslav republics became independent states, and the High Commissioner felt that early engagement was important if UNHCR was to help meet what were clearly going to be rapidly escalating humanitarian needs and have any influence in such a highly charged situation.[5]

One of the High Commissioner's earliest decisions was to appoint a Special Envoy. In part, this was a device that allowed UNHCR to manage the operation coherently within the region by sidestepping questions of the legitimacy of the newly proclaimed republics: new offices "of the

Special Envoy" were swiftly opened in Zagreb, Sarajevo and Ljubljana (UNHCR already had an office in Belgrade). More importantly, this appointment gave the High Commissioner a direct link with the field, including with the political leaderships, and someone on the spot in whom she had confidence, authorized to take decisions on her behalf when necessary. The combination of this confidence, the qualities of the first Special Envoy and the High Commissioner's own commitment to the operation played a major part in the expansion of UNHCR's role and reinforced UNHCR's standing as a negotiator.

UNHCR's first relief consignments reached Belgrade and Zagreb in mid-December 1991. The intended number of beneficiaries was then 500,000, and UNHCR had 19 staff in the former Yugoslavia. On 30 April 1992, the High Commissioner addressed an appeal to 27 foreign ministers, and warned that up to 500,000 more people could be displaced as a result of the conflict in Bosnia. The intended number of beneficiaries was already 1 million, and UNHCR had 80 staff in the region. Two months later, the humanitarian airlift to Sarajevo began. By April 1993 the operation was planning to reach over 3.8 million people and UNHCR had 550 staff. Food needs alone were assessed at over 2,000 metric tons per day, with the majority of the beneficiaries in Bosnia and directly affected by the conflict. UNHCR had access to trucking fleets with a capacity of over 4,000 metric tons. The Sarajevo airlift became the longest-running humanitarian airlift in history. Airdrops by military aircraft delivered relief at UNHCR's request to areas to which land access was denied.

The main actors

As the scale of the needs became evident, UNICEF, the World Food Programme (WFP) and the World Health Organization (WHO) deployed staff and resources to the region, as did the International Organization for Migration. From early 1993, the United Nations High Commissioner for Human Rights had several monitors in the region. From May 1993, a Special Representative of the Secretary-General (SRSG) based in Zagreb coordinated UN activities in the former Yugoslavia. By 1994, the Food and Agriculture Organization, the United Nations Development Programme, the United Nations Educational, Scientific and Cultural Organization, the United Nations Industrial Development Organization, United Nations Volunteers and the United Nations Department of Humanitarian Assistance were also participating in the United Nations' Consolidated Appeals for the former Yugoslavia.

The United Nations Protection Force (UNPROFOR), which reached a military strength of some 30,000 in Bosnia, was mandated to support humanitarian activities, principally by providing escorts, safe routes and transport. In Bosnia and Croatia, UNPROFOR assisted with the delivery of relief items, using convoy teams dedicated to the humanitarian operation.[6]

The ICRC had a major presence throughout the former Yugoslavia; like UNHCR, its operation was its largest worldwide. Over 100 international non-governmental organizations (NGOs) were active in Bosnia and Croatia. National NGOs played an important role in the final distribution of assistance. The European Commission, through its Humanitarian Aid department (ECHO) and the European Community Task Force, implemented programmes throughout the former Yugoslavia. A number of governments provided convoy teams either directly to UNHCR or through NGOs and seconded personnel to UNHCR.

Within the region, UNHCR interacted with the combatants at all levels, from those at road blocks to the overall commanders, and with the authorities from the municipal to the highest levels, as well as with the various associations of civilians affected by the conflict. The great majority of the associations of civilians were simply representing the concerns of their community. Others also had a political agenda, which could include physically blocking the passage of aid to the other side.

UNHCR's monthly Information Notes for former Yugoslavia contained a chart of the relationships affecting the operation. In addition to those already mentioned, this showed the United Nations Security Council, NATO (at both headquarters and regional – Allied Forces South in Naples – levels), the Western European Union, the Conference on Security and Co-operation in Europe (CSCE),[7] the International Criminal Tribunal, the Special Rapporteur on Human Rights, the Co-chairmen of the Steering Committee of the International Conference on the former Yugoslavia and its working groups, the five-nation Contact Group, the European Union Administrator of Mostar, the United Nations Special Coordinator for the restoration of essential public services in and around Sarajevo, and the International Management Group (IMG) for infrastructure in Bosnia.[8]

UNHCR was in close contact with those governments outside the region most directly concerned by the conflict. These contacts, which included meetings between the High Commissioner and the leaders of key countries, allowed UNHCR to address concerns with regard to asylum seekers and refugees from the Balkans, an issue that moved up political agendas as the conflict continued, to mobilize support for the operation, and to highlight the wider issues of the humanitarian toll of the conflict and the importance of political action to bring it to an end.

Operational issues

The aim

UNHCR's negotiations had different immediate objectives but almost all could be linked to one aim. The operation sought to meet the vital needs of all civilians affected by the conflict and, where possible, to help prevent further violations of human rights. However the parties saw this aim in light of their own interests, its motivation was rarely challenged. It remained the foundation on which negotiations were based and to which short-term goals could be linked. The clarity of the aim and the belief of staff at all levels that this was a just cause – though they might differ over tactics – were important positive factors. For UNHCR's national colleagues, in offices that remained multi-ethnic throughout the war and whose role in the humanitarian operation was of critical importance, this was an aim they could share whatever their views on the conflict.

The overriding need was for security. Efforts to prevent ethnic cleansing initially focused on the large-scale displacement that was occurring as territory was overrun by the Bosnian Serbs and Bosnian Croats. These involved challenging the aggressor's local military or paramilitary commanders and officials, and attempts to find safety for those already displaced. Such actions were complemented by high-level interventions and prominent media coverage. As the front-lines stabilized, attention turned to those who had remained in now hostile territory and were at immediate risk and desperate to leave. When it became clear that ethnic cleansing was not going to be halted, the focus shifted to negotiating safe passage for at least some of those whose lives depended on it. With the exception of high-profile evacuations, including medical evacuations, these negotiations were conducted at the local level but required coordination with UNHCR colleagues on the other side of front-lines or borders. Securing the admission to Croatia of non-Croat refugees from Bosnia remained a major problem.

An immediate objective of negotiations was access for relief convoys: one early convoy from Zagreb to Sarajevo had to negotiate 90 checkpoints. As the new authorities became more organized, clearances had to be obtained for convoy plans and crossings of active front-lines.[9] Access often hinged on the nature of the relief consignment and whether it was seen as contributing to the other side's war effort. In many cases this was a pretext for obstruction; sometimes the concern was genuine. At the highest level, formal assurances were on occasions sought from the leaders of the warring parties and texts negotiated.

In addition to clearances and access, the routes on which convoys were authorized to travel had to be agreed. The Bosnian Croat and Bosnian

Serb authorities required convoys to use some indirect and unsuitable routes. Other diversions were dictated by the need to avoid active front-lines and known flash points where possible.

The Sarajevo airlift

An informal coalition of the countries that provided the military aircraft ran the airlift, seconding military personnel to the air operations cell at UNHCR headquarters. Decisions on stopping and restarting the airlift were taken by this coalition, in close consultation with UNHCR. The airlift also involved UNHCR in negotiations. Obtaining approval from the Bosnian Serbs for the onward movement of supplies from Sarajevo airport was a constant problem. The question of what was carried on the airlift and who should have the very limited number of seats gave rise to many difficulties.[10] For example, newsprint for *Oslobodjenje*, the Sarajevo daily newspaper that published throughout the siege, was occasionally given priority over relief. UNHCR's policy of taking decisions rather than seeking consensus reflected operational imperatives but was at times resented by other humanitarian organizations. In deciding priorities, UNHCR had to take into account the wishes of the countries contributing aircraft. The air operations cell could solve most problems by reference to UNHCR's policy but some needed UNHCR's intervention, such as the request from a senior delegation from one country for seats on one of "their" aircraft that were already allocated to parliamentarians from another country.

Relations with the ICRC

Humanitarian operations in war zones fall within the competence of the ICRC. In the initial stages of the conflict in Bosnia, needs far outstripped capacity and the ICRC and UNHCR developed an understanding at field level of who would try to do what and where. Both temporarily withdrew from Bosnia in late May 1992, UNHCR after the hijacking of a convoy and the ICRC after an attack on a convoy that cost the life of its head of delegation in Sarajevo. UNHCR resumed operations in mid-June and re-opened offices in Sarajevo, Mostar and Banja Luka. The ICRC's resumption was delayed and this contributed to UNHCR's further engagement.

The ICRC's responsibilities under international humanitarian law and the UNHCR's mandate for refugees were respected. The division of other responsibilities between UNHCR and the ICRC was never formalized. To an outsider there were marked differences in approach, such as UNHCR's high media profile and the distance the ICRC kept from UN-PROFOR, but there were close informal contacts. UNHCR profited from the ICRC's experience of operating in war zones. Complementary responses might be agreed to specific challenges affecting both organizations, for example on the evacuation of threatened minorities. For much of the period the organizations were headed in the field by staff who already knew each other and understood both the sensitivities of each organization and the importance of informal cooperation in the face of such a daunting task.

The role of the lead agency

Initially, it was foreseen that only displaced persons would need outside assistance. It soon became clear that the needs were much wider, and the operation then sought to assist all civilians affected by the conflict. As the United Nations' lead agency, UNHCR saw its responsibilities as analogous to those in a refugee emergency: to try to ensure that needs were met, either directly or through others. In most cases, UNHCR initiated negotiations, but UNHCR also undertook negotiations with the authorities on behalf of others, for example for clearance for relief consignments (of which the delivery of a field hospital donated to besieged East Mostar by a South African foundation was among the more challenging) or when NGO staff were detained.

UNHCR's role as lead agency was consolidated early on. Some of the highest-profile interventions within the region took place in the first months, as the Special Envoy met with the leaders in Belgrade, Zagreb and elsewhere in an effort to obtain a halt to ethnic cleansing and atrocities, some of which he witnessed. There was global media coverage of what was happening and of UNHCR's efforts. UNHCR remained the only UN presence in much of Bosnia, because UNPROFOR was unable to deploy on territory controlled by the Bosnian Serb Army.

The appointment of an SRSG did not alter UNHCR's role nor did the SRSG seek to limit UNHCR's scope for addressing contentious issues or for negotiating independently, even when so doing might not have helped other UN negotiations. With the appointment of the SRSG, the UN operation as a whole sought to present a common front. As lead agency, UNHCR was from the start well supported by UNICEF, WFP and WHO. The UNHCR Special Envoy was a member of the SRSG's core team. Any differences of approach at this level were usually quickly resolved. There were more difficulties in the field. Some NGOs rejected UNPROFOR's support and advice. Establishing a clear understanding at all levels of UNPROFOR of UNHCR's lead role took time. On occasions, UNHCR argued for initiatives that were not taken. On others, UNPROFOR staff took initiatives that UNHCR saw as ill advised. In most cases, these involved "linkages": offering or agreeing to local concessions that in effect conditioned assistance to one side on meeting the political demands of the other.[11]

Obstacles and opportunities

In these conflicts, suffering was deliberately inflicted on civilians as a means to achieve political ends. In such circumstances, humanitarian action to prevent or relieve that suffering will face opposition. This section outlines the obstacles faced, with examples of obstruction, reviews some of the favourable elements, and concludes that UNHCR's negotiating position was weaker than the level of support for the operation might suggest.

Obstacles

In the same way that the humanitarian negotiations had a clear aim, so the obstacles had a clear cause. In varying degrees, all sides saw the operation as neither neutral nor impartial but as directly helping their enemy. Until early 1994, Bosnian Croat and Serb forces surrounded Bosnian government forces in central Bosnia, as Bosnian Serb forces continued to do in Sarajevo and elsewhere throughout the war. For them, the humanitarian operation was undermining their military efforts by breaking the sieges and thereby delaying their victory. Similarly, efforts to prevent ethnic cleansing ran directly counter to the objectives of those seeking ethnically based control of territory.

The Bosnian government had its own fundamental objection, seeing the operation as an evasion by the international community of its responsibilities. Given a choice between humanitarian aid and progress towards ending aggression, it would choose the latter, even at the price of more suffering in the short term.[12] On occasions, it obstructed the delivery of aid to its own side in order to pressure the international community to change its stance and not treat aggressors and victims as equal. The government objected to being labelled as one of the parties to the conflict and under arms embargo, and resented the fact that, whereas the Security Council resolutions establishing the mandate of UNPROFOR at least identified the aggressor, the humanitarian operation did not. This deeply felt grievance complicated negotiations with the government, though, the closer the authorities were to the beneficiaries, the more likely they were to be understanding of the constraints on UNHCR.

UNHCR became increasingly concerned that the operation would be compromised by NATO action in support of UNPROFOR. Announcing its 2 August 1993 decision to draw up "options for air strikes", the North

Atlantic Council stressed the "humanitarian purpose of the military measures foreseen". The Bosnian Serbs perceived the intent of the Security Council, NATO and UNPROFOR as punitive and directed only towards them. They accused UNHCR of involvement in the use of NATO air power. Their soldiers saw little distinction between UNHCR – anyone in a white vehicle – and UNPROFOR. This increased the security risks run by the humanitarian operation, but it is hard to assess the extent to which it weakened UNHCR's negotiating position. Bosnian Serbs could block access at will, and they developed a better understanding of UNHCR's position than was evident from their public statements.

Efforts to run convoys to Goražde, the closest enclave to Sarajevo, in January 1994 illustrate the problems faced throughout the operation. Planned convoys and their loads were approved for 13 days of the month. The failure of the Bosnian Serbs to authorize the UNPROFOR escort for the last stage into the enclave caused the cancellation of convoys on five days and delayed a convoy by two days, causing the cancellation of another.[13] Twice, convoys had part of their load confiscated at a checkpoint. Inspections at a checkpoint delayed a convoy overnight. Two convoys with shelter materials were blocked. Two convoys turned back rather than accept searches of the drivers' personal belongings. On the second occasion, UNHCR obtained orders from the Bosnian Serb authorities that such searches should not be conducted. The convoy headed for Goražde again but was stopped by Bosnian Serb military police, who denied receiving instructions to let it proceed. One convoy was cancelled because the drivers' visas had expired and new ones were not issued in time.[14]

The provision of fuel for humanitarian purposes created additional problems. This fuel met priority humanitarian needs, such as heating hospitals and the collective centres that sheltered the displaced. UNHCR supervised delivery and monitored use, but this supply indirectly released other fuel for military use. Thus the Bosnian government accused UNHCR of fuelling the Serb offensives on Goražde and Bihać, and its opponents blocked access to government-controlled areas for UNHCR fuel, maintaining that it would be used against them.

Convoys from Serbia to the three eastern enclaves were organized by UNHCR's Belgrade office (which was also assisting 600,000 ethnic Serb refugees from Bosnia and Croatia). On a number of occasions, UNHCR's national staff in Belgrade were able to resolve problems blocking convoys to the enclaves through direct intervention with the BSA at the highest level. The overall intent to obstruct was clear but individual outcomes were not predictable. A convoy that had been blocked by abusive soldiers at a checkpoint might turn back, wait for those soldiers to go off duty, try again and be waved through. Sometimes a BSA officer would offer to drive ahead of a convoy (as long as UNHCR provided fuel) in order to prove that a road was clear of mines.

Among more senior UNHCR staff, understanding of policy and strategy was generally clear and consistent, but the rapid expansion of staff into an environment that was unfamiliar to the organization meant that inexperienced staff found themselves both literally and figuratively on the negotiating front-line. At the same time, there was a rapid turnover. The achievements of new and inexperienced staff were remarkable. Some proved outstanding negotiators, but there was also a lack of consistency and continuity. This was a potentially significant weakness: tactics and arguments may be situation specific, but the requirements and reactions of humanitarian negotiators should be predictable.

Favourable elements

Containment of the consequences of the conflict with a minimum of direct involvement was arguably the real aim of some European governments, which focused on the humanitarian response to a political disaster, not its causes.[15] Action to help relieve the suffering was demanded by Western public opinion. The combination of this imperative and the leadership and initiatives of the High Commissioner ensured strong political and financial support for UNHCR in capitals, had an impact in the field and strengthened the negotiating hand of UNHCR. This allowed UNHCR to play a role and have a profile that was by no means assured at the start. UNHCR's ability to influence events was also strengthened by the close personal engagement of the High Commissioner and the latitude she allowed her senior staff in the field. This helped UNHCR to make interventions with speed and authority, increasing the chances of resolving problems while that was still possible. Although very few of UNHCR's international staff spoke Serbo-Croat, the head of UNHCR's Belgrade office for the first three years of the conflict did. Her effectiveness underlined the importance of language skills in sensitive negotiations.[16]

The views of the international media were of concern to political leaders within the region, whose envoys and lobbyists tried to influence decision makers in key countries. All sides were seeking international recognition. The conflict attracted a high-profile, influential and often partisan press corps. From the start, UNHCR mobilized the media as allies. Staff were encouraged to speak openly and frankly about what they had witnessed. There was an expectation that UNHCR would denounce obstruction and abuses. The first Special Envoy established a particularly close relationship with the media, which resulted in extensive favourable coverage. UNHCR came to be seen as a well-informed and credible source. Although this had little impact on negotiations at the checkpoints or with local officials, it strengthened UNHCR's hand at higher levels.

UNHCR benefited from its position as the UN lead agency and the significant degree of control that this gave the organization over the operation. This was reinforced by the fact that, with the exception of the ICRC, outside humanitarian organizations wishing to deploy staff to and operate vehicles within Bosnia required UNHCR identity cards and number plates. These cards were necessary for travel by air to Sarajevo and were even issued to the first diplomats posted there. The operation had greater coordination and coherence than might otherwise have been the case and was generally felt to have an authoritative voice. This was not necessarily male: UNHCR assigned significantly more women to the field than had occurred previously: for much of the period they held a majority of the key posts. Although this would be unremarkable now, it was not at the time and was seen as increasing UNHCR's effectiveness.

A ministerial-level meeting convened by the High Commissioner in Geneva on 29 July 1992 helped establish UNHCR's international standing. The meeting adopted a plan of action proposed by UNHCR. At that meeting, the United Kingdom, then holding the EC Presidency, announced its intention to convene an International Conference on the Former Yugoslavia (ICFY) in London. This took place in late August 1992. At this conference, the High Commissioner agreed to chair the Humanitarian Issues Working Group (HIWG), one of several working groups established by the conference on issues related to the breakup of the former Yugoslavia. The HIWG allowed humanitarian concerns to be examined with less political polarization than elsewhere,[17] and it provided a means of highlighting these directly to governments. The fact that UNHCR convened regular meetings of the HIWG, set the agenda and prepared documentation, and did so within the framework of the ICFY, added credibility to UNHCR's negotiating position in other forums.

On paper, the greatest support for UNHCR's negotiating position with the parties came from the UN Security Council. Over 80 resolutions were adopted on the former Yugoslavia in the period 1991–1995. From 1992, the majority of these resolutions invoked Chapter VII and many included demands that all concerned facilitate the unhindered flow of humanitarian assistance, honour their commitments to UNHCR and the ICRC, and ensure freedom of movement and security for humanitarian workers. Presidential statements addressed specific UNHCR concerns. In reality, the Security Council itself lost credibility with the parties as the gulf between its repeated demands and its ability and commitment to ensure their respect became clear. Implementation of the sanctions imposed by the Council created a number of problems for the humanitarian operation and required frequent negotiation of exemptions.

The reality

The sum of the favourable elements gave UNHCR and the humanitarian operation a remarkable level of political, financial and material support. However, the declared intent of the international community was not translated into action. The central reality remained that the aim of the humanitarian operation ran counter to the interests of those who had the power to obstruct it. This conditioned negotiations but did not doom all to failure. All sides understood the aim of the operation and, at least broadly, why UNHCR took the actions it did.

Negotiations

This section gives examples of negotiations during the war in Bosnia and the difficulties encountered. Humanitarian negotiators constantly faced attempts to impose conditionality on access and relief – political linkages – and this problem is described. I assess the overall achievements of the operation and outline relevant post-war developments.

Sarajevo

UNHCR was not directly involved in the agreement reached in June 1992 among UNPROFOR, the Bosnian government and the Bosnian Serb authorities on reopening Sarajevo airport for humanitarian purposes. Much of the text covered military aspects, but it provided that aid delivered by the airlift should also go beyond Sarajevo. As a result, throughout the war the Bosnian Serbs conditioned operation of the airlift on the delivery of aid to areas they controlled that had no need of supply by air. The agreement authorized a Bosnian Serb presence at the airport to "facilitate" UNPROFOR's tasks in controlling all incoming personnel and cargo. Whatever the text, obstruction was inevitable, and the agreement in effect gave the Bosnian Serbs control of both the flights and what they could carry. This precedent had immediate and lasting effect on UNHCR's negotiations.

The airlift could not begin until UNHCR and the Bosnian Serb authorities agreed what part of the aid airlifted to Sarajevo would go to areas around Sarajevo that they controlled. Agreement could be reached on the basis only of the estimated populations, not of needs and the degree of dependency on international aid.[18] The Bosnian Serbs then insisted on applying this to land convoys to Sarajevo, which had to pass through the airport. Thenceforth, 23 per cent of all food aid that reached Sarajevo by air or land went to the Bosnian Serb side. The operation of the airport was a cause of understandable resentment on the part of the Bosnian government.

Geneva

Some of the highest-profile formal negotiations initiated by UNHCR followed an attack on 25 October 1993 on an aid convoy as it crossed the front-lines between Bosnian government and Bosnian Croat forces. One Danish Refugee Council driver was killed and one injured, as were nine Dutch soldiers. Convoys in central Bosnia were suspended while new assurances were sought at the highest level. The UNHCR Special Envoy met with the political leaders of the three sides in preparation for a meeting in Geneva on 18 November convened by the High Commissioner. The framework for the meeting covered both formal statements and negotiations on the text of a declaration. The ICRC was present at the formal sessions and conducted its own negotiations.

Agreement on the text of the declaration was finally reached, despite some objections from the Commander of the BSA, present as an adviser to his delegation. The three leaders signed a solemn commitment to ensure the delivery of humanitarian assistance by suspending hostilities and allowing free and unconditional access by the most effective land routes. The leaders also committed themselves to allowing UNHCR and the ICRC to determine, without any conditionality or linkages, the content of humanitarian assistance. As a result, convoys to central Bosnia resumed.

On the ground, the impact was limited and short lived. The fact that UNHCR could convene such a meeting and extract these commitments reflected pressures of international opinion that had little effect on the local military and civilian leadership and even less on those at the checkpoints. The European Union convened a meeting of its foreign ministers with Bosnia's three political leaders in Geneva on 29 November 1993 to try to advance the prospects for peace – an action plan was presented – and in order to have a humanitarian aid agreement signed by the three military commanders. The latter objective appears to have been prompted by a view, espoused by the UNPROFOR Force Commander when he addressed the EU Foreign Affairs Council on 22 November, that the key to aid flow was the commitment of the military commanders with whom UNHCR, or UNPROFOR on UNHCR's behalf, should deal more directly. From early November, the Force Commander had been urging UNHCR to resume convoys in central Bosnia. UNHCR had concerns about this EU initiative, believing that it would make no difference on the ground and would weaken civilian accountability.

The three military commanders signed a declaration that was a more detailed elaboration of the 18 November commitments. Although this had no more impact than the earlier declaration, it gave UNHCR a set of EU benchmarks against which to report non-compliance. Addressing the 29 November meeting, the High Commissioner recalled the commitments made on 18 November and continued:

The reality is that one of the largest humanitarian assistance operations ever undertaken by the international community remains conditional on ever more complicated and arbitrary procedures, imposed at will by the very people who have created the victims we try to reach. These procedures must be radically simplified immediately.[19]

They never were.

Humanitarian assistance?

Negotiating from humanitarian principles in the midst of war could lead to situations bordering on the surreal. Domestic heating and cooking for much of Bosnia depended on power stations fed by coal from surface and deep mines. Mining experts forecast that electricity production might cease across central Bosnia by the end of 1993 unless spare parts for long-overdue maintenance, as well as detonators and explosives for the mines, were delivered.[20] By the autumn of 1993 these were available in UNHCR warehouses. UNPROFOR agreed to transport the detonators and explosives once clearance was obtained. The delivery routes were controlled either by the BSA or by Croatian and Bosnian Croat forces, the latter then being at war with the Bosnian government forces, which controlled the mines and power stations. Clearance for the convoys was consistently refused on the grounds that the supplies would be used by the Bosnian government forces.

Pressure mounted on UNHCR from the increasing threat of a breakdown in power supply and from the UK government, which had made a major investment in the provision of the spares. Requests for convoy clearance were resubmitted without items that could conceivably be seen as having a military use. The UNHCR Special Envoy and the general manager of the International Management Group met the leader of the Bosnian Croats but failed to convince him that the pipes could not make mortars and that the industrial explosives had no military value. In early December, the Bosnian Croat army finally authorized movement of some of the spares. In late December, the UNHCR Special Envoy raised the need for clearance of the remaining spares and the explosives with the foreign minister of Croatia. Fighting between the Bosnian and the Bosnian Croat armies (the latter supported by the Croatian army) was intense in some locations, with significant Croatian casualties. The Croatian government was under domestic pressure to intervene more actively. For the minister, humanitarian logic had been reduced to absurdity. Fortunately, the power stations and mines proved resilient. The problem was solved only after the Washington agreements of March 1994. The last convoy, with 250 metric tons of spares, crossed the border in mid-1994.

Linkages

A major concern for UNHCR in all negotiations was to avoid the linkage of assistance to one side with assistance to or conditions set by another. Non-food supplies, especially those necessary for the winter, were the most at risk. As the winter of 1993 approached, access to the eastern enclaves in Bosnia for such supplies was in effect blocked by Bosnian Serb demands for reciprocity. UNHCR's position was set out in a 25 September 1993 letter to the Bosnian Serb leader, Dr Karadžić:

Linking meeting the humanitarian needs of one group of beneficiaries to meeting those of another clearly cannot be justified, no more than can an arbitrary "fee" for the passage of humanitarian assistance on which lives depend ... if the displaced and refugees within your communities have need of similar assistance in advance of the winter, UNHCR and our partners are ready to assess these needs and meet them on their merits within the limits of our resources.[21]

Three days later, clearance for six trucks carrying shelter and water supply equipment was again refused with the explanation: "we have warned you several times that you cannot request delivery [of such materials] to the Muslim enclave without same request submitted, at the same time, for the needs of the Serb areas."

Even once cleared, convoys came under pressure to give up assistance as a condition for passage. UNHCR convoys had clear instructions to refuse. Despite the policy, which UNHCR urged NGOs to adopt, on occasions assistance was surrendered voluntarily, but this was very rare and became still rarer with time. Convoys remained at checkpoints until free passage was allowed or they were ordered back to base fully loaded. Humanitarian access was denied and obstructed, not purchased or obtained by yielding to linkages.[22] Had it started to be obtained in that way, ever-rising demands would soon have halted the operation. Convoy drivers did, however, usually travel with cartons of local cigarettes, a common demand at checkpoints during the war and sometimes a facilitator of passage.

With the exception of the distribution of aid coming to or via Sarajevo, the aid that was provided to the Bosnian Croats and Serbs was calculated on the basis of needs. These were difficult to assess and generally of lower priority than the needs of others. Most could have been met from sources outside the humanitarian operation. However, UNHCR's readiness to consider these needs gave some leverage in negotiating access.[23]

UNHCR resisted making its own direct linkages, for example by stopping legitimate assistance to the party that was obstructing access to the other side, something on occasions advocated by UNPROFOR. As well as being a matter of principle, UNHCR's policy was based on the assessment that loss of this assistance might be a price the obstructer would pay, and that UNHCR would generally be able to negotiate the restoration of access and, meanwhile, partially compensate with airdrops. In practice, there was some indirect linkage by UNHCR. For example, convoys to the Bosnian Serbs were generally scheduled late in the week and, if the earlier deliveries to the enclaves had been obstructed, these convoys could be cancelled for "technical" reasons.

In late 1994, after weeks of unsuccessful high-level negotiations with the Krajina (Croatian) Serbs who were blocking access to the Bosnian enclave of Bihać, UNHCR decided it would make assistance to them conditional on access to Bihać. Three factors were felt to justify this exception: the shortages were becoming life threatening and airdrops had been suspended because of threats to the aircraft; assistance to areas controlled by the obstructing parties was not vital; and the obstructing parties had further reduced UNHCR's ability to monitor the use of this assistance. UNHCR presented this change not as a linkage but as treating assistance as a package when this was more likely to achieve humanitarian objectives than other approaches. The dilemmas inherent in negotiating from humanitarian principles in the middle of a conflict are evident. Access to Bihać was re-established and denied again several times before military action in mid-1995 lifted the siege.

What was achieved?

Despite the obstacles, much vital assistance reached those in need. In Bosnia alone, almost 1 million tons of relief, the vast majority food provided through the WFP, benefited some 2.7 million people. Although their resilience and determination were surely the most important factors in their survival, the operation helped save many lives. In the circumstances, this was the minimum that was expected of it, however difficult that had proved in practice.

By the measure of the scale of ethnic cleansing and atrocities, the interventions by UNHCR to prevent further human rights abuses had limited impact. Actions by UNHCR field staff, often at considerable personal risk, saved civilians from violent death. Interventions to halt abuses allowed significant numbers who might have been killed to flee instead. The international attention focused on these abuses, the detailed reporting of them to the political authorities that bore the ultimate responsibility, and the presence of international staff throughout Bosnia and in the UN Protected Areas, combined with the actions of the ICRC, moderated behaviour and methods to some degree but could not prevent ethnic cleansing.

As the examples have shown, negotiations were generally successful, in the sense of finally reaching acceptable agreement. In government-controlled Croatia and in Serbia, UNHCR was operating in a broadly familiar context, where legal arguments would at least be considered and where agreements reached centrally might eventually be enforced. This was not the case in Bosnia and the UN Protected Areas. The commitments obtained from the leaders, although achievements in themselves, meant little in practice. There was no accepted legal framework and only a physical presence might have prevented specific abuses (in this sense, any UNHCR field staff might become a protection officer). Even with hindsight, it is not clear that there were alternative approaches that might have had more impact. Rather, the impossibility of humanitarian action alone prevailing over the logic of war is more starkly clear.

After the war

Pressure mounted on UNHCR to repatriate refugees and the internally displaced even when this could not be to their original homes, as was provided for in Annex 7 of the 1995 General Framework Agreement for Peace, on whose wording UNHCR had been consulted. UNHCR's negotiating position appeared stronger, but in reality little had changed. The agreement left those responsible for ethnic cleansing in Bosnia in a position to prevent its reversal. Things were somewhat different for the return of Croatian Serb refugees from Serbia, which the Croatian government initially resisted. The international community had more leverage, given Croatia's desire to join the European institutions. After a period when OSCE and UNHCR sometimes appeared to be duplicating efforts, the two organizations established a joint coordination office in 1998. This was able to develop common positions and responses to the shifting stand of the government on return. Negotiations with the government were coordinated among the diplomatic representatives in Croatia of the European Union, the United Kingdom and the United States, with UNHCR providing the major input where refugees were concerned, and were led by OSCE.

At the working level, an informal but close-knit team from these five was in daily contact, enabling UNHCR to ensure that its concerns were addressed. The arrangement faltered when the Croatian government asked for a list of actions on refugee return that would satisfy the international community. Consensus on a response could not be reached because of concern that the government would find UNHCR's proposed list politically unacceptable. UNHCR finally submitted its list independently, and received broad if reluctant agreement from the government. Follow-up then came back to the team, and a legal group was established with the government to work towards the elimination of discriminatory legislation.

As the conflict that began in Kosovo in early 1998 spread and intensified, the humanitarian operation there started to assume familiar form, with active front-lines to be crossed and clearances to be obtained. UNHCR eventually resorted to international convoy teams. The negotiations were easier, and obstruction of the operation much less, than during the war in Bosnia, although both Belgrade and the Kosovo Serbs saw the operation as partial. By the time the operation was suspended in late March 1999, on the eve of NATO air action, 250,000 Kosovo Albanians had been displaced within the province and another 200,000 had fled it. The response to the expulsions to Albania and Macedonia that followed was in some ways the mirror image of that during the war in Bosnia. In Bosnia, humanitarian action had substituted for political will. For Kosovo, political will had been exercised. A massive new refugee crisis followed, which governments (and NATO) urgently needed to be seen to be containing. The humanitarian operation was at times simultaneously a vehicle for and subordinated to the political concerns of these governments. As a result, UNHCR's negotiating position, for example for asylum in Macedonia, was extremely weak.[24]

Wider implications

This chapter has illustrated why humanitarian action cannot substitute for political resolve and has highlighted some of the difficulties in achieving humanitarian objectives during conflict. This was the case notwithstanding the fact that UNHCR enjoyed high standing and considerable support. UNHCR was also able to operate across what had become separate sovereign states largely without diplomatic constraint, moving staff and material resources as it saw fit. It is unlikely that humanitarians will often enjoy such advantages.

Conflicts involving large-scale abuse of human rights to which the primary response of the international community is humanitarian action are not unique. What was different in the Balkans between 1991 and 1995 was the level of attention demanded of Western governments by public opinion and the media. For at least the first two years, the reply of political leaders when asked what their government was doing concretely about the unfolding tragedy was likely to be that it was supporting the humanitarian action. The deep involvement of humanitarian actors in actions that went well beyond traditional humanitarian concerns and were conducted in an intensely political context yielded lessons of wider relevance.

Some general lessons from past emergencies were reinforced. Clear lines of responsibility and a coherent approach are important foundations for humanitarian negotiations. High-level support, from both within and outside the humanitarian organization, and significant delegated authority to experienced field staff increase the chances of success. Surprise and pragmatism are counterproductive when seeking to ensure respect for humanitarian principles and basic human rights. Negotiations have a greater chance of success if it is clear to all parties that there are things that are not negotiable. Where agreement is possible, it is more likely when negotiations are left to the humanitarians. Difficulties will be compounded – and security may be prejudiced – when humanitarian and political objectives are combined.

The operation highlighted the problems humanitarian action faces in situations of unresolved conflict, where the causes of the suffering it seeks to relieve are not being addressed effectively. Without real commitment by the parties to a peaceful resolution, the gap between the aims of the humanitarian operation and the interests of those who can obstruct it will widen. The task of humanitarian negotiators will thus become more difficult and, perhaps, finally impossible. If the humanitarian operation nevertheless continues, it risks becoming increasingly compromised.

The question of whether the operation prolonged the war in Bosnia began to be raised as the conflict continued. Initially, UNHCR saw its involvement as short term, a holding operation while those seeking a political resolution of the conflict brought the peace they declared to be at hand.[25] For the Western governments that sought to contain the conflict, the operation was an important element in their strategy. It became part of an argument for not taking action that could end the conflict. In that sense, the discharge of a humanitarian mandate may have contributed to prolonging the war. But the absence of humanitarian assistance would not necessarily have forced an earlier political solution and the outcome of a shorter war would not necessarily have been more just, and could have been even more disastrous.

Implicit in the criticism that humanitarian action can prolong conflict is the suggestion that there is a choice between humanitarian action and robust measures to end the conflict. This is rarely the case, and was not the case in the Balkans.[26] UNHCR sought to ensure that the international community understood the limitations of the operation. As the High

Commissioner and the Under-Secretary-General of the United Nations Department of Humanitarian Affairs, Jan Eliasson, put it in the preface to the seventh Consolidated Inter-Agency Appeal for the operation, launched on 8 October 1993:

Humanitarian action is no substitute for peace, but it can mitigate the cruel effects of war. Until firm steps are taken in the direction of peace, we have no recourse but to continue all possible efforts to save the lives of children, women and men now placed at risk by the ongoing conflict.[27]

Early in the breakup of the former Yugoslavia it would have been possible to prevent further gross violations of human rights. The assessment at that time by states with that capacity was that their national interests were not sufficiently engaged. Three years later, their interests were deeply engaged but intervention was far more difficult. Had states appreciated earlier what became evident later, the political will might have been found. Whatever the merits of that argument, it is relevant to a final conclusion in light of the experiences examined here. Without effective political action to end a conflict and stop grave abuses, humanitarian action is likely to face mounting and finally insurmountable problems.

Notes

1. The chapter's focus is the conduct of a humanitarian operation in the midst of conflict, not UNHCR's discharge of its responsibilities towards refugees.
2. This examination is from my perspective as UNHCR Special Envoy for the former Yugoslavia from June 1993 to December 1994 and April 1998 to April 1999. For another examination, see Mark Cutts, *The Humanitarian Operation in Bosnia, 1992–95: Dilemmas of Negotiating Humanitarian Access*, New Issues in Refugee Research, Working Paper No. 8, Geneva: UNHCR, 1999, available at ⟨http://www.unhcr.org/cgi-bin/texis/vtx/research/opendoc.pdf?tbl=RESEARCH&id=3ae6a0c58⟩ (accessed 28 April 2006). For how the operation appeared at the time, see Larry Minear et al., *Humanitarian Action in the Former Yugoslavia: The U.N.'s Role, 1991–1993*, Occasional Paper No. 18, Providence, RI: Thomas J. Watson Jr Institute for International Studies, Brown University, 1994, available at ⟨http://www.watsoninstitute.org/pub/OP18.pdf⟩ (accessed 28 April 2006).
3. There are many detailed accounts and analyses of the origins and course of the conflicts. See, e.g., Laura Silber and Allan Little, *The Death of Yugoslavia*, London: Penguin Books, 1996.
4. European Union (EU) from November 1993.
5. For the High Commissioner's account of this operation, see Sadako Ogata, *The Turbulent Decade: Confronting the Refugee Crises of the 1990s*, New York: Norton, 2005.
6. For a description of the evolution of UNPROFOR's role (and analysis of the political and military interventions in Bosnia and Kosovo), see Nicholas Morris, "Humanitarian Intervention in the Balkans", in Jennifer M. Welsh, ed., *Humanitarian Intervention and International Relations*, Oxford: Oxford University Press, 2004.

7. Organization for Security and Co-operation in Europe (OSCE) from January 1995.

8. The creation of the IMG was a UNHCR initiative endorsed by donor governments on 30 July 1993.

9. Security was an important factor in UNHCR's decision to notify the parties of convoy movements. This led to the requirement for prior clearance, a requirement that was probably unavoidable.

10. A particularly contentious issue was the very restrictive UN policy with regard to seats for Bosnians.

11. One example was the UNPROFOR negotiations over access to Mostar in August 1993, described by Cedric Thornberry in "Peacekeepers, Humanitarian Aid, and Civil Conflicts", in Jim Whitman and David Pocock, eds, *After Rwanda: The Coordination of United Nations Humanitarian Assistance*, London: Macmillan, 1996, also available at ⟨http://www.jha.ac/articles/a002.htm⟩. At the time, the High Commissioner remarked that food for the living had been made conditional on exchanging the bodies of the dead. The problem of linkages is examined later in the chapter.

12. Similarly, in March 1999 Kosovo Albanians welcomed NATO intervention, even knowing that it would halt humanitarian assistance and initially increase their suffering.

13. UNPROFOR escorted convoys across the front-lines into the enclaves. Escorts for Goražde came from Sarajevo. The Bosnian Serb authorities occasionally authorized UNHCR convoys to proceed, but only without UNPROFOR escorts, a condition UNHCR did not accept.

14. Multiple-entry visas were needed for Serbia, where these teams were based, and often they were issued with limited validity.

15. The first error of Western policy identified by the International Commission on the Balkans is: "Definition of the crisis as a humanitarian disaster rather than as brutal aggression" (*Unfinished Peace: Report of the International Commission on the Balkans*, Washington, DC: Carnegie Endowment for International Peace, 1996, p. 68).

16. Most negotiations, whether at checkpoints or with political and military leaders, were conducted with UNHCR national staff acting as interpreters. This is common in humanitarian negotiations and can put the interpreter at risk.

17. After the Federal Republic of Yugoslavia was denied successor state UN membership, the Humanitarian Issues Working Group was the only UN-related forum to which it was invited.

18. There was a precedent. In August 1974, UNHCR had arranged for the Acting President of Cyprus and the Turkish Cypriot Vice-President, who was about to renounce that role, to nominate the most senior officials in their Red Cross and Red Crescent societies as the channel for UN humanitarian assistance, to be apportioned on the basis of the last census. This agreement owed its conclusion in large part to the personal involvement of the High Commissioner, Sadruddin Aga Khan. For more than 20 years thereafter, UNHCR was the only UN body able to operate throughout the island and was the channel for several hundred million US dollars of aid. Unlike the agreement for Sarajevo, the proposed formula was fair and an initiative of, not imposed on, UNHCR.

19. Quoted in UNHCR, "Information Notes on former Yugoslavia", No. 12/93, December 1993, p. i.

20. Security Council Resolution 859 of 24 August 1993, adopted under Chapter VII, included electricity in a demand for the unhindered flow of humanitarian assistance.

21. Quoted in UNHCR, "Information Notes on former Yugoslavia", No. 10/93, 3 October 1993, p. iii. UNHCR convoys had earlier been suspended until the Bosnian Serbs withdrew a demand for payment of a tax for passage.

22. Allegations that access was "bought", or that some 25 per cent of the aid was "skimmed", by the Bosnian Serbs appear to relate to the agreed division of aid coming

through Sarajevo. The United States General Accounting Office (GAO) examined allegations – for which it found no evidence – that the United Nations withheld humanitarian assistance in order to pressure the Bosnian government into an unfavourable peace settlement. The GAO conducted a thorough review of the convoy operation. Its *Briefing Report to the Honorable Robert S. Dole, U.S. Senate* (*Humanitarian Intervention: Effectiveness of U.N. Operations in Bosnia*, GAO/NSIAD-94-156BR, Washington DC: United States General Accounting Office, April 1994) makes no mention of access being bought, but details the obstruction and other problems faced by convoys.

23. Similarly, the Swedish government's agreement, at UNHCR's suggestion, to build a transit camp for displaced Bosnian Serbs helped obtain clearance for the Swedish housing project in the Srebrenica enclave.

24. UNHCR's performance was also criticized. For a brief examination of the negotiating challenges to UNHCR, see Nicholas Morris, "UNHCR and Kosovo: A Personal View from inside UNHCR", *Forced Migration Review*, Vol. 5, August 1999.

25. The report of the UN Secretary-General's High-level Panel on Threats, Challenges and Change defines the core purpose of humanitarian aid in conflict as "to protect civilian victims, minimize their suffering and keep them alive during the conflict so that when war ends they have the opportunity to rebuild shattered lives" (*A More Secure World: Our Shared Responsibility*, New York: United Nations, 2004, para. 234).

26. The Report of the International Commission on the Balkans concludes that: "The primary cause of the failure of negotiations over Bosnia-Herzegovina, until summer 1995, was the refusal of the leading international powers to exert a credible threat of force much earlier in order to impose a settlement" (*Unfinished Peace*, p. 74).

27. Quoted in UNHCR, "Information Notes on former Yugoslavia", No. 11/93, November 1993, p. i.

Bibliography

Active Learning Network for Accountability and Performance (2004) *Annual Review of Humanitarian Action in 2003: Field Level Learning*. London: Overseas Development Institute.

Adibe, Clement (1995) *Managing Arms in Peace Processes: Somalia*. Geneva: United Nations Institute for Disarmament Research.

Africa Watch (1993) *Waging War to Keep the Peace: The ECOMOG Intervention and Human Rights*. New York: Human Rights Watch.

Art, Robert J. and Patrick M. Cronin, eds (2003) *The United States and Coercive Diplomacy*. Washington DC: United States Institute of Peace.

Baitenmann, Helga (1990) "NGOs and the Afghan War: The Politicization of Humanitarian Aid", *Third World Quarterly*, January.

Bales, Kevin (1999) *Disposable People*. Berkeley: University of California Press.

Berger, Jean-François (1995) *The Humanitarian Diplomacy of the ICRC and the Conflict in Croatia (1991–1992)*. Geneva: ICRC.

Berridge, Geoffrey (1994) *Talking to the Enemy: How States without Diplomatic Relations Communicate*. London: Macmillan.

―――― (2002) "Multilateral Diplomacy", in *Diplomacy: Theory and Practice*, 2nd edn. Basingstoke: Palgrave, pp. 146–167.

Black, Maggie (1986) *The Children and the Nations*. New York: UNICEF.

―――― (1992) *A Cause for Our Times*. Oxford: Oxfam.

Bruderlein, Claude with Adeel Ahmed (1997) "Report of the DHA Mission to Afghanistan", United Nations Department of Humanitarian Affairs, May.

Brunel, Sylvie, ed. (1999) *Geopolitics of Hunger*. London: Action against Hunger.

Bryden, Matt (2003) "No Quick Fixes: Coming to Terms with Terrorism, Islam and Statelessness in Somalia", *Journal of Conflict Studies*, Vol. 23, No. 2.

Bull, Hedley (1985) *The Anarchical Society: A Study of Order in World Politics.* London: Macmillan.

Bundu, Abbas (2001) *Democracy by Force? A Study of International Military Intervention in the Conflict in Sierra Leone from 1991–2000.* Boca Raton, FL: Universal Publishers.

Burnett, S. John (2004) "In the Line of Fire", *New York Times*, 4 August, ⟨http:// www.globalpolicy.org/ngos/credib/2004/0804fire.htm⟩ (accessed 2 May 2006).

Carr, E. H. (1984) *The Bolshevik Revolution 1917–1923.* Harmondsworth: Pelican.

——— (1984) *The Twenty Years Crisis 1919–1939.* London: Macmillan.

Carver, Richard (1997) "Sierra Leone: From Cease-Fire to Lasting Peace", *Writenet*, 1 January; reported in *Refworld* at ⟨http://www.unhcr.org/⟩, Geneva: United Nations High Commissioner for Refugees, Centre for Documentation on Refugees (UNHCR/CDR).

Chandler, David P. (1992) *Brother Number One: A Political Biography of Pol Pot.* Boulder, CO: Westview Press.

Chomsky, Noam (2000) *Rogue States: The Rule of Force in World Affairs.* Cambridge, MA: South End Press; London: Pluto Press.

Clarke, Walter and Jeffrey Herbst (1995) *Somalia and the Future of Humanitarian Intervention.* Center of International Studies, Monograph Series No. 9, Princeton University.

Cutts, Mark (1999) *The Humanitarian Operation in Bosnia, 1992–95: Dilemmas of Negotiating Humanitarian Access.* New Issues in Refugee Research, Working Paper No. 8, Geneva: UNHCR Policy Research Unit; available at ⟨http:// www.unhcr.org/cgi-bin/texis/vtx/research/opendoc.pdf?tbl=RESEARCH&id =3ae6a0c58⟩ (accessed 28 April 2006).

Donini, A. (1999) *The Strategic Framework for Afghanistan: A Preliminary Assessment.* Islamabad: UNOCHA.

——— (2003) *Learning the Lessons? A Retrospective Analysis of Humanitarian Principles and Practice in Afghanistan.* A report prepared for OCHA, June; full text available on ReliefWeb at ⟨http://www.reliefweb.int/library/documents/ 2003/ocha-afg-30jun.pdf⟩, accessed 4 May 2006.

Donini, A., N. Niland and K. Wermester, eds (2003) *Nation-building Unraveled? Aid, Peace and Justice in Afghanistan.* Bloomfield, CT: Kumarian Press, December.

Duffield, M., P. Gossman and N. Leader (2001) *Review of the Strategic Framework for Afghanistan.* Islamabad: Afghanistan Research and Evaluation Unit.

Dunn, James (1983) *Timor, A People Betrayed.* Milton, Queensland: Jacaranda Press.

Dunsire, Andrew (1978) *Implementation in a Bureaucracy: The Execution Process.* Oxford: Martin Robertson, Vol. 1.

East Timor and Indonesia Action Network (ETAN) (1998) "Selected Postings from ... East-Timor: Red Cross Visits East Timor's Alas Region amid Massacre Rumours", 23 November, ⟨http://www.etan.org/et/1998/november/22-30/ 23redcro.htm⟩ (accessed 24 April 2006).

Economist Intelligent Unit (2004) *Country Report Nepal.* London: Economist Intelligent Unit, May.

Eguizábal, Cristina, David Lewis, Larry Minear, Peter Sollis and Thomas G. Weiss (1993) "Humanitarian Challenges in Central America: Lessons from Recent Armed Conflicts". Occasional Paper No. 14, Institute for International Studies, Brown University.

Eguren, Enrique (2000) "The Protection Gap: Policies and Strategies", *Humanitarian Practice Network*, 30 October.

Ethics and International Affairs (2004), Vol. 18, No. 2, special issue.

Fisher, R., W. Ury and B. Patton (1981) *Getting to Yes: Negotiating Agreements without Giving in.* Boston, MA: Houghton Mifflin.

Frohardt, Mark, Diane Paul and Larry Minear (1999) *Protecting Human Rights: The Challenge to Humanitarian Organisations.* Providence, RI: Watson Institute.

Gautam, Kul C. (2004) "Cambodia 1974, Nepal 2004: How to Avoid Nepal's Descent towards a Failed State?", 5 April, ⟨http://kulgautam.org/website/index. php?option=com_content&task=view&id=33&Itemid=62⟩ (accessed 25 April 2006).

Geneva Call, in collaboration with the Program for the Study of International Organization(s) (PSIO) of the Graduate Institute of International Studies and the Armed Groups Project (2004) *An Inclusive Approach to Armed Non-State Actors and International Humanitarian Norms: Report of the First Meeting of Signatories to Geneva Call's Deed of Covenant*, at ⟨http://www.genevacall.org/ resources/testi-publications/gc-nsa-report-05.pdf⟩ (accessed 28 March 2006).

George, Alexander (1991) *Forceful Persuasion: Coercive Diplomacy as an Alternative to War.* Washington DC: United States Institute of Peace.

Goulding Report (1988) *Report Submitted to the Security Council by the Secretary-General in Accordance with Resolution 605 (1987).* UN Doc. S/19443, 21 January.

Greenlees, Don and Robert Garran, eds (2002) *Deliverance: The Inside Story of East Timor's Fight for Freedom.* St Leonards: Allen & Unwin.

Hainsworth, Paul and Stephen McClosky, eds (2002) *The East Timor Question. The Struggle for Independence from Indonesia.* London: I. B. Tauris.

Hamilton, Keith and Richard Langhorne (1995) *The Practice of Diplomacy: Its Evolution, Theory and Administration.* London: Routledge.

Hansen, Greg and Larry Minear (1999) "Waiting for Peace: Perspectives from Action-Oriented Research on the Humanitarian Impasse in the Caucasus", *Disasters*, Vol. 23, No. 3, pp. 257–270.

Harroff-Tavel, Marion (2005) "La Diplomatie humanitaire du Comité Internationale de la Croix-Rouge", *Relations internationales*, No. 121, pp. 73–89.

High-level Panel on Threats, Challenges and Change (2004) *A More Secure World: Our Shared Responsibility. Report of the Secretary-General's High-level Panel on Threats, Challenges and Change.* New York: United Nations.

Hinsley, F. H. (1988) *Power and the Pursuit of Peace.* Cambridge: Cambridge University Press.

Hitchens, Christopher (2001) *The Trial of Henry Kissinger*. London: Verso.
Hood, Christopher C. (1976) *The Limits of Administration*. London: Wiley.
Hubert, Don (2000) *The Landmine Ban*. Providence, RI: The Watson Institute.
Human Rights Watch (Americas) (1996) *Colombia's Killer Networks: The Military–Paramilitary Partnership and the United States*. New York: Human Rights Watch.
——— (2000) *The Ties that Bind: Colombia and the Military–Paramilitary Links*. New York: Human Rights Watch, February.
——— (2001) *The "Sixth Division": Military–Paramilitary Ties and U.S. Policy in Colombia*. New York: Human Rights Watch, September.

Ibañez, Juan, Lizzie Brock and Christiane Schwartz (2003) "Evaluación de las Acciones Urgentes como Mecanismo para Frenar Violaciones a los Derechos Humanos", unpublished, Bogotá.
ICRC (International Committee of the Red Cross) (1981) "Action by the International Committee of the Red Cross in the Event of Breaches of International Humanitarian Law", *International Review of the Red Cross*, No. 221, 30 April, pp. 76–83.
——— (1998) "Statutes of the International Committee of the Red Cross", *International Review of the Red Cross*, No. 324, 30 September, pp. 537–543.
Independent Inquiry Committee into the United Nations Oil-for-Food Programme (2005) *Interim Report*, ⟨http://www.iic-offp.org/documents/InterimReportFeb2005.pdf⟩ (accessed 21 May 2006).
Ingram, James (1993) "The Future Architecture for International Humanitarian Assistance", in Thomas G. Weiss and Larry Minear, eds, *Humanitarianism across Borders*. Boulder, CO: Lynne Rienner.
International Commission on the Balkans (1996) *Unfinished Peace: Report of the International Commission on the Balkans*. Washington, DC: Carnegie Endowment for International Peace.
International Commission on Intervention and State Sovereignty (2001) *The Responsibility to Protect: Report of the International Commission on Intervention and State Sovereignty*. Ottawa: International Development Research Centre, December.
International Crisis Group (2002) *Somalia: Countering Terrorism in a Failed State*. Africa Report No. 45, Nairobi/Brussels: International Crisis Group, 23 May.
Iweze, C. Y. (1993) "Nigeria in Liberia: The Military Operations of ECOMOG", in M. Vogt and E. E. Ekoko, eds, *Nigeria in International Peacekeeping 1960–1992*. Oxford: Malthouse Press.

Jackson, Bertha and Joan McLeod-Omawale (1993) "First Baby in Safe Hands", *Keeping the Promise*, No. 5, June.
Jakobsen, Peter Viggo (1998) *Western Use of Coercive Diplomacy after the Cold War*. London: Macmillan.
Jan, Ameen (1996) "Peacebuilding in Somalia". IPA Policy Briefing Series, International Peace Academy, New York, July.
Jaspars, Susanne (2000) "Solidarity and Soup Kitchens: A Review of Principles

and Practice for Food Distribution in Conflict". A joint project by Nutrition Works and the Overseas Development Institute with Nicholas Leader, HPG Report 7, Humanitarian Policy Group, Overseas Development Institute, London, August.

Jönsson, Christer and Karin Aggestam (1999) "Trends in Diplomatic Signalling", in Jan Melissen, ed., *Innovation in Diplomatic Practice*. London: Macmillan, pp. 160–162.

Kamm, Henry (1998) *Cambodia*. New York: Arcade Publishing.

Kellenberger, Jakob (2004) "Speaking out or Remaining Silent in Humanitarian Work", *International Review of the Red Cross*, No. 855, 30 September, pp. 593–610.

Kiernan, Ben and Chan Thom Boua (1982) *Peasants and Politics in Kampuchea 1942–1981*. London: Zed Press.

Knight, Jane (1996) "Sierra Leone: Will Hope Triumph Over Experience?" *One World Link Newsletter*, June.

Kremenyuk, Victor A., ed. (2002) *International Negotiation: Analysis, Approaches, Issues*. Chichester: Jossey-Bass.

Kull, Steven, I. M. Destler and Clay Ramsay (1997) *The Foreign Policy Gap: How Policymakers Misread the Public*. College Park, MD: Center for International and Security Studies at Maryland.

Leader, Nicholas (2001) "Negotiation and Engagement in Afghanistan". Report prepared for the UN Coordinator's Office, Islamabad, 28 May.

Lewis, David and Helen Wallace, eds (1984) *Policies into Practice: National and International Case Studies in Implementation*. London: Heinemann.

Lewis, I. M. (1988) *A Modern History of Somalia: Nation and State in the Horn of Africa*. Boulder, CO: Westview Press.

McNamara, Robert S. (1995) *In Retrospect*. New York: Times Books/Random House.

Macrae, Joanna, et al. (2002) "Uncertain Power: The Changing Role of Official Donors in Humanitarian Action". HPG Report 12, Humanitarian Policy Group, Overseas Development Institute, London, December.

Mahony, Liam (2003) "Colombia's Political Background", unpublished draft.

Makay, Susan and Dyan Mazurana (2004) "Where Are the Girls?", Rights and Democracy, Montreal, Canada.

Mancini-Griffoli, Deborah and André Picot (2004) *Humanitarian Negotiation: A Handbook for Securing Access, Assistance and Protection for Civilians in Armed Conflict*. Geneva: Centre for Humanitarian Dialogue.

Maren, Michael (1994) "Feeding a Famine", *ForbesMediaCritic*, Vol. 2, No. 1.

Marker, Jamshed (2003) *East Timor: A Memoir of the Negotiations for Independence*. Jefferson, NC: McFarland & Company.

Martin, Ian (2001) *Self-Determination in East Timor: The United Nations, the Ballot, and International Intervention*. Boulder, CO: Lynne Rienner.

Mehta, Harish C. and Julie B. Mehta (1999) *Hun Sen: Strongman of Cambodia*. Singapore: Graham Brash.

Menkhaus, Ken (1996) "International Peacebuilding and the Dynamics of Local and National Reconciliation in Somalia", *International Peacekeeping*, Vol. 3, No. 1, Spring.

———— (1998) "Somalia: The Political Order of a Stateless Society", *Current History*, Vol. 97, May, pp. 220–224.

Minear, Larry (1991) *Humanitarianism under Siege: A Critical Review of Operation Lifeline Sudan*. Trenton, NJ: Red Sea Press.

———— (2002) *The Humanitarian Enterprise: Dilemmas and Discoveries*. Bloomfield, CT: Kumarian Press.

———— (2005) "Lessons Learned: The Darfur Experience", in Active Learning Network for Accountability and Performance (ALNAP), *Annual Review of Humanitarian Action 2005*. London: ALNAP.

Minear, Larry, et al. (1994) *Humanitarian Action in the Former Yugoslavia: The U.N.'s Role, 1991–1993*. Occasional Paper No. 18, Providence, RI: Thomas J. Watson Jr Institute for International Studies, Brown University; available at ⟨http://www.watsoninstitute.org/pub/OP18.pdf⟩ (accessed 28 April 2006).

Minear, Larry, Ted van Baarda and Marc Sommers (2000) *NATO and Humanitarian Action in the Kosovo Crisis*. Providence, RI: The Watson Institute.

Morgenthau, Hans J. (1985) *Politics among Nations: The Struggle for Power and Peace*, 6th edn, revised by Kenneth W. Thompson. New York: Alfred A. Knopf.

Morris, Nicholas (1999) "UNHCR and Kosovo: A Personal View from inside UNHCR", *Forced Migration Review*, Vol. 5, August.

———— (2004) "Humanitarian Intervention in the Balkans", in Jennifer M. Welsh, ed., *Humanitarian Intervention and International Relations*. Oxford: Oxford University Press.

NGO Coordination Committee in Iraq (2004) "Bullet Points for Mr Ross Mountain, SRSG a.i. for Iraq: Humanitarian Space in Iraq & Security of Humanitarian Personnel on the Ground", May, ⟨http://www.ncciraq.org/IMG/doc/ NCCI-Bullet_Points_for_Mr._Ross_Mountain_-_Humanitarian_Space_in_Iraq _05-04_.doc⟩ (accessed 2 May 2006).

———— (2004) "Crisis Situation Report", 13 April (SitRep 14.04.04); available at ⟨http://www.ncciraq.org/article.php3?id_article=104⟩ (accessed 2 May 2006).

———— (2004) "NCCI Statement HACC Luncheon (08-05-04)"; available at ⟨http://www.ncciraq.org/article.php3?id_article=135⟩ (accessed 2 May 2006).

———— (2004) "Statements on the Falujah Crisis – Spring", ⟨http://www.ncciraq. org/article.php3?id_article=135⟩ (accessed 2 May 2006).

Nicolson, Harold (1988) *Diplomacy*. Washington DC: Institute for the Study of Diplomacy.

Niland, Norah (2003) *Humanitarian Action: Protecting Civilians. Feedback from Afghanistan*. Prepared for OCHA, United Nations, 30 June; available on ReliefWeb at ⟨http://www.reliefweb.int/library/documents/2003/ocha-afg-30jun2.pdf⟩ (accessed 4 May 2006).

Ofuatey-Kodjoe, W. (1994) "Regional Organizations and the Resolution of Internal Conflict: The ECOWAS Intervention in Liberia", *International Peacekeeping*, Vol. 1, No. 3, pp. 261–302.

Ogata, Sadako (2005) *The Turbulent Decade: Confronting the Refugee Crises of the 1990s*. New York: Norton.

Olaiya, A. (1991/1992) "ECOMOG Mission and Mandate", *The Peacemaker*, No. 1.

Panel of Experts on Somalia (2003) *Report of the Panel of Experts on Somalia Pursuant to Security Council Resolution 1474 (2003)*. UN Security Council, S/2003/1035, 4 November.

Pilger, John (1979) "The Killing Fields of Cambodia", *Daily Mirror*, 12 September.

Ponchaud, François (1978) *Cambodia: Year Zero*, translated by Nancy Amphoux. Harmondsworth: Penguin.

Rashid, Ahmed (2000) *Taliban. Islam, Oil and the New Great Game in Central Asia*. London and New York: I. B. Tauris.

Raynal, Josephine (1989) *Political Pawns*. Oxford: Refugee Studies Programme, Queen Elizabeth House.

Reindorp, Nicola and Anna Schmidt (2002) "Coordinating Humanitarian Action: The Changing Role of Official Donors". HPG Briefing Paper No. 7, Humanitarian Policy Group, Overseas Development Institute, London, December.

Riley, S. and A. Max-Sesay (1995) "Sierra Leone: The Coming Anarchy?", *Review of African Political Economy*, No. 63.

Riordan, Shaun (2003) *The New Diplomacy*. Oxford: Polity Press.

Schultz, Kenneth A. (2001) *Democracy and Coercive Diplomacy*. Cambridge: Cambridge University Press.

Schwarz, Adam (1999) "East Timor: The Little People That Could", in *A Nation in Waiting. Indonesia's Search for Stability*, 2nd edn. Singapore: South Wind Production, pp. 194–229.

Schwarz, Adam and Jonathan Paris, eds (1999) *The Politics of Post Suharto Indonesia*. New York: Council on Foreign Affairs.

Scott, Colin, et al. (1995) "Humanitarian Action and Security in Liberia 1989–1994". Occasional Paper No. 20, Thomas J. Watson Institute, Brown University, USA.

Sen, Amartya (1981) *Poverty and Famines: An Essay on Entitlement and Deprivation*. Oxford and New York: Oxford University Press.

Sharp, Paul (2003) "Mullah Zaeef and Taliban Diplomacy: An English School Approach", *Review of International Studies*, Vol. 29, No. 4, October, pp. 481–498.

Shaw, John and Edward Clay (1993) *World Food Aid*. Rome/London: World Food Programme/James Currey/Heinemann.

Shawcross, William (1979) *Sideshow: Kissinger, Nixon and the Destruction of Cambodia*. New York: Simon & Schuster.

——— (1984) *Quality of Mercy*. London: Simon & Schuster.

Silber, Laura and Allan Little (1996) *The Death of Yugoslavia*. London: Penguin Books.

Slim, Hugo (2004) "A Call to Alms: Humanitarian Action and the Art of War", Centre for Humanitarian Dialogue, Geneva.

Smillie, Ian and Larry Minear (2003) *The Quality of Money: Donor Behavior in Humanitarian Financing*. Medford, MA: Humanitarianism and War Project, April.

———, eds (2004) *The Charity of Nations: Humanitarian Action in a Calculating World*. Bloomfield, CT: Kumarian.

Smith, Hazel (2005) *Hungry for Peace: International Security, Humanitarian Assistance and Social Change in North Korea*. Washington DC: United States Institute of Peace Press.

Sommer, John G. (1994) "Hope Restored? Humanitarian Aid in Somalia, 1990–1994", Refugee Policy Group, November.

Stockton, Nick (2003) "Afghanistan, War, Aid and the International Order", in A. Donini, N. Niland and K. Wermester, eds, *Nation-building Unraveled? Aid, Peace and Justice in Afghanistan*. Bloomfield, CT: Kumarian Press, December.

Strobel, Warren P. (1996) "The Media and US Policies Toward Intervention: A Closer Look at the 'CNN Effect' ", in Chester Crocker, Fen Osler Hampson with Pamela Aall, eds, *Managing Global Chaos: Sources of and Responses to International Conflict*. Washington, DC: United States Institute of Peace, pp. 360–366.

Taylor, John (1991) *Indonesia's Forgotten War. The Hidden History of East Timor*. London: Zed Books.

Terry, Fiona (2002) *Condemned to Repeat: The Paradox of Humanitarian Action*. Ithaca, NY: Cornell University Press.

The Sphere Project: Humanitarian Charter and Minimum Standards in Disaster Response (2004) special issue of *Disasters*, Vol. 28, No. 2.

Thion, Serge (1993) *Watching Cambodia*. Bangkok: White Lotus.

Thornberry, Cedric (1996) "Peacekeepers, Humanitarian Aid, and Civil Conflicts", in Jim Whitman and David Pocock, eds, *After Rwanda: The Coordination of United Nations Humanitarian Assistance*. London: Macmillan; also available at ⟨http://www.jha.ac/articles/a002.htm⟩.

UNICEF (United Nations Children's Fund) (1990) *FIRST CALL FOR CHILDREN: World Declaration and Plan of Action from the World Summit for Children. Convention on the Rights of the Child*. New York: UNICEF.

——— (1995) "Recommendation for Funding for Short-duration Country Programmes and for Additional General Resources and Supplementary Funding to Fund Approved Country Programmes in West and Central Africa Region". Executive Board document, E/ICEF/1995/P/L.28, New York, 13 March.

——— (2002) *State of the World's Vaccines and Immunization*. Geneva: World Health Organization, UNICEF and the World Bank, October.

United Nations (1996) *The United Nations and Somalia (1992–1996)*. Blue Books Series, Vol. VIII, New York: Department of Public Information of the United Nations.

——— (2004) *United Nations Agencies Basic Operating Guidelines*. Kathmandu: United Nations, 16 January; available at ⟨http://www.un.org.np/basic.php⟩ (accessed 25 April 2006).

——— (2004) *United Nations Agencies Guiding Principles*. Kathmandu: United

Nations, 7 January; available at ⟨http://www.un.org.np/basic1.php⟩ (accessed 25 April 2006).

United Nations Country Team (2004) Written statement to the Nepal Development Forum 2004, Kathmandu, 4 May; available at ⟨http://www.ndf2004.gov.np/pdf/chairmanreport.pdf⟩ (accessed 2 May 2006).

United Nations Development Programme (1991) *Human Development Report 1991.* New York: United Nations.

―――― (2001) *Human Development Report: Somalia, 2001.* Nairobi: UNDP.

―――― (2003) *Socio-Economic Survey 2002: Somalia. Report No. 1, Somalia Watching Brief, 2003.* UNDP Somalia with the World Bank.

―――― (2004) *Human Development Report 2004: Cultural Liberty in Today's Diverse World.* New York: UNDP; available at ⟨http://hdr.undp.org/reports/global/2004/pdf/hdr04_complete.pdf⟩ (accessed 15 July 2004).

United Nations High Commissioner for Refugees (1993) "Information Notes on former Yugoslavia", No. 10/93, 3 October.

―――― (1993) "Information Notes on former Yugoslavia", No. 11/93, November.

―――― (1993) "Information Notes on former Yugoslavia", No. 12/93, December.

United Nations Office for the Coordination of Humanitarian Affairs (UNOCHA) (2003) "Guidelines on the Use of Military and Civil Defence Assets to Support United Nations Humanitarian Activities in Complex Emergencies", March, ⟨http://ochaonline.un.org/DocView.asp?DocID=426⟩.

――――, Consolidated Appeals Process (2004) *Humanitarian Appeal 2004: Somalia,* ⟨http://www.un.org/depts/ocha/cap/somalia.html⟩ (accessed 20 July 2004).

――――, United Nations Technical Committee on Humanitarian Assistance (1998) *Protocols Signed between the Government of the People's Republic of Sudan, the Sudan People's Liberation Movement, and the United Nations.* New York: OCHA.

United Nations Office of the Humanitarian Coordinator for Iraq (2004) "Guidelines for Humanitarian Organisations on Interacting with Military and Other Security Actors in Iraq", 20 October, reproduced at ⟨http://www.reliefweb.int/rw/rwb.nsf/db900SID/HMYT-66BQU7?OpenDocument⟩ (accessed 21 May 2006).

United States General Accounting Office (1994) *Briefing Report to the Honorable Robert S. Dole, U.S. Senate. Humanitarian Intervention: Effectiveness of U.N. Operations in Bosnia.* GAO/NSIAD-94-156BR, Washington DC: United States General Accounting Office, April.

Vogt, M. A., ed. (1992) *The Liberian Crisis and ECOMOG: A Bold Attempt at Regional Peacekeeping.* Lagos: Gabumo Publishers.

Von Hippel, Karin (1996) "First Seminar on Decentralised Political Structures for Somalia", Lake Naivasha, Kenya, June.

―――― (1996) "Second Seminar on Decentralised Political Structures for Somalia", Lake Nakuru, Kenya, 16–18 November.

―――― (1997) "The Proliferation of Collapsed States in the Post-Cold War World", in Michael Clarke, ed., *Brassey's Defence Yearbook 1997.* London: Brassey's.

―――― (2000) *Democracy by Force.* Cambridge: Cambridge University Press.

Von Hippel, Karin and Alexandros Yannis (1997) "The European Response to

State Collapse in Somalia", in Knud Erik Joergensen, ed., *European Approaches to Crisis Management*. The Hague: Kluwer International.

Weber, Max (1949) *On the Methodology of the Social Sciences*. Glencoe, IL: Free Press.

Wildavsky, Aaron (1979) *The Art and Craft of Policy Analysis*. London: Macmillan.

World Food Programme (2002) *Food Aid in Conflict Workshop Report*. Rome: WFP.

World Food Programme Office of Evaluation (1999) "Thematic Evaluation of Recurring Challenges in the Provision of Food Assistance in Complex Emergencies: The Problems and Dilemmas Faced by WFP and Its Partners".

Young, Oren R. and Gail Osherenko (1993) *Polar Politics: Creating Environmental Regimes*. Ithaca, NY: Cornell University Press.

Zack-Williams, A. B. (1990) "Sierra Leone: Crisis and Despair", *Review of African Political Economy*, No. 49, Winter, p. 29.

——— (1991) "The Politics of Crisis and Ethnicity in Sierra Leone". Paper presented at the Centre for African Studies, University of Liverpool, February.

Zartmann, I. William (2001) *Preventive Negotiation: Avoiding Conflict Escalation*. New York: Carnegie Commission on Preventing Deadly Conflict and Rowman & Littlefield.

Zartmann, I. William and Maureen R. Berman (1982) *The Practical Negotiator*. New Haven, CT: Yale University Press.

Index